Alternative Food Networks

Farmers' markets, veggie boxes, local foods, organic products, and Fair Trade goods – how have these once novel, "alternative" foods and the people and networks supporting them become increasingly familiar features of everyday consumption? Are the visions of "alternative worlds" built on ethics of sustainability, social justice, animal welfare, and the esthetic values of local food cultures and traditional crafts still credible now that these foods crowd supermarket shelves and other "mainstream" shopping outlets?

This timely book provides a critical review of the growth of alternative food networks and their struggle to defend their ethical and esthetic values against the standardizing pressures of the corporate mainstream with its "placeless and nameless" global supply networks. It explores how these alternative movements are "making a difference" and their possible role as fears of global climate change and food insecurity intensify. It assesses the different positions around these networks from three major arenas of food activism and politics: the UK and Western Europe, the USA, and the global Fair Trade economy. This comparative perspective runs throughout the book to fully explore the progressive erosion of the interface between alternative and mainstream food provisioning. As the era of "cheap food" draws to a close, analysis of the limitations of market-based social change and the future of alternative food economies and localist food politics place this book at the cutting edge of the field.

The book is thoroughly informed by contemporary social theory and interdisciplinary social scientific scholarship, formulating an original integrative framework to understand alternative food production–consumption and offers a unique geographical reach in its case studies.

David Goodman is Visiting Professor, Department of Geography, King's College London, UK, and Professor Emeritus, University of California, Santa Cruz, USA.

E. Melanie DuPuis is Professor of Sociology, University of California, Santa Cruz, USA.

Michael K. Goodman is a Senior Lecturer in Geography at King's College London, UK.

Routledge Studies of Gastronomy, Food and Drink
Series Editor: Michael Hall
University of Canterbury, New Zealand

This groundbreaking series focuses on cutting edge research on key topics and contemporary issues in the area of gastronomy, food and drink to reflect the growing interest in this as academic disciplines as well as food movements as part of economic and social development. The books in the series are interdisciplinary & international in scope, considering not only culture and history but also contemporary issues facing the food industry, such as security of supply chains. By doing so the series will appeal to researchers, academics and practitioners in the fields of Gastronomy & Food Studies, as well as related disciplines such as Tourism, Hospitality, Leisure, Hotel Management, cultural studies, anthropology, geography and marketing.

Published:

The Business of Champagne
A delicate balance
Edited by Steven Charters

Alternative Food Networks
Knowledge, practice, and politics
David Goodman, E. Melanie DuPuis, and Michael K. Goodman

Sustainable Culinary Systems
Local foods, innovation, tourism and hospitality
Edited by C. Michael Hall and Stefan Gossling

Wine and Identity
Branding, heritage, *terroir*
Edited by Matt Harvey, Leanne White and Warwick Frost

Social, Cultural and Economic Impacts of Wine in New Zealand
Edited by Peter Howland

Forthcoming:

The Consuming Geographies of Food
Diet, food deserts and obesity
Hillary J. Shaw

Alternative Food Networks

Knowledge, practice, and politics

David Goodman, E. Melanie DuPuis, and Michael K. Goodman

Routledge
Taylor & Francis Group

LONDON AND NEW YORK

First published in paperback 2014

First published 2011
by Routledge
2 Park Square, Milton Park, Abingdon, Oxon OX14 4RN

and by Routledge
711 Third Avenue, New York, NY 10017

Routledge is an imprint of the Taylor & Francis Group, an informa business

British Library Cataloguing in Publication Data
A catalogue record for this book is available from the British Library

Library of Congress Cataloguing in Publication Data
Goodman, David, 1938–
Alternative food networks : knowledge, place and politics / David Goodman, E. Melanie DuPuis, and Michael K. Goodman.
  p. cm.
Includes bibliographical references and index.
 1. Food industry and trade. 2. Food industry and trade–Moral and ethical aspects. 3. Food supply–Moral and ethical aspects.
 4. Consumption (Economics). I. DuPuis, E. Melanie (Erna Melanie), 1957– II. Goodman, Michael K., 1969– III. Title.
HD9000.5.G658 2011
381′.41–dc22

                                                            2011009477

ISBN: 978-0-415-67146-0 (hbk)
ISBN: 978-0-415-74769-1 (pbk)
ISBN: 978-0-203-80452-0 (ebk)

Typeset in Times New Roman
by Wearset Ltd, Boldon, Tyne and Wear

We dedicate this book to the memory of
Fred Buttel, Tom Lyson, and Jon Murdoch

Contents

Acknowledgments

This book has its origins in the informal debates and work-in-progress sessions of the Agro-Food Studies Research Group (AFSRG) at the University of California, Santa Cruz. Since disbanded, the AFSRG provided one of those moments rarely and fleetingly encountered in academic life: a group of colleagues committed to open, at times fierce, debate in an environment of trust. We are grateful to all who locked horns in those meetings, particularly Patricia Allen, Margaret FitzSimmons, Bill Friedland, Sean Gillon, Julie Guthman, Jill Harrison, Philip Howard, Katie Monsen, Amy Morris, Dustin Mulvaney, Jan Perez, Tara Pisani-Gareau, Tim Vos, and Keith Warner. Themes and ideas that first emerged in AFSRG sessions and subsequently published in academic journals are further elaborated in the main sections of the book. More conventionally, we have all benefited from a wider "invisible college" of scholars who came forward to help us in the course of our research and writing.

David would like to thank Henry Buller, Maria Fonte, Clare Hinrichs, Philip Howard, Moya Kneafsey, Kevin Morgan, Dustin Mulvaney, Michael Redclift, Matthew Reed, Roberta Sassatelli, and Angela Tregear for their advice and help in tracking down research papers. Thanks also to Pierre Stassart for his invitation to attend two stimulating workshops on the Arlon campus of the University of Liege and the opportunity to meet European scholars working on alternative food systems and related topics. David is particularly grateful to Dan Keech, Tim Lang, and John Wilkinson for their valuable suggestions and fresh perspectives.

Melanie presented draft chapters in various academic venues, including CSPACE at the University of Otago, the Department of Geography at the University of Arizona, the Mellon graduate workshop in Food Studies at Brown University, and the Environmental Politics Colloquium at UC Berkeley. She would like to thank all those who invited her to share this work in these contexts, including Hugh Campbell, Nancy Campbell, and Heather Lee. Melanie is particularly grateful to J. P. Jones and Sally Marston at the University of Arizona, who spent a whole morning arguing against her ideas of boundaries and scale and helped her to reach a better understanding of how alternative economies get made. Finally, she wishes to thank Carl Pechman and Christine Williams for reading and commenting on various draft chapters.

Mike would like to thank Chris Bacon, Max Boykoff, Raymond Bryant, Rose Cohen, Ian Cook, Phil Crang, Lewis Holloway, Steward Lockie, Damian Maye, Dustin Mulvaney, Scott Prudham, Colin Sage, Matthias Varul, and Bradley Wilson for engagements over the past few years around fair trade and AFNs more broadly. He is grateful to Matthew Anderson, Amanda Berlan, Matthias Varul, and Dorothea Kleine for sharing their latest work and other information on fair trade movements in Europe, and would like to give particular thanks to Catherine Dolan, Valerie Nelson, Amanda Berlan, Anne Tallontire, and Colin Sage for crucial comments on drafts of the chapters in Part IV.

The (at times cantankerous) MA students in both 2010 and 2011 in the Consumers, Ethics, and the Global Environment class at King's helped him work through and improve much of the material here on fair trade. Finally, Mike would like to express his deep thanks to Twin Trading for the use of the figure in Chapter 11 and to the fair trade organizations in the UK, Europe, and the USA, as well as the producer cooperatives in Costa Rica and the Dominican Republic (CONACADO and Yacao) for their time and energy in helping him learn about fair trade and the good work they are doing to make communities and farmers' lives better in a distressingly unequal world.

Finally, all three of us wish to thank Emma Travis and Faye Leerink at Taylor and Francis for their encouragement, help, and patience in the protracted process of completing this book.

Abbreviations

AFIs	agrifood initiatives
AFN	alternative food network
AFSRG	Agro-Food Studies Research Group
AMAP	*Association pour le Maintien d'une Agriculture Paysanne*
ANT	actor-network theory
AOC	*Appellation d'Origine Controlee*
ATO	Alternative Trade Organization
BBV	BioBourgogne Viande
BSE	bovine spongiform encephalopathy
rBST	recombinant bovine somatotropin
CAFF	Community Alliance with Family Farmers
CAP	Common Agricultural Policy
CCOF	California Certified Organic Farmers
CFE	Community Food Enterprise
CFS	Committee on World Food Security
CIA	Charitable Incorporated Association
CIC	Community Interest Company
CLBA	Country Land and Business Association
CPRE	Council for the Protection of Rural England
CSA	Community Supported Agriculture
Defra	Department of Environment, Food, and Rural Affairs
EC	European Commission
EU	European Union
FAO	Food and Agriculture Organization
FLO	Fairtrade Labelling Organizations International
FMD	Foot and Mouth Disease
FNSEA	*Federation Nationale des Syndicats d'Exploitants Agricoles*
FOS	fructooligosaccharides
FTN	Fair Trade Networks
FTS	farm-to-school
GAS.P!	*Gruppo di Aquisto Solidale di Pisa*
GEPA	Gesellschaft zur Partnerschaft mit der Dritten Welt
GHG	greenhouse gas
GIs	geographical indications

GMO	genetically modified organism
HACCP	Hazards Analysis and Critical Control Point
IAASTD	International Assessment of Agricultural Science and Technology Development
IPCC	Intergovernmental Panel on Climate Change
IPS	Industrial and Provident Society
LEADER	*Liaisons Entre Actions de Developpement de l'Economie Rural*
LFL	Local Food Links
LFN	local food network
LGU	land-grant university
LI/SA	Low-Input/Sustainable Agriculture
MLFW	Making Local Food Work
MNC	multinational corporation
NAT	New Age Traveller
NFU	National Farmers Union
NGO	non-governmental organization
NHS	National Health Service
NOP	National Organic Program
NOPPR	National Organic Program Proposed Rule
NOSB	National Organic Standards Board
OCA	Organic Consumers Association
OFPA	Organic Food Production Act
OLMC	Organic Livestock Marketing Cooperative
OMI	organic marketing initiative
OMSCo	Organic Milk Suppliers Cooperative
OTA	Organic Trade Association
PCT	Primary Care Trusts
PDO	protected designation of origin
PGI	protected geographical indication
RDA	Rural Development Agency
RDR	Rural Development Regulation
SAMs	sustainable agriculture movements
SCA	Stroud Community Agriculture
SFM	Slow Food Movement
SFP	single farm payment
SFSC	short food supply chain
SOP	systems of provision
TN	Transition Network
TPC	third-party certification
TRIPS	Trade-Related Property Rights
UC	University of California
UNF	United Natural Foods
USDA	United States Department of Agriculture
WFM	Whole Foods Market
WTO	World Trade Organisation

Part I
Alternative food networks
Reflexivity and shared knowledge practice

1 Introducing alternative food networks, fair trade circuits, and the politics of food

The end of the twentieth century marked the close of a chapter in the history of social change. In the 1960s, political mobilizations, inspired by revolutionary socialism, reformist social democracy, and identity politics seemed to call into being a brave new world. By the 1980s, these hopes and visions that the world could be transformed by protest-and-projects activity had become distant dreams. Yet social activism is remarkably resilient as revealed by the efflorescence of democracy movements in eastern Europe and the Arab Spring in the Middle East, environmentalist groups, fair trade, the anti-globalization/global justice movement, La Via Campesina, and myriad other expressions of social protest. This "new wave" of social activism includes the burgeoning alternative food movement in its many and diverse forms, from local farmers' markets to fair trade producer cooperatives. Manifestos of this movement, bracketed, for example, by Frances Moore Lappe's *Diet for a Small Planet* (1971) and Michael Pollan's *In Defense of Food* (2008), offer a vision that people, by eating differently, can change the worlds of food as well.

Academic analyses of attempts to transform these worlds of food fall into two broad camps. Some scholars are critical of the failings of activist projects, pointing variously to the powerful mainstreaming forces exerted by a globalizing food industry and the ideological influence of neoliberalism on movement ambition. More recently, academic critique has drawn attention to the exclusionary, often raced and elitist nature of efforts to re-localize food provisioning. Other scholars recognize these failings but also give weight to the promise of the new "pre-figurative" politics created by the alternative food movement as a framework in which these limitations can be addressed and resolved.

The new politics of food provisioning and global fair trade builds on imaginaries and material practices infused with different values and rationalities that challenge instrumental capitalist logics and mainstream worldviews. These alternative projects are seen as templates for the reconfiguration of capitalist society along more ecologically sustainable and socially progressive lines. The discursive and material development of such "spaces of possibility" over the past 30 to 40 years demonstrates that alternative forms of social organization with their own operational rationalities can coexist, and even coevolve, with contemporary capitalist society (cf. Jessop 1997; Leyshon *et al.* 2003; Gibson-Graham 2006; DuPuis and Block 2008).

Our own work has attempted to walk a line between conventionalization arguments that record the rising totalization of food provisioning as alternative political projects, from local food to fair trade, are drawn into the mainstream corporate economy, and celebratory accounts of food movement prefigurations and visions. In steering a course between these positions, we have taken a reflexive view, one that allows a certain critical distance. This stance recognizes that food activists' struggles have failed to meet their own visions but also pays attention to the ways in which, in some cases and in some places, alternative economies have carved out relatively independent positions in the food system.

Taking this reflexive approach, this book focuses on two social spaces where "vanguard" projects of alternative economy have gained more general prominence and are now widely known: alternative food networks (AFNs) and fair trade circuits with the global South. We debate whether or not these developments are precursors of a broader project of social empowerment and progressive change throughout the following chapters.

In this Introduction, we outline some of the underlying problematics of these forms of alternative economy. We suggest that their critiques of conventional or mainstream systems have created a new politics of food as activists struggle to gain greater social control of food provisioning and to reframe notions of what is equitable and fair in trade relations. We then discuss the arenas where these innovative social projects are tested and contested and the principal cross-cutting themes that give the book its analytical and thematic unity: reflexivity, knowledge practices, and alterity.

In their general problematics, alternative food networks and the fair trade movement have emerged in response to the glaring and multifaceted contradictions of the unsustainable industrial food system and the exploitative trading relations embedded in the global supply chains that support its growth and (expanded) reproduction. These contradictions are revealed by the food insecurity and malnutrition of over one billion people, interrelated ecological and livelihood crises, compelling evidence of global resource constraints on intensive, fossil-fuel dependent conventional agriculture, and the crisis-proportions of disease associated with Western lifestyles and diets rich in animal fats and industrially processed foods. Although the magnitude of these global challenges can seem overwhelming, activists are mapping different ways forward by creating new economic and cultural spaces for the trading, production, and consumption of food – organic, fair trade, local, quality, "slow" – whose ethical and esthetic alternative "qualifications" distinguish them from the products conventionally supplied by international trade, mainstream food manufacturers, and supermarket chains.

Unlike the politics of universalism and mass mobilizations to extend and defend public entitlements institutionalized by the state, the collective action of these social movements is directed primarily toward the market. With the "economization" of the political and the accompanying market-embeddedness of morality (Shamir 2008; see also Fourcade and Healy 2007), consumers have become significant agents of change in the social and ecological relations of production, and the pace of this transformation depends on entrenching alternative values ever more deeply in everyday practices of food provisioning and global trade circuits. Inspired in part by feminist theory, activists place the consumer in a *relational* network with other actors, at times provocatively as the "vanguard" of change (Miller 1995c), and including relationships of "trust" with producers, as Whatmore and Thorne (1997) argue in the case of fair trade coffee.

In turn, these commoditized ethical and esthetic values or "qualities" are open to mainstream capture that threatens to neutralize the social projects and critical ambition of the alternative food and fair trade movements. Large-scale retailers, such as Wal-Mart, Carrefour, and Tesco, now provide shelf-space for "alternative" products, often produced and sourced under their own-label brands. These encounters reveal that the interface between "alternative" and "conventional" is becoming highly permeable and confusing as actors compete to control these new income streams. Can the politics, forms, and spaces created by alternative food and fair trade movements resist assimilation and dilution in the miasma of the corporate mainstream and, if not, what kind of social change can "conventionalized" social movements achieve?

These questions immediately "flag" two interrelated and contentious issues that are at the center of debates on market-based social movements: commodity fetishism and political consumerism. In Marx's classic analysis of the commodity form, the exploitation of labor by capital in commodity production is concealed or veiled by the fetishization of the products of that social labor as exchange values. Unless this veil is removed, it is argued, consumers will remain in ignorance of the "real" nature of capitalism as a social relation and accordingly can play no part in bringing about progressive social change. This revelatory strategy underlies much activist discourse and media exposés of industrial food provisioning: once consumers are made aware of this "false consciousness" about food products, they will struggle to create just, humane, and environmentally sustainable food systems.

Other contributors doubt that false consciousness can be so easily and completely dispelled and warn against capital's capacity to re-work the fetish (cf. Bryant and Goodman 2004). David Clarke (2010) is even more forthright and rejects the binary drawn between the false consciousness of the commodity fetishism thesis and the fully conscious subjectivity assumed in some recent analyses of shopping practices and ethical consumption (cf. Miller 1998b). While navigating these dangers, this book understands consumers (and producers) as "imperfect" social actors situated somewhere between these polarized positions and focuses on the politics of consumer–producer relationships that are the bedrock of alternative food and fair trade networks.

A related theme involves the perils of visions of "good food" and ideas of perfecting society – from Michael Pollan's tale of hunting wild pig in northern California to Alice Waters' epiphany when eating a bowl of potage in Paris. Such visions "celebritize" particular ways of life and are easy prey for mainstream branding. Once food politics is caught in the maze of competing definitions of the "real," the "authentic," or the "local" the game is already lost. This book therefore attempts to understand more clearly, and to describe more accurately, the politics of alternative food system-making *as process*.

At the center of our approach is a rethinking of our social world, what it is and how we know it. In particular, we move away from bifurcated Manichean perspectives and a politics of "conversion" that seeks to change the world by embracing a perfect vision of an alternative world based on a fixed, static set of values, whether of the "good life" or "good food." Instead, we rearticulate food politics toward an understanding of the world *as relational and process-based rather than perfectionist.* This relational worldview admits that its vision is never perfect but always can be improved by working in relationship with others, especially when informed by an open, reflexive, and contested view of "improvement" as an idea and a process. The following chapters explore the ways in which the politics of food can be strengthened by relational, process-based approaches.

A reflexive perspective not only changes our ideas of what the world is, but also how we see it. In previous work we have argued that alternative food systems, in fact all alternative ways of life, require different ways of knowing as well. In this book, we examine the politics of knowledge-making more closely and explore how alternative knowledges can work effectively to build a more resilient and vital alternative food system, one that is less vulnerable to mainstream pressures and more capable of dynamism, strength, and growth.

A new food politics: contesting quality

This threat from the mainstream brings us to a recurrent and unifying theme: the politics of quality, or the struggle by activists to confront and transform the values, operational rationalities, and singular pursuit of profitability characteristic of conventional food provisioning and international trade with the global South. The stakes here are greater social control of food and global trade circuits in order to extend civic governance over processes of economic production, valorization, and accumulation. What are the material relations and discursive meanings of quality in food and globally traded products – how, where, and by whom are these commodities produced? Whose values and knowledges determine how these products are commoditized and marketed? That is, which actors and social institutions define the conventions of product quality acceptable to markets? Can the conventions of standardized, industrial products be supplanted by those affirming alternative values of ecological sustainability and social justice?

Such questions immediately reveal the political economic nature of different social constructions of quality since these demarcate the boundaries between markets and establish the conventions or "rules of the game" within these competitive spaces. In the economy of quality, segmented in accordance with different market conventions, only designated production practices and the values they perform will *qualify* products and their producers to participate in specific "defined" markets. Control of the material and symbolic construction of these "qualifications" thus confers competitive advantage by opening up new opportunities for accumulation. As we shall see, especially in Chapters 10 to 12 on fair trade networks, the struggle between mainstream corporate actors and social movements to control the framing of "quality" markets incorporating the new ethical and esthetic conventions of production is at the center of contemporary food politics.

These politics are fought out in many arenas and at different spatial scales. We therefore give thematic prominence to *relational* conceptualizations of place, space, and scalar processes that draw out the asymmetries of power between different actor spaces. These processes articulate the local and the global and we explore their unfoldings at various points along these axes, and particularly in the infrastructural spaces of everyday social practice and reproduction.

Crosscutting analytical themes

We conceptualize alternative food and fair trade networks in relational terms as the organizational expression of recursive material and symbolic interactions between producers and consumers. This theoretical position leads us into "conversations" with a broad range of contemporary social theory as we search for conceptual "bridges" to understand how producers and consumers interact in these emergent "alternative worlds" and what it is that holds them together. By looking at these networks of producers and consumers as relational and mutually constituted in material and discursive practice, we can explore their innovative organizational forms and potential to reconfigure the values, time–space relations, and structures of governance of everyday food provisioning and the global trading system.

Reflexivity

The first of these conceptual bridges is a theoretical and political reading of consumers as critical, self-aware, reflexive actors who articulate and perform ethical, esthetic, and political values in the everyday routines of shopping, food provisioning, and social reproduction. We can then conceptualize alternative networks as reflexive "communities of practice" of consumers and producers whose repertoires create new material and symbolic spaces in food provisioning and international trade. This approach extends to social movements whose critiques of conventional food systems draw on universal ethical values of social justice and ecological sustainability, such as fair trade networks and organic movements, and those adopting a more particularistic esthetic critique based on the conservation of regional food cultures, localism, and traditional farmed landscapes, exemplified by the "gastronomic esthetic" advocated in its formative years by the Slow Food Movement.

In Chapter 2, we develop a reflexive approach to alternative food economies and re-localization movements that is deeply sceptical of utopian imaginaries and their dogmatic politics of "perfection." Supporting an open, process-based and pragmatic food politics, we reject normative portrayals of the local as places with conflict-free, communitarian values of reciprocity and fairness that unproblematically "incubate" alternative economic forms and promote social justice and environmental sustainability. Against such *normative certainties*, we introduce the notion of "reflexive localism" to redress the erasure of politics, difference, inequality, and social injustice.

We argue that a reflexive localism is the foundation of a democratic local food politics that is processual, open-ended, and altogether messier – less dogma and romanticism, greater experimentation, more negotiation, more openness to alternative worldviews. A reflexive approach recognizes this messiness as the stuff of politics and calls for pragmatic compromise and participatory civic governance. In keeping with this perspective, the local is not idealized as a space insulated from power relations and anomic global capitalism but is acknowledged as a publicly contested site of political-economic struggle, exploitation and accumulation. The local thus is formed *relationally* as local and external actors constantly maneuver for advantage in the changing spatial division of labor. We discuss these processes of place-making empirically by examining the parallels and differences in the construction of the local in the USA, Europe, and fair trade networks.

Shared knowledge practices

Practices of knowledge production – how we grow food and how we know what we are eating – provide a second conceptual bridge between production and consumption by revealing the formative linkages between materiality and meaning. *Shared knowledges* between producers and consumers are the foundation of alternative communities of practice and of the collective learning processes behind their growth and consolidation.

This perspective of relational knowledge production was first developed in a 2002 paper, *Knowing Food and Growing Food*, that focused on shared food knowledges as a way of opening up the sociology of agriculture to consumer agency and thus to a significant dimension of contemporary politics (Goodman and DuPuis 2002). On this approach, innovations in the time–space equations of food provisioning reflect cognitive differences from the corporate mainstream in the ways that actors in alternative movements "know and grow" food. The politics of alternative and mainstream provisioning systems can then be located on a terrain of contested knowledge claims, which define material practices and advance competing constructions of quality, modes of governance, and political imaginaries.

We extend these earlier ideas on the "knowledge economy of quality" by drawing out connections with several related literatures, including the recent revival of a theories of practice approach to the sociology of consumption that emphasizes the institutionalized, infrastructural foundations of "ordinary" spending habits, learned routines, and social norms of consumption. Adopting a relational conception of innovation, this research draws attention to the role of alternative food and fair trade movements in testing and disseminating new social practices of consumption. In Chapter 4, we explore several case studies that see innovation through this relational "consumer lens" as change in the daily routines and infrastructures of social reproduction.

This interest in making wider theoretical connections also is central to our analysis of fair trade. The rich literature in this field draws on the "moral turn" in human geography and the vigorous scholarship on ethical consumption but this work has been largely ignored in the sociology of agriculture and food. In our conversations with contributors to these debates, we build a third "bridge" by integrating work on Northern-focused AFNs with that on Southern "development-focused" AFNs.

Alterity

A further crosscutting analytical theme concerns the ways in which these social movements are "alternative" and the economic, socio-cultural, and political foundations of their alterity. We do not see the alternative food and fair trade movements as "oppositional" in the sense that their aim is mass mobilization to seize the state or overthrow the hegemonic capitalist system. Rather, their alterity comes from the development of new ways of doing things that coexist with this powerful system and attempt to change it from within. Although they depend on capitalist markets for their material and social reproduction, alternative economic spaces can develop with different operational logics and value systems, as the growing body of research on "diverse economies" in human geography clearly reveals (cf. Gibson-Graham 1996, 2006, 2010; Leyshon *et al.* 2003; Lee *et al.* 2004). Nevertheless, we need to recognize that the market-embeddedness of many of these projects and social movements does limit their strategic options and room for maneuver.

Within these constraints of social reproduction, the alterity of alternative or diverse economies can take on different forms and meanings, including multiple hybrid expressions. As the analyses in the following chapters demonstrate, alterity and its politics can be found as ecological sustainability, new spatialities, social justice, personalized exchange relations, hybrid market- and non-market mutual forms of social organization, and different modes of governance. These innovations in production practices, social organization, and consumption routines challenge those established by productivist commodity agriculture and corporate food processors and retailers.

In the US case, we suggest that the politics of alterity is bound up with the creation and defence of civic markets based on open, deliberative, public processes to determine who and what is "alternative." As we see in Chapters 8 and 9, the vitality of these processes of civic governance depends on vigilant participation in the politics of object making – for example, the continuing "object conflicts" around US organic standards – and in the politics of boundary maintenance to decide on the scale of the local civic market and who can be admitted.

The comparative perspective we adopt in this book brings a wealth of case material to the debate on alterity and the nature of the challenges to conventional systems from alternative food and fair trade movements.

This debate also raises two compelling structural questions. First, can these movements defend the bases of their alterity from mainstream competition by recalibrating their critique of industrial food systems? In each arena of food activism and politics, we look at the efforts by social movements to get around or "overflow" the pressures of corporate assimilation. For example, by adopting modes of civic governance and going "beyond organic" regulation in the USA, combining market and non-market social organizational forms in Western Europe, and reasserting unmediated, direct buyer–producer relations in fair trade transactions.

Second, can these alternative economic networks in the global North still be regarded as vanguard actors in the struggle to achieve greater social control over the governance of food provisioning and international trade? In other words, are their political imaginaries of sustainable, socially just and re-localized food systems still credible? Or are such "messianic" expectations misplaced and exaggerate their capacity for social change, as some influential scholars now suggest? We reflect on these issues and debates throughout the book.

Taking stock

This introduction emphasizes the importance of a historical perspective in assessing the new politics of food and the significance of the economic and cultural spaces created by the alternative food and fair trade movements. Their present trajectories cannot properly be understood without being aware of the strategic decisions and directions taken in their formative and middle years. After four decades of alternative food networks, and even longer for some fair trade organizations, it is time to take stock of the experience of these social movements and the debates and controversies they have spawned among activists and academics. This is the challenge we have set ourselves in writing this book.

2 Coming home to eat?

Reflexive localism and just food

Books such as *Coming Home to Eat* (Nabhan 2002) and *Eat Here* (Halweil 2004) represent a resounding clarion call among alternative food system advocates. This activist discourse, with its discussion of "foodsheds" and the problems of "food miles," makes strong connections between the localization of food systems and the promotion of environmental sustainability and social justice. In food activist narratives, the local tends to be framed as the space or context where ethical norms and values can flourish, and so localism becomes inextricably part of the explanation for the rise of alternative, and more sustainable, "good" food networks. In Europe, (re-)localization has become integral to efforts to preserve livelihoods, traditional farmed landscapes and rural heritage. In each case, although for different reasons, the local has become "beautiful," as was "small" ("pluriactive" in Europe) in the 1970s and 1980s, and "organic" ("multifunctional") in the 1990s and 2000s.

Localization has also been widely canvassed as a solution to the problems of global industrial agriculture. In the USA, the academic literature on alternative food networks emphasizes the strength of their embeddedness in local norms (Kloppenburg *et al.* 1996; Starr *et al.* 2003; DeLind 2002), such as the ethics of care, stewardship, and agrarian visions. This *normative* localism places a set of pure, conflict-free local values and local knowledges in resistance to anomic and contradictory capitalist forces. US scholarly research engages directly with local food activists and focuses insistently on the capacity of these networks "to wrest control from corporate agribusiness and create a domestic, sustainable and egalitarian food system" (Goodman 2003: 2).

In Europe, the encouragement of local food systems has different roots. It has emerged with the environmental and organic agriculture movements and in the institutional context of new forms of devolved rural governance, paralleling the slow process of reform of the European Union (EU) Common Agricultural Policy (CAP). As we discuss in Part II, the CAP is undergoing a gradual transformation from a centralized, productivist, sectoral policy toward a more decentralized model in which a multifunctional agriculture is a key element of an integrated, more pluralistic approach to rural development (Gray 2000; Lowe *et al.* 2002). In addition, episodic food "scares" and heightened consumer health and food safety concerns in Europe have stimulated a "turn" to quality in food provisioning and reinforced support for less intensive, multifunctional agriculture. Supporters of local food systems in Europe, while arguably less prone to the radical emancipatory idealism and normative communitarianism of US social movements, regard re-localization and re-embedding as strategies to realize a Eurocentric rural imaginary and defend its cultural identity against a US-dominated, corporate globalization.

Our own work certainly supports the view that global industrial agriculture has succeeded through the creation of a systemic footlooseness, and that place has a role in the building of alternative food systems (DuPuis 2002, 2004b; Goodman and Watts 1997). Yet we are critical of an emancipatory food agenda that relies primarily on the naming and following of a particular set of norms or imaginaries about place (Goodman and DuPuis 2002; DuPuis *et al.* 2006; see also Gaytan 2004).

As this chapter will show, an "unreflexive" localism can have two major negative consequences. First, it can deny the politics of the local, with potentially problematic social justice consequences. Second, it can lead to proposed solutions that are based on alternative standards of purity and perfection, making them vulnerable to "standards-based" alterity and so to corporate cooptation (Guthman 2004a; DuPuis 2002).

We therefore join a growing number of agro-food scholars who have acknowledged with David Harvey (1996) that the local is not an innocent term, observing that it can provide the ideological foundations for reactionary politics (Hinrichs 2000, 2003; Hassanein 2003). We agree with the many recent thoughtful critiques that have called for a closer examination of local food systems to "explore the ambiguities and subtleties of the ideas of 'localness' and 'quality'" (Holloway and Kneafsey 2000: 296, quoted in Winter, 2003; see also Allen *et al.* 2003). In common with these scholars, our critique is meant to be constructive and cautionary, not destructive of the alternative food agenda (against global, big, conventional, environmentally degrading food systems). Our intent is to put localist actions on a better political footing, one that can contribute to a more democratic, reflexive, and socially just local food politics.

In this vein, we will question a localism that is based on a fixed set of norms or imaginaries. In particular, we show how an "unreflexive" localism arises from a perfectionist utopian vision of the food system in which food and its production are aligned with a set of normative, pre-set "standards." This kind of food reform movement seeks to delineate standards of what is acceptable as "alternative" food practice rather than to support democratic political processes and local participation in making changes to the food system.

With these aims in mind, we begin with overviews of the current food localism discourse in the USA and localist rural development studies in Europe that reveal their lack of reflexive attention to local food networks. To address this question, we suggest how the reflexive practice of politics and social justice can be brought into the analysis of these networks. In developing this argument for a reflexive localism, we draw on critical social theory and notably recent debates on the theory of justice. This will also help us to interrogate claims that localism offers a counter-strategy to globalization.

Throughout this chapter, we argue for a reflexive and processual understanding of local food politics and food justice. Our central argument is that a normative, values-based localism leads to an elitist, undemocratic politics of perfection marked by problematic conceptions of social justice and civic tolerance. A major, if not, indeed, the foremost, challenge facing local food movements today is how to articulate localism as an open, process-based, and inclusive vision rather than a fixed set of values and standards shared by self-appointed groups of those who "know what is best" for everyone.

The romantic antipolitics of localism studies

There are strong parallels between the academic literature on alternative, localized food networks, particularly in US contributions, and the rhetoric of food activism built on alternative social norms or a kind of "alternative ethic." Many of the arguments speak about "re-localizing" food systems (Hendrickson and Heffernan 2002) into local "foodsheds" (Kloppenburg *et al.* 1996), thereby "recovering a sense of community" (Esteva 1994) by "re-embedding" food into "local ecologies" (Murdoch *et al.* 2000) and local social relationships (Friedmann 1994). Norm-based and ethical narratives also have become one pillar of a questionable scalar binary of global–local relations, as we observe below (Holloway and Kneafsey 2004).

These positions are based in a counter-logic to the political economy of agriculture arguments about the rise of capitalist agriculture as a global corporate regime (McMichael 2000). As Hendrickson and Heffernan (2002: 349) describe it:

> As people foster relationships with those who are no longer in their locale, distant others can structure the shape and use of the locale, a problem that is being explicitly rejected by those involved in local food system movements across the globe.

Localism becomes a counter-hegemony to this globalization thesis, a call to action under the claim that the antidote to global power is local power. In other words, if global is domination then in the local we must find freedom. Friedmann (1994: 30), a trenchant observer of the globalization of food, makes this point forcefully: "only food economies that are bounded, that is, regional, can be regulated" because they bypass the "corporate principles of distance and durability."

Pointing to Habermas' idea of the "colonization of the lifeworld" by the instrumental reason of capitalism, Hendrickson and Heffernan (2002) correspondingly embrace the local as the normative realm of resistance, a place where caring can and does happen. This echoes much of the US local food system literature, in which care ethics, desire, realization, and a sustainable vision become the explanatory factors in the creation of alternative food systems. In these norm or ethics-based explanations, the "local" becomes the context in which cultural values work against anomic capitalism (see also Krippner 2001). In Europe, the local is invested with similar hopes as a rampart against globalized mass consumption of "placeless foods" (Murdoch and Miele 1999, 2002; Murdoch *et al.* 2000).

But who gets to define "the local"? What kind of society is the local embedded in? Who do you care for and how? What exactly is "quality" and who do you trust to provide it? As Hinrichs, Winter and others have noted, "the local" as a concept intrinsically implies the inclusion and exclusion of particular people, places and ways of life. The representation of the local and its constructs – embeddedness, trust, care, quality – privileges certain analytical categories and trajectories, whose effect is to naturalize and thereby conceal the politics of the local.

Unreflexive localism includes the defensive localism described by Hinrichs (2000, 2003), Hinrichs and Kremer (2002) and Winter (2003). The research on alternative agrifood initiatives (AFIs) in California by Allen *et al.* (2003) also reveals that localism is by no means inextricably associated with efforts to implement more socially just "care ethic" agendas. These studies demonstrate that localism is not always democratic and fully representative of local communities. The fundamental point was made by Clare Hinrichs (2000: 301): simply to *take it for granted* that locally embedded economic activities necessarily involve non-instrumental, ethics-based interpersonal relations is to "conflate spatial relations with social relations." In this respect, Hinrichs and Kremer (2002) show that local food system members are mainly white, middle-class professionals and warn that the movement is socially homogenized and exclusionary. In a case study of AFIs to relocalize the food system in Iowa, Hinrichs (2003: 37) cautions that these attempts to construct regional identity can be associated with a "defensive politics of localization," leading to reification of the "local" and becoming "elitist and reactionary, appealing to nativist sentiments."

Nevertheless, the view that localist solutions resist the injustices perpetrated by industrial capitalism is widely held by food activists in the USA and advocates of agrarian-based rural development in Europe. But is localism in itself more socially just? As the studies of AFIs in California and the Mid-West demonstrate, localism can be based on the interests of a narrow, sectionalist, even authoritarian, elite (see also Harvey 2001). A politics that supports an absolute standard of "the good" without examining how that standard will affect others in the community we call an "unreflexive" politics. To formulate a more reflexive politics of localism, we build on the idea of an "open politics" of reflexivity to envision a localism that is more socially just while leaving open a definition of social justice.

We reject a politics that holds up an ideal utopian "romantic" model of society and then works to change society to meet that standard. Instead, we advocate open-ended, continuous, "reflexive" processes – what Childs (2003) calls "transcommunal" and Benhabib (1996) "deliberative" politics – that bring together a broadly representative group of people to explore and discuss ways of changing their society. Rather than a "politics of conversion," we follow Childs (2003) in arguing for a democratic "politics of respect." These processes also take account of the unintended consequences, ironies, and contradictions involved in all social change, and treat ongoing conflicts and differences between various groups not as polarizing divisions but as grounds for respectful – and even productive – disagreement (cf. Hassanein 2003). That is, we place fully deliberative democratic processes squarely at the center of our formulation of an open politics of localism.

A politics of perfection

These critiques reveal that the politics of localism can be problematic and contradictory. However, these critiques are not made to de-legitimize localism but to provide a better understanding of the complexity and pitfalls of local politics and the long-term deleterious effects of reform movements controlled primarily by particular groups of local people. The social history of urban middle-class reform has shown that these movements, bent on "improvement," whether of "degraded" urban environments or "unhealthy" working-class families, tended to create a "sanitarian" germ politics (Hamlin, 1998), which separated the "dirty" from the "clean" and, in the same way, established a welfare system that distinguished between the "deserving" and the "undeserving" poor. Several feminist social historians have critiqued these welfare reform movements for their narrow race, class, and gender "maternalist" politics based on a particular norm or "standard" as the "right" way to live (Baker, 1991; Mink, 1995). DuPuis (2002, 2007) shows that the middle-class controlled the agendas of both the US food reform and welfare movements by *universalizing* particular ways of living as "perfect."

Furthermore, this "politics of perfection" of US reform movements stems not only from a class hegemonic politics but also incorporates the racial representation of whiteness as the "unmarked category." Lipsitz (1998) calls US white middle-class politics "the possessive investment in whiteness." This possessive investment has a material aspect in the monopolization of resources, with mortgage credit and education being two instances that Lipsitz emphasizes (see also Cohen 2003). This is accomplished by a sleight of hand in which institutionalized racism is hidden behind a representation of what is "normal," with all variations from this norm represented as "deviations." For example, a coalition of white middle-class reform groups, health officials, and farmers elevated milk to the status of a "perfect food" that would improve the general health of all bodies when, in fact, milk is a culturally, genetically, and historically specific food (DuPuis 2002).

A reflexive local politics of food would take into account the ways in which people's notions of "right living," and especially "right eating," are wrapped up in these possessive investments in race, class, and gender. Such a politics would actively seek to expose and undermine the tendency of specific groups to work from this "politics of perfection," which universalizes and designates particular ways of eating as ideal when, in fact, all eating – like all human action – is imperfect and contradictory, as recent analyses of obesity in the USA clearly demonstrate (Guthman and DuPuis 2006).

The power and effectiveness of white middle-class reform movements – from abolition to Alar – cannot be denied. These movements have accomplished much, especially in terms of providing US cities with water and sewer systems, without which they would have continued to be places of extremely high mortality (Tarr 1996; Platt 2005). However, particularly with the rise of a new, more fractured middle-class politics in the USA, it is important to pay more attention to the ways in which possessive investments in racial privilege influence how we define problems and solutions (cf. Slocum 2006, 2007; Holloway 2007; Guthman 2008b).

One way to do this is to consider recent reinterpretations of US history that have put race squarely at the center of the story, particularly those histories that examine the creation of local rural places. For example, Matt Garcia's *A World of Its Own* (2001) and Herbert's *White Plague* (1987) show how white middle-classes created systems of local racial domination in some rural areas of California and Texas, respectively. In fact, one of the most shocking aspects of Matt Garcia's history of Los Angeles' orange production regions in the early part of the twentieth century is the juxtaposition of political rhetoric describing orange growers as democratic yeoman with cheerful pictures of them dressed up in Ku Klux Klan robes. Orange growing communities put Hispanic workers "in their place" in more ways than one, burning crosses on lawns if Hispanic families tried to move into neighborhoods beyond the labor camps and *colonias*, while allowing them to provide "ethnic" entertainment in exclusive white supper clubs.

Localism and the "new paradigm" of European rural development

Needless to say, local food movements in Europe arise from very different class, racial, and gendered histories. Calls for the re-localization of food systems reflect a perceived need to protect European rural economy and society from the damaging consequences of international agricultural trade liberalization and the global reach of standardized industrial food provision. As we discuss in more detail in Part II of this book, these calls resonate with a growing perception in EU policy circles that the consumer-driven "turn" to quality has created a wider range of farm-based livelihood opportunities for those producers who can adopt conventions of product quality that emphasize territorial provenance in localized socio-ecological processes. This market-oriented approach emerges strongly in the European academic literature on local food systems, placing great emphasis on the economic viability of new, farm-based sources of value-added and related processes of territorial valorization, as we see below.

However, the European rural imaginary also embraces a distinctive "possessive investment" in national traditions, although it is expressed in an "unmarked" discourse of small family farms, local markets where producers and consumers interact, regional food cultures, vibrant rural communities, and ecologically diverse rural environments. To varying degrees, this rural imaginary also has influenced several recent thematic contributions to European rural sociology.

It is particularly salient in the notion of endogenous rural development, which builds on the empirical observation that European agriculture is entangled in a diverse constellation of socio-ecological, economic, cultural, and historical relations. This diversity is conceptualized in terms of "styles of farming," and it is argued that "Europe's countryside (should) be safeguarded as precious 'cultural capital'" by promoting "farming styles based on the optimal use of local resources" (Ploeg and van Dijk 1995: xii). This normative position is underpinned by the economic claim that "endogenous development patterns tend to materialize as self-centered processes of growth: that is, relatively large parts of the total value generated through this type of development are re-allocated in the locality itself" (Ploeg and Long 1994: 2).

A rural imaginary also infuses the characterization of "alternative food networks" and "short food supply chains" (SFSCs) as sources of *resistance* against the homogenizing effects of "placeless," globalized, industrial modes of food provisioning and the "McDonaldization" of regional food cultures (Murdoch and Miele 1999, 2002; Marsden *et al.* 1999; Murdoch *et al.* 2000). The Slow Food movement, with its efforts to counter the march of the "golden arches" by valorizing regional cuisines and their rural networks of provision, has established itself as a prominent expression of this oppositional, "militant particularism."

Unlike its US counterpart, however, the normative idealization of the "rural local" – the re-localization and re-embedding of agro-food practices in local eco-social relations – is attenuated and obscured, at least in part, by a complementary discourse of economic performance and competitiveness, which has attracted policy support. The prominence of this framing has grown as the reorientation of the EU's CAP toward a wider notion of rural development involving more decentralized policymaking, multifunctionality, and territoriality has gathered momentum (Lowe *et al.* 2002: 14–15).

The claims articulated earlier to buttress the concept of endogenous rural development re-emerge with AFN/SFSC now seen as new sources of value added that can be retained locally and hence as catalysts of rural economic regeneration and dynamism. As argued elsewhere: "The ability of quality food products to secure premium prices and so generate excess profits is a central plank of (this) market-led, value added model" (D. Goodman 2004: 8). However, apropos our theme of a reflexive food politics, these formulations of a market-oriented, "economic" localism ignore the inequalities of place politics, not least who gains in the struggles to appropriate and sustain the flows of economic rent arising in the "new economic spaces" created by AFN/SFSC (Ploeg *et al.* 2000; Marsden *et al.* 2002; Ploeg and Renting 2000; Renting *et al.* 2003).

This framing of the local as a new site of surplus value generation usefully reminds us of the dynamism of valorization processes. However, these analyses do not address the political driving forces behind the reconfiguration of space and scale and the new forms of commodification of territoriality – as *terroir*, traditional skills, landrace species, for example. The local as an arena of political-economic struggle and socially constructed scale of accumulation remains an opaque category, conceptually and empirically, a veritable black box.

Territoriality, a cipher for the local, similarly is unexamined, figured by land-scape, habitat, or craft knowledge in ways which naturalize the social relations underlying its production and reproduction.

Rethinking the idea of the local: taking politics seriously

The purpose of our critique is not to deny the local as a powerful political imaginary in the struggle against the forces of globalization. Our real goal is to understand how to make localism into an effective social movement of resistance to globalization rather than a way for local elites to create protective territories that narrowly serve their own interests. This requires letting go of a local that is fetishized as intrinsically moral and more just. *We have to move away from the idea that food systems become just simply by virtue of making them local and toward a conversation about the work needed to make them more just.*

In seeking to bring politics "back in" to analyses of local food networks, we are drawn to Amin's (2002: 397) proposal for a new politics of the local. Thus he argues for a "shift in emphasis from the politics *of* place to a politics *in* place" (original emphasis). The former "sees cities and regions as performing a kind of place-based politics,... a distinctive politics of place based on the powers of proximity/particularity in a world of displaced and multi-scalar happenings and power geometries" (ibid.: 396–397). Politics *in* place, by contrast, is

> a non-territorial way of viewing place politics in an age of global connectivity. Instead of seeing political activity as unique, places might be seen as the sites which juxtapose the varied politics – the local, national, and global – that we find today. What matters is this juxtaposition.
>
> (Amin 2002: 397)

The merit of Amin's conception is "to see political activity in places as plural, open, and contested" (ibid.: 397), thereby avoiding the normative contradictions to which a politics of place is prone (see also Castree 2003a, 2004).

To forge our understanding of the local as an imperfect politics in place, we need to open up the black box of "trust" and ask: where does that trust come from and is it always intrinsically good? In some cases, such as local food systems controlled by organized crime, trust involves the certainty of harm if one does not follow the rules. The historical relationship between organized crime and New York's Fulton Fish Market comes immediately to mind here (*New York Times* 1997), although there are undoubtedly many other examples.

Trust, therefore, like all other social interaction, is political. It is not necessarily based on equitable relationships nor on reflexive democratic processes. Nevertheless, the re-localization literature has tended to treat trust as intrinsically just, another way of depoliticizing an activity by purifying it. This "perfect" politics is embedded in social narratives of salvation and degradation that have been a part of US middle-class, romantic, reformist culture since the early nineteenth century (DuPuis 2002; DuPuis and Vandergeest 1995).

Instead, we seek to free food reform movements from control by consumers of a particular class and ethnicity who have historically set the agenda for "saving" the food system. In the following sections, we "depurify" ideas of the local and of trust by re-admitting politics into an understanding of food re-localization as a social movement. This enables us to rethink the local, not as a romantic move toward emancipation but as an "open," inclusive, and reflexive politics in place.

To do this, we need to understand the ways in which localization might relate to various existing forms of power. Interestingly, there are substantial bodies of research on these issues that have been largely neglected in the local food studies literature. A brief overview of work in three of these areas – urban studies, regionalism, and the politics of scale – will reinforce the case for analyzing local food systems as a politics in place.

Urban studies

The politics between city elites and food producers in their rural hinterland has been almost entirely ignored, arguably due to a disciplinary split between urban and rural sociology, and urban and rural geography. Rural sociologists, perhaps not surprisingly, tend to be particularly unfamiliar with urban sociology. While this lacuna may have been of less significance in earlier studies of rurality, it becomes particularly problematic in the study of local food systems, which are characterized by relationships both within and between the urban and the rural. For example, there has been little attention to the urban political interests around farmers' markets. Yet, if only for purely demographic reasons, food politics, whether the "urban–rural food alliances" of the 1970s and 1980s (McLeod 1976; Belasco 1989) or today's "food policy councils," are based in urban activism. Nearly all food councils – the Kansas City Food Circle, the Toronto Food Policy Council, for example – are named after the city that contains the consumers, not the region that contains the producers. Similarly in Europe, the ethos and organization of food politics typically are urban (cf. Lang 2007).

This suggests that we need to examine these dimensions of the urban to understand local food systems. Better analysis of local urban–rural politics will lead, we believe, to less reliance on normative – *gesellschaft/gemeinschaft* – explanations and give greater weight to the opening up of political processes. While many areas of urban studies have something to offer to the analysis of local food systems, we will draw very briefly on only two subdisciplines here: community power studies and urban environmental history.

Studies of community power began with Robert Dahl's (1961) historical analysis of political power in New Haven, Connecticut, continued with John Gaventa's (1980) study of power and powerlessness in Appalachia and are most evident today in the analyses of city growth politics initiated by Logan and Harvey (1987). The findings of these community power studies make it difficult to conceive of the local as the ethical guarantor of an egalitarian "politics of care." These analyses reveal how local urban elites go about controlling city and regional politics, although often constrained by the increasingly global competition over economic growth. One of the classics of urban community power research – Dahl's (1961) study of New Haven, *Who governs?* – reveals the power of elites in that city even as the social composition of that elite group changed over time. At first, old patrician families maintained political control, later to be replaced by local industry leaders, and then by an ethnic political regime. A key question worth exploring is to ask how the urban–rural interface varied in the patrician, industrial, and ethnic political eras identified by Dahl. Did agrarian–patrician politics differ from agrarian–industrial politics, and to what effect? To what extent did the different political interests – industrial, artisan–agrarian, ethnic – clash or coincide?

So far, US urban environmental historians have come the closest to answering these questions. They emphasize the role of local institutions, elites and political coalitions in the construction of urban ecosystems that "connect" cities to nature (Cronon 1991). Middle-class urban consumer reformers in the USA emerge as a powerful political force in this process (Tarr 1996; Platt 2005; DuPuis 2004a), including the creation of food systems (DuPuis 2002).

For much of the modern urban period, white middle-class consumers – in alliance with the growing class of government professionals – actively supported the growth of large-scale urban provisioning systems because they saw this system as cheaply and efficiently meeting their needs (cf. Cohen, 2003), part of the larger Fordist "bargain" that defined modes of urban livelihood "systems of provision" (Fine and Leopold 1993). Now, however, this Fordist triangulation between urban consumers, government professionals, and large-scale global capitalism – the old sanitarian Fordist regime – has unraveled. With the disintegration of this modern consumer–government–industrial food alliance, some urban consumers are seeking new allies.

In the USA, many of these new middle-class urban consumer movements – notably those inspired by Alice Waters and Carlo Petrini – are looking to Europe – particularly France and Italy – as a kind of "city on a hill" vision of a different kind of political alliance between cities and the countryside. The extent to which European urban–rural relationships in fact fulfill this ideal, whether it can survive untarnished as Spain becomes the new California and Africa becomes Europe's global garden (Freidberg 2004), and whether or not US consumers can successfully re-create Europe in their backyards are all key questions in understanding the contemporary politics of food localism.

Regionalism and sectional politics

Human geographers have long understood (cf. Harvey 1985; Cox 2002) that localism, rather than being a romantic movement of resistance, can be mobilized as a powerful strategy of territorial competition between regions. For the most part, localism is as much about the protection of particular places against other places as it is a form of resistance to some abstract conception of "the global." Two literatures are particularly applicable here: the economic geography literature on regional economic development, and the historical literature on sectionalism and regional urban–rural/farmer–consumer alliances.

In some cases, sectionalism can walk a thin line between a regional development effort and a form of xenophobia. For example, in California, one commercial for the state cheese industry features two cows, one of which is embarrassed because it has a spot on its flank that resembles the rival cheese-producing state of Wisconsin. "Is that why Marge acts so weird to me," it asks its friend and fellow cow, "because I thought it was because of the time I backwashed in the water trough." As this case shows, sectional competition and xenophobia can become political bedfellows. Local social movements supporting environmental goals need to ask whether there are costs to allying themselves with xenophobic sectionalism or "defensive localism" (Winter 2003). There may also be unacceptable costs to alliances with local elites that stand to benefit from localization. While these may seem obvious points, they often get missed in homogenous references to "community" and "trust" in the localist discourse on food.

In Europe, the prospect that greater interregional competition may lead to disequalizing – if not zero-sum – outcomes, also offers a serious challenge to the notion of re-localization as a new rural development paradigm. As Buller and Morris (2004: 1078) observe, "once territoriality becomes a component of value, it also becomes a commodity in itself, to protect and exploit, a source of differentially commodified relationships," leading to, in Marsden's words, "new rural geographies of value" (Marsden 1999: 507). The dimensions and expressions of this new competitive territoriality of value, and its implications for processes of rural development, are only just beginning to be explored.

One possible point of departure, as agro-food studies "meets" regional economic development, is to affirm, with Cox (2002), following Harvey (1985), the importance of "territorial coalitions" in contesting and improving local positions in the geographic division of production and consumption. Brunori and Rossi's (2007) research on the struggles between different coalitions of local and external actors to demarcate the "Chianti" region in Tuscany and appropriate the economic rents of its symbolic capital is an insightful illustration of this approach (as discussed in detail in Chapter 4).

In other words, and this is a deceptively simple point, when we attempt to implement a local food system strategy, we need to pay attention to local institutional interests. We need to ask: which local institutions are more successful in promoting democratic, reflexive localist solutions and which merely perpetuate local inequalities? In this respect, historical scholarship on the organization of regional institutions in US and European political development is revealing (Sanders 1999; Bensel 1984). For example, Elizabeth Sanders has examined the interconnections between different forms of agrarian and urban politics in several US regions to explain why "farmer–labor alliances" were more salient in some regions than others. Following Sanders, DuPuis (2002) and DuPuis and Block (2008: 15) show how different urban–rural political alliances in the Chicago and New York milksheds contested the boundaries of the dairy milk market orders created by the 1937 federal legislation "in locally specific ways." As DuPuis and Block (2008) demonstrate, these boundary struggles resulted in the coexistence of two agroecologically distinct dairy (farming) styles of resource use.

Such a historical perspective on the politics of regionalism could greatly improve the understanding of local food systems today. For example, if the racial or ethnic composition of cities differs significantly from the characteristics of the rural hinterland, how will this affect potential political alliances? Agrarian politics, at least in California, also entails a landlord class – often living in local cities – whose interests often differ not only from those of producers but also from those of other city residents (DuPuis 2004b). In these cases, the perspectives gained from urban studies and economic geography may help provide explanations for the relative strength or weakness of urban–rural food alliances.

Localism and neoliberal globalization

Several influential social constructionist formulations of contemporary global–local relations argue that globalization processes are producing a new "scalar fix" in the geographic division of labor of the state (Jessop 2000). In this reconfiguration of political scales, the subnational and global levels are gaining prominence at the expense of the nation-state, a process that has been characterized as "glocalization" (Swyngedouw 1997a, 1997b) and the "hollowing out of the state" (Jessop 1999, 2000). A number of authors (Jessop 1998; Lovering 1999; Lawrence 2005; Dean 1999) have suggested that the embrace of localist forms of control "are experiments in sub-national regional governance that are themselves a response to wider problems in managing global capitalism" (Lawrence 2005: 3).

Re-localization can be seen as part of the restructuring of government toward "governance": the devolution of some autonomy in decision making to networks of local actors but with coordination still exercised through multilayered, top-down institutional structures. From this more critical perspective, re-localization appears to be not so much about resistance to neoliberal globalization as an intrinsic part of it because it has "endorsed and fostered the self-regulation of individuals and communities which, at the regional level, equates to the acceptance of programs, techniques and procedures that support market rule, productivism and global competition" (Lawrence 2005: 9). In other words, re-localization can be part and parcel of what Dean (1999), drawing on Foucault, calls "neoliberal governmentality."

In the face of these new arguments about global governance, the presumption that localization intrinsically stands as a force against globalization seems, at best, naive. In fact, in the absence of specific case studies, it is arguable that localization most recently has been deployed to further a neoliberal form of global logic, a refashioning of agricultural governance that plays on both left ideals of political participation and right ideals of non-interference in markets (cf. Allen *et al.* 2003). This is a dangerous political bargain, which in other arenas has led to the dismantling of hard-fought government institutional capacities in utility regulation, antitrust and state protection of citizens' health and welfare. It would be equally presumptuous, of course, to argue that all localism is the handmaiden of neoliberalism. However, only by looking at the local as a "politics in place" is it possible to understand the ways in which localism is deployed for or against global forces.

Local politics as the "new politics of scale"

The largely apolitical approach to place construction in the agro-food literature on the quality "turn" and local food systems contrasts vividly with the lively debates on the politics of space and place found in human geography. These debates bring out the importance of spatial and scalar political processes in the social construction of place, emphasize the contingent nature of socio-spatial structures and scalar orderings, and direct analytical attention to the "winners" and "losers" in these struggles.

Despite its potential complementarity, the agro-food literature on local food systems curiously has ignored this challenging body of work in human geography. Indeed, the quality "turn" literature takes the ontology of the local as given, not as a category to be explicated in terms of societal processes. This stance is certainly idiosyncratic, if not myopic, when "the proposition that geographical scale is *socially constructed* (is) an established truism within contemporary human geography" (Brenner 2001: 592, original emphasis). In this perspective, territories and scales are "*contested social constructions*" (Herod 1991: 84, original emphasis) and the ontology of scale, from the "local" to the "global," is not preordained but can be reconfigured through socio-political struggle (Smith 1993; Swyngedouw 1997a, 1997b).

AFN/SFSC scholarship could productively engage with the socio-spatial practices of scale construction to theorize the *contested, relational processes* constituting the local and the dynamic interaction between local forms of socio-spatial organization and trans-local actors and institutions. Instead, the local in agro-food studies is currently taken for granted as a "purified" category, as somehow given in the "order of things," and treated as a context or locale that is conducive to the emergence of new economic forms incorporating "alternative" social norms.

The relevance of the new politics of scale for explorations of power and politics in local food systems lies in the centrality it gives to social struggle and contestation in the *making* of place and scale. This analytical focus also undermines reductionist global–local binaries and the tendency to concede the global as the domain of capital while paradoxically framing the local as a site of empowerment (Herod and Wright 2002). This emphasis on contested socio-spatial processes draws on the wider point that "Interests are constituted at many different scales and contest scale divisions of labor that are equally varied and equally subject to re-definition" (Cox 2002: 106).

So far in this chapter we have cautioned against the reification of the local found in normative and market-oriented perspectives and its naturalization as a bulwark against anomic global capitalism. Instead, an inclusive and reflexive politics in place understands local food systems not as local "resistance" against a global capitalist "logic" but as the outcome of mutually constitutive, imperfect, political processes in which the local and the global make each other on an everyday basis. In this more "realist" open-ended story, actors are allowed to be reflexive about both their own norms and about the structural economic logics of production. We now extend this reflexive open-endedness to ideas of social justice in local food networks. How can we work towards just food in local food politics?

Social justice and reflexive food politics

We have suggested that food activists and scholars conflate "the local" and "justice" but this ignores another larger conversation about the meaning of justice itself. The alternative food movement would be more effective, we argue, if it worked with a more reflexive notion of justice, one based on a clear understanding of the complexities of justice in its various and contradictory meanings. In developing this argument, we look at the pervasive but unexamined conceptions of justice – communitatarian, anticorporate, and liberal egalitarian – underlying much food activism, as well as the current embrace of a more cultural notion of justice in food movement agendas. We will focus on how the conversations about justice in political theory deal with the tensions between the universal and the particular, and how local food movements have ignored these issues.

Theories of justice

Recalling our earlier discussion of "perfectionism," we need to ask some of the basic questions that have pervaded political philosophy since its inception. Is justice a matter of determining "the good" – such as "good food" – and then attempting to move society toward this ideal? Or is the adoption of a single set of universal values intrinsically non-egalitarian, insofar as some members of society determine a singular set of ideals not necessarily shared by others, values that are resisted as a violation of their freedom? Even those professing the best of intentions can create particular visions of "the good life" that unconsciously exclude some people. These tensions between the democratic ideals of individual autonomy and sovereign notions of "the common good" constitute a central debate in modern political theory. Understanding this debate on the meaning of justice can help us clarify questions of local food and social justice as well.

Since the time of Plato, philosophers have sought to discover the ideals that would lead to a perfect – just – society. In the Middle Ages, religious and royal authorities determined these ideals for society as a whole. Beginning in the seventeenth century, however, Enlightenment political philosophers, such as Thomas Hobbes and John Locke, rejected religious authority and instead saw the ideals of justice as human rights for democratic participation in the creation of a social contract. In *The Social Contract*, Jean-Jacques Rousseau argued that individuals, through democratic processes, could define just ideals of "the common good" and "the good life" for a particular society (Rousseau 1986). Jefferson enshrined the ideas of natural rights and universal truths in the Declaration of Independence, translating the democratic ideals of a just society through his understanding of Locke and Rousseau.

But some political philosophers responded skeptically to the idea of a social contract. Utilitarian political philosophers Jeremy Bentham and John Stuart Mill rejected social contract idealism as injurious to an individual's personal freedom to choose his or her own idea of the good, just life. For utilitarians, the perfectionist vision of "the good life" was inevitably authoritarian, since it imposed a particular idea of good living on everyone and did not admit alternative views. In other words, perfectionist idealism is undemocratic – unjust – denying the individual's own rationality and ability to determine "right living." Bentham and Mill's utilitarianism was specifically aimed at overcoming this platonic, social contract-based, perfectionist view of justice. Adam Smith took this a step further, arguing that involvement in market exchange was the way in which individuals pursued their interests, fulfilling both their individual notions of the good life and creating greater wealth for all. From this perspective, the market facilitates social justice by enabling individuals to choose the life they wish to lead.

In response to the utilitarian critique, social contract political philosophers have argued that a world based solely on individual interests would lead to a war of all against all – a state of social chaos first depicted by Thomas Hobbes – making the creation of a social contract imperative. Hobbes argued that in a society without traditional hierarchies like the Church or the Crown, a social contract was necessary to avoid this anarchy, a dystopian view of society often depicted nowadays in post-apocalyptic movies like *Blade Runner*. Ever since Hobbes first developed the idea of a social contract – and the Hobbesian nightmare of social chaos – tensions between individual liberty and social order have pervaded the political theory debate about social justice.

John Rawls' seminal work, *A Theory of Justice* (Rawls 1971, 1999), represents the most prominent attempt to reconcile these tensions. Rawls' liberal egalitarian theory of justice revived the Enlightenment ideas of equal rights and individual freedom while taking seriously both social contract ideas of fairness and utilitarian critiques of perfectionism. Rawls formulated a universal political philosophy of right action that did not rely on a pre-formed, perfectionist set of ideals or values, except for a basic social commitment to equality (Rawls 1971, 1999). In other words, Rawls' theory of justice acknowledged the utilitarian notions of liberty from authority while maintaining the social contract idea that there is one universal idea of justice as "fairness."

Rawls demonstrated how to reconcile liberal ideas of equality with utilitarian ideas of freedom through a thought experiment: what would the social contract look like if people agreed to an idea of justice under a "veil of ignorance" about their own economic and social position in society? He argued that, under those (theoretical) circumstances, people would agree to the maximum possible liberty and equality – including equality of access to political institutions – but that they would accept an unequal distribution of wealth if that inequality benefited the least well-off members of society. In other words, you deserved more if your efforts and talents were dedicated to improving the lives of those who have the least.

Rawls' work initiated an intense debate over the nature of justice in contemporary society and critiques of his ideas tend to come from three alternative perspectives: political economy, communitarian, and cultural.

Political economy perspectives

These approaches place the onus for injustice on the structure of capitalism, particularly global industrial capitalism and its market-based individualism, as celebrated by libertarians. The political economy perspective draws on Marx's critique of commodity fetishism as casting a veil over the real inequalities in capitalist society. That is, market exchange and economic goods – rather than being what utilitarians see as a source of individual freedom – are in fact a "fetish," an illusory form of freedom. For Marx, social injustice arose from private ownership of the means of production, which constituted the material basis of the exploitation of labor by capital. From this perspective, one of the goals of a social justice movement is to unveil this "truth" since it is assumed that awareness of these exploitative relationships will to lead to social action. Contemporary critiques of global corporate control and monopoly power tend to follow this line of argument.

Yet, both Marx and Rawls critiqued perfectionist ideas of social justice, agreeing with utilitarians that the solution to social problems was not to re-establish particular normative values, but to adopt better political processes (although they disagreed on the nature of those processes). Marx advocated a radical restructuring of society, but he did not paint a vision of the "perfect society" that would result from that process. Both Marx and Rawls agreed with Smith that perfectionist visions of social ideals were inimical to freedom. Marx was famously critical of the communitarians, especially Proudhon, and other utopian visionaries for their attempts to imagine and create such alternative, ideal societies. Unlike Rawls, however, Marx railed against liberal egalitarian ideas as part of the fetishization – the veiling – of politics under capitalism.

Communitarian perspectives

Communitarian theorists of justice begin by re-embracing ideas of "the good life" as community shared values. Communitarian notions of justice are based in the particular, although the definition of this particularity tends to be spatial (as in a particular neighborhood) or voluntary (as in a particular group joined together for a common goal and with common values). Communitarians seek to re-establish moral economies (Scott 1976) that are informed by a larger set of social and cultural values (Etzioni 1995), a move both utilitarians and liberal egalitarians criticize as perfectionist and authoritarian, and therefore inimical to individual freedom.

Communitarian concepts of social justice are embedded in particular relationships of trust, often based on the physical proximity of living in the same place. In most, but not all, cases, "communitarians tie their notions of a good society to a good place. In other words, justice and territory go hand-in-hand" (DuPuis *et al.* 2006: 259). As Kymlicka 1990: 209) observes, communitarians "are united by the belief that political philosophy must pay more attention to the shared practices and understandings within each society." Proponents of communitarian forms of social justice, such as Michael Walzer (1990) and Michael Sandel (1982), argue in favor of community-based autonomy in which people join together to articulate decisions about the good life and how to go about making a good society. Their stance counters the individualism predominant in egalitarian liberal notions of social justice, which define the good life as equal political representation within a "neutral state." For communitarians, in contrast, the roots of social justice are to be found in the "politics of the common good," which

> is conceived of as a substantive conception of the good life which defines the community's "way of life." This common good, rather than adjusting itself to the pattern of people's preferences, provides a standard by which those preferences are evaluated. The community's way of life forms the basis for a public ranking of conceptions of the good, and the weight given to an individual's preferences depends on how much she conforms or contributes to this common good.
>
> (Kymlicka 1990: 220)

Cultural theories of justice

Cultural perspectives on justice add to the complexity of the debate on perfectionism. Perfectionist ideals, culturalist theorists argue, are cloaked in false notions of rational, scientific objectivity that underlie liberal notions of rights. Instead, feminists, postcolonial and critical race theorists argue that universalist notions of justice are exclusionary, as are particularist notions of social justice advocated by communitarians. Both universal and particularist ideas of justice tend to make a particular type of person, generally the Western white male citizen, into a universal category (Lipsitz 2006; Omi and Winant 1986). While they may agree with the communitarians that justice must include considerations of group autonomy, cultural theorists argue that this should recognize racial, religious, and ethnic "group differentiated rights" *within* communities. Cultural theorists and communitarians, therefore, both agree that justice requires shared norms, although in different ways.

Cultural approaches to justice stem from identity-based group definitions of "the good life," whether from a gender, race, or religious perspective. These more particularistic and contingent notions of justice emphasize differences in group epistemological standpoints derived from histories of oppression and exclusion (Collins 2000). Culturalists criticize liberal egalitarian forms of justice for imposing an idea of the individual, autonomous subject, whether as intrinsically white (Lipsitz 1998), Western civilized (Said and Sjöström 1995) or predominantly male (Butler 1999; Scott 1988).

Yet cultural theorists also agree with utilitarians that a single, universal idea of "the good life" is authoritarian as it does not recognize the diversity of viewpoints. Identity-based theories of justice begin by uncovering the racialized aspect – "whiteness" – of seemingly universal ideals of the good life, and argue that all universal ideals are, in fact, embedded in particular forms of racial dominance.

From a culturalist perspective, historical analyses of local politics by critical race scholars show that localism has been used as a tool for exclusion rather than inclusion. For example, Lizabeth Cohen's history of US consumerism (Cohen 2003) demonstrates that localism was implicated in non-egalitarian local agendas in many different arenas, particularly housing, access to financial capital, and education. Her work on the rise of consumerism after World War II reveals that localism was instrumental in the creation of "stratified communities with mass suburbanization" (ibid.: 230). In her historical study of the State of New Jersey, Cohen argues that the rise of local "home rule" led to increased segregation and an inequitable distribution of state resources toward white neighborhoods. Critical race scholars have also shown how moral notions of health and rightness serve as instruments of power and exclusion. For example, Shah (2001) finds that moral notions about community public health represented particular ways of life and particular groups practicing those ways of life as "healthy," which set other groups apart as vice-ridden and unsanitary.

Communitarianism as group autonomy is not always defensive, however. Sometimes it is linked with tolerance of other cultures and practices within a community, as with the Amish communities. Yet, even the most well-intentioned communitarians sometimes clash with cultural theorists, especially when definitions of "community values" exclude definitions of the "good life" embraced by other groups in a locality (Guthman 2008b; Slocum 2007).

Some scholars have sought to envision a multicultural "transcommunal" ideal (Childs 2003) that takes Bentham's perfectionist critique into account, yet accepts a coexistence of different group-based ideals. This reflexive approach tends to focus on the discovery of good *processes* rather than *visions* of good life. From this perspective, processes of collaboration can emerge between groups that have different conceptions of "the good life," or even of life itself. This scholarship has revealed how certain civil rights groups that identify as autonomous communities nevertheless also work with the tension of practicing egalitarian decision making within the wider group, combining liberal and communitarian notions (Polletta 2002). The reflexive approach we discuss below draws much of its inspiration from this perspective.

Food justice

In their rhetoric and practice of social justice, food movement activists tend to draw upon one or other of these perspectives without reflexively recognizing the tensions between them. Instead, they tend to work at a nexus between communitarian, anticorporate globalization, and egalitarian perspectives, without acknowledging these different views of justice. This juxtaposition also is evident in the localist advocacy of such popular authors as Gary Nabhan (2002), Brian Halweil (2004), Michael Pollan (2006), Barbara Kingsolver *et al.*'s *Animal, Vegetable, Miracle* (2007) and Francis Moore Lappe and Anna Lappe's *Hope's Edge*, (2002), who call for the rebuilding of local food systems as a way to fight the global industrialization of the food system. For these writers, as well as the "New Agrarians," such as Wendell Berry and Wes Jackson, grassroots democratic processes promise to (re-)create community values as the basis of a just society, with the capacity to resist the universal, instrumentalist juggernaut of industrial food provisioning.

The maxim "Think Globally, Act Locally" brings together the antiglobalization critique of corporate food with a communitarian notion of values-based food systems founded on group interconnections in local moral economies. "Think Globally," in the food politics context, means a critique of the industrial food system that begins with a Marxian unveiling of the true nature of food production, showing in particular "where your food comes from," as in the popular documentary, *Food, Inc.* Food activist discourses then tend to "Act Locally" through the communitarian "coming together" of people in local food networks. Yet, this second part of the equation leads antiglobal food activists away from Marx's revolutionary ideas of radical social restructuring and his vigorous rejection of the market as a vehicle of change, and toward communitarian relocalization through consumer support for local farmers – and the utilitarian solution of the market – as the ideal.

The political alliance between Marxian anticorporatists and communitarians is therefore subtle: communitarians see the local as the remaking of community connections while anticorporatists see localism as fostering greater transparency and smaller production structures. For the anticorporatists, food is better if you get to see how it is made. Once you know the truth, you will opt to buy your food from a local system of smaller farms. For the communitarians, food is better if you create a personal connection of trust and shared values with the person who produces your food. Either way, *local* food solves the "justice problem" as defined from both perspectives.

However, as we have already cautioned, the pursuit of local food as justice can lead to key alliances with more conservative groups whose idea of community integrity may involve the exclusion of particular groups induced, for example, by a "politics of fear" (Davis 1998). In other words, this lack of reflexivity about the meaning of local food justice can create common purpose between odd political bedfellows of communitarians, Marxists and the "crunchy conservatives" described by popular social commentator, Rod Dreher (Dreher 2006).

In practice, the "moral economy" of local food systems embedded in communities with shared values may therefore be more of a pragmatic alliance between different political interests that conceals substantially different ideas of social justice.

In fact, this pragmatic alliance politics can be in conflict with liberal, Marxist, and cultural notions of justice. A pragmatic local food politics that ignores exclusionary practices and local elite control violates the liberal egalitarianism notion of individual equality, that is, the right of everyone to pursue their notions of the good life. If, as Hassenein (2003) argues, work on local food systems is a type of "participatory democracy," then this participation needs to take Rawls' liberal democratic ideas of equal access to political voice into account. Such pragmatic food politics also ignores Marxian critiques of market exchange as intrinsically exploitative of labor and runs counter to culturalist notions of justice as inclusive and tolerant toward different cultural viewpoints of "the good life."

However, from a reflexively localist perspective, these contradictions are regarded not as a reason to abandon local food activism, but instead as an argument for a new kind of localist practice, one that includes more careful "reflexive" interrogation of the relationships between "the local" and "justice." What kinds of justice can a localist food movement strategy pursue, and what tends to be left out of such strategies? Can food re-localization movements overcome these limitations, and if so, how?

Toward reflexive food justice

The answers to these questions are certain to be incremental, messy and bound up in imperfect politics (DuPuis 2002). In this section, we will explore how to rebuild localism along more just lines, through a more "reflexive localism" that takes into account different visions of justice, community, and good food (Staeheli 2008). Reflexivity is not a set of values, but a process by which people pursue goals while acknowledging the imperfection of their actions. Nor is it a particular, fixed process, but rather one that responds to changing circumstances, imperfectly, but with an awareness of the contradictions of the moment. Here is an imperfect start to a description of reflexive localism as a practice.

Reflexivity begins by admitting the contradictions and complexity of everyday life. As we have seen, a number of contemporary scholars have been attempting to formulate a theory of justice that both takes into account reflexive notions of equality while maintaining rights of group or community autonomy. Several influential political theorists, for example, are exploring the idea of "reflexive" or "dialectical" equality (Benhabib 1996, 2002; Young 1990; Beck *et al.* 1994). These theorists see reflexivity as a way to escape a politics of perfection that both hides and perpetuates hegemony. The challenge, therefore, is to discover practices that make society "better" without reinforcing inequalities (cf. DuPuis *et al.* 2006).

Reflexive approaches emphasize process rather than vision. That is, reflexivity is achieved through "open" collaborations that do not insist on shared values or even shared views of the world. Of course, it is just such alliances – between groups with different interests but some overlapping agendas – that make politics work. Local politics will always require collaborations between people with different, sometimes countervailing, interests (Hassanein 2003). A reflexive local politics works within, and not against, the awareness of these differences in political viewpoints, what Paola Di Maio refers to as "open ontologies" and critical race scholar John Brown Childs calls "transcommunality" (Childs 2003; Di Maio 2007).

Reflexivity does not favor any one scale of political practice. Born and Purcell (2006) suggest that localism is a "trap" that causes political movements to rely on a particular scale to further the goals of environmental sustainability, human health, and social justice. They argue that localism should be seen as one possible strategy and not as an intrinsic solution to the problems of the global food system. Reflexive approaches to food justice would assess the value of localism as a strategy on a case-by-case basis.

Our earlier discussion of "defensive localism" emphasized that economic boundaries erected at this scale, whether a local food system or other "buy local" initiatives (Hess 2009), can create and maintain social exclusion, economic inequality, and injustice. As a way to put reflexive social and environmental justice into practice, food justice activists have much to learn from New Regionalist and Smart Growth initiatives that attempt to reunite inner city and surrounding suburban and ex-urban interests and emphasize political inclusion and region-wide decision making (Clancy and Ruhf 2010; Pastor *et al.* 2000). This political approach also goes beyond the idea that city–country connections occur only along the commodity chain. A just and inclusive city–rural politics would give voice to political interests that go beyond consumers' interest in local farmers. Those we buy from are not the only rural people worthy of our thoughts.

Reflexivity works within multiple notions of privilege and economy. A reflexive food politics would address the ways in which racial notions of purity and privilege have helped to construct both our spatial and our dietary inequalities. We have seen that perfectionist, *unmarked* ideas of "good food" and "community values" have been used to marginalize certain groups, who are fully aware of such discrimination, as the sociology of deviance and social control has demonstrated (Becker 1997; Merton 1972). This reflexive awareness also would extend to recognition of the adverse effects of the inequitable rural–urban power relations in the USA (cf. Block and DuPuis 2001).

With this historical political economic perspective, activists could forge local food systems that are products of political relationships that cut across categories of economy and identity, making for a more inclusive metropolitan regionalism promoting equitable distribution of resources and services across the board. Food system re-localization could also contribute to New Regionalist political agendas by expanding beyond the suburban "rings" around cities. Ideas about "smart growth" and intelligent planning then become part of larger housing, nutrition, and economic development policies, which would include active partnerships with rural hinterlands.

Perpetuation of the ambiguous and mythic history of American Agrarianism in opposition to American Urbanism is also a disservice to localist food politics (Hofstadter 1955; Jacobs 1961). It entangles impersonal *gesellschaft* views of the city and value-filled *gemeinschaft* views of rural life with less idyllic views of the countryside as degraded "crackerdom" (Bell 1997) or spaces of racial exclusion (Agyeman 2002), and cities as the realm of tolerance and progressive thought (Jacobs 1961). Food movement activists must reject these distorted perspectives and combat their influence, for example, on farmers' market policy (McPhee and Zimmerman 1979; Alkon 2008), and other spheres of urban–rural relations. To pretend that foodsheds avoid such entanglements is a potentially fatal blindness of the local food movement.

Conclusion: embracing imperfect politics

From this more reflexive, non-perfectionist viewpoint, true reform of our food system requires that we muck ourselves up in the imperfection of political contestation over food. To start, we need to recognize the diverse yet always "situated" (Haraway 1991) productions of knowledge about "good" food. This will enable a more complex and inclusive discussion about what a just food system would look like, rather than pressing for certain "community values" as if all communities were defined by some identical monolithic set of values. A reflexive and imperfect open politics would also make us more aware of inequalities beyond the local that affect the range of choices we have closer to home, such as food industry monopolies, United States Department of Agriculture agency capture, nutrition policy, agricultural subsidies, food dumping, and food deserts, as well as extraordinary inequalities in wages and access to health care.

A reflexive food politics can include re-localization in a larger struggle over the global food system, combining a "not in my body" politics of boycotting and a "yes in my body" politics of 'buycotting' within a more realist perspective of local and global power. Reflexive justice brings activism back to the imperfect politics of process and away from the perfect and privileged politics of standard setting. Rather than creating an alternative economy for the homogenous few, reflexive localism could work across difference, and thereby make a difference, for everyone.

3 Bridging production and consumption

Alternative food networks as shared knowledge practice

Introduction

In the 1970s and 1980s, social activists and progressive scholars drew attention to the deep and intensifying contradictions at the heart of the industrial food system, ranging from environmental degradation and the disappearance of the iconic "family farm" to concerns about food safety and unhealthy processed foods. While activists gave new impetus to building alternative food networks (AFNs), academics developed critical analyses of industrialized food systems and began to systematize the experience of these newly-emerging forms of food provisioning, whose proliferation reached phenomenal proportions by the mid-1990s. To understand these turbulent changes in food provisioning, many scholars relied on the theoretical toolbox of political economy. Others, however, moved away from the dominant optic of production relations, workplace politics, and capital–class relations of power. Instead, they found new ways to understand the problematics of food by drawing on the "turn" to the cultural in poststructuralist and postmodernist social science.

Activists, for their part, turned to market-centered approaches to food system change by politicizing food consumption, epitomized by organic and fair trade products (cf. Wilkinson 2009, 2010). Taken in tandem, the cultural turn in academic thought and activist pragmatics have focused attention on the joint, constitutive role of production *and* consumption relationships in the construction of alternative forms of food provisioning; that is, the relational and iterative processes that link consumers to (alternative) producers and vice versa.

A food consumption politics has become increasingly salient in public arenas, arising from awareness of the environmental and animal welfare harms of industrial agriculture and systemic anxieties about food provisioning. These public concerns attracted the attention of academics in two fields with significantly different intellectual traditions: political economy and cultural studies. For example, recurrent food "scares," notably the "mad cow disease" (BSE) pandemic in Western Europe and sequential E. coli 0157:H7 outbreaks in the USA, led political economists, particularly in Europe, to analyze the economic structures producing these risks, whereas cultural studies scholars focused more on the "culture of anxiety" they created among consumers.

Yet our review of this work shows that scholars from these two analytical perspectives have been slow to recognize each other. Indeed, despite calls for more integrated approaches to production–consumption relations (Tovey 1997; Goodman 2002), political economy has only partially recognized the "turn" to consumption, with the result that the questionable academic "division of labour" between agricultural "production" sociology and the consumption "cultural" sociology of food has remained alive and well. In other words, the treatment of production and consumption in agro-food studies is still highly asymmetric. This asymmetry needs to be addressed if we are to engage and understand new progressive forms of food politics, ranging from diffuse, often localized, struggles over alternative modes of food provisioning to more formal alliances between producers and consumers.

Recent interpretations of the politics of milk illustrate these divergences. Buttel (1998, 2000) argued that the social resistance to rBGH milk in the USA and the introduction of "no rBGH" labelling was merely a product of class-fractured consumption and did not qualify as political action. DuPuis (2002), on the other hand, saw the rise of recombinant-free BGH milk as an example of reflexive consumption, a social and political act even if that action was not part of an organized social movement. This divergence arises from deep-rooted differences in understanding the constitutive roles of production and consumption in contemporary society. These emanate, in turn, from a larger theoretical disagreement between Marxian and production-oriented perspectives and more cultural and consumption-centered views of society that are now prominent in the social sciences. This chapter explores the tensions between these contending frameworks by looking at recent attempts to bring consumption and consumers "back in" to agro-food studies. We review this work as a first step toward articulating a more integrated framework that can bridge the "fault-line" which now exists between the "production" and "cultural" sociology of food and its provisioning (Whatmore 2002).

The reluctance to cut loose from analytical perspectives that privilege either production or consumption means that they appear as autonomous, "purified" categories of social life, as sites only briefly and tenuously linked through the act of exchange. The analytical challenge is how to move beyond the theoretical asymmetries and linearities of these frameworks, with their implicit alignment of power relations and loci of agency, and "acknowledge" consumers, along with producers, brokers, and supermarkets, as relational actors in recursive, mutually constituted networks. This chapter argues for the rethinking of both production-centered and cultural approaches to food politics in ways that recognize the contested processes of interaction between how we "grow food" and how we "know food."

To do this, we will address head-on a long-standing question in sociological theory regarding the nature of commodity exchange: are commodities illusory *fetishes* hiding true social relationships, as Marx would argue? Or are they, as Durkheim would have it, meaningful *totems* representing society itself? In other words, how do we "know" food: as fetish or as totem? If commodities are merely fetishes, then the politics of consumption is a chimera and does not help us to grasp the realities of food politics. Alternatively, if food is a totem, it provides us with symbolic messages that we can read to better understand these politics. In short, in the food-as-fetish framework, consumption does not qualify as a form of knowledge: we cannot "know" food through consumption since all consumption is based on illusions about the nature of society. However, from a food-as-totem perspective, an understanding of the role of consumption is necessary for a fuller understanding of society and of social change.

A focus on food knowledges therefore opens up the analysis to consumer agency and thus to a central dimension of contemporary food politics. Alternative and mainstream provisioning systems can then be located on the terrain of contested knowledge claims, which define both the conventions of material practice and advance competing constructions of quality, modes of governance, and political imaginaries. These issues take us to the heart of this book as we seek to understand the interactive dynamics and relational hybridities emerging from these material and discursive struggles.

Accordingly, in this chapter, we will critique some attempts to "bring consumption in" to agro-food studies, showing how these efforts remain embedded in the Marxian politics of food as fetish. We will then point to work that suggests more promising pathways are to be found in cultural Marxism, feminist standpoint theory, and material culture studies. These sections draw heavily on a 2002 co-authored article published in *Sociologia Ruralis*: *"Knowing and growing food: beyond the production–consumption debate in the sociology of agriculture."* This chapter, as we note in section VI, initiated an exploration of food knowledges as a promising conceptual bridge between production and consumption and as formative linkages of alternative "communities of practice."

We then build on our past analysis and look at more recent work that takes this knowledge approach to AFNs in interesting new directions. We explore how current research on food as material and cultural practice extends our understanding of different food provisioning systems as socio-ecological assemblages of contested knowledges and collective learning. This focus on contested knowledges opens up fruitful engagements with several related literatures, including recent contributions by Alan Warde, and Elizabeth Shove and her colleagues on a theories of practice approach to "ordinary" consumption, work in institutional and evolutionary economics on "routines," learned practices and innovation, and French convention theory. We trace these connections and points of convergence in the final section of the chapter.

Lost in production: the elusive consumer in agro-food studies

In agro-food studies, especially in the USA, discussions of food provisioning have been heavily influenced by William Friedland's (1984) pioneering work on commodity systems analysis. Following a Marxian reading of commodity fetishism, commodity chain analysis has been directed principally to "uncovering" the social relationships behind the production of a particular commodity.

The storylines of such popular documentaries as *Food, Inc.* and *Supersize Me* take this approach, seeking to lift the veil of the commodity fetish and thereby expose the exploitation of workers, consumers, and nature. Rather than giving workers freedom and consumers health, the commodity in fact destroys both of these. In *Food, Inc.*, it is the packaging that conveys this distorted image, projecting a view of farming that is the antithesis of the actual production system, the source of what is inside the package.

Production-centered theorists, following Marx's analysis in *Capital*, see domination and power struggles as arising primarily in the ways capitalists seek to extract surplus value by exploiting labor. Marx insisted that political power is located in the sphere of production only, and commodity exchange *per se* accordingly has no "politics." Consumer choice in a market society is an illusion, as is liberal democracy. The power to shape society comes from control over the means of production, not consumption. This schema is reproduced in the Marxian sociology of agriculture, which views production as the locus of power and the privileged terrain of political agency, with the commodity form acting as a "veil" that conceals exploitative social relations from consumers. From this perspective, consumers are passive because they interact only in the illusory sphere of circulation – the market. Correspondingly, the role of commodity chain analysis in food studies and related fields is to awaken the consumer to true political consciousness by revealing these unequal power relations. As we observed in the previous chapter, the politics of knowledge here involves the exposure of "the truth" about these production relationships, which will then stimulate collective consumer action to change the food system.

The strong, continuing influence of the production-oriented Marxian legacy in agro-food studies and rural sociology is exemplified by several recent contributions that purportedly assign consumers a key role in their analytic schemas. In these cases, scholars deploy consumption to explain trends and directions of change in agro-food sectors, yet these studies are not "about" consumption practices themselves. Consumers emerge briefly as a causal category, only to disappear again into a production-centered framework. A few examples from work in this field will show that, despite increasing attention in the agro-food literature, the consumer continues to be elusive.

Marsden and Wrigley's (1995) study of corporate retailers' increasing control of the British food market was one of the first analyses in agro-food studies to take consumers seriously. However, despite their focus on the realm of exchange, they conclude their discussion by stating that the extent of consumer action in the future "will depend upon the development of a social and political consciousness of the consumers themselves. This in turn depends upon on an ability to overcome the types of commodified individualism and positionality much of the contemporary system attempts to promote" (Marsden and Wrigley 1995: 1911). From this perspective, consumers have an "undeveloped" consciousness, which will remain undeveloped – that is, unpolitical – until they acquire the collective awareness to articulate an effective challenge to the corporate domination of food provisioning. A broadly similar conclusion regarding the powerlessness of "the 'individualised' consumer" constructed by corporate interests emerges from Marsden *et al.*'s (2000) more detailed investigation of British food retailing and regulatory policy.

Murdoch and Miele's (1999) analysis of the increasingly varied and contested nature of contemporary food provisioning presents a more complex view of the consumer. Their approach is based on Eder's (1996) proposition that nature in modernity is experienced as an ambivalent "double" structure, oscillating between a view of nature as moral authority and as "utilitarian object." This duality is used analytically to distinguish between "non-standard food production/consumption practices," identified with alternative, "more localised and differentiated forms of production," and "a set of increasingly globalised mass consumption food patterns" (Murdoch and Miele 1999: 466–467). On the premise that this dichotomy corresponds to "two general production areas" in which "socio-natural relations are differentially constructed," Murdoch and Miele (1999: 469) explore how the tensions in "Eder's double structure might be reconfiguring the relationships between producers and consumers."

However, the dynamics of these new production–consumption patterns are explained in structuralist terms, as a response to external societal shifts and transitions. Thus Murdoch and Miele (1999: 466) see mass food consumption as the counterpart of standardized production processes "or perhaps driven" by these. Conversely, the expansion of localized, differentiated, more "natural" food production networks is attributed to "key trends now sweeping through the agro-food sector," namely, rising affluence and enhanced food safety concerns, resulting in the "growth of discerning food consumers" (ibid.: 469). This account is not only looking "back to nature" but also to the two "worlds of production" of its title, which command analytical attention. Thus, "new trends in food consumption" and "the rise of a new culture of consumption, centred upon the search for a healthier diet and the rediscovery of traditional cuisines" (ibid.: 473), emerge as unexamined categories, foils for the theorization of production, even though they are assigned explanatory power.[1]

The figures and conceptual categories found in Murdoch and Miele (1999) – "discerning food consumers," "new cosmopolitan consumers" and "greater consumer awareness" – appear as common tropes in a literature that uses consumption mainly to talk about production. The "new culture of consumption" seen developing around "traditional products and organic animal-friendly foods" (ibid.: 473) is articulated theoretically with production only in the economistic terms of growing demand and market expansion.

In short, the reconfiguration of producer–consumer relationships is overwhelmingly one-sided, with consumers cast in stratified, market research terms, changing practices as their "world of food" changes, but without "agency" to influence these changes.

Consumers thus appear as an amorphous, shadowy presence in the literature on the construction of "quality" in food networks, and are largely absent from the constellation of forces advanced to explain these changing "conventions" of production (Arce and Marsden 1993; Marsden and Arce 1995; Marsden 1997;

Murdoch *et al.* 2000; Wilkinson 1997). For example, Murdoch *et al.* (2000: 108), observe that a "growing number of discerning consumers" have "concerns about food safety and nutrition" and "increasingly are linking notions of food quality to notions of nature in the agro-food system." Again, despite the apparent causal primacy attributed to consumers in these analyses, theoretical development is dominated by the behavior of producers and their "worlds of production," whose markets are characterized in terms of two continua: "standardised-generic products" and "specialised-dedicated products." Alternative categories of food consumption are then "added on" or associated with these new niche markets as, for example, with the "growing market of specialised consumers (those who are opting out of the mass markets of generic food-stuffs)" (ibid.: 121). Guthman's (2003) use of the term "yuppie chow" to characterize the specialty niche markets for organic baby greens is one example of this type of analysis: alternative food systems simply fit into, and exemplify, consumer class positions.

As this brief discussion reveals, not only are production-centered frameworks still pre-eminent in agro-food studies but also the "turn" to consumption as a meaningful social category is largely illusory. Under-theorized notions of consumption become exogenous structural categories and are granted "agency" or transformative power only in the economistic, abstract terms of niche demand, In these analyses, consumption emerges, to paraphrase Appadurai (1986: 31), as private, atomistic, and passive rather than as "eminently social, relational and active."

These reconstructive efforts effectively reaffirm the analytical centrality of production and labor as the crucial loci of politics and social change. Much of this work, following Marx and later writers of the Frankfurt School, conceals an implicit, rarely acknowledged notion of consumers as manipulated, blinkered individuals, whose political epiphany will come only when the scales of commodity fetishism have been removed from their eyes. The consumer escapes theoretical attention since politically conscious action cannot occur in the sphere of circulation, where the only apparent relationships are those between things. Commodity fetishism precludes politics in this sphere, or makes political what is really just bourgeois ideology. Activists and their upper-class supporters may paint these alternative economies as real social change but, in reality, it is implicated with capitalism, since only those with substantial income can afford these "niche market" products

The promise of symmetry in production–consumption analysis

A number of authors have made the move away from the production-centered analytics of commodity fetishism toward ways of understanding food systems that integrate both production and consumption practices. Thus Lockie and Kitto (2000) adopt an actor-network (ANT) perspective to theorize food provisioning and consumption as being co-determined; that is, "worlds" that are conjoined and mutually constitutive. They argue that food production–consumption practices should be theorized without recourse to *a priori* causal schemas which distinguish classes of phenomena "that drive from those that are driven" (Law 1994: 12). Analogously, producer cultures and consumer cultures are not "purified," separate categories of social life but rather are relational and mutually constitutive.

In an earlier paper, Lockie and Collie (1999) prepare the ground for this symmetrical approach to food networks by building on disparate, unintegrated elements of contemporary theorizations of food consumption, notably Ben Fine's "systems of provision" (SOP) approach (Fine and Leopold 1993; Fine 1995; Fine *et al.* 1996). Seeking conceptual tools to explore the social practices that hold agro-food networks together, Lockie and Collie (1999: 64) call for greater understanding of "the whole material culture surrounding food production and consumption" (cf. Dixon 1999). As Lockie and Kitto (2000: 5) note, this important dimension is recognized by the SOP approach but they argue that it is "poorly developed in both theorisation and operationalisation." Furthermore, production activities are privileged in SOP analysis as "*determinants* of consumption practices" and the "role of agency is marginalised" by giving primacy to structural tendencies in the shaping of SOPs (ibid.: 5).

The search for conceptual resources to more fully comprehend production–consumption interactions brings Lockie and Kitto (2000: 8–9) to ANT, which, they note approvingly, is aligned "with the broad trend towards relational theories of power within contemporary sociology." However, these authors are dissatisfied with the ways in which ANT has been deployed so far in agro-food studies. These earlier uses are variously criticized for not improving on commodity systems analysis (Busch and Juska 1997; Sousa and Busch 1998), formulating a "linear set of metabolic relational processes" that gives primacy to production and erases consumption (Goodman 1999), and for "the continued 'black boxing of the consumer'" in Whatmore and Thorne's (1997) analysis of fair trade coffee production–consumption networks (Lockie and Kitto 2000: 13–15).

Lockie and Kitto (2000) critique these previous uses of ANT for failing to give adequate weight to the recursive relational organization of socio-material networks, reflecting the constitutive material and symbolic interactions between production and consumption. In their view, closer attention to these recursive relationships is needed to avoid linear characterizations of production–consumption networks that are corrupted by the modernist search for the locus of power, typically identified with upstream producers and intermediaries, who apparently can "unproblematically dictate the situation in which food is consumed materially and symbolically" (ibid.: 15–16). In their support for ANT's relational ontology, theories of power, and conceptual resources, Lockie and Kitto (2000) helped to pave the way for agro-food studies to engage with other recent theorizations of consumption in the social sciences which hitherto had been disregarded.

However, this exploration quickly revealed to agro-food scholars that reconstructed commodity systems analysis and ANT were by no means the only candidates in the quest to bridge the divide identified by Tovey (1997) and Whatmore (2002) between the production and cultural sociology of food. For example, ANT's commendable rejection of the locus of power as the overriding analytical concern is counterbalanced by its avowed discomfort with "critical theory" and its questionable agnosticism on issues of politics (Casper and Clarke 1998; Murdoch 1997a). In contrast, other post-Foucauldian approaches to politics and society have extended conceptual and social understandings of "the political" beyond the search for the locus of power, without rejecting the political as a focus of study. In our view, agro-food studies can fruitfully broaden its analytical horizons beyond the current limiting choice between commodity systems analysis and ANT. As conceptual arsenals of consumer politics, one disarms consumers and the other disarms politics.

Moreover, these approaches fail to take into account the significant conceptual and empirical work that has taken place in cultural food studies in the last few decades. Most importantly, agro-food analyses have not escaped the conceptual silo of political economy to bring in more cultural approaches to food and eating. To lead agro-food theory toward these wider horizons, therefore, we need to make a brief historical detour to consider analyses of consumption in cultural food studies.

The consumption turn in social theory

To understand how the fault line between agro-food studies and cultural studies of food has developed requires a broader perspective on the recent intellectual history of the social sciences in general. Over the past two decades, consumption as a focus of study has gained a high profile in the social sciences, driven in part by the current sociological interest in "pop culture." Food and its consumption figure prominently in this new and burgeoning literature, finding expression in the rising tide of "food and society" courses currently being taught in US universities. Much of this work emerges from decidedly non-Marxian social science perspectives. A seemingly endless number of recent books and films explain food more in terms of Durkheim's idea of "totem" – as a symbol that represents social relationships and cultural notions of belonging (Douglas and Isherwood 1978). Food also features strongly in critiques of globalization and industrialization. For example, Ritzer's (2000) enormously popular *The McDonaldization of Society* fits strongly into a Weberian analytical tradition, showing how the logic of rationalization creates the monster of fast food. These studies see food as a mirror of social relationships and social meaning, while Marxian approaches view the food commodity as "fetish," a symbol that hides social relationships. Thus a "totemic" perspective infuses studies of food with analyses of cultural identity and solidarity. Jeffrey Pilcher's (1998) *Que Viven Los Tamales!*, Stephen Mennel's (1985) *All Manner of Food*, and the collected articles in *Golden Arches East* (Watson 1997) all represent food as a mirror of social relationships, rather than as a Marxian veil. In addition, feminist scholars have studied food as illuminating everyday gendered practices (DeVault 1994), as material culture involved in the creation of gendered identity (Bynum 1991), or as a reflection of the contradictions surrounding food and gender (Bordo 1993).

Nevertheless, despite its major contribution to our understanding of food as meaning, the cultural studies literature so far has failed to provide analytical tools for agro-food studies since it tends to ignore, under-theorize or simply explain away production–consumption relationships. This failure is part of a more general "turn" away from the material, the economic and production in cultural studies as a field. For example, Ritzer (2000) finds "McDonaldization" everywhere he looks, thereby eliminating the need to study production as anything other than a mere exemplar of the same trend. Taken to extremes, cultural studies of food can become a "soft" appendix to marketing initiatives or exploit the "food as entertainment" trend in popular publishing. This is simply the obverse of our critique of food production sociology since now the analysis is "all about consumption" (Gregson 1995), an equally unacceptable asymmetry in food studies.

As this discussion reveals, although cultural food studies have made significant progress in understanding food as meaning, much work is still needed to build a better theoretical bridge between the production and cultural sociology of food. One way forward is to focus on those scholars who have attempted to reconcile political economy with cultural studies. Many of these scholars come out of the "cultural Marxism" tradition pioneered by Raymond Williams and E. P. Thompson. Surprisingly, these well established cultural Marxist approaches have been widely ignored in current attempts to "acknowledge" consumption in agro-food studies. A brief overview of three of these approaches – the "New Times" analyses of the Birmingham school, the "material culture studies" perspective, and the standpoint feminists – reveals their potential fruitfulness in agro-food studies. These literatures provide useful links between culture/identity studies of consumption and the more production-centered focus of commodity systems analysis.

"New Times" analyses grappled with the rise of working-class support for Margaret Thatcher in 1980s Britain. Stuart Hall, one of the founders of this intellectual movement, argued that late capitalism represented a new era, that is, a new set of interactions between the forces of production and social relations. "This is not to argue that New Times are necessarily and inevitably good times.... Capitalism is still deeply entrenched – in fact, more so, globally than ever before. And the old inequalities associated with it remain" (Hall 1989: 17). However,

> another feature of New Times is the proliferation of the sites of antagonism and resistance, and the appearance of new subjects, new social movements, new collective identities – an enlarged sphere for the operation of politics, and new constituencies for change.
>
> (Hall 1989: 18)

While the multiplicity of antagonisms makes a revolutionary mass politics difficult, new forms of agency and arenas have emerged, including consumption.

Moreover, although consumers may not possess the revolutionary capacity of a proletarian class, this group can aspire to power, if power is defined as the ability to set parameters, such as rights, obligations, and rules governing processes (Mulgan 1989).

This rethinking of the definition of power echoes similar theoretical developments in Marxist feminism. Feminist standpoint theory (Hartsook 1983; Smith 1987), for example, arose in conversation with Marxist epistemology. From a Marxian perspective, the proletariat, because of its class position, can "see" the reality behind commodity fetishism and understand class struggle as the true emancipatory politics. Standpoint theorists argue that women, socially positioned as responsible for the reproduction of social worlds, similarly have a capacity to understand and know a reality beyond the bourgeois ideology of exchange. This expanded epistemological potential can lead to a women's form of emancipatory politics. Building on these foundations, feminist political theory has transformed the notion of "political" beyond more Weberian or Marxian notions of domination and the "locus of power." In particular, feminist theory has added the "private" sphere of everyday life and of reproduction to concepts of politics (Gordon 1990). This has led to a re-conceptualization of the political as a more de-centered "capacity to act" (Baker 1990), to encompass the diverse ways in which actors influence the construction of future society.[2]

Drawing on the Gramscian tradition, Hall, his New Times colleagues, and the standpoint feminists advocate a more diffuse definition of politics that sees any form of influence as political action. Their view is closer to Gramsci's "war of position" than to the outright revolutionary "war of manoeuvre" more common to Marxist political economy perspectives. Consumer activism may never lead the revolution, but as a form of political action, it does wield power to shape the food system.

The third approach to thinking about consumption is the material culture framework of Arjun Appadurai and Daniel Miller (1995b). Rather than rejecting production, Appadurai (1986) dismantles the distinction between traditional and "modern" societies that typifies social science explanations of modernity. By examining the nature of material culture in the Durkheimian intellectual tradition of Marcel Mauss, Appadurai finds that capitalist and pre-capitalist relations are not as distinctively different as Marx would have us think. Instead, he shows that exchange relationships in both traditional and modern societies are a complex mix of (non-market) use and (market) exchange values, an analysis that makes the idea of the commodity fetish as veil problematic.

From Appadurai's perspective, consumption practices have always possessed significant power to change society, no matter the economic period. By looking at consumption with different eyes than those of Marx, it is possible see the mutual constitution of social relationships between producer and consumer, and the ways in which market and non-market activities are continually embedded within each another, rather than being contained in separate spheres.

We can also find common ground between the material culture approach advanced by Appadurai (1986) and Lockie and Kitto's (2000: 15) insistence on the "centrality of non-humans" in the theorization of food production–consumption networks. The convergence between these perspectives is seen in their critiques of ontologies that fetishize "society" and the epistemological importance each attributes to materiality and material objects in actively constituting social worlds. Each approach seeks to elaborate a sociology of things, a sociology of relational materialism in Law's (1992) lexicon, as central to a theory of social action (Long 2000). In short, both ANT and material culture studies reject theoretical perspectives in which material worlds are socially constructed and which treat these domains as being ontologically separate. As Miller (1998a) notes, the key theories of material culture developed in the 1980s demonstrated that social worlds were as much constituted by materiality as the other way round (cf. Bourdieu 1977; Appadurai 1986; Miller 1987). Or again, the work of Douglas and Isherwood (1978) and Bourdieu (1977, 1984) suggested "an active role for objects in the constitution of social relations" (Miller 1995a: 148).

Looking at the "life of things" in society, a life that goes on beyond the fetishized sphere of exchange, brings both people and things together in reproductive and meaningful relationships. For Miller, this has resulted in more sensitive, nuanced attention to the complexities of the world of consumption – not just how things are bought but how they are used for most of their "lives," that is, outside the world of commodity exchange. Using Hegelian Marxism as a framework, Miller's (1987) analysis of the consumer is strikingly similar to feminist standpoint theory: the consumer, as reproducer of culture, has epistemological access to a world beyond the commodity fetish. This is not a world of production but a world of meaning in which things are embedded, and in which people and things interact (Miller 1987). While this may seem ontologically similar to ANT, what distinguishes the material culture approach is its emphasis on systems of meaning, stemming from its explicit re-embrace of Durkheim, particularly through the work of his disciple, Marcel Mauss. ANT, in contrast, is antagonistic to the idea of external systems of meaning, focusing more on meaning as an emergent property of particular networks in specific times and places.

Lost in consumption: over-shooting the cultural "turn"

These literatures and their ongoing development give a glimpse of the array of theoretical resources available to agro-food studies as it contemplates theorizing consumption in all its material and symbolic diversity. With these tools, we can approach consumption as other than a "lumpen" appendage to production and distribution or, at best, as a superstructural "automatic pilot," redirected by exogenous factors – "life-style changes," post-Fordism – that serve principally to refocus attention on worlds of production. Although this reconstructive work has barely started, agro-food studies might draw more explicitly from these approaches. Yet this must be done with care to avoid the danger of "over-shooting," thereby widening the divide between the sociologies of food production and consumption.

Such over-shooting apparently is common in anthropological studies of consumption, according to Miller (1995a: 151), who suggests:

> It is not surprising that earlier studies had this tendency, because in many cases they were aimed specifically at repudiating what was seen as an obsessive concern with relations of production as opposed to consumption. By the 1990s it has become evident that neither of these pursuits is best carried out in isolation.

Commentators in human geography give a more oppositional portrayal of the analytical costs of over-shooting, with Gregson (1995: 139) making the following observation:

> "The geographical literature on consumption highlights the ascendance of cultural, as opposed to social, theory in social geography ... and cultural theory in the tradition of Gramsci, Williams, Hall and Said ... these writings bring with them a particular interpretation of consumption grounded in meaning, identity, representation and ideology." [In her view, such approaches] "require a firmer grounding in structural social inequalities (the significant differences of gender, class, race, sexuality, (dis)ability, etc.) and in material culture ... it is precisely this social-theory derived agenda which the cultural 'turn' in geography has left behind and which has brought about a crisis in social geography."

A related but more moderate "progress report" in human geography acclaims "the beginnings of the much-needed fusion of materialist analyses with more culturally derived approaches" (Crewe 2000: 280).[3]

However, in our view, the answer to over-shooting is not to revert wholesale to production-centered analytical categories but rather to demonstrate that cultural Marxist perspectives enable effective political engagement with a broad range of social questions, extending beyond the immediate production arena. In short, for agro-food studies, the challenge posed by Tovey's (1997) division of labor is how to combine the sociologies of production and consumption in ways "that do not privilege the agency and power of either producers or consumers" (Lockie and Collie 1999: 270).

Such an integrated, symmetrical perspective is a very tall order indeed. However, one step in this direction is to follow culturally derived approaches to the point of recognizing that food politics encompasses worlds *beyond* the classical sociological terrain of the labor process, exchange, and meaning. In particular, food is also a realm of knowledge. Growing and eating are both practices imbued with ways of knowing the world, and with knowing the ways to construct the kind of world we want to inhabit. It is to a conceptualization of food as knowledge that we now turn.

Knowing and growing food: rethinking food politics

Of the many possible ways of building bridges between the sociology of food and agro-food studies, we find the current focus on knowledge systems in agriculture extremely promising. Discussion of sustainable agriculture has turned increasingly to "growing" as a practice that is constructed through struggles between agricultural knowledge systems (Kloppenburg, Jr 1991; Hassanein 1999; Kaltoft 1999; Campbell and Liepins 2001; Ploeg 2003). These in-depth studies describe the practices of alternative farmers and their struggle to build and reproduce alternative knowledge systems. However, once again, the consumer, whose values, subjectivity, and activity are intrinsic to the making of alternative food systems, remains uni-dimensional. Yet from the epistemological position of cultural Marxism, how the consumer goes about "knowing" food is just as important as farmers' knowledge networks in the creation of an alternative food system.

By linking these struggles over knowledges, we begin to see the politics of the food system as involving alternative "modes of ordering" of material and cultural resources in which food is an arena of contestation rather than a veil over reality. It is clear, therefore, that any attempt to integrate how we "know food" and how we "grow food" will require rethinking both production- and consumption-centered notions of politics and formulating new ways to articulate the relationships between the two. The difficulties of embarking on this integrative challenge, as well as the insights it brings, can be seen by reviewing some recent work on the politics of organic agriculture and food.

Allen and Kovach's (2000) study of social movements in the US organic food sector provides substantial evidence of an organized, activist consumer–producer politics around the creation and growth of alternative food systems (cf. Buttel 1997; Buck *et al.* 1997; Reed 2001).[4] These authors also regard natural food stores as spaces in which political organizing can and does occur, as in the marshalling of opposition to the United States Department of Agriculture's (USDA) Proposed Rule for the National Organic Program in 1999–2000 (cf. Vos 2000).

These examples of food politics as direct public contestation and organized social movements clearly fall into the realm of politics as traditionally defined. Not only is the consumer "awakened" to political action, but this awakening includes a defence of what Allen and Kovach call consumers' "right to know" or the "defetishization" of production. Consumers demand labels that attest to how their food is grown and, in the case of the US National Organics Standards debate, they contest any attempt by the State to promote what is perceived as "refetishized" industrialization. Organic movements can be seen as the praxis of commodity systems analysis, although here consumers rise to defend the "defetishized" transparency of the ecological production process rather than to unmask exploitative labor relations (Allen 2004). Through alternative food politics based in ecological transparency, organic food becomes the totem of mutuality, mirroring the collective action of food and agriculture movements.

In these characterizations of the organic movement in the USA, the consumer is clearly a political actor in the food system, practicing a "form of politics" that has been widely accepted since E. P. Thompson's (1968) *The Making of the English Working Class*. But where should boycotts be situated, such as the consumer boycott of table grapes in support of the United Farm Workers' organizing in the 1980s? In this case, some actors were part of an organized movement while others' political activity only occurred at the point of sale (or non-sale). Here, the definition of politics as organized social movement starts to blur, and different notions of politics begin to emerge.

Thus new studies of organic food and fibre systems are addressing the fact that the struggle over questions of "knowing" food – for example, "what is organic?" – involves more than merely making the system more "transparent." As Chapters 7–9 will demonstrate, whether or not a food will be certified – that is, known as "organic" – has been and remains a source of significant political struggle in the USA. Examples of these contestations include Allen and Sach's (1993) call for forms of certification that take into account the social conditions of farm workers (cf. Brown and Getz 2008b), the already noted controversy over the USDA's organic standards, and studies of the construction of "quality" as an arena of struggle in food networks (Guthman 1998; Murdoch and Miele 2002; Marsden 2004; Wilkinson 2009, 2010).

These conclusions resonate with earlier work in social theory in general. Thus both critical race and feminist theorists have been especially insightful in their studies of the formative power of meaning and representation in society – of identities and imaginaries – and their critique of structuralists for ignoring these factors (cf. Hall 1989; Gordon 1990). This point comes to the fore in studies of the racialized aspects of alternative food politics in terms of representations of clean vs. contaminated food (Alvarez 2005) and the "whiteness" of alternative food spaces and practices (Slocum 2006, 2007; Holloway 2007; Guthman 2008a, 2008b). This research builds on earlier contributions in this area that reconceptualized notions of identity as "both a matter of social structure and cultural representation" (Omi and Winant 1994: 56). Drawing on Gramsci, this work revived the emphasis on the study of "formations": that is, historically contingent social and economic "blocs." The notion of formation bears some resemblance to Law's (1994) concept of "modes of ordering," although in contemporary studies there is an explicit awareness that food politics is embedded in broader political struggles over identity (Guthman 2008a).

In this respect, alternative discursive and material projects, such as those represented by organic agriculture, fair trade, anti-rBST groups, eco-labelling, or the Slow Food movement, for example, seek to reconfigure the hegemonic formations or "orderings" of the socio-ecological in industrial or conventional agrofood networks (Goodman 2001). Using ANT to analyze fair trade networks, Whatmore and Thorne (1997: 301) argue that "what is analytically distinctive" about these alternative geographies of food, "is *how* they strengthen relationships amongst formerly 'passive' actants in commercial networks – the producers and consumers – through a mode of ordering of connectivity which works for non-hierarchical relationships framed by 'fairness'." Food is no longer polarized conceptually as either totem or fetish, but becomes a terrain of contested orderings, as well as a realm of connectivity. That said, more recent critical approaches problematize this connectivity in a food movement that retains a pronounced white, middle-class demographic (Slocum 2006, 2007; Holloway 2007; Guthman 2008a, 2008b).

As this discussion emphasizes, the notion of cross-sphere alliances bridging production and exchange, private and public spaces (or even erasing these distinctions altogether), is at the core of this more discursive, yet eminently material, notion of politics. These alliances include consumers as both actual and potential actors, and the social relations formed in consumption – both with and between producers and with and between consumers – are regarded as more than just "private," that is, a-political action. Discursive perspectives "see" politics in places where a production-centered framework finds only a failed attempt to overcome capitalist forces.

For example, from a production-centered viewpoint, Community Supported Agriculture (box schemes in the UK) may appear to be an epiphenomenal and transitory utopian entertainment for higher income customers and their fortunate few farmer friends, although recent research reveals that the demographics are far more complex (cf. Kneafsey *et al.* 2008; Lockie 2002, 2009). Alternatively, this movement can be seen as bearing the seeds of a political struggle to realign consumer–producer relationships on alternative eco-social foundations that conceivably may succeed in creating a broader farmer–consumer (or even broader class) alliance. Similarly, the Monsanto web pages can be seen as the strategic discourse of large-scale capitalists, marshalling the power/knowledge of hegemonic biological science in an attempt to create its own alliance with consumers. In other words, the "politics" of food get played out in many ways that include both the struggles of contested knowledges and the struggles to form political alliances that will become the more stable political formations of the future. Each of these arenas has an ability to influence the other, and each deserves analytic attention.

From this perspective, the fact that organic food consumption is still largely a well-educated, middle-class privilege – a "class diet," if you will – and is not based on a formal social movement should not deny the politics of this activity. Of course, the middle class is only one voice in the overall discursive political framework around organic food, and how it chooses to "know" the organic may ignore other actors in the system, such as farm laborers, food service workers and poorer consumers. Nevertheless, "class diet" or not, the knowledge practices of reflexive consumers are expressions of agency and so constitute a politics of food. If a "broad church" approach is adopted, the consumer politics of organic food can be admitted without prejudice to other modalities of food politics.

Returning to the questions posed earlier, both production and consumption spheres contain struggles, intrinsic contradictions and, ultimately, interactions across the boundary of the commodity "veil." Whether using the notions of New Times, material culture studies, or standpoint theory, a relational production–consumption perspective on food provisioning sees the political possibilities of consumption as less than the revolutionary overthrow of capitalism but more than merely a niche marketing opportunity. Consumers can be seen as political actors when they exercise the "capacity to act" in any way that affects the future form of society. For this reason, the turn by some consumers to organic milk and the introduction of non-rBST milk in some parts of the USA represent a political response to the aggressive tactics of Monsanto. In turn, Monsanto's reaction to this political pressure by lobbying against labelling and promoting antifood disparagement legislation reflects the importance this company attributes to this consumer-based political activity.

More generally, the most cursory look at today's food advertisements shows how deeply food is embedded in a contested discourse of knowledge claims. Contemporary food industry marketing seeks to combine common consumer aims with profit goals, by enrolling consumer bodies ("Healthy Choice"), ideals of nature ("Hidden Valley") or both ("Healthy Valley"). Some consumers have displayed a robust scepticism of the brightly colored signs – "natural" or "fat-free" – that lead to Healthy Valley. Instead, they have become reflexive, interrogating industry claims and refusing a passive role in the food system (DuPuis 2000).

Despite the experience of numerous "food scares," anti-genetically modified organism (GMO) movements and animal welfare campaigns, integrative analytical work on food provisioning and consumption and its potential as a terrain for progressive food politics has been slow to emerge in agro-food studies. Such an integrative, more expansive notion of food politics would embrace a broad range of activities, from diffuse, capillary modes of social action to more formal alliances between producers and consumers, and the contested material and discursive orderings of the social and ecological which articulate everyday bio-political contestations and connections. Parts II–IV of this book explore these broader notions of food politics in three major arenas of alternative food praxis: the UK/Western Europe, the USA, and the international fair trade economy.

From knowledges to practices: innovation in consumption

With some revision and updating, this chapter has covered the terrain mapped out in the 2002 co-authored paper, "Knowing food and growing food." In this final section, we extend the idea of AFNs as orderings of material and cultural resources anchored in contested knowledge claims. This is done by teasing out connections with several other intellectual traditions and approaches to social reproduction and change. In pursuing these linkages and tangencies, one of our aims is to understand the growth and consolidation of these alternative orderings as *processes of innovative behavior*. That is, we explore AFNs as processes that integrate new complexes of production–consumption, with their distinctive material, cultural, and moral economies – organic, local, fair trade, or animal-friendly foods, for example – into the practices and routines of daily life. Since these other traditions and subdisciplines have their own intellectual purposes and trajectories, this exercise inevitably is rather opportunistic and short on exposition as the main purpose is to uncover points of tangency that illuminate our conceptualization of AFNs and their role in the contemporary politics of food.

One of these perspectives arises from recent re-statements of theories of practice, whose antecedents can be traced to earlier contributions by Bourdieu, Foucault, Lyotard, and Giddens, for example (Reckwitz 2002; Schatzki 1996, cited by Warde 2005). Although its current advocates recognize that these roots are rather tenuous and fragmentary, fresh attempts have been made to revive this approach to the sociology of consumption (Warde 2005; Watson and Shove 2006; Hand and Shove 2007; Shove *et al.* 2007). Our interest in this recent literature stems from its dissatisfaction with exclusively symbolic, representational approaches to consumption and "methodological individualist accounts of 'the consumer'" (Warde 2005: 132). Instead, it emphasizes the practice of consumption as recurrent performance that is "shaped by and constitutive of the complex relations – of materials, knowledges, norms, meanings, and so on – which comprise the practice-as-entity" (Shove *et al.* 2007: 13). Such a nexus describes "the more complex practices found in and constitutive of particular domains of social life" (Schatzki 1996: 98, cited by Warde 2005: 135), such as those of farming, cooking, or business. In such domains, the individual is

> a carrier of patterns of bodily behaviour, but also of certain routinized ways of understanding, knowing how and desiring. These conventionalized "mental" activities are necessary elements and qualities of a practice in which the single individual participates, not qualities of the individual.
>
> (Reckwitz 2002: 250)

If practices are viewed as the "bedrock of consumption," as Warde (2005: 144) contends, then "it is impossible to understand the dynamics of consumption without also understanding how practices emerge, stabilise and disappear" (Watson and Shove 2006: 1–2). This turns attention toward innovation and change in the social practices of consumption, particularly when it is recognized that "consumption is embedded in relatively inconspicuous routines occasioned by the characteristically mundane socio-technical systems of everyday life" (Shove *et al.* 2007: 10).

The expansion of AFNs, for example, thus depends on their capacity to reconfigure these routines and, if they are to move from niche into the mainstream, to undermine the inertial forces represented by the ubiquitous role of supermarkets in conventional socio-technical systems of food provisioning. A practices approach also focuses on the many varied "competences" that comprise the different domains of social life and the role of tacit knowledge, collective learning, and routine in social reproduction (Warde 2005: 138–141), a lexicon which resonates with heterodox economics perspectives on institutional rigidities, path-dependence, and innovation, as discussed below. As Warde (2005: 140) observes: "The principal implication of a theory of practice is that the sources of changed behaviour lie in the development of practices themselves. The concept of practice inherently combines a capacity to account for both reproduction and innovation."

An interesting bridge between theories of practice and institutional economics is provided by several recent analyses of initiatives to re-localize food provisioning (Brunori *et al.* 2008; Kneafsey *et al.* 2008) and promote sustainable production–consumption more generally (Seyfang and Smith 2006). Each of these contributions builds upon a broader, more inclusive notion of innovation by extending the conventional focus from production technologies in the market economy to embrace innovation in consumption and in the social economy of non-profit enterprises and community organizations, as well as initiatives which straddle these "divides." Identifying collective rather than individual action as a "potentially powerful force for change," Seyfang and Smith (2006: 1–2) view these local, community-level developments as "innovation niches" and examine the nature of their contribution in promoting a transition toward more sustainable patterns of production and consumption.

To specify the difficulties of this transition, Seyfang and Smith (2006) turn to the economics of innovation literature and the concept of large-scale "socio-technical regimes," which emerge following systemic "paradigm shifts" and whose particular "technological trajectories" are consolidated by mutually-reinforcing, embedded macro- and meso-level processes, comprising path-dependent innovation, cognitive frameworks, collective learning, institutional change, social norms, and infrastructural development. In some respects, the potential role of grassroots "innovation niches" is formulated in directly obverse terms: how to create viable spaces to incubate alternative practices and "generate socially-embedded changes in behaviour" that subsequently can be taken up in the transition toward sustainable mainstream development (Seyfang and Smith 2006: 4). Brunori *et al.* (2008) also adopt this framework of niche innovation and socio-technical regimes but focus more explicitly on innovation in consumption in the form of box schemes and farmers' markets established in Italy by voluntary organizations.

Informed by theories of practice and the economics of innovation, Brunori *et al.* (2008: 5–6) stress that looking at innovation through the "consumer lens" brings daily routines to the fore and the obstacles "consumers face when they try to act according to their values." These constraints, they suggest, are

> part of their lifeworlds. Purchasing and consumption routines, in fact, are based on socio-technical systems that link systems of provision together with consumer goods (a house, white goods, a car) and public goods (road infrastructures, parking, public services).... Behind these goods, there are people, knowledge, values, skills, rules [and] norms.
>
> (Brunori *et al.* 2008: 6)

Brunori *et al.* (2008: 6) go on to suggest that collective action by organized reflexive consumers to remove the constraints imposed by mainstream socio-technical systems of provision "can be a driver for producers to innovate accordingly." We examine the empirical findings of Gianluca Brunori and his colleagues in Part II below.

This integrative, relational approach to agro-food innovation is very much in agreement with our basic premise that the socio-natural practices of food production and consumption are interactive and recursive. Emerging socio-technical *projects*, such as organic agriculture, local food networks, fair trade, and the Slow Food movement, can thus be seen as assemblages of production–consumption practices, knowledges, routines, and imaginaries, which seek to reconfigure the "orderings" of the socio-ecological engendered by conventional agro-food provisioning. A leading question, then, is whether or not these projects will come together to constitute a *radical* innovation, as understood in evolutionary, neo-Schumpeterian economics, with the potential to provoke a systemic paradigm shift, revolutionizing the previously dominant or incumbent socio-technical regime and its technological trajectory (cf. Freeman and Perez 1988).

In contrast to their technologically path-dependent counterparts in manufacturing, the "spaces of innovation" for these alternative socio-ecological projects reflect the *polyvalent* heterogeneity of food production–consumption practices. These heterogeneous orderings are found in the survival of different "styles" of farming, their associated skills and routines, organizational forms, and their co-evolved expression in cultures of food preparation and cuisines. The persistence of these alternative "spaces of innovation" in the shadow of the conventional hegemon involves, at least in part, the recovery of collective socio-ecological learning and repertoires of performance, as the Slow Food movement and the revival of regional cuisines have shown (Miele and Murdoch 2002). That is, of a "collective memory" of both codified and tacit knowledges once more widely embodied in diverse skills, routines, competences, and institutions of "field and table" (cf. Stuiver 2006; Fonte 2008).

This discussion resonates with the conceptualization in institutional and evolutionary economics of "habits and routines as *durable* repositories of knowledge and skills," which are often tacit and context-dependent (Hodgson 1999: 63, emphasis added; see also Hodgson 1997, 1998). However, since routines are transferable through learning and replication, they provide a mechanism of innovation and diffusion. This notion of knowledges embedded in the habits and routines of "communities of practice" (Lave and Wenger 1991), performed and reproduced in the daily round of lived experience, lends conceptual clarity to the *durable* polyvalence of food production–consumption practices.

The idea of routines as repositories of learning, skills, and innovative potential recalls Jack Kloppenburg's (1991: 529) seminal paper on local, experiential knowledge, which the hegemony of scientific knowledge has "pushed to the epistemic peripheries." Yet these "reservoir(s) of local knowledge ... at the margins and in the interstices between technological convention and scientific orthodoxy" support "alternative farmers and alternative institutions ... who continuously produce and reproduce a landscape of alternative agricultural possibilities" (Kloppenburg 1991: 535). The clash between local, tacit learning and scientific orthodoxy also is at the heart of Hassanein's (1999) study of sustainable farming networks in Wisconsin. In their role as producers and disseminators of alternative practices, these *learning* networks are conceptualized as "informal social movement communities ... that are connected to a wider effort to transform agriculture" (ibid.: 7).

Although the relationships between traditional ways of knowing and scientific knowledge have not been entirely neglected in the European literature, as work on expert systems demonstrates, for example (cf. Ploeg 2003), the main focus has been on understanding agri-environmental problems, with a marked preference for Latourian actor-network approaches rather than social movement analysis (Murdoch and Clark 1994; Clark and Murdoch 1997). In this book, we lean in the other direction and later sections add empirical substance to the framework of contested knowledges outlined in the preceding discussion. That is, we concentrate on the social movements leading these struggles over the knowing and growing of food and on the political economic challenges facing the wider diffusion of alternative production–consumption practices and their innovative time–space patterns of provisioning.

The analytical importance of habits, collective learning, ingrained practices, and routines in the dynamics of social behavior and economic activity found in a theories of practice approach to consumption (Warde 2005) and in institutional and evolutionary economics (Dosi and Nelson 1994; Hodgson 1997) also can be seen in French convention theory. We engage with this perspective at various points in the book, as it has become an influential meso-level analysis of the quality "turn" in food provisioning. Convention theory addresses the "economy of quality" more generally and offers typologies that distinguish the quality of products in terms of "orders of worth" or "worlds," which correspond to the processes of "qualification" experienced by the human and non-human entities involved in their production and reproduction. These "worlds" define different conventions of quality – industrial, domestic, civic, for example – their logics, production techniques and organizational forms. The tangencies noted above are seen particularly in the centrality of rules, norms, and conventions as necessary mechanisms of economic coordination of these "worlds" of quality, and in the role of collective learning in the dynamics of institutional and social change (Wilkinson 1997).

Convention theory has been used to conceptualize the quality "turn" to alternative food provisioning networks as a contested process of transition between, say, the "industrial" world and its standardized norms of quality and the "domestic" world, with its conventions of trust, tradition, and place (Murdoch and Miele 1999, 2002; Murdoch *et al.* 2000). However, since this analysis focuses primarily on the production sphere, we suggest that convention theory be "opened out" to incorporate the material and symbolic performance of its product "worlds" *in consumption*. In the case of "alternative" provisioning networks – civic, domestic, or green – the quality conventions whose performance "qualifies" producers would also be shaped recursively by, and be incorporated into, consumer practices based in routines of "knowing" food. Alternative food networks or particular orderings of the socio-ecological can then be conceptualized as cognitive structures embedded in routines, which create and stabilize relational "communities of practice" of mutually "qualified" producers and consumers.

Conclusion

This chapter lays some of the groundwork needed to understand AFNs as socio-ecological assemblages formed by practices and routines which mobilize and "qualify" material and cognitive resources in particular ways. This understanding is enhanced by drawing together analytical threads and lines of inquiry from other social science disciplines, as we have done here. Once AFNs are approached as relational, recursive "communities of practice" of producers and consumers sharing ways of "knowing and growing food," we can go on to explore how these communities and social movements have set about building alternative "worlds of food."

Part II

Alternative food provisioning in the UK and Western Europe

Introduction and antecedents

This introduction situates the rise of alternative food provisioning practices in Britain and Western Europe on a broad canvas by identifying some of the many pathways whose convergence is carving out political-economic and discursive spaces for their development. Some paths, initially seen as rather minor, eccentric byways, such as organic farming, have grown into major thoroughfares of political, economic and institutional change, while others remain as narrow, winding tracks yet contribute to the range of social experimentation and more radical discourse, as in the case of New Age Travellers (NATs), for example. These pathways are discussed in relatively short, thumbnail sketches to describe how the confluence of social movements, institutional processes and contingent events occurring on multiple levels has given rise to alternative food provisioning networks and influenced their contemporary trajectory.

Counter-culture movements

Although the commune movement has strong historical roots in both the US and Europe (Bramwell 1989), the counter-cultural "back-to-the-land" movement of the 1960s and 1970s has particular significance for alternative food networks (AFNs) in the USA, where it was the cradle for the early growth of organic agriculture from the 1960s (Belasco 1989; Vos 2000). However, the formative years of the organic farming movement and the Soil Association in Britain and the biodynamic movement in Germany, for example, are the 1920s when, following World War II, "the belief in the regenerative power of contact with the land took on an even greater force" (Bramwell 1989: 104). The parallels are much closer in the 1960s and 1970s when Western European back-to-the-land movements shared many of the same political concerns as their contemporaneous US counterparts, including antimaterialism, pacifism, feminism, antiurbanism, ecologism, and radical green visions, inspired in some cases by earlier experiments in rural communal living with roots in agrarian socialism (Pepper 1991) and anarchism (Bramwell 1989). As Pepper (1991) reminds us, rural communes and relatively self-sufficient, small-scale communities were advocated by writers of very different political hues, from Goldsmith (1972) and Sale (1980) to Bahro (1986) and Gorz (1980).

Abrams and McCulloch's (1976) and Rigby's (1974) studies of communes in 1960s Britain, as discussed by Pepper (1991), reveal that their communards, despite their individualistic and idealist politics, believed that wider awareness of their values and lived practice contributed to social change. That is, they were playing an "'exemplary' role in the vanguard of change for the whole society" (Pepper 1991: 56). This idea of the "exemplary" project as a strong influence on the political imaginary of alternative rural "futures" springs to mind when considering Keith Halfacree's (2007b: 131) work on the changing spatiality of the British countryside and the possibility that an emergent "radical rural spatiality" might survive Lefebvre's "trial by space" against "the gravitational pull of dominant spatialities."

This recent statement builds upon earlier research on nomadic groups or New Age Travellers (NATs), who gained media notoriety in the mid-1980s and early 1990s, and whose composite identity covers "back-to-the-land'ers," "hippies" and direct action environmental protesters (Halfacree 1996). The subsequent repression of NATs by the state is explained in terms of the perceived threat these "parasitic" groups posed to the sedentary "rural idyll" and the conformity of capitalist spatiality. Nevertheless, Halfacree (1996: 66) still sees the seeds of alternative rural spatialities in the NATs and associated groups, and argues that "whether these seeds germinate remains open."

Back-to-the-land movements represent a second counter-cultural challenge to the hegemony of productivist agriculture and its appropriation of rural space. In a series of papers on the UK, Halfacree (2001, 2006, 2007a,b) disentangles these movements from mainstream, middle-class counter-urbanization, inextricably embedded in capitalist relations, property structures and power. Resisting "the strong cultural mythologizing and essentialising" of the "'American 1960s'," Halfacree (2007a: 3) observes that back-to-the-land experimentation "was found across the global North, including France and the UK." Although values and organizational practices from 1960s and 1970s projects have survived, together with some of the earlier settlement sites, Halfacree (2007a) argues that contemporary back-to-the-land exponents differ significantly as "they are much less concerned with any (mythical) 'dropping out'" (ibid.: 4). With rising social engagement, Halfacree (2007a: 3) suggests that back-to-the-land is becoming "a very diffusive concept," making it difficult to distinguish between initiatives with counter-cultural influences, "and more bourgeois forms of counter-urbanisation, on the one hand" – for example, self-build settlers – and, on the other, "more traditional forms of agricultural activity," such as organic smallholding.

This proliferation and the danger of framing counter-culture projects too rigidly in opposition to counter-urbanization is illustrated by Mailfert's (2007) analysis of "neo-farmers" from urban backgrounds in France, Rivera Escribano's (2007) work on urban–rural migrants in Navarre, Spain, and Meijering *et al.*'s (2007) survey of almost 500 intentional communities throughout the global North. In the British case, Halfacree (2001) discusses the difficulty of positioning contemporary back-to-the-land (re-)settlements as increasingly they practice sustainable agriculture, permaculture, and low-impact development. This complexity is exemplified by new crofting initiatives in Scotland, which advocate empowerment, land ownership, and conservation. The demand for easier means to gain secure, permanent access to land, articulated with an explicit critique of the planning system and property relations, also is the key priority of "new settlers," including some "former travellers," living on three rural cooperative settlements in south-west England (ibid., 403; cf. Fiddes, 1997; Fairlie, 2000). This demand resonates strongly with rural community movements operating in the social economy and developing innovative forms and mechanisms to obtain land to grow food locally and to build affordable housing. These counter-culture-inflected "communities of practice" are supported by the political praxis of larger social movements and umbrella groups, such as Making Local Food Work, as we see in a later chapter.

The argument running through this research is that back-to-the-land movements in the twenty-first century should be situated as protagonists in the process of "ongoing contested rural change," which is constructing an increasingly diverse, "differentiated countryside" (Murdoch *et al.* 2003). As the contradictions of productivist agriculture become increasingly acute, space is created for alternative socio-spatial imaginaries and, for Halfacree (2007a: 4–5), "Back-to-the-land is a player in the game of producing rurality/ruralities for the new millennium." This brings us back to the role of "exemplary" projects in catalyzing social change, which in this case depends on the success of these nascent "radical ruralities" in Lefebvre's "trial by space" with "other species of post-productivism that clearly are emerging" (Halfacree, 2007b: 138).[1] Conveniently, this struggle is illustrated by mainstream pressures to undermine organic agriculture as a "localized" practice. The following section explores the origins of the organic movement in the UK as one of the major catalysts of the contested transition to alternative food provisioning.

Organic agriculture

The historical antecedents of the organic agriculture movement in Britain in the 1920s and 1930s, and its foundations in an extraordinarily eclectic range of political philosophies, from proto-Fascism and Nazi peasant ideology to social credit, guild socialism, and various strands of anarchism, have attracted wider attention in recent years, largely because of its influence on the growth of modern environmentalism (Bramwell 1989; Conford 2001; Reed 2001, 2002). Christian (particularly Anglican) theology, with its ideas of a natural order, natural laws, and reverence for nature, is identified by Conford (2001) as one unifying thread in the advocacy of organic farming, running from the ferment of these early years to the first decades of the Soil Association, established in 1945 following the publication of Lady Eve Balfour's *The Living Soil* (1943). These foundational ideas coalesced into a powerful critique of industrial society and its reckless exploitation of nature and passionate advocacy of small-scale, locally-centered organic husbandry and its contributions to ecological and human well-being, nutrition, health, and the vitality of rural life.

Despite this rich history, Reed (2002: 481) recounts that the Soil Association and the organic movement in Britain spent the next 40 years "in the wilderness" before starting to "break through in the late 1980s" as it became the organizational locus of protests against the introduction of genetically modified organisms (GMOs) in agriculture. However, these wilderness years witnessed a major strategic shift in its discursive and institutional trajectory, which greatly facilitated its later rise to prominence. Thus, under the leadership of Fritz Schumacher from the late 1960s, the "prolonged search for scientific validation for organic farming" (Reed 2002: 483) became a secondary preoccupation and was superseded by a normative discourse couched in Gandhian moral terms. "Organic food was to become both morally and chemically safe" (Reed 2001: 141). Other themes from the past, "such as the importance of locally grown and processed food remained," but their original far-Right, fascistic, and elitist trappings were quietly abandoned (Reed 2001: 141). Nevertheless, some of Schumacher's ideas were resisted, including land re-distribution and "his call for land to be held in trust for the benefit of the community," and "it remains a lacuna in the discourse of the British organic movement that *questions of social justice are constantly elided*" (ibid.: 141, our emphasis).

If scientific validation proved elusive, the Soil Association continued as a sorting-house of practical knowledge and in 1966 it introduced a set of common production standards based on practices and normative values acceptable to its members. This flexibility has allowed its standards to evolve "since the 1960s to include greater emphasis on wildlife protection, animal welfare, and the banning of genetically modified products" (Reed 2002: 492). The Soil Association is now the leading organic certification body in the UK and receives state funding to operate an information service for prospective organic farmers. Institutionally, it is a complex amalgam of "a business, a farmer's union, a consumer group, as well as a campaigning group" (ibid.: 492). Despite this apparently central position, Reed (2001, 2002) argues that the Soil Association only moved into the mainstream of UK environmental and food politics following the "mad cow disease" (BSE) crisis of 1986 and subsequent food "scares" and, more decisively, with its determined and very public opposition to GMOs in the later 1990s. With its accumulated experience and knowledge of *alternative* ways of "knowing and growing food," the Soil Association offered an authoritative voice in this anxious period of food "scares" and mistrust of science, creating discursive space and support for local organic food and its other initiatives (Reed 2001).

This authoritative position was enhanced by tactical alliances against GMOs with mainstream environmental movements, including Greenpeace and Friends of the Earth, and its support for direct, non-violent, action to destroy trial plots and commercial plantings of GM crops (Reed 2005). Analyzing this watershed period, Reed (2008: 215) characterizes the wider organic movement as a "range of *informal interaction networks* ... (with) a strong set of *shared beliefs* about the importance of organic farming and food ... (leading) to a strong sense of common identity that is displayed in a sense of *solidarity*" (original emphasis). Under the threat of GM foods, these networks engaged in forms of collective action, direct protest and consumer boycotts, temporarily obscuring but building upon their more routine, capillary processes of knowledge dissemination and advocacy of local organic food. Reed (2008: 215) makes the significant point that "The social stake that is being contested – the social control of the provision of food – has remained constant." Furthermore, as we argue throughout this book, on this contested ground it is "the alliance between producers and consumers that is the generative basis of the organic movement" (Reed, 2005: 234).

Territorializing the Common Agricultural Policy (CAP)

The persistent but still tentative process of reforming the CAP, and the greater discretion this has allowed in national farm policies, gradually has created institutional "spaces" and budgetary allocations for local food initiatives and other forms of alternative food provisioning. In this process, the narrow sectoral focus of the CAP, enshrined in its original structural emphases on supporting commodity prices rather than farm incomes, and the accompanying centrality of commodity regimes and productivist agricultural modernization, is now being challenged by a more territorialized model of multifunctional agriculture and diversified rural development. This contested opening up of agricultural policy to new voices and social actors, which also is evident at the European Union (EU) level, has weakened the dominance long enjoyed by national corporatist farm organizations, such as the National Farmers Union (NFU) in the UK and the *Fédération Nationale des Syndicats d'Exploitants Agricoles* (FNSEA) in France (Roederer-Rynning 2002; Coleman and Chiasson 2002). In the UK, these new actors are represented by such broad alliances of conservation, environmental, and urban consumer groups as Wild Life and Countryside Link and Sustain and, in France, by the *Confédération Paysanne*, with its campaigns for a greener, more "social" agriculture and its central role in the *Alliance Paysans-Ecologistes-Consommateurs*.

However, despite the greater pluralism of agricultural policy at supranational and national levels, the end of CAP support for large-scale commodity agriculture is still an uncertain and distant prospect. Although current levels of support are due to be re-negotiated by 2013, the outcome is clouded by the intransigence of powerful national commodity lobbies, the fractious collapse of the Doha Round of international trade negotiations in 2008, and the canvassing of protectionist forms of food security following the intense bout of global food price inflation in 2007–08 and its resurgence in 2010–11.

The process of CAP reform is frequently attributed to the increasingly neoliberal ideological thrust of trade liberalization, exemplified by the Uruguay Round of 1986–94, when agriculture was first subjected to the disciplines of the international trade regime. While this influence undeniably is central, it is easy to lose sight of the well-orchestrated public opposition to the environmental degradation and loss of wildlife caused by intensive monocultural farming – despite the rhetorical positioning of farmers as "stewards of the land" – the concentration of subsidy payments in the hands of a tiny minority of large-scale farmers and corporate actors, and the fiscal strain of the CAP on EU budgetary resources (cf. Cunha and Swinbank 2009). The initial steps of CAP reform include the introduction of dairy production quotas in 1984, the 1988 agreement to increase the so-called Structural Funds for regional development by constraining CAP expenditure, and most notably the MacSharry reforms of 1992, which reduced commodity support prices and began the shift toward direct farm payments as the principal mechanism of support.

In response to the trade liberalization pressures of the Uruguay Round and, subsequently, the World Trade Organisation (WTO), the MacSharry measures gave real momentum to the diversification of farm income support by moving to "de-couple" subsidies from direct production-related activities, the so-called "first Pillar" (Pillar I) of the CAP. These commodity payments were to be replaced by alternative forms of support, such as agri-environmental stewardship schemes and more broadly "rural" programs, which are considered to involve non-trade-distorting or "green box" payments under WTO rules (Potter and Burney 2002). This strained duality at the heart of the CAP found further expression in the Cork Declaration of 1996 and the Agenda 2000 reforms,[2] which repackaged Pillar I, commodity-related support for international consumption as "green box-compatible" by appealing to the concept of multifunctionality as grounds for claims of European *rural exceptionalism*. This notion – part economic, part esthetic – attempts to mediate this duality by acknowledging both the socio-economic functions of agricultural production, such as income and employment generation, and its delivery of public goods in the form of agri-environmental services and rural development.

The Agenda 2000 reforms articulated this "public goods" approach – "public payments for public benefits" – by bringing together a range of previously separate programs under the Rural Development Regulation (RDR), known as the "second Pillar" (Pillar II) of the CAP. Although no additional EU resources were allocated to its implementation, member states were permitted to "modulate" or redirect up to 20 percent of production-related payments to measures designated under the RDR (Falconer and Ward 2000).[3] Commenting on this new landscape and the rebalancing of supranational and national agricultural policy, Lowe *et al.* (2002: 14–15) identified three major new developments: "…subsidiarity and the increasing decentralisation of agricultural policy within the European Union," multifunctionality, which is "challenging the classic sectoral vision of farming as an exclusively productive enterprise," and territoriality.

Additional steps toward the "WTO-proofing" of the CAP were taken in 2003, when the so-called Fischler reforms further decoupled payments from commodity production and reconfigured basic income support into a "single farm payment" (SFP), which was made conditional on undemanding "cross-compliance" with several EU agri-environmental directives (Rutherford 2004). With Pillar I farm income support protected until 2013 under the terms of the 2002 agreement between French President Jacques Chirac and German Chancellor Gerhard Schroeder, the wider social legitimacy of the CAP for the time being rests squarely on the "public goods" approach embodied in the RDR (Falconer and Ward 2000). However, the tensions between these different, though still agro-centric, visions of the future of the CAP are deeply entrenched and fiercely contested (Buller 2004). For example, in December, 2005, under pressure to reduce overall EU expenditure levels in the 2007–13 budget, EU leaders left Pillar I funds unchanged, respecting the Franco-German accord, but made significant cuts in Pillar II resources for national rural development programs, slowing down further "greening" of the CAP.[4]

The unresolved contradictions of this bimodal structure have prompted suggestions that the CAP now accommodates

> two agricultures, one orientated toward world markets, the other constructed as "agriculture in a region," (with) the need to increase competitiveness ... presented ... alongside the continuation of some sort of "social agriculture," sustained through a combination of income diversification, policy support and the capture of growing consumer demand for quality products.
>
> (Potter and Tilzey, 2007: 1297; cf. Coleman, 1998)

Similarly, analyzing the evolution of agricultural policy in France, Buller (2004: 102) observes that "it has been able to nurture and develop across the entire national space these twin models of farming, the one de-territorialized and industrialized, the other locally and socially embedded" (cf. Coleman and Chiasson 2002). These tensions, articulated in the different economic and politico-institutional setting of the UK, can be seen in the report of the 2002 Policy Commission on the Future of Food and Farming, set up in response to the 2001 foot-and-mouth crisis, which recommended that producers reconnect with consumers by developing quality food products and re-embedding food systems in local space, as we discuss in Chapter 4.

Against this general background, we now briefly consider several specific EU programs that, in a loosely cumulative way, have encouraged the growth of "social agriculture" and territorialized local food systems. One important piece in this unfinished jigsaw of re-territorialization is the European Structural Funds, which "evolved from a modest initial European regional policy devised in the mid-1970s" to reduce spatial economic disparities toward a set of programs with *targeted territorial* funding criteria (Ward and McNicholas 1998: 28). Thus the so-called Objective 1 and 5b funds focused on stimulating local rural development in poor, peripheral agricultural regions, bypassed by modernization and Pillar I CAP support.[5] Discussing the central role of territoriality and provenance in alternative food networks, Ilbery *et al.* (2005) approvingly cite Dwyer's (2000: 7) conclusion that "support from EU structural funds is a common factor in the development of many new countryside product initiatives across Europe." This is put in much stronger terms by Gilg and Battershill (1998) in their study of the direct marketing ("*vente directe*") of quality foods in Brittany and Vendee, who suggest that EU Social and Regional funds are vital to the survival of these French producers, as well as their counterparts in marginal farming areas elsewhere in Europe.

The strong influence on the rationale of Objective 1 and 5b programs of endogenous regional development theory, with its emphasis on building local capacities, adding value to local resources, capturing economic rents locally, and "bottom-up," participatory governance, also is apparent in the case of LEADER *(Liaisons Entre Actions de Développement de L'Economie Rurale)*. With a backward glance to *gemeinschaft* village culture, this local community program also originated in the first Structural Funds reform (1989–93), when more specific territorialized targeting was adopted. Introduced as a three-year pilot initiative in 1991 in Objective 1 and 5b regions, it was extended for two further five-year periods in 1995 as LEADER II and in 2000 as LEADER+.[6] As Ray (2000: 164) observes:

> Existing or ad hoc organisations ("Local Action Group" – LAG) could apply for LEADER funds … (for) proposed development actions based on the valorisation of indigenous resources … and on the active participation by the public, voluntary and business sectors in the territory designated.

Characterized by the European Commission as a rural development "laboratory," the three LEADER programs have funded over 2,000 LAGs (Silva Rodriguez 2005) in the "disadvantaged rural Europe" of Objective 1, 5b, and 6 regions (Ray 2000).

Recent national case studies of LEADER projects have challenged the optimistic official rhetoric and suggested a range of alternative interpretations (Ray 2000). These analyses variously interrogate the political project behind LEADER and its politico-institutional capture, the realities of "community participation," the role of local economic and political interests, and ask whether or not the LAGs inhibit more radical approaches to rural development. More generally, these projects abrogate the responsibility of the local and national state for local economic regeneration, substituting weaker, and spatially more uneven, forms of support. Nevertheless, despite the pertinence of these questions, LEADER clearly is an integral element of the contested but perceptible shift from a sectoral perspective toward a broader, territorial understanding of rural development.

A territorial imperative also is the fundamental characteristic of EU Regulation 2081/92, which established an integrative framework for the different national practices of certifying the geographical origin of specialty food and drink products and the use of quality labels, with a view to their eventual harmonization. As Barjolle and Sylvander (2000) observe, this regulation was intended to encourage the diversification of agricultural production and promote rural development in less-favored regions through the provision of mechanisms of state legal protection for quality products which "qualified" as either a "protected designation of origin" (PDO) or a "protected geographical indication" (PGI).[7]

This EU legislation institutionalizes systems of geographical indications (GIs) that have a much longer history in southern member states, including the analogous system of *Appellation d'Origine Contrôlée* (AOC) used for French wines since 1935 (Parrott *et al.* 2002). Geographical indications as a form of intellectual property gained global recognition under the Trade-Related Property Rights (TRIPS) agreement of the World Trade Organisation (WTO). In theoretical terms, GIs provide a juridical framework for the "translation" of co-evolved, biocultural traditions and values into the commodity form and enable the "local" to trans(act) at a distance, notably in urban markets. In the EU, PDO/PGI registrations have expanded at a rapid rate since the early 1990s, providing tangible evidence of the "turn" to localized quality foods and the rise of territorialized supply chains, which are the subject of the next chapter.

This highly condensed discussion conveys an understanding of the awkward and difficult journey toward territorialized rural development and food systems characterized by sustainability, traceability, animal welfare, and local provisioning. We have focused on the multiple spatial dimensions of this social struggle to challenge the hegemonic rurality of productivist commodity agriculture and its globally extended supply chains. As we have seen, these challenges occur in many different arenas, from the supranational level of the CAP to countercultural experiments in various localities. In national space, forms of alternative settlement and organizational practice can differ significantly, but organic agriculture and back-to-the-land exponents of low-impact development share a "toolbox" of sustainable knowledges. Across the UK and Western Europe, there is a ferment of ideas around small-scale, locally-grown organic food circulating through what Reed (2008: 215) calls "informal interaction networks."

In the different arenas, room is being created for alternative socio-spatial imaginaries of food provisioning, ranging from more regionalized, multifunctional ruralities to Halfacree's (2007b) "radical ruralities." At the supranational scale, the halting and still fragile progress from a narrow sectoral perspective of agricultural policy toward more territorialized, regionally-embedded rural development provides eloquent evidence of the entrenched resistance and political power of commodity interests. In Buller's (2004: 102) words, the EU is riddled with the contradictions of pursuing "twin 'models' of farming," with France, the "inventor" of the CAP, the most skilled practitioner of the balancing act to maintain an internationally-competitive commodity agriculture alongside a "social agriculture" to meet wider rural development goals.

Nevertheless, processes of change are clearly evident on many different scales. The question of the moment is whether these are sufficiently powerful to bring about a real *transition* in rural policy, or will it remain partial and incomplete, or even be set in reverse? We seek answers to this question in the following chapters, beginning with recent developments in local food networks and claims that their emergence marks a paradigm shift in European rural development.

4 Rural Europe redux?

The new territoriality and rural development

How can we grasp the proliferation of alternative food networks (AFNs) since the 1990s? How can we understand the many different ways in which they are organized? Does the growth of these networks mark a watershed change – "back to a future" of re-localized, re-embedded quality food production–consumption and away from globalizing industrial food systems, with their "placeless and nameless" supply lines encircling the world? How "alternative" are these re-localized networks? What are their relationships with mainstream food provisioning? Is re-localization an oppositional move, articulating a new moral politics of food informed by ecological sustainability, social justice, and animal welfare? Are these moral politics grounded in a Putnamesque (re-)valorization of social community or is the quality "turn" to the local rather a new form of cultural capital in Bourdieusian status wars for social "distinction?" This chapter does not answer all these questions but it does provide us with analytical tools and contextual materials to move toward a better understanding of the issues at stake.

The Introduction to Part II presented a broad-brush sketch of the farm and policy structures which shaped the rise of AFNs in Western Europe. To recapitulate, the Common Agricultural Policy (CAP) policy has evolved to support a bimodal structure of "two agricultures": an internationally-competitive, de-territorialized commodity sector and a multifunctional, territorialized "social agriculture" to meet wider rural development goals, including income and employment generation, the production of "quality" foods and the conservation of culturally-valued farmed landscapes, biodiversity and other "public goods." This differentiated policy approach, incorporating elements of agricultural "exceptionalism" and loosely equivalent to the first and second Pillars of the CAP, is viewed by Coleman (1998) as a response to the uneven, disequalizing impacts of the modernization paradigm, which became increasingly evident in the later 1960s and 1970s. Measures to mitigate these impacts by providing support for "social (cohesion) agriculture" varied between member states, emerging initially at the *Lander* level in Germany, for example, but this policy orientation was strengthened by the accession in the 1980s of Greece, Spain, and Portugal, with their predominantly small-scale farm sectors, and provided the rationale for the 1985 reforms redirecting EU Structural Funds toward disadvantaged, lagging rural regions (Coleman 1998).

This case is made in even stronger terms by Potter (2006), who suggests that concern for the social welfare of economically marginal producers and the public goods dimension of agricultural production can be traced back to the foundational principles of the European Community (EU) and the inception of the CAP rather than marking a deliberate attempt to attenuate the neoliberalizing assault on agricultural protectionism from the 1980s onward. In much of Western Europe, this bimodal policy paradigm also demarcates many vectors of difference in socio-spatial ruralities, including large- and small-scale production, mixed dairy farming and cereal monoculture, and between intensive commodity agriculture in lowland areas and the more extensive systems found in economically disadvantaged upland regions.

Niche development, transition pathways, and alterity

Alternative food networks have emerged within these different, mainly disadvantaged, ruralities, establishing niches and bases for reproduction and expansion, whether closely integrated in mainstream food supply systems or growing in parallel alternative markets. One way to understand the many organizational forms adopted by AFNs is to use a heuristic framing as a means to systematize this empirical diversity. The approach we have chosen builds on the notion of niche development and recalls our earlier discussion in Chapter 3 of innovation and transition between socio-technical regimes.

If we conceptualize AFNs as a form of niche development, we can draw on the multilevel framework devised by Geels and Schot (2007) to analyze the range of possible relationships between niches, the dominant socio-technical regime of industrial food provisioning, and what they designate as the socio-technical landscape. This is "an exogenous environment beyond the direct influence of niche and regime actors" (ibid.: 400), somewhat akin to Braudel's *longue durée*, though also subject to sudden "shocks." Adopting this "multi-level perspective," Geels and Schot (2007) elaborate a typology of transition pathways between socio-technical regimes, which raises some interesting conceptual questions about the nature of niche development relevant to the analysis of AFNs in Western Europe.

Within this array of transition pathways whose trajectory is determined by interactions between these "nested levels," niche-innovations can "have a *competitive* relationship with the existing regime, when they aim to replace it ... (or) ... *symbiotic* relationships if they can be adopted as competence-enhancing add-ons in the existing regime to solve problems and enhance performance" (ibid.: 406, original emphasis). One of these ideal-typical transition scenarios is of particular interest to our discussion as it describes a situation where "moderate landscape changes create pressure on the regime" but niche-innovations are not sufficiently developed to take full advantage of this opportunity to transform the socio-technical regime (Geels and Schot 2007: 406).

In this pathway, which is illustrated by Smith's (2006) study of organic food, considered in more detail below, pressure groups and social movements and the demonstration effects of viable alternatives change public opinion and the perceptions of regime insiders, notably here supermarkets, leading to the reorientation of development trajectories. Based on this adaptive capacity, "new regimes grow out of old regimes through cumulative adjustments ... regime actors survive ... (and) may import external knowledge if the 'distance' with regime knowledge is not too large. Such symbiotic niche-innovations *add* to the regime and do not disrupt the basic architecture" (Geels and Schot 2007: 407, original emphasis).

This approach brings out the relational, contingent, and dynamic character of alternative economic institutions, while also recognizing the central role of social agency. It also reveals the *dialectic pressures* between niche development or "growth from below" and the political economic mainstream (cf. Smith 2006), and how these processes can affect the *positionality* of alternative economic forms: symbiotic, competitive, oppositional, for example. These ideal-types are helpful as we attempt to grasp the rich empirical complexity and variety of AFNs and their relationships with mainstream food provisioning.

A more explicitly spatial perspective on alternative economic forms is found in Fuller and Jonas' (2003) study of British community credit unions. Specifically, they warn against the representation of alternative economic spaces in static, idealist, and bounded terms, arguing that "this begs the question of how these places and spaces in practice preserve such (distinctive) values and ideals, their local autonomy, and the social, economic and political bases of their 'alternative' nature" (ibid.: 56). On this point, Leyshon *et al.* (2003: 8), commenting on Gibson-Graham's (1996) project of "the proliferative economy" as an alternative to the hegemonic discourse of global capitalism, observe that

> all economic geographies must (always) be constrained by the requirements of materially effective circuits of consumption, exchange and production. [If] ... they are incapable of sustaining the means of social reproduction [they] are doomed to fail. But to say this is not to say that effective economic geographies are reducible to a singular model. The scope for proliferation, though constrained, is still very wide.

This statement again focuses our attention on interactions between alternative economic geographies and the mainstream political economy, and "on the social relations and relations of power through which all economic geographies take place and by which they are shaped" (Leyshon *et al.* 2003: 4).

This is a timely reminder for two reasons. First, as we argue below, social relations have been neglected in many analyses of AFNs in Western Europe, which have tended to privilege their ecological relations and material outcomes, despite "the inseparable and mutually formative relations between the material and the social in the construction and functioning of economic geographies" (Leyshon *et al.* 2003: 8). Second, a focus on social relations problematizes ideas of alterity and challenges us to clarify widespread assertions that alternative

economic forms are in some sense "oppositional" even though their social reproduction depends on capitalist market relations and/or the state.

Our position in this chapter is that AFNs are not "oppositional to capitalism
in general" (Leyshon *et al.* 2003: 18). Indeed, such is the tenacity of this *idée
fixe* that we have ignored other alterities, which find expression, for example, in
the redistribution of power and social justice or new forms of spatiality. We
grapple with these issues below and throughout the book as we interrogate the
meanings of "alternative" in food provisioning and ask where alterity is to be
found. Is it found in sustainability (organic agriculture), social justice (Fair
Trade), new rural spatialities (quality foods), or more open, participatory governance (local foods) when these activities in many cases are reproduced through
capitalist markets?

Locality and local food networks

We now turn to the empirical core of this chapter and examine the European literature on AFNs and a wide range of case studies in light of the heuristics and analytical questions discussed above. As a rather crude approximation of the ideal-types
of "competitive" and "symbiotic" alternative economic geographies or niche-
developments, we begin with the distinction between "local" and "locality" foods
first drawn by the UK 2002 Policy Commission on the Future of Farming and Food,
known as the Curry Commission. This distinction is hardly watertight as locality
foods frequently are consumed locally, but this term does emphasize the ability of
certain foods to "travel" by mobilizing cultural signifiers or "qualities" of "place"
that have commercial and cultural traction in distant, mainly urban, markets. The
local/locality distinction thus is useful as a shorthand taxonomic device, which also
brings out an important difference between the USA and Western Europe.

In Europe, academic and policy discourse characterizes AFNs primarily as re-
localized or territorialized value chains linking producers of quality, often for-
mally certified, foods of known provenance with distant consumers, which the
Curry Commission regards as locality foods. It states that "the time has come for
locality food marketing to become mainstream in Britain as it is in France and
elsewhere," and recommends that state agencies, including Rural Development
Agencies (RDAs) and Regional Food Groups, seek to realize the "full benefits of
local branding" by promoting "The European 'Protected Names' Scheme" for
quality regional foods (Curry Commission 2002: 46). Such locality products are
seen as "opportunities for farmers to add value" (ibid.: 43), as sources of more
diversified farm livelihoods and, more broadly, as catalysts of rural regeneration
via local income and employment multipliers. This is but one, though admittedly
influential, example of the strong economic inflection to the discourse of quality
foods and re-localization. In the European arena, "just value" is the policy mantra,
rather than an "alternative" focus on "just values" embedded in a normative communitarian discourse of social justice more commonly encountered in the USA.

This economistic emphasis also pervades the European academic literature on
AFNs and this is heightened in more recent contributions by what we describe

below as a "*new realism*." This more pragmatic stance displays greater awareness of the competitive dynamics faced by locality foods and deploys an entrepreneurial analytics to understand quality struggles with mainstream actors over
territorialization and its commoditized attributes. Although "local food – which
comes from near the purchaser" (Curry Commission 2002: 43) is not entirely
neglected in this policy–academic discourse, particularly with the rapid growth
of farmers' markets and box schemes since the late 1990s, the "grey" literature
produced by national and local campaign groups and social enterprises engaged
in this sector is a major source of information. In *a priori* terms, these "horizontal" local food initiatives are more likely candidates as "competitive" or "oppositional" organizational forms than the "vertical" supply chains of locality foods.
Is this impression confirmed by case studies?

One of the few explorations of the local/locality food spectrum is Maye and
Ilbery's (2007) study of regional development strategies in the Scottish Borders
and Northumberland, two "lagging rural regions" of the UK. This analysis is situated in the context of regionalization and devolved rural governance, an institutional background sorely neglected hitherto in agro-food studies and rural
geography (cf. Winter 2006). Although the regionalization agenda in the UK has
a long gestation, the 1997 New Labour government added to its institutional
foundations with the creation of RDAs in 1998 and regional assemblies from
2000 onward.[1] This process of state rescaling gained further impetus following
the 2001 Foot and Mouth Disease epidemic and the Curry Commission's recommendations that RDAs adopt regional foods strategies, reinforced by other influential reports supporting regionalized rural governance structures and food
re-localization initiatives.[2] If we put aside the complex, often overlapping and
conflicting, activities of the institutional actors involved in multilevel governance, this study reveals that regional development policy and local project
support are strongly biased toward locality products, which Maye and Ilbery
(2007: 164) attribute to the influence of the regional economic agencies that
"drive the local food agenda, promoting regional branding and value-added strategies as tools to help improve competitive advantage."

Of particular interest here is that this institutional dominance has created
"*tension between locality foods and local foods*" (ibid.: 164, original emphasis).
Although Maye and Ilbery's (2007: 165) research focused mainly on locality and
specialty products, they report that

> some interviewees argued that such a narrow economic focus potentially
> ignores the diverse nature and potential of local food economies, character-
> ised by different types of food provisioning that include 'quality' food pro-
> duction but also involve local food community projects, public procurement
> initiatives and so on.

They go on to call for more attention to local food initiatives that "offer economic *and* social development potentials" and "espouse an avowedly community or politically-based agenda" (ibid.: 165, original emphasis). We follow this

line of thought and the tensions it reveals as we explore the diverse case materials on AFNs, and again in the discussions of mainstreaming and community social enterprises in Chapters 5 and 6.

A second general point before we turn to these materials is that locality foods entering supply chains to distant consumers construct quality using "immutable mobiles," such as *Appellation d'Origine Contrôlée* (AOC) labels and protected designation of origin/protected geographical indication (PDO/PGI) designations, as signifiers of "product, process and place" (Ilbery *et al.* 2005), whereas for foods produced and consumed locally the nature of network relations and interpersonal "regard" (Sage 2003) arguably are more significant (Watts *et al.* 2005; Maye and Ilbery 2007; see also Winter 2003). Without pushing this point too far, while locality foods are inescapably enmeshed in commodity relations, local foods can take on more ambivalent characteristics, with the potential to engage in non-market production–consumption relations or, indeed, to "shuttle" between these two circuits. Such considerations clearly should weigh heavily in conceptualizing alterity. A related issue concerns the dangers of drawing too firm a line between conventional food provisioning and alternative food networks when research, at least in the UK, indicates that actors in these networks move easily between "mainstream" and "alternative" markets to ensure their social reproduction (Ilbery and Maye 2005a, 2006). As Morgan *et al.* (2006: 2) observe, "the border between these systems is becoming more and more porous."

Locality foods: some case study evidence

We have suggested that locality and local foods represent twin dimensions or interwoven strands of the quality "turn" by consumers away from industrial food provisioning and toward socio-ecologically embedded local foods whose provenance is common (local) knowledge or is assured by labelling schemes and certification, as in the case of organic products. We have also seen that these strands, in practice, are difficult to disentangle since many "alternative" producers participate in both local and extra-regional markets. For ease of exposition, however, we begin with case studies of locality foods, which can be the focal point of territorial rural development policy or, more narrowly, of efforts by local producers to capture economic rents or even, as we shall see, a contradictory combination of the two.

Each of these elements emerges in the study by Angela Tregear and her colleagues of the PDO/PGI product qualification process in three cases of regional food production: the cured ham of Culatello di Zibello near Parma, the cherries of Lari in Tuscany, and Beacon Fell Traditional Lancashire Cheese from northwest England (Tregear *et al.* 2007). Endogenous, and neoendogenous approaches to rural development (Ploeg and Long 1994; Ploeg and van Dijk 1995; Ray 2000) and culture economy formulations (Ray 1998; Kneafsey 2000) broadly maintain that regional foods provide opportunities to (re)localize economic control by valorizing local cultural identity embedded in socio-ecological resources and *savoir faire*. But, as Tregear *et al.* (2007: 14, our emphasis) observe more analytically, the key point is that "How such assets are valorised … may vary according to the *types of actor* involved and the strategies they choose to pursue." These options are described conceptually as a *supply chain strategy* or, alternatively, as a *territorial quality or extended territorial strategy*. Under the latter,

> it is the territorial identity and associations of the product that are the bases of value generation, rather than the physical outputs of a single production network and supply chain. The identities and associations are seen to be utilisable by a broad range of actors … resulting in a wide distribution of economic rent.
>
> (Treagar *et al.* 2007: 14)

The conflicting strategic interests of different actors are most apparent in the Culatello case, where there are strong tensions between a Consortium of small artisan producers employing traditional methods and two industrial producers, while wider territorial initiatives adopted by local government actors lack coordination and are poorly supported by producers. Tregear *et al.* (2007: 16) conclude that the economic rent from PDO qualification "has only been distributed amongst a certain set of firms" (and) "new industrial initiatives linked to Culatello (have brought) the associated risks of damage to the environment (due to the presence of industrial pork breeding), as well as threats to small producers." In the case of Cherry of Lari, although the still incomplete PDO qualification process has stimulated collective action by the part-time, non-professional growers, it has been "captured" by local and regional government actors as part of a territorial development strategy to promote regional identity and encourage tourism in the area. PDO qualification for Beacon Fell cheese was gained successfully by the largest of nine local producers in a straightforward case of rent-seeking. "The strategy adopted is clearly not territorial, but neither is it supply chain, as de facto, little or no collective action exists. The qualification is used as part of a marketing strategy pursued by one individual firm" (Tregear *et al.* 2007: 19).

This comparative case study is a welcome step forward insofar as it highlights the tensions between supply chain and territorial quality strategies, yet it only hints at the struggles to gain control of the valorization process and the distribution of economic rent. This reluctance to give greater salience to social relations and power structures replicates analytical silences and omissions characteristic of much of the early European AFN literature on the quality "turn" and AFNs.[3] Arguably these stem from the reification of the "local" and the associated failure to interrogate its conceptual building blocks of embeddedness, trust, and close personal interactions (Goodman 2003). Thus, reiterating Hinrich's (2000, 2003) perceptive insight, to assume that local economic embeddedness precludes exploitative relations is to confuse spatial relations with social relations and "can inadvertently produce an *overly benign view of economic relations and processes*" (Sayer 2001: 698, our emphasis).

On this point, many of these early AFN analyses (cf. Ploeg *et al.* 2000; Renting *et al.* 2003) acclaim the "strategic" or "central" role of farmers in generating and appropriating the higher income flows accruing from rural innovation, often by re-allocating existing resources between on-farm activities. Yet, although these processes are seen as the centerpiece of a new, "alternative" rural development,

> this literature fails to subject farm-level innovation and AFN-centred strategies to critical sociological analysis. [These] case studies do not systematically engage issues of power within the farm enterprise, as variously configured by social relations of production, domestic labour, gender relations and patriarchal property structures. Beyond the farm household, the ways in which these strategies will mitigate such long-standing rural problems as income inequality, low paid employment, rural poverty, social exclusion, and more general questions of uneven development receive negligible attention. At each level, enthusiasm for an alternative, socio-ecologically embedded rural development model overrides Sayer's (2001) warning and occludes exploitative capitalist processes of domination.
>
> (D. Goodman 2004: 7)

The continued failure to break this analytical and empirical silence sustains doubts about the alterity of locality foods and their potential as progressive solutions to entrenched rural problems. In addition, early AFN studies have little to say about relations between enterprises in "alternative" networks and mainstream provisioning systems. This "blindspot" has proved remarkably stubborn, despite well-publicized evidence that, at least in the UK, supermarkets have dominated sales of organic products for many years.[4] Consumer research in the north of England indicates that consumers also prefer to buy local foods at mainstream supermarkets (Weatherall *et al.* 2003). Relatedly, Ilbery and Maye's (2005a) work cited earlier on farm-based and other small and medium-sized rural enterprises in the Scottish/English borders reveals that these specialist food producers source inputs from upstream suppliers located outside the region, in some cases using the same suppliers as "mainstream" producers, and sell some of their output through "conventional" wholesale and retail outlets in the UK and European markets. "Hybrid" spatial patterns of input sourcing and marketing also emerge from a detailed analysis of 61 sampled organic farm businesses in England – Sussex and the south-west – and south-west Wales (Lobley *et al.* 2009a, 2009b). As Ilbery and Maye (2005a: 12) observe, these "hybrid food geographies" problematize "an increasing tendency to readily conflate terms such as 'local', 'speciality', 'quality', 'alternative' and 'sustainable', *all part of some oppositional camp to agro-industrial production*" (our emphasis).[5]

Following this detour into the microanalytics of locality foods, we can return to the meso-level distinction drawn by Tregear *et al.* (2007) between (sectoral) supply chain and territorial development approaches. This convenient distinction gains much greater analytical purchase if the actors advancing these different

strategies are seen explicitly as struggling for control over processes of valorization of the capital – economic, cultural, symbolic – represented by biocultural
heritage or *terroir*. This brings the power dimension directly into the analysis
and problematizes the "local" by adopting a relational concept of place that
recognizes the key role of *external* networks and actor spaces in these struggles
(cf. DuPuis 2002). In these power politics of scale, external actors are "enrolled"
to reinforce local alliances in competing to appropriate economic rents generated
by territorial forms of capital.

Disputing rurality: the case of Chianti

This wider approach is developed in detail by Brunori (2006), drawing on
Bourdieu, actor-network theory and neo-endogenous development theory, and
illustrated by the power struggles to control the territorial symbolic capital
vested in the name of "Chianti" in Tuscany, which is at once a region and
famous wine appellation (Brunori and Rossi 2007). The main protagonists in this
struggle to "align" local and external actors around different social representations of rurality and so "shape rural change in (their) own interests" (ibid.: 184)
are the Consortium (*Consorzio*) of producers of *Chianti Classico* wine and a
grouping of eight local municipalities, the Permanent Conference of the Mayors
of Chianti, which emerged in the 1990s as a political counter-weight to the
Consorzio.

The struggle between these "fields of power" was brought into sharp focus by
the 2001 Italian Agricultural Act which, "on the wave of a growing interest
in strategies of relocalisation of agricultural production and ... endogenous
development," permits regional governments to establish "rural districts,"
thereby translating "an analytical concept into a governance pattern" (Brunori
and Rossi 2007: 185–186). The central bone of contention involves the boundaries of the proposed "rural district" of Chianti, neatly encapsulating the conflicts
between a sectoral supply chain concept of localization and the wider concerns
of territorial development. Thus, for the *Consorzio*, which defends boundaries
that coincide with the area of the *Chianti Classico* appellation, "the rural district
is a producers' network and its recognition is an instrument of territorial marketing" (ibid.: 190). However, this proposal would exclude significant parts of four
of the eight municipalities, inhibiting administrative coordination and the use of
the rural district to promote "the whole economy of the area through a valorisa-
tion of all local resources," (and to re-balance) "the role (and the power) of local
actors in managing development" (Brunori and Rossi 2007: 190).

With the battle lines drawn around a "wine monoculture" image of local economy, society and identity, this case study "follows the actors" in the processes
of building networks, forming alliances between local and external actors, and
creating discourses to advance competing visions of territorial development.
These represent different political articulations of economic interests, social relations, and power structures, with each of the protagonists continually working
"to strengthen its local networks around specific interests – the Consorzio with

the wine producers and the landowners, the Mayors mainly with non-agricultural actors" (ibid.: 203). This fascinating study demonstrates the significant insights of a relational conceptualization of territoriality, which draws attention to the formative significance of power relations in determining who has access to, and who benefits from, specific social constructions of place. As Brunori and Rossi (2007: 203) emphasize, in "post-rural" Chianti, with its "highly complex civil society," this "complexity is further increased by an intense inside/outside interplay, which contributes to an endless redefinition of local identities and changes in the balance of power within the area."

This emphasis on the "*intense inside/outside interplay*" between rival social representations of place addresses a second analytical limitation of the early European AFN literature: the treatment of the "local" as a "purified" entity, that is,

> as a spatial configuration that is ontologically given rather than the contingent outcome of ... social processes and relations of power that produce, reproduce and restructure the scale of the local. In other words, the local tends to escape sociological and socio-spatial analysis.
>
> (D. Goodman 2004: 5)

This purification of the scale of the local is diametrically opposed to the work in human geography on the contested social construction of place and the "winners" and "losers" in these "politics of scale," as we noted in Chapter 2. There are now welcome signs that agro-food studies is beginning to redress the earlier neglect of these contested, relational processes (cf. DuPuis and Goodman, 2005; DuPuis *et al.* 2006). In addition to Brunori and Rossi's (2007) analysis, other contributors to the "new realism" in research on locality foods also are paying more attention to spatial dynamics and scalar politics, as we see in the following section.

The "new realism" in locality food research

The "new realism" in locality foods research refers to the greater salience of socio-spatial processes, competitive dynamics, innovation, and the role of entrepreneurship in some recent analyses of the production and reproduction of locality foods suppliers, whether these are collective entities or individual enterprises. This *analytical shift* interrogates and qualifies rural development imaginaries by placing locality AFNs squarely within the highly contested political economic and institutional spaces they inhabit. In the British case, this shift is of a piece with the institutional changes provoked by the 2001 outbreak of Foot and Mouth Disease (FMD), which "derailed Labour's 'grand project' of rural policy reform" (Ward and Lowe 2007: 416). For these observers, the market-oriented policies adopted in the aftermath of the FMD crisis have restored a "farm-centred view of the rural world" (ibid.: 418), which has left wider rural development "as the poor relation of agricultural policy" (ibid.: 417).

The "new realism" is a shorthand description for a loose amalgam of elements which, taken together, point toward the use of different lens and metrics in assessing locality food projects and their potential to generate rural income and employment. Although it is therefore impressionistic and far from constituting a "school," it does mark a new, more pragmatic stage in academic research on the quality "turn." Earlier talk of locality food production as the spearhead of paradigm change in rural development is now being restated in less idealistic, more contingent terms (cf. Ploeg *et al.* 2000; Marsden and Sonnino 2008).

A central feature of the "new realism" is the growing emphasis on *entrepreneurial approaches* to rural development in different arenas, ranging from locality food production and interregional competition (Sylvander and Kristensen 2004; Valceschini 2002) to the rescaling of rural policy, proliferation of rural partnership and "stakeholder" initiatives, and other dimensions of the "new" culture of rural governance (Murdoch 1997b; Little 2001; Woods and Goodwin 2003). As we have seen, the entrepreneurial "turn" in the UK was sharply accentuated by the 2002 Curry Commission report and its "highly sectoral, supply-chain perspective on the future of the farming industry" and insistence that farm businesses "reconnect" with consumers (Ward and Lowe 2007: 417).

In a large-scale survey of organic marketing initiatives (OMIs) conducted in 2001–03 in 19 European countries, "success" as defined by economic and ethical criteria is attributed to entrepreneurial vision and "internal competencies" (inherited skills, path dependence, "learning by doing") rather than external contextual factors (Sylvander and Kristensen 2004). In a related paper, Sylvander and Schieb-Bienfait (2006) situate their analysis of this OMI survey in heterodox economic theories of the firm and argue that these approaches need to be complemented by an "entrepreneurial perspective." In the case of OMI leaders, this involves taking "into account their personal project and the enterprise's global project (both on ethical, economical and technical levels) in order to understand how their entrepreneurial actions have created new resources or combined existing resources in new ways" (ibid.: 349).

The emphasis Sylvander and Schieb-Bienfait (2006: 348) give to the "political talent" demonstrated by the networking activities of OMI leaders has close parallels with Marsden and Smith's (2005) analysis of the partnership-building and network creation needed to capture a greater share of the value stream generated from local resources. Such "network-based forms of *ecological entrepreneurship* can foster the wider development of 'socio-technical niches' in particular geographical spaces" (ibid.: 3, original emphasis). Entrepreneurial skills also are prominent in Ilbery and Maye's (2005a: 341–342) case studies of small "speciality" food producers in the Scottish–English borders, which "demonstrate quite clearly that the key to success is the dynamism and personality of the entrepreneur, together with their own network of contacts." However, as these authors stress, such skills are made even more vital by the intensely competitive and harsh economic conditions encountered in "quality" food markets, which brings us to a key dimension of the "new realism."

In a general statement of these dynamics, Goodman (2004: 8–9) observes that, "the ability of quality foods to secure premium prices and so generate excess profits is a central plank of the market-led, value-added model.... Since rents attract rent-seekers, the *durability* and magnitude of these income flows and the *location* of the actors who capture them become key issues" (original emphasis). More specifically, corporate food retailers in the UK and elsewhere in Europe have introduced policies of imitative expansion and strategic convergence, including the sourcing and labelling of "local" foods and own-label territorial identity products, in attempting

> to shift economic rents away from the farm and local level.... Examples here are Tesco's sale of over 100 locally-sourced products with some form of Welsh label in their supermarkets in Wales, the development by Waitrose of 'Welsh Organic Lamb' (Banks and Bristow, 1999), and "Carrefour's *filières de qualité* ... and another major distributor's *Reflets de France* product line, which banks on the regional tie" (Valceschini 2002: 25).
>
> (D. Goodman 2004: 9)

These comments reflected a concern expressed earlier by Marsden *et al.* (2000: 426) that the "*key influences upon the attribution and allocation of economic value across the different actors in the supply chains* ... (is) ... a significant research gap in recent literature" (Original emphasis). Marsden (2004) reiterates this concern in his analysis of the new quality food "spaces" and the struggle to dominate their material and discursive construction. "Competitive control of quality," he observes, confers power to demarcate "'competitive spaces,' boundaries and markets" between retailer-led commodity chains and AFNs (ibid.: 147). In short, appropriation of the material and cultural meanings of quality can be translated into flows of economic rent. Marsden argues that the large retailers in the UK hold an unfair advantage in this struggle given "the continued institutional and regulatory dominance of retailer-led food governance "(ibid.: 144; cf. Flynn *et al.* 2003). Nevertheless, empirical evidence of these supply chain processes continues to be a "significant research gap" and impedes clear assessment of the re-spatialized, territorial, value-added model of rural development.

Re-ordering rural space: "bio-regionality" and alterity in south-west England

These issues are revisited from a different, more geographical perspective in two recent papers by Terry Marsden and Roberta Sonnino (2006; Sonnino and Marsden 2006b), which open up agro-food studies and rural geography to relational conceptualizations of place and space and scalar processes. One of these papers begins as a range-finding exercise on the now familiar ground of quality struggles and value capture and observes that in the "first phase" of research on alternative food networks "their competitive relations with (and their alternative embeddedness from) the conventional sector have been largely ignored"

(Marsden and Sonnino 2006: 194). In setting an agenda for a "second phase," they broaden the terrain of competition between standardized and localized food systems to include spatial and scalar relations and conceptualize "rural spaces ... (as) multilayered phenomena which hold and play out the competitive tendencies between conventional and alternative food networks" (ibid.: 197). These spatial valorization struggles delineate "*competing agri-food geographies* operating within the same regions, built as they are upon different sets of quality and commercial conventions..." (ibid.: 196, original emphasis).

This theme of the potential of "bio-regional" AFNs to recapture and revalorize rural space in competition with the dominant conventional sector is developed further in Sonnino and Marsden's (2006) study of south-west England. However, the complex interdependencies and power asymmetries that characterize these dynamics of spatial and product quality competition call the value of this sectoral distinction into question. Also, regionally branded, traceable agricultural production, often using more extensive practices, may be "recapturing" rural space but this process is intimately connected to the marketing strategies of corporate retailers and their quality demands.

Sonnino and Marsden (2006) examine three regional food networks: Cornish clotted cream, granted PDO certification in 1998 under the leadership of Rodda's Creamery, which has an 80 percent market share; the Steve Turton Meats Network, whose watchwords are regionality, traceability, and quality, and which supplies and manages meat counters in 15 Sainsbury's supermarkets in the region; and the PDO-certified West Country Farmhouse Cheddar Cooperative, whose members variously sell their cheese under the collective brand and several individual own farm labels, although 50 percent or more is sold to large local cheese processors. The branded cheeses, whose distinctive quality derives from "the local milk base and the handmade nature of the cheese" (ibid.: 315), earn premium prices from the supermarkets.

Although scathing in their indictment of the weak, often obstructive, state policies toward AFNs following the "bio-security crisis" of "mad cow disease" (BSE) and the dismantling of regulated dairy markets, Sonnino and Marsden (2006) suggest that this hiatus has created opportunities for "horizontal embeddedness" in which the individual "ecological entrepreneur" plays an instrumental role, epitomized by Rodda's Creamery and Steve Turton. These actors have the ability to innovate by recasting "*bio/local/regional reconnections*" and reinventing tradition in ways that meet and exploit "the new circumstances agriculture finds itself in. These new circumstances involve high levels of privatised competition associated with gaining access to large retailers for value-added products" (ibid.: 316–317).

Here, these new "bio-regional" quality food producers are selling into "quite closed and highly coordinated networks ... (with) ... their own dynamic conventions, qualities and prices. These are regularly re-negotiated around retailers' variable commitment to meeting quality/premium markets" (ibid.: 318). These market conditions indicate that regional food networks need to be accomplished in the arts of "boundary maintenance" as they compete for room on supermarket shelves with retailers' own-label quality products, other quality suppliers, and cheaper "space-less" products (Sonnino and Marsden 2006: 318–319).

These case studies bring out the complex entanglements – "a 'nested Russian doll' of interactions" (ibid.: 318) – created by the quality turn in consumption and the related vulnerabilities of locality food producers to the marketing and pricing decisions of corporate retailers.[6] Nevertheless, despite this highly pragmatic analysis and recognition of these hybrid "nested hierarchies" in quality food provisioning, Sonnino and Marsden (2006: 320) make the normative claim that these three networks are not merely "alternative niches associated with local branding" but rather "represent sustained attempts to create a new agrarian eco-economy." Moreover, this claim is not buttressed by discussion of the possible pathways that would allow these bioregional forms to disentangle themselves from the supermarkets' close embrace. Indeed, this compact is fully accepted as the reproduction strategy of these networks, although the authors do acknowledge their "inherent fragility" and vulnerability if corporate retailers decide to "reassess their portfolios" (ibid.: 320). In short, this claim rests on the premise that the alterity of locality food networks is separable from the processes of their economic reproduction.

This is a fine line, however, and it brings us back to the ideal-types discussed earlier in this chapter and the observation by Leyshon *et al.* (2003: 8) that all economic geographies, whether based on capitalist relations, mutuality, or environmental sustainability, are constrained by the "requirements of materially effective circuits of consumption, exchange and production." As we have seen, the "effective economic geographies" of locality food networks in south-west England and elsewhere are deeply implicated in capitalist commodity markets and can hardly be regarded as "oppositional to capitalism in general" (ibid.: 18). Their claims to alterity thus would seem to rest on their "offer" of commodities inscribed with esthetic and ethical values that are "alternative" to the standardized, generic foods of mainstream provisioning. Yet these values clearly are open to mainstream capture and assimilation in processes that are *collapsing* this distinction. In terms of Geels and Schot's (2007) categorization of niche-innovations presented above, these market-oriented alternative food networks are in transition from an initially *competitive* relationship to *symbiosis* with the existing socio-technical regime.

This is not to deny the esthetic and ethical norms of locality food networks and the significant consequences of "internalizing" attributes of territoriality and place in the commodity form. As Buller and Morris (2004) observe, the quality "turn" has stimulated the commodification of socially valued externalities, such as landscape and habitat conservation, biodiversity, and sustainable farm environments. To take one example, the AOC *Comte* cheese network has been instrumental in the survival of "traditional low-density dairy farming" and the conservation of "species-rich natural grasslands" on the chalk uplands of the Jura massif in eastern France (Ilbery *et al.* 2005: 125). The esthetics of extensive farm husbandry, tacit artisan food processing knowledges, and culinary traditions similarly find expression in the Slow Food Movement's (SFM) project to protect "endangered foods" as a way to enhance the ecological sustainability and socio-economic vitality of rural areas in Europe and elsewhere (Miele and Murdoch 2002; Leitch 2003; Murdoch and Miele 2004a, 2004b).

It is in this restricted, though nonetheless significant, sense of the spatial reorganization of rural production, with its "defensive" and expansive dimensions recalling Lefebvre's "trial by space," that Sonnino and Marsden (2006) can legitimately entertain claims of alterity and "a new agrarian eco-economy."

Local food networks (LFNs)

LFNs, insofar as producers are profit-seekers and depend for their economic reproduction on market relations, display many of these same ambiguities. Indeed, the few case studies presented above cannot do justice to the rich research literature on how erstwhile local producer networks, using semiotic markers of place, have "jumped scale" by translating the quality norms of the interpersonal, local "domestic" world to the extra-regional "commercial" and "industrial" worlds, with their respective quality conventions of price and standardized products (Murdoch and Miele 1999). These relationships between scale and quality conventions are nicely elucidated by Fonte's (2006) analysis of the SFM's recent agreement with Italy's largest supermarket, *Coop Italia*, which involves "requalifying" local products for distant consumers. This process of codification – quality logos, AOC labels, PDO/PGI designation – "implies a shift from a *domestic convention*, based on face-to-face relations, to a civic/market convention that necessitates 'general forms' in order to communicate with *distant* people" (ibid.: 215, original emphasis, see also Lotti, 2010).[7]

However, for a variety of reasons, many food producers are refocusing on their local markets, often as a deliberate decision to disengage from extraregional corporate worlds, by taking up new forms of direct marketing, such as box schemes, farmers' markets, farm shops, and on-farm sales. These organizational forms also are less adapted to "jumping" scale, although several mega box schemes with complex supply networks serving the national market have emerged in some countries, including Abel and Cole, Riverford Organic, and Daylesford Organic in the UK, and *Bio-Paris* in France (Lamine 2005), as we see in Chapter 5.

Direct marketing as an alternative means of economic reproduction for farmers and an alternative mode of provisioning for consumers has become a Europe-wide phenomenon in the last ten years or so, complementing existing retail circuits in some cases and reviving local market traditions in others. The incredibly diverse organizational forms of these new local food system initiatives are impossible to capture in a few pages, although the greater weight of direct interpersonal relations in exchange processes provides some (variable) common ground.

In France, for example, where the first box schemes were created as recently as 2001, the diversity of geographical scale and organizational form is already apparent, ranging from national and regional schemes managed by private organic wholesalers, cooperative farms, and social enterprises to what Claire Lamine (2005) calls "local partnerships," which ideally incorporate closer inter-actions and *reciprocal* obligations between farmers and consumers, though these typically are drawn mainly from the urban middle class (cf. Girou, 2008). Such partnerships or AMAPs (*Associations pour le Maintien d'une Agriculture Pay-sanne*), "quite similar to the US Community Supported Agriculture model, were initiated in southern France and represent today 500 local consumer groups..." (Lamine and Deverre, 2008: 1). This commitment to smaller-scale, family farm-based food production reflects the institutional support of the *Confedera-tion Paysanne*, coordinated through the *Alliance Paysanne-Consommateur-Ecologiste*, "which took the initiative to promote the AMAPs" (ibid.: 3).

In these local partnerships, alterity is expressed through their more localized and personalized exchange processes and the *potential* scope this allows for ethical and political engagement, including commitments to sustainable produc-tion, animal welfare, more equitable producer–consumer relations, local public procurement, and small-scale, "peasant" agriculture (cf. Dubuisson-Quellier and Lamine, 2008). However, there is typically less concern with equitable food access for poorer, disadvantaged social groups, and Lamine and Deverre (2008) warn that the social relations of consumption of AMAPs reproduce local structures of wealth and power. Similarly, Girou (2008: 11) comments on the "relative social homogeneity" of "Amapians" revealed by research in the Midi-Pyrénées region. Reflecting on these uneven social geographies of consumption, Lamine and Deverre (2008: 7) observe that "there are almost no AMAPs in less favoured urban or rural areas." They also question whether this new form of market governance does, in practice, deliver more equitable exchange relation-ships, suggesting that

> there is a risk that such systems might generate new asymmetries between producers and consumers. The AMAPs can become structures within which consumers have most of the decision-making power, and the producers become their "suppliers".
>
> (Lamine and Deverre 2008: 7)

Echoing Laura DeLind's (2003) lament about the passivity of community sup-ported agriculture (CSA) members in the USA, Girou (2008) finds a similar lack of symmetry in the lukewarm participation of "Amapians" in farm activities and open days, apart from a core group of members. A related point concerns the polit-ical limitations of local particularism as engagement in local food politics is not matched by interest in "larger transformations of the agro-food system" (Lamine and Deverre 2008: 7), who add that "some AMAPs might be highly involved in local debates about the future of agriculture or urbanisation, but most of them are 'only' alternative systems of exchange." Despite these disappointments, however, AMAPs offer participating farmers and consumers livelihood and provisioning options outside corporate supply chains and so contribute to the processes that are slowly re-ordering rural space in accordance with the territorialized esthetics and ethics of "quality" food. As the contract for consumers joining the *Bio-Paris* box scheme states, " 'with this system you will contribute to the conversion to organic production of *x* hectares of land' " (Lamine 2005: 340).

Moya Kneafsey and her colleagues offer a different perspective on these issues, finding alterity in the challenge to corporate food provisioning represented by "alternative" local food schemes, whose persistence in time and space "allows the practical expression of a particular vision of food production–consumption" (Kneafsey *et al.* 2008: 64). On this transformational approach, participants in these local networks are helping to "build the knowledge and positive relationships that create the capacity for change" (ibid.: 177) by "subscribing" to a particular set of values incorporating environmental ethics and relational "arenas of exchange," which engender new forms of social agency and identity. The sheer diversity of local food schemes is emblematic of "a proliferation of different ways of thinking and doing things within a wider capitalist economy" (ibid.: 64).

One illustrative example is EarthShare Community-Supported Agriculture, located in Nairn in north-east Scotland and the longest running CSA in the UK, whose members can reduce their monetary subscription fees by doing three work shifts a year and paying up to 20 percent of their fees using currency units obtained by offering services in kind through the Local Exchange Trading System (LETS). In addition to supplying organic food "embedded with ethical value … part of what EarthShare represents then is the possibility of a challenge to the purely money exchanges which are prevalent within capitalist food production–consumption…" (ibid.: 63). More "orthodox" farmer–customer exchange relations characterize Waterland Organics, a 49-hectare farm in Cambridgeshire, which operates a home-delivery box scheme and also supplies produce to other organic networks. Waterland's conversion to organic and entry into direct marketing reflects a combination of environmental concerns, fears for the survival of the family farm, a desire to retain a greater share of the retail value by opting out of supermarket supply chains, and the satisfaction derived from direct contact with consumers (Kneafsey *et al.* 2008: 66–67).

Salop Drive Market Garden, occupying a three-acre site in Sandwell, "an economically depressed urban borough" in the West Midlands region of England, is a box scheme embodying a much broader concept of "reconnection" than "supplying local food to local people" (Kneafsey *et al.* 2008: 61). Indeed, the line between producers and consumers is intentionally blurred by the project's heavy reliance on volunteers and its wider agenda to promote community interaction. These activities, in line with national programs, are "first and foremost concerned with encouraging healthy eating and healthy living, with a specific focus on involving disabled people" (ibid.: 60). With the economic imperatives of reproduction relaxed by public funding, Salop Drive illustrates "the diversity of agendas and activities which can be pursued within differently structured producer–consumer relationships" (ibid.: 60–61).

Reviewing these relationships in their five UK case studies of box schemes, farm shops, and farmers' markets, Kneafsey *et al.* (2008: 161) conclude that "we have engaged with people who have found solutions, even if only partial, to the practical and ethical problems they are confronted with in their daily lives." This social practice approach to alterity resonates with Brunori *et al.*'s (2008: 4) view of "alternative" local food networks as "laboratories for experimenting new solutions to problems emerging in society," which "put on trial concrete alternatives to the conventional ways of producing, selling and consuming" and "challenge dominant values and behaviour norms."

Brunori *et al.* (2008) conceptualize alterity as the transition between reflexivity and routine, which describes the passage from individual reflexivity to the collective action needed to resolve contradictions between ethical and political values and the patterns of daily life in conventional food systems. This transition is illustrated by a case study of a consumer-initiated CSA or weekly box scheme in the Italian city of Pisa, *Gruppo di Aquisto Solidale di Pisa: GAS.P!* This is a network of 180 families supplied by small-scale, mainly organic or bio-dynamic, producers, including some "drop outs" from industrial agriculture and others who are new, "lifestyle," entrants to farming. Brunori *et al.* (2008) analyze the innovations by consumers and producers in new provisioning networks as a collective process of social learning to "scale up" the values underlying individual reflexive consumption into organized social practice. This analysis places Brunori and his colleagues in the transformational "camp" on the basis of the demonstration effects that can radiate from successful "alternative" experiments and stimulate further "restructuring of daily patterns and technologies of consumption and distribution" (ibid.: 17). They would probably also agree that a microinitiative such as *GAS.P!* or EarthShare in north-east Scotland can "raise an explicitly oppositional voice against the majority of food provisioning practices in its locality" (Kneafsey *et al.* 2008: 64).

The studies of local food schemes reviewed here reinforce a more general point we discussed earlier in Chapter 3. That is, patterns of social practice embedded in these new forms of production–consumption coevolve in interactive, contingent processes of social learning and innovation. Producers and consumers must acquire knowledges and skills, both new and revived, before these novel patterns can be "normalized" in everyday routines. To paraphrase a previous suggestion, producers *and* consumers need to be seen as active, relational, and political "partners in the contested knowledges of 'knowing and growing food'" (D. Goodman 2004: 13).

The "social economy" of food

In closing this discussion of "alternative" local food networks, an important caveat is to recognize that its institutional boundaries are narrowly circumscribed. As suggested by the case of Salop Drive Market Garden, with its focus on strengthening the linkages between food, health, and community, a wider institutional understanding of the local food economy would extend beyond the market-embedded nexus of locality/local foods to the myriad social enterprises, non-governmental organizations (NGOs) and other organizations working to reduce inequalities in health and access to fresh, nutritious food, alleviate "food poverty," and build sustainable local procurement systems (Morgan and Sonnino 2008; Kirwan and Foster 2007). Many of these organizations, like Salop Drive, inhabit the so-called "third sector" or "social economy" and sit somewhat uneasily between the private sector and the state, between market and non-market relations, and profit-making and non-profit structures, often combining elements of each.[8]

The third sector and social enterprises expanded rapidly under New Labour after 1997 as a localized approach to social exclusion and deprivation that was represented as a "Third Way" between direct state welfare provision and the competitive tendering for public services delivery introduced by the Conservative governments of the 1980s and 1990s. This "social economy" of food includes "'local food projects' funded by the statutory services" and targeted to disadvantaged communities, notably through food cooperatives and school-based initiatives (Dowler and Caraher 2003: 57), but also rural social enterprises, community interest companies, local buying groups, urban farms, and a variety of voluntary organizations.[9] These forms also can combine volunteer and paid workers and draw their funding from public authority grants, current operating revenues, donations, and charitable sources.

In comparison with the empirical and theoretical work on the quality "turn," this sprawling, unwieldy world of the social economy of local food has been sorely neglected. However, the role of the "third sector" at the local level more generally has attracted critical attention since it is seen by "many academic commentators ... as fracturing the principle of national welfare provision" (Lee and Leyshon 2003: 33). Similarly, Amin *et al.* (2003: 49) suggest that the social economy is a means of devolving state responsibility "that simply replaces older forms of welfare provision with more precarious, weaker and uneven forms." While not rejecting the efficacy of "local food projects" in hitherto excluded communities out of hand, Dowler and Caraher (2003) broadly agree with this view and suggest that the social economy is not up to the structural challenge of equalizing access to healthy food. That said, these lines of analysis need to be explored more fully as part of a comprehensive assessment of this more broadly conceived local food economy that still remains to be done.

Conclusion

The debates and case materials reviewed in this chapter reveal how difficult it is to place locality and local food networks unequivocally under the rubric of "alternative." As we have suggested, although exceptions possibly exist, the economic reproduction of these networks indicates that they are not, in any meaningful collective sense, "oppositional to capitalism in general" (Leyshon *et al.* 2003: 18). Can we then consider varying degrees of alterity in the context of capitalist relations of production and exchange? Locality and market-oriented local food networks certainly can be conceptualized as new organizational interventions in the production and distribution of value which, in different ways, *challenge* patterns, spatial scales, and structures previously consolidated by productivist commodity agriculture and downstream corporate actors. Having discarded the notion of alterity as "oppositional," we are left to consider the nature of this challenge.

In the case of locality foods, this challenge resides in the ecological, ethical, and esthetic values ascribed to the production process. Of course, locality foods can be marketed directly, but "jumping scale" to distant consumers more typically requires integration into corporate distribution channels and "quality" product portfolios. In terms of exchange and distribution, these networks have a symbiotic relationship with the conventional socio-technical regime. In the space-economy of production, however, we have seen that locality foods are competitive with intensive commodity agriculture and their expansion is reclaiming rural space and so redistributing flows of value within rural economies. Locality food networks are "hybrids," combining competitive and symbiotic relationships with conventional food provisioning, depending on the sphere of economic activity in question.

It is important to acknowledge that "bio-regional" and locality food networks are recapturing rural space for more extensive, sustainable farming practices, but claims for "ecological alterity" must be qualified explicitly. For example, we learn very little about who *inhabits* the reclaimed spaces of Sonnino and Marsden's (2006) "new agrarian eco-economy" in south-west England, other than livestock suppliers, cheese producers, and creamery operators. In what ways are the protagonists in these recaptured spaces contesting, rather than reproducing, "embedded" structures of wealth, property, privilege, and power? Such structural questions are obscured and left unanswered by the representations of the (reclaimed) rural space and rurality of locality food networks.

Local food networks engaged in innovative forms of direct marketing are more competitive with the mainstream, appropriating flows of value that otherwise would have been channelled through corporate circuits of production and exchange. Both Kneafsey *et al.* (2008) and Brunori *et al.* (2008) find alterity in this competitive relationship with corporate food provisioning and the scope this creates for "alternative" experiments in social learning that attempt to reconcile particular ethical and political values with everyday routines. These are "hopeful" political geographies, as well as "materially effective" economic geographies.

This discussion of alterity revolves around dimensions of difference from the mainstream but, as with the academic literature and policy discourse, it is silent on its counterpart question: *alterity for whom?* Who is enfranchised and who is disenfranchised by the quality "turn" to locality foods and innovative forms of direct marketing? Salop Drive Market Garden and other publicly-funded "local food projects" to strengthen the food–health nexus in poor neighborhoods provide an incomplete but indicative answer to this question. In short, the social relations of consumption of market-oriented "alternative" food networks have long been ignored by those asserting their alterity. This is not to say that these foods are only a "class diet" for the privileged; case study evidence undermines this reductive view (cf. Kneafsey *et al.* 2008; Dowler 2008). However, social justice is the Achilles heel of these networks as the poor and disadvantaged continue to be ill-served.

5 Into the mainstream

The politics of quality

With a strong but not exclusive focus on the British case, this chapter broadens our exploration of a central theme of this book: the contested politics of quality, or who defines how food is grown and how it is known. This deceptively simple question eludes a definitive answer but opens up large, complex issues regarding the social control of food provisioning, which help us to grasp what is at stake in these struggles.

The now routine appearance on supermarket shelves of organic, local, and other quality foods presents difficult dilemmas for alternative food networks (AFNs) and social movements. Are corporate retailers' volume requirements and supply chain management practices shifting income streams and economic rents away from quality food producers and their rural economies? Does the mainstream subvert the values and "moral geographies" of locality foods as they enter the market and industrial "worlds" of corporate retailers? Can mainstream retailing provide wider social access to quality foods and stimulate the gradual transformation of food provisioning toward a more equitable, ethical, and sustainable future?

In previous chapters, the new agro-food networks galvanized by the quality "turn" were characterized as innovative socio-ecological "projects" whose practices potentially challenge those of the "incumbent" regime (Smith 2006). Their emergence and rapid growth have triggered strategic adjustments in conventional provisioning systems and these, in turn, have brought responses from quality food networks. We suggest below that the politics of quality construction is an "open," ongoing process, or what John Wilkinson (2009: 20) represents as a "dialectics without synthesis" to capture "the permanent tension … between markets and social movements in the case of transactions heavily laden with values."

In examining these dynamics, we look first at the rise of corporate retailers to their hegemonic position in the contemporary food system. Next, drawing on several case studies, we consider the experience of different quality food networks in their efforts to fit into the "offer" of these corporate actors or, on the other hand, to resist and retain a degree of autonomy. A final section discusses the theoretical and empirical traction of a two-sector framework in capturing the interactions between "alternative" and "conventional" actors in the contested "spaces" of quality.

Corporate retailers ascendant

This section provides a brief historical background to the rise of supermarket chains as the leading actors in the modern food system and suggests why this leadership will be difficult to "resist" and dislodge.

Taking the long view, the locus of value capture and market power in the product complexes and supply chains linking farming, primary food processing, food manufacturing, and retail distribution has moved inexorably downstream toward retailing. At different times in the historical evolution of this system, these downstream sectors have developed very similar industrial structures, characterized by high production concentration, oligopolistic competition, and transnational operations. Led by such firms as Unilever, Nestlé, and Cargill, these were already well-defined features of primary food processing before 1914, whereas the internationalization of food manufacturing occurred mainly after World War II (Goodman *et al.* 1987).

In turn, the power of the giant processors and manufacturers was countered and superseded in the 1950s and 1960s during the long "golden age" of Fordist, mass food consumption, which provided the platform for the growth and consolidation of an independent retail sector of large, oligopolistic supermarket chains. According to contemporary observers (Burns 1983; Lang and Wiggins 1984), these chains have held the ascendancy in the UK food system since the 1970s.

Two dimensions of this dominance are of particular interest to us here. First, despite great efforts to diversify their feedstocks of raw materials and product ingredients, the competitive position of food processors and manufacturers is still closely tied to particular agro-food complexes – dairy, oilseeds, cereals, livestock, for example – and their respective supply chains. Thus "even after decades of diversification from their original product base, industrial capitals can still be identified by their historical location in the food chain" (Goodman and Redclift 1991: 90). Corporate retailers, on the other hand, must respond to the shifting patterns of consumer demand and have no primordial commitment to specific agricultural supply chains or production technologies, which gives them the upper hand in relations with suppliers, processors, and manufacturers.

In the sociology of markets (Fligstein and Dauter 2007), these asymmetrical relationships are conceptualized as *resource dependence*. That is, power in markets is unequally distributed if one side of the exchange is more dependent on what is being exchanged than the other party (ibid.: 114). This asymmetry is thrown in bold relief by estimates that already in the late 1980s the top four British supermarkets accounted for 50–80 percent of most major food manufacturers' sales, whereas no single food manufacturer represented more than 1 percent of Sainsbury's or Tesco's turnover (Martin 1990). This low level of resource dependence on suppliers, enhanced by the introduction of supermarkets' own-label product lines, had great strategic value for corporate retailers as it allowed them to respond flexibly as markets changed. More specifically, it enabled them to maintain their dominance as the era of "cheap" mass food consumption and price competition gave way in the 1980s to non-price competition with the "turn" to quality and increasingly differentiated, segmented, and demand-driven markets.[1] In short, quality and its construction became the new basis of competition in food provisioning.

Such room for maneuver is invaluable in an industry where the original, pre-industrial, "natural" product, whether fresh or traditional artisan foods, is still widely regarded as a benchmark of quality (Goodman and Wilkinson n.d.). These survivals, in turn, reveal the persistence and coexistence of remarkably heterogeneous, interstitial forms of production, distribution, and consumption within the modern food system. More than this, such knowledges and their material praxis demonstrate the system's latent capacity for *polyvalent* responses to economic and socio-cultural trends, such as changing priorities between "value-for-money" and "values-for-money," for example (Lang 2010). The quality "turn" expresses this polyvalence and retailers are in a much stronger position to adapt to these new consumer values than other, more product-specific, actors in the food industry. This flexible positioning also emphasizes why it is so difficult to "resist" the challenge of corporate retailers. For example, by attempting to establish autonomous, large-scale production and distribution networks for quality foods when supermarkets' infrastructural logistics are already so deeply embedded in our daily routines of "getting and spending."

This "turn" also is an expression of the increasingly active role of consumers in the politics of quality construction. The UK and Western Europe have been assailed by successive food "scares" since the mid-1980s, creating widespread mistrust of conventional, chemical-dependent farming and industrial food processing, notably in livestock production. These episodic food crises are epitomized by the 1986–87 pandemic of "mad cow disease" (BSE), the 2001 foot-and-mouth outbreak in the UK, recurrent food contamination events and periodic incidents of food poisoning. In the UK, public anxieties and media attention have focused particularly on intensive, "factory" livestock practices, strengthening support for ethical animal husbandry. Anxieties about the quality and safety of intensively-reared chicken, for example, drew a direct response from Marks and Spencer with the introduction of their "Oakham White" chicken brand in the early 2000s (Jackson *et al.* 2007, 2010). In this way, without commitments to specific commodity sectors, supermarkets have again been able to further consolidate their market dominance by mediating such consumer concerns, although this mediation is driven primarily by commercial self-interest and tends to be reactive in most cases.

With post World War II agricultural modernization policies and corporatist governance now widely discredited by these "extreme food events," a hybrid regulatory model has emerged in the UK. This model combines state-defined baselines of food safety, European Union (EU) standards, such as the application of HACCP (Hazards Analysis and Critical Control Point) risk control methods in food processing, and private "corporate retailer-led supply chain regulation of food quality," which dovetails neatly with retailers' competitive strategies of product differentiation and market segmentation (Flynn *et al.* 2003: 40). In this climate of food "scares" and threats to consumer trust in their brand image, retailers have responded by raising their standards of supply chain coordination above statutory baseline levels and imposing more rigorous traceability requirements and quality management systems on their suppliers. Moreover, such measures have allowed retailers to represent themselves as advocates of the "consumer interest," creating new opportunities to enhance brand "loyalty," pre-empt consumers' agency and promote corporate constructions of food quality. On the other hand, in the UK's highly concentrated retail sector, with the leading four supermarkets accounting for 75 percent of the grocery market in 2010, corporate regulation exposes retailers' investment in brand reputation to greater risk and provides social movements with sensitive points of leverage.

Qualifying (for) the mainstream

The shift in the balance of power toward large-scale retailers, the retreat of the state to baseline food safety regulation, and greater consumer reflexivity induced by food anxieties converged to create favorable conditions for the "turn" to quality (Murdoch and Miele 2004a; Wilkinson 2009). Traceability from "field to fork" became the mantra of public and private food quality standards which, in turn, raised the salience of "process" characteristics, both to ensure food safety but increasingly to match growing consumer interest in foods whose production reflects such values as sustainability, biodiversity, artisan practices, culinary traditions, fair trade, and animal welfare. These concerns, as we have seen, open up new opportunities for retailers to further differentiate and segment their markets, but also give social movements, such as the Soil Association, Slow Food and Fair Trade, a much broader platform to mobilize support for the values and practices incorporated in alternative quality products.

However, to reconcile the ethical and esthetic values embedded in the process characteristics of organic, locality, and other quality foods with the demands of mainstream provisioning for traceability and food safety has required "new forms of qualification" involving "novel systems of recognition – certification, labelling, auditing" (Wilkinson 2009: 4). These mainly private standards are becoming "a dominant form of governance" in food provisioning (Henson and Reardon 2005: 251) as corporate pressures for standardization and codification continue to intensify.

Much of the work in the social sciences on these novel systems of supply coordination has focused on the global food industry and how transnational actors, including food retailers, have incorporated ethical values into their governance of global value chains and global production networks (Hughes *et al.* 2007, 2008; Humphrey 2006). In the case of the UK and Western Europe, an "audit culture" of supply chain governance is linked to rising levels of concentration in food retailing. The buying power concentrated in the hands of supermarkets in Europe is illustrated by Grievink's (2002) widely cited estimate that 110 buying desks are the "gatekeepers" between three million producers and 160 million consumers. Exploiting this buying power, supermarkets have gained more direct control over the supply chain by reducing their reliance on the arm's-length transactions of spot markets and wholesale brokerage and distribution networks in favor of more centralized coordination involving direct contracts and close working relationships with lead suppliers and other members of the chain (Dolan and Humphrey 2001; Humphrey 2006; Soler 2005; cf. Menard and Valceschini 2005, in the case of the giant food retailer *Carrefour*).

Supermarket concentration, buying power and non-price competition have set the stage for the rise of private food safety and quality standards in the global food industry, a trend reproduced in the UK's hybrid regulatory model, as we have seen. At the global level, these increasingly ubiquitous standards are widely recognized as "drivers of change in the structure and *modus operandi* of agri-food systems" (Henson and Reardon 2005: 242). Such "quality-centred competition," it is argued, is (re-)structuring food markets by "standardising product requirements over suppliers," harmonizing product and delivery attributes, and creating new institutional arrangements to "qualify" producers and their products (ibid.: 244). As a number of authors have emphasized, public accountability is diminished as governance of the global food industry is transferred to the private sphere (Busch 2000; Busch and Bain 2004; Konefal *et al.* 2005).

In the EU, Humphrey (2006: 579) similarly regards concentration as the driving force behind the growth of private regulatory power, which is "a direct response to the increased stringency of public standards" and "the (legal) obligations they place on food companies" (cf. Codron *et al.* 2005). He goes on to suggest that both sets of standards share common principles: "controls over processes rather than products, the maintenance of identity and traceability, and a 'whole chain' approach" (Humphrey 2006: 577). As we noted earlier, these principles also are expressed globally in the Trade-Related Property Rights agreement of the World Trade Organisation (TRIPS/WTO) legislation recognizing "geographical indications," which builds on the Appellation d'Origine Controlee (AOC) system originally developed in France and Italy and its later extension to the EU as PDO/PDI designations under EU Regulation 2081/92. Superficially, this shift to process-based controls and standards would seem to have created a regulatory framework tailor-made for food sectors that valorize process- and place-related constructions of quality, such as organic agriculture and Slow Food products. However, this rosy view completely ignores the power relations behind the rise and enforcement of private regulatory standards in closely managed supply chains.

We have seen that process characteristics provide fertile ground for product differentiation as a source of added value, a competitive strategy that is open to various actors, including "branding from above" by supermarkets and food manufacturers:

> Such branding is seen in private company standards such as Tesco's Nature's Choice, which is also based on third-party inspection and certification of suppliers, creating new forms of control along the value chain, while at the same time establishing credible bases for claims about environmental impact, food quality, etc.
>
> (Humphrey 2006: 579)

In France, Carrefour has implemented a similar mode of process governance and quality certification for its own-label beef, *"filière qualité Carrefour"* (Menard and Valceschini 2005).

These so-called "credence goods" (Reardon *et al.* 2001) clearly are the life-blood of strategies of "branding from below" adopted by AOC producer groups, non-governmental organizations (NGOs) and market-centered social move-ments, such as the Soil Association and Fair Trade, and other collective and indi-vidual actors. Concomitantly, this "turn" to quality or credence goods differentiated from generic commodities has given rise to an "industry" of third-party certification (TPC) agencies and an increasingly bewildering variety of labels and logos intended to verify process-based claims in the marketplace.

Although not pursued here, there is a substantial body of research on TPC, its asymmetrical power relations, and unequal distributive effects in terms of eco-nomic rents, compliance costs, and risk (Mutersbaugh 2005a, 2005b; Muters-baugh *et al.* 2005). Other authors draw attention to the use by supermarkets of third-party certified private quality standards as

> strategic business tools. In other words, businesses use private standards today *strategically*, whether it is to gain access to new markets, to coordinate their operations, to provide quality and safety assurances to their consumers, to complement their brands, or to define niche products and markets.
>
> (Hatanaka *et al.* 2005: 356, original emphasis)

At the same time, widespread recourse to TPC and its strategic importance to supermarkets provides NGOs and activists with a target for reform when seeking to recalibrate their demands or defend their identity from mainstream cooption, as John Wilkinson (2009, 2010) argues.

Adopting a social movement perspective, Wilkinson (2009) explores the danger that mainstreaming will weaken the ethical and esthetic critiques mobi-lized by alternative food networks against the dominant values represented by conventional food provisioning. That is, once collective action is directed more toward the market than the state, these radical critiques are open to cooption "as mainstream marketing adopts the values of counter-cultures and social move-ments" (ibid.: 7). Following Boltanski and Chiapello (1999), he notes that

> "endogenisation" of the aesthetic critique via market segmentation is evid-ent in the adoption of values associated with nature/tradition/artisan produc-tion by food industry and retail leaders. A parallel endogenisation of the ethical critique can be seen also in the extension of corporate social respons-ibility to include strategies of ethical trading.
>
> (Wilkinson 2009: 7)

However, as we discuss later in this chapter, Wilkinson (2009, 2010) suggests that market endogenization is a continuing process rather than an endpoint insofar as social movements can successfully rearticulate their demands and new forms of collective action emerge to take up the banner of progressive change.

These recent trends in the mainstream food industry reveal significant points of convergence with alternative, quality food provisioning, notably the use of common principles and monitoring practices to maintain the identity and integrity of value chains. But, although mainstream and alternative credence goods converge on a *shared* terrain of competition, it is one that clearly is unequally structured by the concentrated buying power of supermarkets and their strategies of product differentiation. On entering this highly asymmetric terrain, alternative quality food producers face the risk that their identity, and therefore premium prices, will be lost or diminished by competition from other alternative producers, supermarkets' own-label credence goods and product portfolio decisions, and their control of access to shelf space.

One final point is that European analyses of organic mainstreaming, perhaps not surprisingly, tend to be drawn to the overwhelming importance of supermarkets in the retailing of organic fresh fruit and vegetables, often neglecting the fact that the same dynamics of global competition, concentration, and consolidation are also found in the mainstream food processing and distribution of organic products in general. In the USA, where these actors have a more powerful structural role, several researchers have documented how these acquisitive corporate giants – Kraft, Cargill, Pepsi, Tyson, ConAgra, General Mills – are diversifying their portfolios by taking over smaller organic companies, as we discuss in more detail in Chapter 7 (Sligh and Christman 2003; Howard 2005, 2009a, 2009b; Sayre 2006).

Furthermore, in keeping with the global contours of competition, these food conglomerates are introducing "organic product lines originally developed in the US into European markets," including M&M Mars' Seeds of Change label, Hain Celestial's organic Rice Dream and organic ketchup from Heinz (Sayre 2006: 21). In turn, huge European food companies, such as Nestlé, Unilever, and Danone, have responded by launching their own organic product lines, while leading distributors, such as the Dutch conglomerate, Koninklijke Wessanen, and the Aldi supermarket chain, owner of Trader Joe's, have significant shares of both the European and US markets for organic and natural foods (ibid.: 23). In short, the organic "spaces" in all segments of mainstream food chains are becoming increasingly crowded as transnational food corporations consolidate their global reach.

Experiencing the mainstream

The two previous sections have laid the groundwork to examine how different individual and collective actors have fared in their encounters with mainstream supermarkets. Some salient, if not necessarily commonplace, features of this territory were identified in the case studies discussed in Chapter 4. These revealed the hybrid food geographies of the sourcing and marketing practices of "alternative" food producers (Ilbery and Maye 2005a, 2006) and the highly competitive conditions of access to large retailers facing locality or "bioregional" producers and their networks (Marsden and Sonnino 2006a, 2006b). We have seen that retailers in the UK and elsewhere in Europe have responded to the new esthetic and ethical values now constructing quality by introducing private own-label locality foods and new product ranges for such generic "alternative" categories as organic, Fair Trade, animal welfare, and "local" foods. These values, and the economic rents they can represent, are open to appropriation and "endogenisation" through imitation, the most sincere form of flattery.

Local food networks might be located, at least for now, on a parallel pathway. However, the relationship of those "alternative" food networks that engage with the mainstream to secure their economic survival is something of a paradox, a kind of "competitive symbiosis," whose stability and future development are unclear at this point. These constitutive uncertainties are illustrated below by several case studies of "mainstreaming," although these are not claimed to be representative of the wider universe of AFNs.

Rachel's organic milk and yoghurt

Against a background of long-term decline, farm closures, privatization of dairy processing and manufacture, and "continual downward pressure on farm-gate prices" of conventionally-produced liquid milk, Rachel's Organic Dairy developed from a family farm in Aberystwyth in West Wales into a nationally-recognized brand (Straete and Marsden 2006: 277). The UK's first certified organic dairy farm in 1952, Rachel's began to produce organic yoghurt as an on-farm strategy to add value in 1984, before building an off-farm plant in 1992 to process locally-supplied milk to meet the growing demand from Sainsbury's and other nationwide distributors. However, rather than borrow to finance further expansion, the family owners sold the business in 1999 to Horizon Organic Dairy, the leading supplier of organic milk in the USA.

Following its sale, Rachel's "have loosened their local relations and produced generic (organic) brands" (Straete and Marsden 2006: 289). More pointedly, Rachel's has moved

> towards a more "placeless" design built upon a personalised story. The raw milk comes still from dairy farms localised in the area of origin ... but it is no longer bounded by this area. Dairy farms may easily be replaced – or rather their number enlarged – with dairy farms from other areas that may be closer to the larger markets in England.
>
> (Straete and Marsden 2006: 291)

Shades of Ben & Jerry's ice cream! In 2004, Horizon was acquired by the US transnational conglomerate, Dean Foods, and Rachel's changed hands yet again in July, 2010 when it was sold to the French company, Groupe Lactalis, a subsidiary of BSA International. In this cautionary tale of mainstreaming, only the Rachel's Organic brand name and "narrative" packaging recall its origins as a distinctively Welsh locality food.

Organic foods

The case of Rachel's can be seen as a phased transition from local to locality food to generic or standardized organic product. As it "scaled-up and out," it has become progressively "locked-in" to a "more conventional organic system" with standardized industrial conventions of designed quality (Straete and Marsden 2006: 293). Leaving aside its brand design, Rachel's illustrates an intrinsic problem confronting organics in mainstream corporate retailing, namely, *anonymity*. In mainstream channels, organic foods are "dis-embedded" and "de-localized," losing the distinctive local connections and "regard" for their producers associated with direct sales through farmers' markets and small-scale box schemes.

In these mainstream channels, moreover, certification is the handmaiden of standardization. With its institutional codification, "certified organic" is reduced to a generic, technological production claim, providing scope for supermarkets to create their own-label organic brands, such as the "SO: Sainsbury's Organic" product range launched in 2005. The combination of rapidly growing corporate markets and codified standards, in turn, has encouraged producers to specialize and scale-up to meet retailers' volume, price, and quality requirements, replicating some of the features of conventional agricultural production. Although applied specifically to the USA, Michael Pollan (2006) has suggested that the corporate dominance of organic foods is promoting "industrial organic": large-scale operations based on an "allowable inputs" approach, subverting the organic imaginary of small-scale, holistic farming "in nature's image" and localized food production–consumption networks.

Of the three main retail marketing channels for organic foods – supermarkets, specialist organic and health food shops, and direct sales – we have already observed that supermarkets have the dominant share of the market. In 2001–03, this share averaged 55 percent of sales in 19 European countries and exceeded 70 percent in Austria, Denmark, Finland, Sweden, and the UK (Sylvander and Kristensen 2004). To take the case of Sainsbury's, of its roughly 800 organic product lines, 450 are marketed under its own-label "SO" organic range. Yet organics represent only 2 percent of its total sales of food and drink (Soil Association, 2009a), neatly illustrating Fligstein and Dauter's (2007) point about "resource dependence" and the distribution of market power. *A priori*, this concentration of buying power indicates that both organic producers and consumers are vulnerable to exploitation, which the sparse evidence available certainly bears out.

In one of the few analyses of power relations in organic supply chains, Smith and Marsden (2004: 352) look first at the "micro-realities" encountered by domestic UK producers of organic milk, lamb, horticultural products, and cereals and argue that the large corporate retailers exert "downward pressure on farm-gate prices" in these markets. This pressure is exacerbated by the combined effects of an excess supply of domestically-produced organic milk, lamb, and vegetables and competition from imports, with supermarkets "being able to 'pick and choose' between suppliers" (ibid.: 355).[2] Consequently, as fierce competition between the major UK food retailers for a larger share of the lucrative organic market grows ... there is a real danger ... that retailled organic supply chains will exhibit many of the long-standing features of conventional food chains, particularly concerning the operation of a *farm-based cost-price squeeze.*

(Smith and Marsden 2004: 354–355, original emphasis)

Moreover, the accompanying shift of value added toward retailers threatens the potential of organic agriculture as "an engine of rural development" (ibid.: 355). This shift reflects the profitable mark-ups between farm-gate prices paid to their "anonymous" suppliers and high retail prices, and Smith and Marsden (2004) report complaints that supermarkets are over-charging their customers.[3]

The argument that organic market conditions since the late 1990s have given UK corporate retailers much greater scope to "pick and choose" is reinforced by Smith (2006: 451): "supermarkets could become more discerning ... Contracts were exacting. Deliveries could be rejected if they did not meet the grade." These changes have had unequal distributive effects as "they posed a particular challenge to smaller growers who produced a variety of crops on their mixed farms. Even after specialization and consolidation through wholesale suppliers, supermarket specifications for quality and appearance remained demanding" (ibid.: 451) As Smith (2006: 451) observes, mainstream actors – large conventional farmers, international food processors, supermarkets – "came to organics in ways which confounded the wholefood origins of the movement" and its affirmation of decentralized networks of local production–consumption.

To a lesser or greater degree, these same issues emerge from a survey of organic marketing initiatives (OMIs) in 19 European countries reported by Sylvander and Kristensen (2004) but in more circumspect language. Thus in comparison with direct marketing, we are told that "Hyper- and supermarket sales impose clear constraints" on OMIs, particularly in countries where buying power is highly concentrated, as in Switzerland, with two large distributors, Migros and *Coop*, controlling 70 percent of food sales, or where supermarkets hold major shares of organic markets, which is the rule in Scandinavia and other north-western European countries, as we have seen (ibid.: 86; Soil Association 2010: 35).

These constraints are illustrated by the case of the farmer cooperative *Bio-Bourgogne Viande* (BBV) located in the Burgundy region of eastern France, which sells its Charolais beef under the regional organic brand, *BioBourgogne*. This OMI has attempted to diversify its marketing policy but one major supermarket, Auchan, still accounts for 70 percent of its sales, and this throughput is vital to the profitable operation of BBV's new meat-cutting plant. Despite this dependence, Sylvander and Kristensen (2004) are doubtful that BBV can find more promising alternatives by forging alliances with actors outside conventional marketing channels. They note that other farmer associations, conventional meat processing firms, and downstream competitors, all of whom could recruit farmers from BBV, are developing rival organic product lines. Moreover, reminiscent of competition between organic lamb and the cheaper yet "green"

Welsh Mountain lamb in the UK, organic beef competes with that sold under the *Label Rouge* label, "the official quality system in France, perceived as being close to organic standards" (ibid.: 105).

With competition intensifying in organic markets and supermarkets' strong preference for large-scale partners able to meet their volume, product range, and quality requirements, the dilemma for BBV, as for other OMIs in similar circumstances throughout Europe, is how to retain some independence "while remaining faithful to its principles" (ibid.: 123).

Organic farming markets in England and Wales

Some effects of these forces at work on the structure of organics emerge from a recent survey of England and Wales that is "arguably one of the most integrated studies of organic consumption, production and marketing conducted to date"(Lobley *et al.* 2009a: 22). This research reveals a significant level of concentration in organic production, which is sharply bifurcated between the largest 10 percent of farms with more than 50 percent of sales, and "a group of highly committed, typically small-scale and locally orientated, organic producers who manage a more diverse range of marketing channels compared to those with a more regional and national market focus" (ibid.: 1).

Competitive pressures felt specifically by these smaller producers arise from "the appropriation of the box scheme concept by supermarket chains" (ibid.: 19) and the market penetration of so-called "mega-box schemes," which are causing some to abandon this form of direct marketing. More broadly, other "recurring concerns regarding the viability of the sector … and place of individual producers within it" include the impact on organic premium prices of "the escalating cost of primary organic inputs … the rapidly rising cost of fuel and electricity … (and) the low availability and high cost of land for rental…" (ibid.: 19). These findings resonate with earlier research on farmers who had left organics in the years 2000–03 (Harris *et al.* 2008). The squeeze on profit margins arising from difficulties in marketing their organic produce and lower price premiums emerge as the main reasons for the "significant outflow of farmers from organic farming from 2000 onwards, especially amongst smaller farmers" on holdings under 50 hectares (ibid.: 108).

Drawing on a detailed sample survey of organic producers, Lobley *et al.* (2009a) report that marketing cooperatives (26.4 percent) and contracts with processors (24.0 percent) are the principal marketing channels by sales value. The study

> found that some organic commodity producers sold their raw products directly to supermarkets, processors and organic cooperatives, such as OMSCo (Organic Milk Suppliers Cooperative) and OLMC (Organic Livestock Marketing Cooperative), and were not trying either to add value and/ or sell their produce locally.
>
> (ibid.: 11)

In terms of spatial distribution, farms with a regional or national market focus, suggesting integration in "longer and more complex supply chains," accounted for 35.4 percent and 50.9 percent of total organic sales, respectively, with the remaining 13.7 percent shared between locally-orientated farms, which "are much more likely to emphasise, and differentiate, their produce through appeals to 'localness,' freshness,' 'organicness,' 'healthiness' and 'traceability'" (ibid.: 9). These producers "sell most of their output through local marketing routes such as farm shops, farmers' markets and cooperative ventures" (ibid.: 20). While this survey does not explore whether or not these marketing orientations are a reflection of different philosophical commitments for "going organic," this bifurcated structure is consistent with Smith's (2006) analysis of organic mainstreaming in terms of niche fragmentation.

Although related less directly to the discussion of mainstreaming, Lobley *et al.* (2009a) provide an unequivocally homogeneous portrait of consumers of organic food, one that is strikingly similar to that of their US counterparts, as we see in Chapter 7. Their survey data suggest that

> organic consumers are *highly educated and predominantly white* ... 63.8% ... were educated to at least degree level and/or were members of a professional institute ... The equivalent figure is 25.0% for those who do not buy organic food. For this latter grouping, 30.8% of respondents were educated to school leaving age level only. In the case of three box schemes, 98% of organic consumers ... described themselves as white. Of those who do not buy organic food ... 13.2% [describe] themselves as having a non-white origin.
>
> (Lobley *et al.* 2009a: 5, original emphasis)

The authors caution that a poor response from customers of the specialist retailer, Planet Organic, resulted in the over-representation of box scheme members, which possibly has skewed the sample "towards well-educated, white women.... That said, highly educated women probably do account for the bulk of committed organic consumers" (Lobley *et al.* 2009b: 72).

In spite of these biases, behavioral differences between organic consumers depended mainly on where they made the bulk of their purchases. For example, metropolitan customers served by regionalized "mega-box schemes," such as Riverford Organic Vegetables, "were more likely to buy organic produce at a range of outlets including farm shops, health and whole food shops, butchers, bakers, greengrocers and local convenience stores" (Lobley *et al.* 2009b: 44). Nevertheless, 84 percent of all organic consumers purchase some organic food from supermarkets and almost 50 percent agreed that these retailers met all their needs (ibid.: 46–47). Among the reasons given by organic consumers who did not purchase directly from the producer were high prices (38.7 percent), inconvenience (36 percent) and the lack of local suppliers (30.7 percent), while 31.7 percent had never thought about doing it. The survey also found that most of the regular consumers of organic food ... do not appear to be particularly price sensitive. That is, they do not expect organic food to be comparable to non-organic food in terms of price and the quantity of organic food that they purchase is not particularly sensitive to their income level.

(Lobley *et al.* 2009b: 73–74)

Of the survey respondents who did not currently buy organic food (21.7 percent), high prices were identified by 78.6 percent as the main deterrent, although "57.8 per cent also agreed that more income would encourage them to purchase organic food" (ibid.: 66). These results cast serious doubts on arguments that supermarkets are a democratizing force for organics.

The 2008–09 credit "crunch": interlude or the future of organic mainstreaming?

In many ways, the sudden credit "crunch" of mid-2008 and the ensuing severe global economic recession is an instructive episode in the mainstreaming of organic food, with possibly deeper, long-run consequences. Certainly the prospect implicit in the papers by Smith and Marsden (2004) and Smith (2006) that mainstream organic markets would continue their recent dynamic expansion can no longer be taken for granted. Rates of growth of organic retail sales in the UK in 2008 and those of the multiple retailers were significantly lower than in previous years, although still positive at 1.7 percent and 1.85 percent, respectively (Soil Association 2009a). These increases also may be the result of food price inflation rather than higher sales volume. At a more disaggregated level, this picture of flat growth becomes mixed and more difficult to gauge. For example, organic sales at farmers' markets rose by an estimated 18.7 percent whereas, in the supermarket category, sales by the groups with the largest market shares – Sainsbury's, Tesco, and Waitrose – all declined, with those of the market leader, Tesco, falling by 8.9 percent. Despite this volatility, senior product category managers stated that the leading supermarkets remain fully committed to their organic lines and the organic sector more generally (Soil Association 2009a).

The media told a different story, however, as the leading multiples refocused on price competition and "value for money" lines – the so-called "Aldi effect" – to stem the loss of market share to specialist discount retailers, such as Aldi and Lidl. The difficult times facing quality organic products were strikingly illustrated by the faltering fortunes of the Prince of Wales' Duchy Originals farming and food company, a standard bearer for organic practice. In what was described as "a very up-market marriage of convenience" (Smithers 2009: 15), Waitrose announced in September, 2009 that it had reached a licensing agreement with exclusive rights to manufacture, distribute, and sell Duchy Originals products in the UK. Waitrose plans to expand the Duchy Originals line from 200 to 500 products and these "will, in effect, become the supermarket's luxury range" (ibid.: 15).

Not so newsworthy as Prince Charles, but no less real signs of these economic pressures, were reports of organic products being "crowded out" as supermarkets expanded their value ranges – "Tesco Value," "Sainsbury Basics," "Essential Waitrose," and Asda's "round pound" deals – to retain their now more budget-conscious customers. As one disgruntled organic supplier said: "If it's not there, you can't buy it." Other stories suggested that organic producers were being "squeezed" to accept lower prices, contribute to promotional support, and pay for shelf space. Consumer surveys reported in the press also indicated that roughly two-thirds of shoppers polled planned to continue cutting back on organic food after the end of the recession (*Guardian* July 6, 2009). On the other hand, the Soil Association (2009a: n.p.) identified a strong core of committed consumers "who may be tightening their belts but are determined to stick to their organic principles" and also notes that the proportion of households eating organic increased in 2008.

Nevertheless, these recent events have dispelled a certain mystique with the demonstration that, in the crunch as it were, shelf space for organics is subject to supermarkets' marketing strategy and profit targets, just as it is for any other product range. Moreover, these pressures intensified in 2009 as organic sales declined by 12.9 percent and those of supermarkets, with a 74 percent share of the market, fell by 12 percent (Soil Association 2010). Organic sales by non-multiple retail outlets, including box schemes, were far more volatile, falling precipitously by 26 percent. Although the Soil Association anticipates a return to modest growth in 2010, the credit crunch has well and truly deflated the "bubble" of organic agriculture in the UK and its future both in the mainstream and direct marketing channels is now clouded with uncertainty.

"Mega-box schemes": branding localism, escaping the mainstream?

In the cold prose of marketing, the Soil Association (2009a: no page) makes the following observation:

> In recent years the market for organic box schemes has become more competitive. Alongside individual producers latching on to the opportunity to sell direct, bigger operators such as Riverford Organic Vegetables and Abel & Cole have expanded significantly. This increased competition, coupled with the effects of the economic downturn, suggests that 2009 will be a challenging year for many box operators.

The *Organic Market Report 2010* reveals just how challenging conditions have been as sales by "medium-sized box schemes," with a turnover of £62–171,000, fell by 23 percent in 2009, whereas those of the largest schemes with a turnover exceeding £1 million declined by only 7 percent (Soil Association 2010). The competitive impacts of these large firms and accompanying concentration in direct selling on the long-term viability of smaller, more locally-orientated, organic box scheme operators also are emphasized by Lobley *et al.*'s (2009a) detailed investigation of organic marketing, as we noted earlier. In England and Wales, this study found that

> some producers originally committed to different forms of direct marketing were now struggling in the face of competition from the large scale "alternative" forms of direct marketing ... The rise and power of these "alternative" businesses further contests straightforward divisions between "commodity" vs. "alternative" markets.
>
> (Lobley *et al.* 2009a: 12)

Riverford Organic Vegetables, with its regional network of five "sister farms," including its "home farm" in Devon, a new production site in France, and franchised distribution, delivers around 47,000 weekly boxes to households in England and Wales, while Abel & Cole supply some 35,000 boxes, mainly to customers in south-east England. Of particular interest here, these firms have sought to transcend the largely *anonymous* features of organic produce once it is sold beyond the "local" by developing brand names and sophisticated logistical systems. Without being local or having face-to-face contact with their customers, the "organic" is branded to convey a (re-)localized food supply and a sense of social and ecological "re-connection" with "the farm." The discursive themes of re-localization and connection are particularly strong in the case of Riverford. Both companies nevertheless source produce overseas to meet seasonal limitations or, as Abel & Cole's website puts it: "We have some fantastic European and international farmers who help us fill the gaps when, due to our cooler climate, the UK fields are in between harvests.... In these circumstances we never air-freight and, obviously, our first choice is always British."[4]

In the Riverford value chain, the cachet of "local food" is captured and re-fetishized by "regionalizing" a nationally-branded distribution network of box schemes comprising the home farm and four regional franchised "sister farms," franchised home delivery agents and joint ventures. According to the Riverford website:

> As demand for our veg boxes grew, we didn't want to grow any larger from the original Devon farm. So we joined up with organic farmers around the country who share our obsession for growing great-tasting affordable organic vegetables for local people. The regional sister farms help us keep food miles down, support local farmers, provide local employment and help us build a strong link between grower and consumer.
>
> (www.riverford.co.uk, accessed July 10, 2009)

This business model shares some characteristics of that of multiple retailers – national distribution, regional "depots," overseas sourcing, branding, market research, information technology, for example – but its commercial originality is to mainstream organic production–consumption outside the aisles of supermarkets and still lay claim to the quality of the local.

According to Clarke *et al.* (2008: 4), "the long-term plan is to advance the Riverford business model and brand across the UK while simultaneously retreating back into the South-West as producer and distributor."[5] At first, this regional "export" base comprised the Riverford farm and nine other members of the South Devon Organic Producers cooperative but in 1999 "10 producers became one producer-marketer (Riverford) and nine straight producers. Today, Riverford acts as sole marketing agent for the co-operative" (ibid.: 3).

Riverford and other "scaled up" box schemes not only have replicated certain organizational features of the multiple retailers but also have been similarly adept, if not more so, in marketing the organic imaginary of reconnection, re-localization and sustainability. Their highly specialized product range also may give greater legitimacy to their positioning as innovative mediators between their customers' ethical and political values and habitual patterns of daily life. However, despite the marketing spin on the meaning of local, this role does not put them in the same category as *collectively* organized, interpersonal, and spatially circumscribed box schemes discussed in Chapter 4, such as EarthShare in Scotland, *Gruppo di Aquisto Solidale de Pisa* (*GAS.P!*) in the Italian city of Pisa and local *Associations pour le Maintien d'une Agriculture Paysanne* (AMAP) partnerships in France. Riverfood and the like are much closer to what Johnston *et al.* (2009: 512) call the "corporate-organic foodscape" than to the collective action initiatives at the local scale that inhabit the organic vision. Although Riverford reportedly is to become a not-for-profit enterprise, Abel and Cole revealed its corporate face in October, 2007, when it sold an interest in the business to Phoenix, a private equity company.

While Riverford adds value with its sustainable provenance and regionalized distribution network, there are so far no research studies of its supply chain relations, farm-gate/retail price markups, earnings, labor conditions, clientele by social group, or competitive impacts on other box schemes, although Clarke *et al.* (2008) do provide some general information. That said, Riverford has successfully scaled up the box scheme model and evaded entanglement and loss of identity in the logistical structures of the supermarkets. Riverford thus can lay claim to "ecological" and "spatial" alterity since its market growth, albeit in competition with smaller box schemes, is expanding the spaces of sustainable organic production, as in the case of locality foods, but with the significant difference that its economic reproduction lies outside the conventional food system.[6]

Niches and dialectics

We have seen that Smith (2006) approaches the mainstreaming of organic in the UK from a socio-technical regime perspective, viewing it as a process of niche fragmentation. This is creating an "organic *industry* ... quite like the conventional industry – and quite unlike the organic *movement*" (ibid.: 453, original emphasis) and a "renewed niche" that is reaffirming the organic imaginary. Fragmentation has occurred by "piecemeal appropriation" because "elements of the socio-technical configuration" could be "stripped of the more rounded practices contained within the original vision. Less radical elements have been absorbed without requiring wider transformation in the incumbent socio-technical regime" (ibid.: 452).

Niche renewal is identified with "direct, community-based, food initiatives" and "direct marketing routes," which "are seen as rescuing the organic vision and bringing the niche back to its founding ideals" (ibid.: 452). This process of niche renewal is being led by the rapid proliferation of local farmers' markets, box schemes, public procurement policies and myriad social enterprises, as we see in Chapter 6. The "revived local organic food niche" continues to reproduce more holistic, localized practices and "its committed actors ... remain advocates of more radical systems innovation" (ibid.: 455). This dynamic tension between the reformed mainstream and the radical niche then may persist until "shifting social contexts" initiate a "new round of incremental reconfigurations. In sum, the relationship between niche and mainstream is dialectic" (ibid.: 456).

A dynamic relational approach also is advocated in a recent study of the organic sector in Denmark to demonstrate that the "organic field is constantly evolving and continues to add new meanings to terms like 'mainstream' and 'alternative'" (Kjeldsen and Ingemann 2009: 168). The Danish case mirrors the general trajectory toward mainstream consolidation, with retail chains accounting for roughly 80 percent of organic sales. However, it would be hasty "to say that the overall result has been the conventionalisation or disembedding of the organic movement" because a variety of new alternative organic food networks have emerged to exploit "new means of consumption ... as a resource for opening up new economic spaces" (ibid.: 165–166).

These dialectical responses include several web-based box schemes, notably Aastiderne.com, and new cooperative enterprises, such as a consumer-owned farm and cooperative sales outlet, that "differ from conventional Danish agricultural co-operatives in being consumer-driven and rooted outside the agricultural sector" (ibid.: 163). As Kjeldsen and Ingemann, 2009, 166) observe, "there are still efforts taking place to fight back (against) conventionalisation." These processes are not without casualties since "Following the entry of Aarstiderne.com, several small-scale sales outlets in Copenhagen, mainly farmers' markets, were shut down, indicating increasing competition in the alternative retail market" (ibid.: 162).

John Wilkinson (2009, 2010) also turns to dialectics to analyze the response of alternative food networks and social movements to mainstream pressures to coopt and trivialize their "projects" to achieve greater civic governance of food provisioning. His approach is inspired by conversations between social network analysis, economic sociology, convention theory, and actor-network theory, and particularly Michel Callon's (1998, 1999) work on commoditization and the configuration of organized markets. Callon (1999: 186) uses the metaphor of framing to theorize the processes by which spaces of calculative agents or markets emerge and become institutionally stabilized by allowing "coordination through calculation." In Callon's (1998: 15–16) analysis of framing as a "mechanism of inclusion and exclusion," he draws on economic theory for the notion of externality, which denotes "all the connections, relations and effects which agents do not take into account when entering into a market transaction" (Callon 1999: 187).

In common with economists, Callon (1999: 188) argues that "there are always relations which defy framing"; that is, externalities, and, even when agents "decide to reframe them – in other words to internalise the externalities – other externalities appear. I would suggest the term 'overflowing' to denote this impossibility of total framing. Any frame is necessarily subject to overflowing."

Wilkinson (2009, 2010) adapts the "framing/overflowing" metaphors to the analysis of relations between corporate actors and the "new economic social movements," such as organics, Fair Trade and Slow Food, "whose novelty (is) the centrality of markets rather than the State in achieving the objectives of the movement" (Wilkinson 2009: 4). Mainstream adoption of the values and practices of these movements, epitomized by the "turn" to new forms of qualification based on codified process characteristics, involves negotiation to reframe or internalize and purify market relations, at least temporarily. Such reframing is evident in the commoditization of what were previously treated as public goods or externalities, including landscape and habitat conservation, sustainable farm practices and animal welfare.

Of course, these negotiations can be highly contested as actors seek to control the framing of the new "quality" markets. Thus territorial provenance denoted by "place" or *terroir* is a major target of corporate reframing and an important component of retailers' market segmentation strategies, which can have the effect of trivializing it through a combination of own-label quality supply chains, proliferation, and "label fatigue," and by encouraging mass consumption of "origin" foods. In Wilkinson's (2009: 12) words, "the particularist values of 'origin' products are challenged either by territorial competition as supply outstrips demand or by de-territorialisation as demand strains the established demarcations of supply."[7] At perhaps the extreme end of this spectrum, cheese producers and supermarkets in Brazil sell "*Tipo Camembert*" and "*Tipo Brie*" and other similar offerings.

In Wilkinson's (2009, 2010) analysis, corporate efforts to reframe and thereby "endogenise" certain social movement values are answered by a regrouping around those values that "overflow" this reframing and so provide the platform for new demands. Values still excluded or "externalized" by markets become the new focus of social mobilization and provide the movements with continued political traction. As Wilkinson (2009: 5) puts it,

> behind the NGOs … stand social sectors and issues which, in the language of Callon, represent the factors which are excluded in the process of framing the markets. To the extent that the market implies exclusion through framing and it rather than the State becomes the central object of social and environ-

mental demands, *the market itself increasingly becomes a forum of continuous negotiation and contestation.*

(Wilkinson 2009: 5, our emphasis)

Mainstreaming does not involve the once-and-for-all absorption of alternative networks, "rather, these movements should be understood in the more dialectical perspective of a continuous process of 'framing' and 'overflowing'" (Wilkinson 2009: 5).

In this perspective, mainstream and social movement actors are engaged in a process of "permanent negotiation and conflict" to resist the disempowering effects of cooption and makeshift compromise. "In practical terms, this would mean campaigning for higher standards ... establishing new connections (GMO-free products), integrating an increasing number of alternative characteristics (organic + fair trade + sustainability + local distinctiveness), or developing new distribution channels" (Wilkinson 2010: 113). One example of such "overflow" movement responses to mainstream "framing" would be organic farmers going "beyond organic" to focus on local direct marketing following the technocentric codification and institutionalization of the organic in the USA, as we discuss in Part III (Goodman and Goodman 2007).

A second case of "overflowing" is the repositioning of the Slow Food Movement's (SFM) initial agenda to revitalize artisan food production and local culinary traditions to now embrace biodiversity, conservation, and sustainability. This move, captured by SFM's call for "eco-gastronomy," forges links between culinary heritage and biodiversity and brings a new dimension to the notion of *terroir* (Leitch 2003; Sassatelli and Daviolo 2008; Andrews 2008). The SFM consolidated this change in 2003, when it established the Foundation of Biodiversity to promote and fund projects to strengthen the commercial viability and market access of "endangered" small-scale food products or *presidia* and their associated gastronomic traditions, agroecological practices, and bio-diverse cultural landscapes.

In the lexicon of Boltanski and Chiapello (1997), this "overflowing" has brought together the particularistic, esthetic critique of mainstream industrial food systems with universalistic ethical values. In the UK, the Soil Association reportedly is considering incorporating fair trade values of social justice into its organic certification practices, and Jaffee *et al.* (2004) have made a similar proposal for alternative food products in the USA. More generally, this discussion points toward the much wider problematic of "critical consumerism" (Sassatelli 2006; Sassatelli and Davolio 2008) and notions of civic consumers and socially responsible consumption, which are not entirely encompassed by a social movement framing (Brewer and Trentmann 2006).

Conclusion

Putting this problematic aside for now, we can return to the opening theme of this chapter: the contested politics of quality, or who defines how food is grown and how food is known. Our discussion here suggests not only that these politics are indeed highly contested but also that the terms of engagement are constantly in flux. Despite its narrative convenience, it is simplistic to decant these arenas into a two-sector opposition between alternative food networks and mainstream food provisioning. Similarly, characterizations of these alternative social movements in terms of the general nature of their critiques of the mainstream – particularist esthetics or universalistic ethics – can be revealing but it is easy to forget that each of these categories encompasses a "family of issues." Moreover, as in the case of the SFM, these movements are evolving hybrid strategies and changing organizational morphologies.

Although power is unequally distributed in these politics of quality construction, the processes of "framing/overflowing" create, as Wilkinson (2009, 2010) argues, a permanent state of contested negotiation and changing forms of civic association and collective agency. This framework of the interface between markets and social movements conveys a strong, dynamic sense of these dialectical processes, whereas the socio-technical perspective (Smith 2006) suggests a more protracted, less active dialectic, with the "renewed niche" waiting hopefully "in the wings," as it were. Whether these dialectics continue "without synthesis" or some stable accommodation is reached in the future is an open question. Such a settlement could possibly arise in more extreme circumstances if sudden "shocks" to the exogenous socio-technical landscape (Geels and Schot 2007), such as binding ecological resource constraints or the unforeseen acceleration of global climate change, put food security in real jeopardy. These possibilities and likely responses are the subject of the next chapter.

6 Changing paradigms?

Food security debates and grassroots
food re-localization movements in the
UK and Western Europe

The discussion in Part II has explored the much-heralded but still largely unrealized transition from globalized, "faceless and placeless," industrial food systems toward more territorialized rural economies and food networks built on "alternative" eco-social values of sustainability, provenance, animal welfare, and localized provisioning. As we have seen, these ethical and esthetic values infuse the main currents of contemporary food politics, underpinning shared producer–consumer knowledges and their "communities of practice" and carving out new economic and cultural spaces for organic agriculture, quality foods, and innovative forms of direct provisioning. We have also traced the many resistances and challenges to transition and paradigm change encountered in different arenas, from the halting process of the Common Agricultural Policy (CAP) reform to adaptive corporate retail strategies that uphold the cultural authority of industrial food systems and their central place in the social infrastructures of household food provisioning.

In this chapter, we turn first to recent developments at the global level and the growing evidence that profound changes are occurring in the fundamental parameters of global agricultural eco-systems. This scientific prognosis entered the wider public domain with startling suddenness in 2006–08, when rapidly rising world food prices and export restrictions imposed by leading commodity producers revealed the precarious state of food security in a globalized, interdependent world. This inflationary episode and the continuing high level of international commodity prices have created mounting pressures to re-order the internationalized political economies of food provisioning in ways that reconcile the goals of global and national food security.

This chapter examines how policymakers perceive these spatial food economies and their re-ordering, the measures being considered to achieve national food security, and the role they see for re-localized food networks in this process of adjustment to more binding resource constraints. As we shall find, the growing prominence of national food security on political agendas in the UK and the European Union (EU) has exacerbated tensions between supporters of localized provisioning and policymakers and food industry stakeholders who see the ecological modernization of conventional systems as the foundation of national food security.

We begin the discussion of these re-spatializing forces by reviewing reactions to the food price inflation of 2006–08 before turning to contemporary policy debates on food security in the UK and the EU. We then consider responses to these global and national developments by two UK social movements: the organizations collaborating in the Making Local Food Work initiative and the recently formed Transition Movement.

Global food security and paradigm change: new directions in UK policy?

The remarkable upsurge of international food price inflation in 2006–08 and the events it set in train aroused widespread fears that global and national food security are severely threatened by deep-seated changes now underway in international agricultural markets. Food price inflation accelerated at the fastest pace seen for three decades, provoking food riots in over 30 countries and leading to the overthrow of governments in Haiti and Madagascar. Major surplus-producing countries, such as Argentina, Thailand, and Vietnam, introduced export restrictions to stabilize domestic prices and ensure local supplies, exacerbating the volatility of international commodity markets.[1] In these turbulent conditions, some food-importing countries are attempting to bypass these markets by negotiating bilateral contracts with exporters, as in the case of the Philippines, the world's largest rice importer (*The Economist* November 21, 2009: 63). Other richer food-importers, including Saudi Arabia, the Arab Emirates, China, and South Korea, have responded to predictions of long-term global shortages by purchasing farmland in poorer countries, particularly in sub-Saharan Africa, a practice widely condemned as "land grabbing" (GRAIN 2008; von Braun and Meinzen-Dick 2009; United Nations 2009) and "agro-imperialism" (Rice 2009).

The inflationary surge in staple food prices brought the number of people considered to be "food insecure" or "undernourished" to over one billion for the first time, leading to the June, 2008 Rome summit on World Food Security called by the United Nations Food and Agriculture Organization (FAO) and the creation of a United Nations High-Level Task Force and the inter-governmental Committee on World Food Security (CFS). Subsequently, meeting in L'Aquila in July, 2009, the G-8 nations pledged to implement the World Bank Global Partnership for Agriculture and Food Security program and to commit an additional US$20 billion to agricultural development over the next three years. The potential of the CFS as a more open, democratic process of global governance was enhanced in October, 2009 by successful reform efforts to extend membership to social movements and civil society organizations, although much remains to be done to realize this promise (People's Food Sovereignty 2009). These institutional developments prefaced the second UN Conference on Food Security held in Rome in mid-November, 2009, but few firm commitments were made, despite recognition that global climate change will aggravate the global crisis of hunger and child malnutrition.

Analysts have been quick to identify the *proximate* causes of the 2006–08 global food price inflation, emphasizing rapidly rising incomes and dietary change toward increasing consumption of red meat and other livestock products in such emerging economies as China and India, record high energy prices, changing land use from food to renewable fuel crops, especially the diversion of US maize to ethanol production, and the effects of increased financial speculation attracted by the international commodity price "bubble" (von Braun 2008; Evans 2008; HM Government 2010a; Baffes and Haniotis 2010).

However, as the two UN "summits" have demonstrated, the crisis of food security is perceived as a *structural* problem, with roots in the global resource limits now facing intensive, fossil fuel-dependent, industrial agricultural systems.[2] That is, the current crisis is revealing the structural parameters of *a new international eco-political economy.* These parameters or "new fundamentals" (Barling *et al.* 2008) include global climate change, the imminence of "peak oil," water scarcity, soil degradation, and global population growth. Before the galvanizing events of 2006–08, politicians and many policymakers chose to ignore or underplay the risks to food security posed by these global resource constraints and their unequal geopolitical impacts, despite the accumulation of increasingly pointed reports emanating from international agencies, such as the Intergovernmental Panel on Climate Change (IPCC), the International Assessment of Agricultural Science and Technology Development (IAASTD), and the FAO.

Some recent contributions to UK food security debates

In the UK, these reports now provide the evidential foundations for what has become a seemingly unstoppable torrent of programmatic statements, discussion papers, and publications from government ministries, public agencies, a Parliamentary Select Committee, and prominent think tanks evaluating the country's food security and how best to ensure it in the future.[3] While there is growing acknowledgement that the "new fundamentals" herald the end of the era of "cheap food" in the global North, though not, it should be noted, of industrial agriculture, there are important points of disagreement on the steps needed to ensure national food security in these changing circumstances.

We review the paths of adjustment to these new realities articulated in these reports, with emphasis on adaptations in corporate food supply chain management and consumption patterns. In particular, we ask whether or not this new trajectory of food policy will significantly enhance the role of organic agriculture and localized food networks in provisioning. Where markets – mainstream and "renewed niche" – seem to have failed, will paradigm change be delivered instead by policy instruments and regulative fiat? What a quixotic idea! The following discussion reveals how deeply the conventional food system is entrenched in political economic and cultural terms, and the policy distance that must be navigated before sustainable re-localized food networks and food justice come within reach as accepted goals in fairer, open societies.

At present, the principal aim of protagonists in these British debates is to establish the future "direction of travel" for food policy. This struggle is exemplified by attempts to define what "sustainability" means in the context of national food security and how to address generic issues of availability, access, and affordability. These polemics tend to overshadow detailed discussion of the structural changes that will be needed in farming, supply chains, and consumption patterns to make progress toward this goal. The question of sustainability has gained new prominence from the volatile events of 2006–08, which have given increasing credence and legitimacy in policy circles to the thesis that the "new fundamentals" pose an urgent and novel challenge to food policy.

The record prices reached in world food and energy markets in 2006–08 severely damaged the credibility of what might be called a global market-based approach to food security. Despite these events, the UK Department of Environment, Food, and Rural Affairs (Defra) has been remarkably loyal in following the UK Treasury in the confident belief that the UK essentially could "buy" "access to food and food security through open and competitive markets" (The Strategy Unit 2008: 1; cf. HM Treasury and Defra 2005; Defra 2006). This policy prescription is neatly encapsulated in the following statement:

> We produce much of our food, and because the UK is a developed economy, we are able to get the other food we need for a nutritious diet by buying from abroad. However, these recent increases in food prices have sparked a debate about self-sufficiency, food security and the resilience of our food supply network.
>
> (Defra, 2008: 1)

Proponents of dependence on globalized supply chains still draw a certain reassurance from the fact that "In 2006, 68 percent of food imports into the UK were from other members of the EU *i.e. from low risk, stable trading partners*" (ibid.: 15, our emphasis). The Defra 2008 discussion paper also reiterated the UK Treasury position that "effectively functioning markets are fundamental to ensuring global food security. The Government is committed to continuing to liberalise markets through the Doha Development Round of trade negotiations and reform of the EU's Common Agricultural Policy" (Defra 2008: 27). This line of thinking similarly permeates the conceptualization of the resilience of food supply chains, which is defined mainly as retailers' and food manufacturers' flexible access to international markets and less in terms of their agroecological properties. For example:

> Our openness to trade makes the UK very resilient in terms of disruptions to one or a few sources of supply. In particular, food retailers are able to switch sources of supply rapidly in case of disruption, as has been seen during animal disease episodes.
>
> (Defra 2009a: 1)

Nevertheless, it is abundantly clear that food security concerns have weakened the case for outright reliance on liberalized global markets and introduced new uncertainties into British food policy.

Of course, there have long been tensions between reliance on conventional, distantiated food systems and demands by social movements and concerned consumers for more sustainable, "short chain" localized networks. Furthermore, food security and sustainability can also be conflicting goals and difficult trade-offs will have to be made if food security is severely threatened. At present, however, calls for autarkic solutions have been resisted but there is growing support for selective efforts to attain higher levels of national food self-sufficiency (cf. Defra 2009b). In the words of Hilary Benn, then Secretary of State for Environment, Food and Rural Affairs, addressing the Oxford Farming Conference on January 6, 2009,

> I want British agriculture to produce as much food as possible. No ifs. No buts. And the only requirements should be, first, that the consumers want what is produced and, second, that the way our food is grown both sustains our environment and safeguards our landscape.
>
> (Benn 2009)

These remarks gloss over the potential conflicts between food security and sustainability that are likely to appear if international markets experience prolonged and intense periods of rapid price inflation and supply disruptions.

As this discussion indicates, what is meant by "sustainable food security" is highly contingent and this introduces a significant degree of ambivalence and generalization. This may explain why it is difficult to glean many specifics about what a strategy of sustainable food security would look like from these policy statements and debates. Thus the farm sector and food supply chain tend to be discussed only in unitary terms, with the focus on the general requirements of adaptation – lower carbon, methane, and nitrous oxide emissions, resource conservation, biodiversity, waste reduction – to the "new fundamentals" for sustainability. This is evident, for example, in the Cabinet Office Strategy Unit's advocacy of a low-carbon food sector:

> Reducing the food chain's dependence on energy, water and other resources will reduce its exposure to future increases in resource prices. Reducing the quantity of waste and GHG emissions can improve resource efficiency and anticipate the changes required for the transition to a low-carbon economy.
>
> (The Strategy Unit 2008: 6)

While such generality is perhaps acceptable as an initial over-arching statement of the UK government's vision for the food system and its role in the UK's response to the challenges of global food security and global climate change, the flurry of reports and discussion papers it has elicited fails to go much beyond this vision and flesh it out in greater detail. Instead, these sources seem content to sketch out what will be needed to improve the resource efficiency, sustainability, and resilience of conventional agriculture, mainstream food supply chains and centralized retail distribution systems. Movement toward greater sustainability is not envisaged as a root-and-branch transition from one organizational template to a radically different model, such as localized organic production–consumption systems. Rather, the impression given is that real progress toward reducing current high levels of external input dependence by stimulating more efficient resource use would itself constitute a radical step.

Evidence for this view can be found in the written submissions and public hearings before the Select Committee of Inquiry into *Securing Food Supplies up to 2050: The Challenges Faced by the UK*, conducted by the All Party Parliamentary Group on Food and Agriculture for Development in 2009. In these hearings, Defra representatives replied to questions about moving to a low-input form of agriculture by advocating measures with conventional systems presumably in mind, such as better soil conservation, greater efficiency in water and nitrogen use, integrated pest management, and integrated natural resource management (EFRA 2009b: 224). In supplementary written evidence, Defra suggested that "experience from farming organically has much to offer to agriculture generally in terms of reducing reliance on inputs, in particular nitrate fertilisers, and making the best use of on-farm resources" (ibid.: 235). But following this short preamble, the focus is quickly broadened since "the Government wants all UK agriculture – organic or otherwise – to produce as much as possible, as sustainably as possible.... Ultimately, UK food security depends on the contribution of all our farmers" (ibid.: 235).

When asked directly, "What use could be made of local food networks?" Defra responded by noting the buoyant growth in 2003–08 of locally produced food and the success of direct selling by farmers. The European Commission's reply was even more non-committal, stating that it is "already promoting local production through the EU labelling schemes PDO and PGI" (EFRA 2009b: 192). A detailed reading of the evidence submitted to the Select Committee demonstrates that such lukewarm responses are the rule, not the exception. In fact, with support from Friends of the Earth, the Biodynamic Agricultural Association and the Council for the Protection of Rural England, the Soil Association was the only organization to present a strong case for organic agriculture and to argue that "more localized food networks are key to enhancing the resilience of the UK's food security" (EFRA, 2009b: 172).[4]

In its final report, the Select Committee notes the "increasing enthusiasm among consumers" for local food and home production, yet these essentially are regarded as a sideshow rather than a key pathway in the transformation of conventional provisioning.

> In terms of overall production, *these trends are a small contribution to a huge challenge*, but they are a way of reconnecting people with food production and have an important part to play in encouraging the sort of

changes in consumer behaviour that will be necessary for a sustainable system of food production.

(EFRA 2009a: 30, our emphasis)

The dominant position is that "sustainable food security" can be achieved, not by expanding the "renewed niche" of localized food networks, but by promoting the *ecological modernization of the incumbent industrialized food regime.*

This view of "transformation from within" is elaborated in slightly more detail in the Chatham House report, *Food Futures* (Ambler-Edwards *et al.* 2009). This analysis develops four global food supply scenarios based on different responses to the "seven (new) fundamentals" and examines how to manage the transition of the UK/EU food systems "to a sustainable system that can also deliver the desired volume of food" (ibid.: 23). Such a system, identified here with the "Into a New Era" scenario, would involve a gradual shift away from the existing agricultural paradigm as the binding nature of long-term resource supply constraints is recognized, leading to the diffusion of "eco-technological approaches" and "small-footprint technology" to reduce greenhouse gas emissions across food supply networks.

Lest this future system be confused with organic agriculture, the authors admit that "The term 'agro-ecological approaches', as originally conceived within the scenario *Into a New Era* (it was later changed to 'eco-technological approaches'), was intended to embrace a wide range of systems." It is telling that this change was made after consultation with corporate interests since "*within the industry* the term 'agro-ecological' was seen to be synonymous with organic systems and engendered little confidence that there was any convincing prospect of these types of systems delivering the yields required" (Ambler-Edwards *et al.* 2009: 23; our emphasis).[5]

To achieve "the new normality," a new framework of policies, institutions and supply system capabilities will be needed to reconcile four characteristics that will be "of increasing significance in a future food supply system: resilience, sustainability, competitiveness, and the management of consumer expectations" (ibid.: 26). In this framework of ecological modernization, the reduction of the food system's resource footprint will "require a step change in innovation, one akin to the 'double Green Revolution' (Conway 1997) ... – in effect a new agricultural paradigm." Innovation in the development of new food supply models will follow the managerial principle of eco-efficiency: "instead of production at lowest levels of cost, eco-efficiency aims at production with least environmental cost" (Ambler-Edwards *et al.* 2009: 28). In common with its notoriously ambiguous predecessor, "sustainable development," eco-efficiency appears to offer a "win-win" scenario in which "business as usual" as agricultural modernization can continue only now more respectful of its ecological conditions of production and reproduction. Sustainable food security is framed as a techno-scientific "paradigm shift" between different forms of environmental managerialism, not as a progressive societal project that combines low-carbon futures with social justice and other transformative values.

Given its preference for "eco-technological approaches" over organic systems, the Chatham House report, perhaps not surprisingly, is equivocal about the role of localized food production–consumption networks in this era of "a new bio-economy" and "a new agricultural paradigm" (Ambler-Edwards *et al.* 2009: 28). On the one hand, it suggests that "as resources come under pressure, and in a low-carbon economy, food grown and consumed locally will provide much more significant benefits to the national economy" and recommends that "the role of more regionally-based systems and assets in providing a greater degree of resilience will need to be considered" (ibid.: 36–37). On the other hand, this support for more territorialized provisioning is immediately qualified since "any benefit must be offset against potentially significant environmental and cost trade-offs" (ibid.: 37), arising from scale diseconomies, "additional (storage) facility costs and ... less efficient transport systems" (ibid.: 30).

Reflecting the received view of the Whitehall food policy community, the report is far more sanguine about conventional food systems and their capacity to adapt to the new imperatives. Thus "supply chain arrangements will need to be restructured ... to deliver a wider set of criteria – carbon reduction, resource utilisation, environmental and social impacts, etc." (Ambler-Edwards *et al.* 2009: 35). This "etc." speaks volumes as these impacts – on social justice, for example – clearly have not been thought through in detail. Nevertheless, the assessment is that "retailers and food service providers will remain key ... in driving forward the new models and standards" (ibid.: 35). Overall, the report anticipates "an extended transition period in which a patchwork of the old and the new will be evident" (ibid.: 37) but, despite the fine labels, the new food supply models apparently will continue to feature the same familiar powerful corporate actors concentrated at the nerve center of the now "redundant" existing paradigm.

"Mind the gap": UK and EU food security

Although attempting to finesse it in various ways, typically by calling on government to exercise leadership, UK debates on food security and transition to more sustainable food systems take place in something of a political vacuum. For all their insights, contributors chafe under the powerful institutional hold exerted by the EU over the direction of national food policy and its regulation.

This "European dimension" is stated in the baldest of terms by the Country Land and Business Association (CLBA):

> all the major policy levers affecting food security in this country are decided at EU level. We refer to the Common Agricultural Policy, the EU Common External Tariff (i.e. trade policy) and the fact that nearly all environmental policy affecting land use is based on EU directives. [In addition], the EU Budget ... provides the principal public financial support for the policies which shape our food and environmental security.
>
> (EFRA 2009b: 119)

For the CLBA, on the assumption that intra-EU trade in the Single European Market will not be disrupted "in times of severe supply-stress ... *food security has to be considered primarily as an EU issue*" (EFRA 2009b: 119, our emphasis). In the CLBA's view, "the EU as a major economic and political power bloc ... has responsibilities and self-interest in demonstrating how to rise" to the interrelated challenges presented by climate change, the anticipated addition of 2.5 billion people to the world's population by 2050, and the need to respect "far higher environmental standards" in meeting the ensuing "huge growth in food demand ... these issues must be addressed through a common EU approach and our suggestion is that the CAP evolves to become Europe's Food and Environmental Security Policy" (ibid.: 119).[6]

The Select Committee recognized the overriding influence of the CAP and EU directives but nevertheless recommended that Defra develop its own food strategy as a means to shape and lead emerging EU policy (EFRA 2009a: 32). In other words, it accepted that the struggle for sustainable food security must be fought out in the framework of a common EU policy, and particularly as negotiations get underway to determine the size and composition of the new EU budget after 2013. Preliminary skirmishing is already underway as protagonists begin to stake out their positions. Some of the fissures and dissident voices that might emerge in these negotiations surfaced in 2008 during the CAP Health Check at the height of food price inflation and fears for food security.

These disputes broadly center around the future of First Pillar direct farm support payments, subject to environmental cross-compliance requirements, on the one hand, and whether and, if so, how quickly, to continue the decoupling process of shifting these payments to Second Pillar rural development programs, on the other.[7] For example, with global food prices accelerating, press reports suggested that UK support for further decoupling was opposed by the French, who were in favor of reframing the CAP around food security and a renewed focus on production, with the French Agriculture Minister's advocating "protection, not protectionism" for EU consumers and producers (*Financial Times* October 25, 2007, cited in Barling *et al.* 2008: 26). In its inimitable style, the *Daily Telegraph* (May 20, 2008) polarized these positions as follows: "Britain argues that high food prices make subsidies for growing food even less necessary, while France is using precisely the same issue to argue precisely the inverse – that the food crisis makes farm supports more vital than ever" (cited in EFRA 2009a: 40).[8]

The recent bout of food price inflation clearly has concentrated minds about the future of the decoupling process. Thus following the CAP Health Check, which further reduced First Pillar direct payments, a resolution passed by the European Parliament in January, 2009 firmly stated that it was "opposed to the dismantling of market management measures and cuts in farmer's support payments" (EFRA 2009a: 40). Although voiced less strongly, the UK food security debates also reveal that the case for a decoupled CAP is coming under increasing scrutiny. For example, EFRA (2009a: 41) sees a robust domestic production capacity as "a necessary condition for food security" and deftly recommends that

Defra "consider whether its stance on the elimination of all direct payments and its new position on the contribution made to food security by domestic production are reconcilable." This "new" position has inescapable fiscal implications if it is determined that UK food security depends on raising domestic food output using sustainable methods. Arguing for "a common sustainable food policy" *via* "a *recoupling* of sustainability into *food production*," Tim Lang (2009a: 19, our emphasis) notes that the danger of a decoupled CAP is that it is involves "paying for environmental goods instead of paying for food to deliver those environmental goods."[9]

This concern that decoupling is over-shooting at the expense of production is reflected in EFRA's recommendation:

> The CAP is a way of rewarding farmers for the provision of environmental services. However, the focus of the post-2013 CAP should be on *sustainable food production, rather than land management itself.* Europe has a responsibility to contribute to global food supplies and the EU must ensure that European countries are in a position to respond to increased demand.
>
> (EFRA 2009a: 42, our emphasis)

This is a long way from the confident belief that "open and competitive" markets will deliver global, European, and UK food security. Nevertheless, the UK government reaffirmed this stance in its response to the recommendation by EFRA noted above (see EFRA 2009c: 20–21; see also HM Government 2010b). This position continues to divide EU member states and these differences are likely to become more acute as the negotiations of the new seven-year EU budget for 2014–21 enter the final decisive phase in 2011–12.

Placing these food security debates in the context of our earlier discussions of niche development, socio-technical regime change and the impact of systemic "shocks" (Geels and Schot 2007; Smith 2006), we have seen that the prevailing policy response to the "new fundamentals" is to encourage the ecological modernization of the conventional food regime through a series of cumulative adjustments. These will be catalyzed primarily by "eco-technological innovations," including possible recourse to genetic engineering, that do not radically undermine the basic architecture of this regime. Under the guise of EU food security and responsibility to meet increased global demand, the next decade is likely to see *a new expansionary cycle of agricultural intensification* that revitalizes the productivist model, if no longer in its stereotypical "cheap food" mode.

Ecological modernization that attempts to reconcile continuing output growth with more efficient natural resource management promises to become the guiding principle of the post-2013 CAP. Indeed, a recent report recommends precisely that – "a sustainable intensification of agriculture" – as the basis of the future CAP (House of Lords 2010: 22). Moreover, as the growing scrutiny of decoupling indicates, there are already pressures to refocus *both* Pillars I and II more narrowly and explicitly on agricultural production and income support activities (IEEP 2009a). This emphasis on fiscal issues reflects a wide consensus that significant segments of EU agriculture are broadly uncompetitive and in no position to contribute to European food security and global needs using sustainable "small-footprint technology" without substantial continued income support payments from the public purse. As the CLBA observes, "direct payments under the CAP account for a significant share of net farming income. *Without this assistance, a very large proportion of EU farming businesses will not survive*" (EFRA 2009b: 120, our emphasis).

In short, as it faces the challenges of the "new fundamentals" to historical patterns of food security, the EU must find ways to develop new, more endogenous supply capacities that build on the bifurcated structural legacy created by over 50 years of the CAP. That is, how will the transition to ecological, social, and economic sustainability be managed in a sector characterized, on the one hand, by an "industry" of internationally-competitive, external input-intensive commodity producers and a long "tail" of low income, under-capitalized, CAP-dependent "social agriculture," on the other? (cf. Coleman 1998; Buller 2004; Potter and Tilzey 2007). This industry has the financial capacity to undertake the cumulative process of ecological modernization, and may even draw on some of the sustainable *production* knowledges and practices found in the "alternative" sector, as the Geels and Schot (2007) model of socio-technical transition suggests.

But the larger question concerns the fate of the people, livelihoods, rural communities, and landscapes of "social agriculture" – *un desert rural*? The outcome hinges on the post-2013 CAP settlement and, in the current climate of public expenditure cuts and fiscal austerity, whether or not income supports for sustainable production will be strategically targeted and sufficiently generous to ensure the economic viability and social vitality of these communities and their traditional landscapes.[10]

Sustainable diets and governance

Before the implications of the 2006–08 food price inflation were fully appreciated in policy circles, IPCC research and other studies had already raised awareness that agriculture and food are a significant source of global anthropogenic greenhouse gas (GHG) emissions. The links subsequently made between climate change, food security, industrially processed foods, rising rates of obesity and diabetes, and other diet-related public health risks (cf. Lang 2009b; Sustainable Development Commission 2009b; Popkin 2009) have focused particular attention on emissions from intensive livestock production.

There is now a broad consensus that livestock products are more GHG intensive than other food groups and that these emissions are concentrated at the farm stage rather than in downstream processing and distribution activities (Garnett 2009; FAO 2006). The meat and dairy sectors contribute approximately 18 percent of global GHG emissions and account for about four-fifths of global *agricultural* GHG emissions (FAO 2006), while the saturated fat in livestock products is an established risk factor in cardiovascular disease (Friel *et al.*

2009).[11] In the UK, where the meat and dairy sectors generate an estimated 40 percent of food-related GHG emissions, they hold the key to an accelerated transition to a more sustainable, lower carbon, and healthy food system (Stern 2006; Millward and Garnett 2009; Garnett 2008, 2009). Moreover, these sectors rely heavily on imported supplies of intensively produced animal feed, particularly soya from Latin America, increasing the global "emissions" footprint of the UK food system and its vulnerability to high energy prices and possible export embargoes.

In this emerging, "joined up" policy discourse (cf. Defra 2009b), sustainably produced food must find its mirror image in a sustainable diet if the circle is to be closed. This requires a truly revolutionary transformation of consumer dietary behavior and the consumer culture built since the end of rationing in the early 1950s on the twin pillars of "cheap food" and freedom of individual choice (cf. Jackson 2004, 2009). This theme has prompted an increasing flow of government reports and research studies on what is meant by a sustainable diet and outlining possible trajectories of transition (cf. Sustainable Development Commission 2008, 2009a, 2009b; Thankappen and Flynn 2007; Scott and Phillips 2008).

If a transition from the economically- and culturally-embedded "cheap food," globally-sourced provisioning model is to be undertaken fairly and equitably for all citizens, sweeping changes to contemporary EU multilevel, hybrid public–private structures of food governance will be needed (cf. Marsden *et al.* 2010). The power over food supply chains devolved earlier to the corporate sector must be clawed back and national and supranational institutions given regulatory oversight mechanisms with real sanctions to counter and manage market forces in the social interest. It is naive to think that the UK state needs to do little more than provide clear, unequivocal signals of the new, low-carbon "direction of travel" and the lightly-regulated, growth- and profit-centered, and highly concentrated industrial food system will then voluntarily undergo an internal metamorphosis to emerge as one capable of delivering food security to households in sustainable, healthy, and equitable ways.

Yet confidence that corporate retailer supply chains can be "nudged" in the desired direction is at the heart of current UK thinking (EFRA 2009a, 2009b, 2009c; Ambler-Edwards *et al.* 2009; HM Government 2010b; cf. Dowler 2008). In our view, such confidence is badly misplaced and a much more powerful *dirigiste* state apparatus is needed to ensure that social equity and justice are given priority when assessing and regulating the performance of the food system. Given the bleak reality of food poverty in the UK and the pronounced inequalities in income, nutrition, and health revealed by recent inquiries, it is difficult, not to say impossible, to imagine how substantive progress toward these goals can be made without strong state intervention (Marmot 2010; Hills 2010; Sustainable Development Commission 2010). Yet the new Con-Lib Dem coalition's ideological "slash-and-burn" approach to the state and welfare services suggests that these entrenched social injustices will become even more severe.

The "mirror" transition to a sustainable diet likewise implies coordinated public policies, possibly including mandatory measures, to redirect purchases to low-carbon foods and oblige consumers to reduce their intake of meat and dairy products (cf. Darton *et al.*, 2009).[12] Lower consumption of these products can indeed provide a "fast track" to immediate reductions in GHG emissions but the *politics* of such profound cultural and behavioral change, and the lower material living standards implied by a transition to sustainable consumption more generally, are completely ignored and "black-boxed."

This black box is transported unopened into the most recent statement of UK food security strategy, *Food 2030* (HM Government 2010b), that responds to the call for a cross-government, more joined-up approach to food policy by the Cabinet Office Strategy Unit's 2008 report, *Food Matters – Towards a Strategy for the 21st Century*. In the first *national* Food Strategy to be formulated since the immediate post-World War II Attlee government, consumer choice is identified as the engine that will lead the transition to sustainable food security:

> *People power* can help bring about a revolution in the way food is produced and sold. Food businesses, including supermarkets and food manufacturers, (will) follow consumer demand for food that is local, healthy and has been produced with a smaller environmental footprint – just as consumers have pushed the rapid expansion of Fairtrade products and free range eggs over the past decade.
>
> (Benn 2010, our emphasis)

With preference for corporate self-governance, mediated by self-interest, the state effectively is written out of this story, despite caveats: "The Government will favour voluntary industry-led and owned measures wherever possible, but we recognise that regulation may be required in some instances" (HM Government 2010b: 8).

This people-powered, industry-led individualistic approach to sustainable food security is supported by little more than the usual weak props of such free market rhetoric: consumer education, better nutritional labelling, and more information on the geographical origin of food. The neoliberal flourishes, belief in "nudging" and "light touch" regulation of this Panglossian vision of 2030 apparently are all that is needed to achieve its goal of food justice in a fairer food system: "People from all parts of society should be able to choose and eat a sustainable diet with reliable access to affordable, healthy and safe food" (HM Government 2010b: 16). Yet the politics of the journey to this idyllic world of equal and fair access to sustainable, affordable food are again neglected, an oversight made all the more galling by repeated reference to the marked income and diet-related health inequalities in the UK (cf. Defra 2010).

This neglect of the politics of sustainable food security is matched by the silence on the concentrated oligopolistic structures of the UK food system and the glaring asymmetries between corporate power and "people power." The current food industry architecture is simply left out of this discussion since it is taken for granted that the retail food giants will respond and adapt to the desired "direction of travel" without state-led restructuring and regulation.

But, as a recent synthesis report on encouraging "pro-environmental" consumer food behaviors observes, although supermarkets "play the central role in determining contemporary diets ... it is far from clear that (they) are ready to engage in a pro-environmental agenda based on a low impact diet" (Darton *et al.* 2009: 10).

The market-led trajectory of transition to sustainable food security advocated by *Food 2030* also skates over views that a lower hydrocarbon future is unlikely to be realized without strong regulatory measures to direct demand away from high GHG systems of dairy and livestock production. Disingenuously, *Food 2030* avoids this issue by arguing that "the evidence to inform appropriate consumer choices and policy responses is unclear" (ibid.: 48). It is widely mooted that food rationing in some form, such as the "soft paternalism" of "choice-editing" by supermarkets and other "expert" interventions to modify consumer behavior, will be required in the drive for sustainable food security but these issues receive far too little attention in *Food 2030*. (cf. Barnett 2010b; see http://governingtemptation.wordpress.com/).[13]

What "command-and-control" powers will the state need to achieve low carbon transition and how and by whom will the activities that can be left to the market and profit-seeking actors be decided? In a fuel-depleted, low carbon economy, how will equitable socio-spatial structures of food distribution be established? By reviving corner shops and street markets in "food deserts"? Subsidizing Ocado-style store-to-home delivery for all households to reduce individual grocery shopping journeys? What are the politics of such restructuring, how can social justice and fairness be achieved and what will this new system of sustainable food production–consumption look like? It is cold comfort that the Food Ethics Council (2010) regards the neglect of the social justice or, at best, its superficial treatment, as typical of UK food policy debate. Yet "social justice is so central to the aims of ensuring sustainability, food security and public health that those goals cannot be met without making our food system fairer" (ibid.: 21).

In short, transition to a sustainable food security strategy will usher in a period of draconian change and raise tough political questions about production, land use, property relations, food justice, social practice, and accumulation in food systems. So far, these questions have not been formulated let alone confronted in UK and EU discussions of food security.

Alternative pathways to sustainable food security in the UK: mapping the "new" UK food relocalization movement – Making Local Food Work and the Transition Network

> The principal implication of a theory of practice is that the sources of changed behaviour lie in the development of practices themselves. The concept of practice inherently combines a capacity to account for both reproduction and innovation.
>
> (Alan Warde 2005: 140)

The preceding discussion reveals some of the emerging contours of current policy thinking on the magnitude and imminence of the challenges presented by the "new fundamentals" and how their impacts can best be mitigated at different geopolitical scales. As we have seen, sustainable food security is now the new watchword, despite acknowledged tensions between self-sufficiency, sustainable production, and global provisioning. In the UK, and, one suspects, in the post-2013 EU, ecological modernization of conventional industrial agriculture and centralized corporate retailing is emerging as the preferred strategy. However, to equate ecological modernization unequivocally with notions of sustainability and "sustainable growth" is to be reminded that these are all notoriously plastic, if not oxymoronic, concepts and, on the ground, this strategy is likely to mean different things to different actors.

In prioritizing the ecological modernization of conventional food provisioning, Whitehall food policy circles effectively marginalize organic agriculture and localized food networks with indulgent but faint praise. By implication, these activities are laudable – "a way of reconnecting people with food production" (EFRA 2009a: 30) – but peripheral to the real business of achieving sustainable food security at the *national* scale. The corollary is that the current highly centralized, just-in-time food distribution system, with suitable adjustment, is also the preferred way to ensure *local* food security.

This dismissive view of localized food provisioning is firmly embedded in the techno-centric and technocratic optimism nurtured by corporate stakeholders "within the industry." Yet this lack of support may come to be seen as a costly missed opportunity as the future unfolds. Rather than adopting an absolutist, unconditional position, it is enough to accept that re-localized systems have a role to play in meeting food needs and providing a proving ground for the behavioral changes that will be required for a low-carbon society. At the very least, the creative responses by social movements and grassroots groups in the UK to the *same* impending constraints on hydrocarbons and ecosystem services are galvanizing public support and encouraging collective action at a time when public disenchantment with conventional party politics and policy channels is widespread. Moreover, there is growing evidence that these networks can contribute significantly to climate change mitigation and a low-carbon food economy (Soil Association 2009b; MLFW 2010).

Such imaginaries and social experiments form what John Urry (2010) describes as "low carbon vanguards." In the context of recent debates, these activists see their efforts as ways of taking responsibility for local food security and as practical demonstrations of how to make the transition to more sustainable and resilient food systems. We begin with "first generation" strategies of food re-localization but, in practice, these are facets of a much more diverse movement to extend the reach of local provisioning.

The earlier chapters in Part II explored such "first generation" initiatives as regional PGO/PDI locality foods, organic agriculture, and local food networks involving farmers' markets and CSA/box schemes, illustrated by case studies of French AMAPs (*Associations pour le Maintien d'une Agriculture Paysanne*), the GAS.P! (*Gruppo di Aquisto Solidade de Pisa*) scheme in Pisa, and the UK projects analyzed by Kneafsey *et al.* (2008). Of course, localized food provisioning extends well beyond these relatively formal, market-oriented activities. It encompasses myriad community self-help projects, including community allotments, gardens, orchards, land and crop share schemes, food co-ops, shops and cafés, as well as organizations combining these alternative forms of sourcing and distribution in different ways. This list also would cover more individual activities, such as home gardening, allotments, and garden share schemes and there is great popular interest in "growing your own food." Projects across this diverse spectrum are now proliferating in the UK and their "demonstration effects" are mobilizing support for the spatial reorganization of food provisioning.

Making Local Food Work (MLFW)

In the UK, this "first generation" arsenal is now being replenished and renewed in highly imaginative ways using a variety of new legal and organizational instruments to set up local provisioning networks that combine market and non-market forms (see Soil Association 2005; MLFW 2009). Arguably, these collective, non-market innovations straddling production and consumption practices are opening up a new dimension in the contemporary politics of food. While there is a groundswell of individual activist groups experimenting independently with these new operational approaches, this process of renewal has gained greater momentum under the leadership of a broad consortium of six social and environmental organizations engaged in the MLFW program, established in 2007.

With £10 million in Big Lottery funding for five years, the different project strands of the MLFW are coordinated by the Plunkett Foundation and implemented by its consortium partners: the Council for the Protection of Rural England (CPRE), the Soil Association, Co-operativesUK, Country Markets Ltd, the National Farmers' Retail & Markets Association, and Sustain (the alliance for better food and farming). These organizations also draw the activities and resources of their own networks into the orbit of MLFW to create supportive synergies and extend its scope. In 2008, for example, Sustain, formed earlier by a group of national organizations, established the Local Action on Food network, which "builds on the work of the former Food Links UK and its own Food Access Network (and) serves as a means of strengthening and disseminating the national Making Local Food Work programme" (www.sustainweb.org/localactiononfood, accessed October 21, 2009). The reach of these activities can be gauged from its January, 2010 Newsletter, where MLFW states that by 2012 it "aims to have supported 650 community food enterprises to increase awareness and access of local food for a million people" (info@makinglocalfoodwork.co.uk).

In tracing the changing contours of the food re-localization movement, we pay greater attention to newer strategies, particularly community-based projects, although the MLFW is actively supporting the growth of farmers' markets and box schemes. As we saw in Chapters 4 and 5, these older, "first generation" forms are vulnerable to mainstream cooption or "endogenisation," as well as to competition from "scaled up" box schemes, such as those operated nationally and regionally by Riverford Organic and Abel and Cole. A crucial question, therefore, is whether the "second generation" localization initiatives are any less exposed to these forces, particularly once MFLW support comes to an end in 2013.

Public procurement, food re-localization, and economically vulnerable communities

Efforts to re-localize public food procurement also have drawn support from rising popular interest in local food, although these initiatives have struggled to gain a secure institutional foothold, and particularly now in the aftermath the "credit crunch" and the deep cuts to central government and local authority budgets. This strategy, a kind of "reverse" endogenization, involves political initiatives to reclaim "the power of the public plate" from "placeless" food service corporations by using local authority procurement policies to support local food networks and widen access to nutritious food (Morgan and Sonnino 2008; Kirwan and Foster 2007; East Anglia Food Link 2008; Camden Sustainability Task Force 2008). Thatcher and Sharp (2008: 256) quantify this power by pointing out that public sector catering represents 7 percent of total UK food expenditure and the National Health Service (NHS) is the largest single purchaser of food.

After much ground work by activists and several government programs, public procurement was catapulted into the political arena in 2005 by celebrity chef Jamie Oliver's "muckraking" TV series, "Jamie's School Dinners," exposing the poor quality of processed school meals and passionately advocating healthier menu options, including local fresh foods. There is now a large and growing number of encouraging initiatives in this area, such as the national Food for Life Partnership program coordinated by the Soil Association and embracing almost 3,000 schools, and a wide variety of innovative smaller schemes.

As an illustration of these activities, Local Food Links (LFL) organizes a hot meal delivery service for 12 schools around Bridport in West Dorset and a further eight schools in the Blandford area following its decision to take on the management of a local authority-owned kitchen in early 2009. This social enterprise is now extending its catering services to four care homes for older people and a day care center. LFL received the Food for Life Partnership's highest catering award in 2009 for its use of locally sourced food, organic produce, and fair traded products. However, like many such projects, LFL is grant dependent and finding it difficult to achieve stability by building up relatively secure income streams (Crabtree 2009).

These local fresh food procurement schemes supplying schools, hospitals, and other public institutions also are vulnerable to competition from corporate, often transnational, food service companies whose "scale arguments" can be persuasive in terms of "bottom line" reasoning and the administrative simplicity of a "one-stop shop." The funding of local food procurement under discretionary rather than statutory programs is a further source of instability, and particularly now following the severe expenditure cuts announced in October, 2010 by the Con-Lib Dem coalition. As these cuts bite into local government budgets, it is feared that groups of local authorities will seek to make fiscal economies by combining their procurement needs, leading to "demand aggregation" and higher minimum scale requirements that are beyond the capacity of local fresh food procurement projects (Crabtree 2009; Morgan 2009).

Another broad category of local food procurement involves projects initiated and supported by local NHS Primary Care Trusts (PCTs) to provide fresh local produce to community food co-ops and buying groups in poor, vulnerable communities, often located in "food deserts," where it is difficult to buy fresh fruit and vegetables. In one example, Blythe PCT in north-east England set up Blythe Valley Food Co-op Ltd in 2003 to supply local buying groups with better access to fresh produce and this later merged with North East Land Links to create Food Chain North East, which incorporated as a Community Interest Company (CIC) in 2006. This social enterprise, now with support from MLFW, is developing growing and supply contracts directly with local producers and delivers produce that is "as local as possible" to some 50 buying groups, which are mainly publicly funded. Again, grant dependence and uncertainty about the continued availability of public funds are sources of potential instability.

Food Chain North East is just one example of an expanding number of cooperative organizations working with PCTs and other statutory bodies throughout the UK to deliver fresh fruit and vegetables to networks of food co-ops, school food clubs, and buying groups. However, the priority given to local food in these provisioning schemes for low-income communities can vary. In East London, for example, Community Food Enterprise (CFE), a registered charity, has addressed the problem of "food deserts" in the Borough of Newham and surrounding areas by setting up a retail network of Social Food Outlets in schools and operating a mobile food store. While fresh produce originally was purchased at the conventional New Spitalfields wholesale market, CFE is now collaborating with MLFW to establish a "distribution hub" for local, sustainably-produced food supplied by farmers from nearby rural counties. On the other hand, a similar organization, East London Food Access, is less committed to local sourcing than making fresh produce available to economically disadvantaged groups and elderly and disabled people living on housing estates in Hackney and nearby areas where no other access exists.

These examples provide glimpses of a more "autonomous" pathway to local food provisioning, albeit one where its embryonic organizations often require grant aid and public funding. In turn, this pathway highlights the gaps and "deserts" left by corporate retailing and the direct support that will be needed to deliver socially just and equitable food security.

Community social enterprises and food localization projects

In analytical terms, "first generation" localization strategies based on direct selling, though primarily market oriented, sought to offset the competitive advantages of scale enjoyed by supermarkets and food service companies. While still dependent on the market for social reproduction, this was achieved by adopting modes of governance where success is measured not by "scaling up" and the hierarchical concentration of market power but by *ubiquity* in space.

Local farmers' markets spring immediately to mind here and their rapid reproduction in the UK since the first prototype was opened in Bath in 1997 represents a major, highly visible step toward food re-localization. This expansion, supported by customers appreciative of the alterity of locally produced food and face-to-face interaction, reveals the possibilities of horizontal growth in spaces less easily occupied by mainstream actors. Of course, farmers' markets are exposed to indirect price competition from supermarkets and street markets and yet must be commercially viable in order to attract and retain producers offering a variety of produce (Kirwan 2004). Some assurance of a reasonable quality of life also is vital for the spatial diffusion of farmer-led community supported agriculture (CSA)/box schemes.

Farmers' markets, CSA/box schemes and local public procurement still represent the main profile of the food re-localization movement in the UK, and these channels also provide an important outlet for small-scale organic producers.[14] However, this familiar localized "foodscape" is now being reinvigorated and extended by a variety of community self-organized schemes, including some that are operating fully or partially beyond the market, often on land owned by community land trusts or leased out by local councils.[15] This quiet "revolution" involves legal forms and organizational types that can be scaled at the community level and vest ownership and control in community hands, insulating them from corporate "endogenisation." These new structures also provide the "raw material" that is being synergistically integrated by the MLFW consortium so that the whole is rapidly exceeding the sum of its parts.

Although informed by this "revolution" and the rising discursive profile of local food, many of these initiatives stand outside formal networks, such as MLFW, and typically are the work of individual actors and small groups. This grassroots effervescence is exemplified by the Futurefarms not-for-profit growers' cooperative established in 2004 in the parish of Martin, Hampshire. According to one of the co-founders, the co-op was organized "to cut out the middlemen" and provide fresh, nutritious food for the village. "Farmers' markets tend to be expensive niche providers for the few. I wanted a system to provide local food for the many" (*Guardian* February 3, 2010). Production initially relied exclusively on volunteer work rotas but these are now supplemented by four part-time workers and the hope is to employ a full-time farmer eventually. The co-op rents land owned by members and supplies a wide variety of fresh vegetables and free-range chickens, lamb, and pork to 126 families in the village, whose annual membership fee of £5 can be commuted by seven hours of volunteer labor (personal communication).

Local food projects such as Futurefarms attracted fulsome praise at the 2010 annual conference of the Soil Association, which is seeking both to dispel the image of organic food as elitist and expensive and to challenge the technocentric ecological modernization approach advocated by Whitehall as the future of British food provisioning. According to Bonnie Hewson, the Soil Association's project director,

> "People … need to feel empowered. We know of lots of alternative local food systems that are sustainable, resilient, viable and principled." … "The Futurefarms experiment is an inspiring example of how a small group without much funding can do its own thing in a small corner of England, and do it well."
>
> (*Guardian* February 3, 2010)

The legal status of these new social enterprises can reflect the long history of community activism, as in the case of the Industrial and Provident Society (IPS) – in the form of IPS (*bona fide* co-op) and IPS for the Benefit of the Community – and Charitable Incorporated Association (CIA). The two forms of IPS, based on the democratic principle of "one member, one vote," are by far the most common legal status adopted by social enterprises active in local food networks (Seymour and Simmonds 2009). Other social enterprises have arisen under more recent initiatives, including the CIC legislation introduced in the UK in 2005, or are organized as public limited companies, associations, partnerships, and trusts. These different legal structures encompass a bewildering range of organizational types of social enterprise, although on the simplest definition these are businesses trading for a social purpose (www.socialenterprise.org.uk). Again, there is the revival of the old – workers' cooperatives, consumer cooperatives, farmers' market cooperatives, food co-ops, buying groups – and the new – community land trusts, community-supported agriculture, community-run agriculture, urban farms, development trusts (MLFW 2009).

However, merely listing these different types of social enterprise conceals how much their structure can vary in practice. Even relatively well-known models, such as CSA schemes, are difficult to categorize empirically. Thus a recent survey of seven trading CSA enterprises reveals significant divergence from the ideal-type in terms of organization and governance (Keech *et al.* 2009). For example, the principle that box schemes mitigate and more equitably distribute production risk between producers and member consumers is often regarded as a key distinguishing feature. Yet this review finds that consumers may have little exposure to risk and, in two cases, "their farmers have, respectively, shouldered considerable personal financial burdens, or written off any hope of an income, in favour of carrying out their CSA innovations" (ibid.: 13). This study for the Soil Association, which is charged with supporting the development of CSAs under the MLFW program, concludes with the suggestion that "it is possibly a mistake to hook CSA emergence to grant-giving" (ibid.: 14).

In this uncertain context, the confident trajectory of Stroud Community Agriculture (SCA) marks it out from its peers. It is often used by local food activists to demonstrate the social and ecological benefits that can be generated by a successful community-led box scheme. Established as a social enterprise with community shareholders following a public meeting in 2001, SCA changed its structure in 2002 to become an industrial and provident society (Pinkerton and Hopkins 2009). The enterprise has some 200 subscribing members, rents 50 acres of certified organic land, employs two full-time farmers and recently extended its activities to livestock. Although SCA accepts some grant aid, subscription income is sufficient to ensure that it is self-financing. This financial stability and social cohesion distinguishes SCA from the many recently established community box schemes that are still finding their feet.

Another pioneering organization in the inner London Borough of Hackney, Growing Communities, which became a non-profit company limited by guarantee in 1997, sources organic produce as locally as possible, primarily from small peri-urban producers and farms nearby in rural Essex and Kent. Its core activities include London's first organic box scheme, an urban farm shop, the UK's first organic farmers' market established in 2003, and three organic market gardens in Hackney. The inner city sites on public land in parks and an allotment are cultivated by volunteer work teams and supply salad vegetables and fruit for the organic box scheme. Growing Communities has been independent of external grants since 2005 and its core projects are now fully self-financing through the market (Pinkerton and Hopkins 2009: 161). The priority it gives to the sustainable use of urban sites, back gardens, and peri-urban land also has inspired activists devising strategies for lower carbon communities.

The Transition Network (TN)

Such planning underlies the explosive growth of the Transition Town concept as a way for communities to respond to a lower energy future implied by the passage of "peak oil," and which suddenly has become a very significant catalyst of environmental activism. As a first step, each local Transition group envisions a low-carbon future and then gradually develops pragmatic ways of adjusting to its new circumstances. The Transition movement began in Kinsale in County Cork in Ireland in 2005 with the preparation of the Kinsale Energy Descent Plan, followed by the launch of Transition Town Totnes in Devon in 2006 and the Transition Network in 2007. With its "viral spread" to many other centers in the UK and beyond, the TN has "become one of the fastest-growing community-scale initiatives in the world" (Hopkins 2008: 133).

Collective action to broadly promote economic re-localization is the driving force of this new social movement, whose philosophical foundations are based on permaculture design principles. This lineage helps to explain the movement's focus on agricultural sustainability and the recent groundswell of community-led food projects. These microscale, self-reliant food provisioning practices are valued for their collective learning and demonstration effects as communities begin to prepare for what is billed as the approaching "perfect storm" of climate change, fossil-fuel depletion, water shortages, and economic crisis.

Transition food activists draw on the same diverse repertoire of alternative operational tools as the food re-localization movement – community gardens, allotments, garden shares, community orchards, box schemes, food co-ops, and school projects – and embrace its vision of sustainable and resilient local food systems. One of the lead partners in MLFW, the Soil Association, has welcomed the Transition movement and the idea of low hydrocarbon "Transition food." In the words of its then director, Patrick Holden:

> To anyone who still questions the importance of food in the transition process I would say this – in relation to climate change and fossil-fuel depletion, there is likely to be a serious food crisis long before the effects of global warming impact on our lives.
>
> (Cited in Pinkerton and Hopkins 2009: 26)

On the other hand, as Bailey *et al.* (2009: 1) note, the Transition Network is extending "its appeal beyond 'hardcore environmentalists' (by) ... bringing together ... a collection of linked but otherwise disparate concerns – about peak oil, energy security, climate change, and globalisation...." However, these authors, one of whom is widely acknowledged as the moving spirit behind the TN, are critical of the revival of early 1970s survivalist "limits-to-growth" discourse. They suggest that this will make it be difficult for the movement to find political traction outside "the demographic silo of middle-class pro-environmentalists" since it appeals "mainly to 'post-materialist' groups whose wealth and values (are) unrepresentative of broader populations" (ibid.: 7). If this characterization of the TN constituency is accurate, other activist organizations must be alert to the dangers of the "lifeboat ethics" of an exclusive localism that would subvert MLFW principles of open and equal community access to healthy, sustainable food.

A further question involves a "rural bias" of the TN movement insofar as larger, more socially and ethnically stratified urban communities and metropolitan, built-up inner city areas will experience much greater difficulty in finding sites for *collective* renewable energy projects and re-localized food production. Purely for illustrative purposes, in the case of the totemic inner London organization, Growing Communities, 95 percent of the produce for its organic box scheme is grown outside Hackney and most of the producers trading in its organic farmers' market are located within 70 miles of the borough, with a small number coming from over 100 miles away (Keech 2007). As these distances emphasize, how sustainable and equitable distribution systems will be structured under low carbon constraints is also a key issue for local food activists that deserves far more attention than it has received. Organic CSA schemes nevertheless seem to be the Soil Association's answer to this issue of "rural bias" as "CSAs can be established in rural areas or in urban settings, on municipal land, farms, allotments or gardens" (Daniel 2009: 105).

It is also unclear whether the present "bottom up" community-scale structures of the TN will evolve ways and means to engage with central government, although the "new localism" is prompting politicians on both the Left and the Right to invoke their radical traditions of civic mutualism (Bunting 2009; cf. Blond 2009). More pragmatically, TN is attracting interest from local government and the number of Transition Local Authorities is rising. Funding and planning support at this scale is vitally important if the TN is to become a real force in building sustainable and more resilient local economies. While it has yet to have any appreciable impact beyond the proverbial parish pump, the TN is very much in its formative phase and it would be premature to dismiss its politics out of hand as merely elitist green parochialism. This fledgling organization is giving impetus and a broader rationale to MLFW strategies by creating an increasingly *multifaceted* economic re-localization movement whose evolution will be fascinating to follow over the next few years.

Community food enterprises: the end of the market "niche" model?

The newer, "second generation" forms of re-localization reviewed very briefly here illustrate how activism "overflows" the market in the process of evading cooption and "framing" by the mainstream (Wilkinson 2010). On the other hand, while noting the dialectics of these moves, the forms of community-led provisioning around which alternative food movements are regrouping, exemplified by MLFW and the TN, no longer seem to constitute a market "niche." That is, in the sense that they possess a latent commercial potential that can be "appropriated" by mainstream actors if market and political economic conditions change radically enough to throw the incumbent regime from its current trajectory.

If anything, the danger comes from the opposite quarter insofar as community self-help projects in food, healthy eating, and related areas of public welfare begin to be seen even remotely as an alternative to the provision of collective state services of care and community support. Intimations of a "proxy state" can be found in the use of largely volunteer but market-based local fresh food procurement projects to address food-related health inequalities. The Con-Lib Dem advocacy of an altruistic, voluntary "Big Society" to mask its ideological attacks on the welfare state and public provision magnifies this concern.[16] Moreover, the socio-spatial distribution and "thickness" of associative networks are unequal and tend to be closely correlated with income and wealth. Local food activists must engage directly with these wider politics and resist attempts to confine their activities to these two extremes for that will ensure their marginalization. That is, resist becoming an inadequate proxy for collective welfare provision or contributing to the social stratification and divisive cultural hierarchies characteristic of contemporary corporate food systems. The key struggle is to place re-localized food systems at the center of progressive collective solutions to the welfare and sustainability of society at large, not only the economically disadvantaged, on the one hand, or wealthy "post-materialist" groups, on the other.

Conclusion

In this chapter, we have suggested that twin concerns for UK food security, aroused by warnings of global food shortages and social movement initiatives for sustainable local provisioning, are converging in growing pressures to re-order spatial political economies of food. Of course, social movements have long campaigned for more sustainable food systems based on shorter supply chains embedded in localized production–consumption networks. Nevertheless, apart from mainstream efforts to "endogenise" profitable segments of organics, locality, and local foods, these campaigns have made relatively little impression on conventional food systems and the prevailing ideology of "cheap food," with its foundations in the distantiated patterns of global sourcing developed by trans-national food manufacturers and supermarkets. This ideology and its correlate that national food security can be secured through "open and competitive" global markets has defined the received wisdom of UK food policy for the past 50 years.

As we have seen, these cherished assumptions were badly shaken by the international price inflation of 2006–08 and the magnitude of the global food crisis that these events exposed. Old ideologies die hard, however, and recently HM Government (2010b) re-affirmed its confidence that access to open markets represents the most effective way of ensuring UK food security in the years 2010–30. Since the EU currently accounts for 69 percent of UK food imports, this policy stance amounts to a political calculation that intra-EU trade flows will be maintained even in periods of supply shortages when individual Member States will be under pressure to give first priority to the food security of their own citizens. Despite urging by the CLBA (EFRA 2009b: 119), there is no public evidence that contingency plans are in place to deal with the possible breakdown of the EU Single Market.

In the case of the UK and, by extension, the EU, we have discussed the policy debates and arguments over the "direction of travel" to take to safeguard national food security against further disruptions in international agricultural markets arising from global resource constraints and climate change. In the UK, few concrete steps in this adjustment process have been taken beyond proposals for a certain "re-nationalization" of food supply chains to improve self-sufficiency ratios by stimulating domestic production – for example, in horticulture – and encouraging the ecological modernization of food provisioning in accordance with the principles of eco-efficiency.

At this early stage, it is difficult to evaluate the real substance and transform-ative potential of this new trajectory of ecological modernization and its resil-ience if external "shocks" again threaten the stability of international commodity markets. However, despite the campaigning efforts of the Soil Association and its MLFW partners, it seems that re-localized food networks are still out of favor as a key building block in mounting an effective response to the challenges of sustainability and uncertain global supplies as the long reign of "cheap food," if not industrial agriculture, finally draws to a close.

Part III

Alternative food movements in the USA

Formative years, mainstreaming, civic governance, and knowing sustainability

7   Broken promises?

US alternative food movements, origins, and debates

This chapter surveys the development of alternative agriculture movements in the USA and the challenges they now face following the institutionalization of a standards-based, "allowable inputs" conception of organic food and its governance. We suggest that this fundamental conceptual shift has created a *fault-line* in alternative food movements by marginalizing process-based approaches embedded in a political imaginary of holistic agroecological practices, personal and equitable interactions between farmers and consumers and localized democratic governance. There is no doubt that the "allowable inputs," norm-based standards of United States Department of Agriculture (USDA) organic certification has encouraged the entry of large-scale specialized growers, facilitating monocrop production and integration in mainstream processing and distribution networks controlled by powerful corporate actors. From this perspective, the counter-cultural origins of the organic farming movement and its radical critique of conventional food provisioning have been transcended by the rise of a mimetic, multibillion dollar industry.

Yet this unilinear narrative of ineluctable mainstream pressures neglects the dialectical responses of alternative food activists, who are "reframing" their struggle to gain greater social control of food provisioning, as we suggested in Chapter 5. Thus in the USA, as in Western Europe, local food movements are articulating initiatives that "overflow" or escape corporate framing by building networks of civic agriculture based on direct marketing and open, deliberative processes of governance. These renewal efforts can be seen as attempts to reclaim the vision of localized food networks and revitalize food politics by moving into material and discursive spaces that are less easily assimilated into the corporate mainstream and beyond standards-based USDA regulation. The rapid growth of farmers' markets, community supported agriculture (CSAs), "beyond organic" logos, region of origin labels, and local Food Policy Councils are testimony to this process of resistance and renewal.

In recent debates in agro-food studies, some protagonists have called these responses to corporate mainstreaming into question for failing to recognize that their "possessive investments" in class, race, and gender severely inhibit their ability to promote social justice in food provisioning and thus narrowly circumscribe the "politics of the possible." We explore the nature of this challenge by following recent debates on farm-to-school programs and the "white," racially coded spaces of civic agriculture projects. This critique is accompanied by demands that the "transformative" or "emancipatory" potential of local food networks be reassessed. In the final section, we examine the mainstreaming of organics in some detail and argue that the distinctiveness of the US case arises from the economic opportunities created by standards-based regulation and the subsequent capture of this process by the giants of US agribusiness.

Taken together, the chapters in Part III analyze the tensions between markets and alternative food movements, exacerbated by the corporate-USDA rejection of a process-based organic vision (Chapter 7), investigate the "object conflicts" and crisis of legitimacy triggered by corporate lobbying to weaken the deliberative civic governance of organics (Chapter 8), and examine the ecological and institutional challenges facing the production of sustainable knowledge in the case of organic strawberries in California (Chapter 9).

Sustainable agriculture movements: emergence, transformative potential, and localist alternatives

Organic farming began to emerge as a relatively coherent set of production and land management practices in the USA only after World War II, building on the indefatigable propagandizing of J. I. Rodale and the Rodale Press, whose magazines, *Organic Gardening and Farming* and *Prevention*, both "enjoyed a very wide circulation in the post-war years" (Vos 2000: 246), and especially in the 1970s (Belasco 1989). Rodale was strongly influenced by Lady Eve Balfour, author of *The Living Soil* (Balfour 1943), Sir Alfred Howard, known as the "inventor" of compost (Reed 2001), the nutritionist Sir Robert McCarrison, and Rudolf Steiner, whose ideas underpinned the biodynamic movement in Western Europe and the USA in the inter-war period (Conford 2001). These early proselytizers of the unity of ecological and human health were joined in the late 1960s and early 1970s by a cacophony of more radical, disaffected voices drawn from the civil rights campaign, anti-war activism, the embryonic environmental movement, anti-consumerism, and the diffuse currents of a growing counter-culture.

This formative period saw an explosive, though short-lived, growth of rural or country communes, numbering around 3,500 in the years 1965–70, before this "lyrical stage" of subsistence-based living gave way to the development "under the rubric of Appropriate Technology ... (of) ways to make small-scale farming viable" (Belasco 1989: 83). An early participant describes the organic agriculture movement in the late 1960s and 1970s as "a fugitive subculture of urban refugees ... (and) part of a broader reaction to the bland ... conformist, post-war lifestyle..." (Jolly 1998: 1). These dissident voices in the pluralistic coalition, collectively known as the back-to-the-land movement, articulated a militant social and ecological critique of industrial agriculture and the giants of American agribusiness, as we see below in the case of the Agriculture Sustainability Project. One influential current of academic scholarship continues to judge sustainable agriculture movements (SAMs) and local food networks (LFNs) by this (historical) metric of oppositional activism and discursive militancy on the national stage and to lament what is seen as a retreat into localism and accommodation with entrepreneurialism.

The gradual transition from idealistic country communes to small-scale local provisioning is a classic case of innovation embedded in learning-by-doing and informal mechanisms of knowledge transmission (cf. Hassanein and Kloppenburg 1995), complemented by Rodale magazines and a host of counter-culture, often ephemeral, "underground" publications, such as *Whole Earth Catalog* and *Mother Earth News*. This transition is illustrated by the appearance in 1978 of *New Farm*, a Rodale magazine of "regenerative agriculture dedicated to putting people, profit and biological permanence back into farming" (Belasco 1989: 84). In short, those seeking to make a living on the land gradually engaged with local markets and forged relationships with supportive, like-minded groups of urban consumers, who shared the vision of alternative food provisioning. This solidarity, in turn, spawned novel organizational forms, ranging from urban food cooperatives, buying groups and natural food stores to communal-restaurant businesses symbolized by *Alice's Restaurant* and the *Moosehead Cookbook* (1977) whose names continue to evoke memories of those hopeful times (Belasco 1989).

As these growing producer–consumer linkages brought organics to the fringes of the mainstream, grassroots farmers' organizations, such as California Certified Organic Farmers (CCOF) and Oregon Tilth, developed mechanisms of self-governance and organic certification standards. Such private regulation remained the norm until the federal legislation in the 1990s. Although several states introduced legal codification, including the California Organic Foods Act of 1979, for example, these production codes were not harmonized and lacked adequate state enforcement mechanisms, leaving this role by default to private groups, such as the CCOF.

In tracing this trajectory from pluralistic social movement informed by radicalism and romanticism to nascent sector and, in the 1990s, to an institutionalized, multibillion dollar organic *industry* structured by federal organic standards, many academic commentators see a parallel political transition from radical social critique and transformative politics to a narrow, technocentric production politics. These transitions describe the central tension that historically has divided the US organic agriculture movement. Its contemporary manifestation can be seen in the economic and political fragmentation between specialized "minimalist" farmers, processors and mainstream supermarkets, and localized grassroots *movements* supporting holistic "beyond organic" networks. Indeed, for Vos (2007), commercial success has created an identity crisis between social movement and expanding industry.

"Hightowerism" and research activism[1]

The ascendancy of production politics from the later 1980s also arises from another formative influence on the organic farming movement: the agricultural scientists whose social activism gradually was eclipsed by claims of scientific legitimacy and demands that the federal government fund organic agricultural research in the public land-grant university (LGU) system. Fred Buttel finds the roots of this "technology-led vision" in the social mobilizations of the 1970s and 1980s contesting the institutional "capture" of the LGU system by "a largely invisible, but powerful ... 'productivist coalition' ... (of) the elites of several key institutions – farm commodity groups, land-grant administrators, agribusiness firms and federal agricultural agencies..." (Buttel 2005: 276).

In his analysis of "Hightowerism," Buttel (2005) discusses the activism unleashed by the Agricultural Accountability Project and crystallized by co-founder Jim Hightower's book, *Hard Tomatoes, Hard Times* (1973), that mounted a broadside attack against the inequities and structural bias embedded in the public agricultural research and extension "complex." Hightower's root-and-branch *social* critique accused the USDA/LGU complex of misusing public subsidies to underwrite and accelerate agribusiness logics of technological modernization based on the scale economies of farm consolidation, specialization, and intensification to the neglect of small farmers, farm workers, and widespread rural poverty.

SAMs at first were caught up in this Hightower-type research activism challenging the priorities of the LGU and agricultural science establishment, but the original emphasis on social justice and the biased use of public funding gradually was superseded by competing claims of scientific authority and demands for greater recognition of agroecology and sustainable agriculture *within* this system. Furthermore, in Buttel's (2005) account, activist campaigning for a progressive research policy agenda failed to mobilize the very constituency of small-scale and "family" farmers that Hightowerism claimed to represent, sowing the seeds of its later split into two quite separate social movements organized around food re-localization, on the one hand, and anti-agbiotech and antifood globalization, on the other. The campaign for the public funding of agroecological research achieved some initial success in the 1980s when the Low-Input/Sustainable Agriculture (LI/SA) program was included in the 1985 Farm Bill. This focus on production technology continues to characterize federal sustainable agriculture programs, with the social role of farming receiving only faint recognition (Allen 2004: 82–84).

In his typology of environmental ideologies and discourses, Buttel (1997: 355) categorizes this kind of agricultural research activism as "alternative technologism," which is "an increasingly influential expression of environmentalism in agriculture." In this imaginary, the technoscientific rationalism of conventional agriculture is displaced by an equally science-based but *alternative* rationalism in order to persuade "public research institutions to emphasize 'sustainable,' 'low-input,' or 'alternative agriculture'" (ibid.: 355). In short, this once progressive current of research activism in the SAM eventually settled for greater institutional legitimacy and fiscal traction by advancing sustainable agriculture as a scientific "knowledge claim" rather than a societal socio-ecological project or political agenda.

Pursuit of this technocentric alternative managerialism, Buttel (1993: 32) argues, meant that sustainable agriculture in US policy circles was defined primarily in LISA-like terms of lower chemical use and represented as technology that can readily be *"grafted onto the knowledge base of otherwise conventional agronomy"* (our emphasis). The template of the USDA "Organically Grown" label and the "organic-industrial complex" (Pollan 2001) could hardly be clearer. In Allen's (2004) blunt assessment, the "framing of sustainable agriculture in a natural science discourse" (ibid.: 104) and the adoption of its epistemological positivism are at the root of the failure to interrogate the assumption "that achieving agricultural sustainability is possible without changing social relations" (ibid.: 99). Opposition not only to rationalist scientific discourse but also the "re-rationalist" LISA-like "allowable" inputs approach enshrined in the federal organic standards has led one strand of Hightower-inspired research activism to promote experiential local farmer knowledge as a cornerstone of sustainable agriculture, an approach that Buttel (1997: 356) characterizes as "indigenism."

These heirs of Hightowerism thus began to identify with the localist/agricultural sustainability movements that "arose in a limited way in the late 1970s, largely in continuity with the organic farming movement, and also as a reflection of the growing interest of mainstream environmental groups (such as the Sierra Club) in rural and agricultural environmental issues" (Buttel, 2005: 279). While the agricultural technoscience establishment and the disproportionate funding of conventional agriculture are still contested, activists increasingly are focused on building

> an alternative locally-based food system involving more direct linkages (such as direct marketing, farmers' markets, community-supported agriculture) between farmers and consumers ... [some] important segments of the sustainable agriculture community stress the development of green "value-added" labelling and marketing strategies, while others stress issues such as community food security.
>
> (Buttel 2005: 280)

Although maintaining a quite separate identity, community food security movements have extended this remit of "indigenism" to encompass urban farms and retail food spaces and incorporated a more explicit social justice, antihunger dimension by including low-income and marginalized consumers and/or forging rural–urban food networks between small-scale farmers and urban consumers (Gottlieb and Fisher 1996a, 1996b; Anderson and Cook 1999; Bellows and Hamm 2002).

A localist, entrepreneurial "turn"

This narrative of displaced militancy and retreat from national agendas, so evident in Fred Buttel's work, has become an increasingly dominant theme of US scholarship on sustainable agriculture movements. Explicitly or implicitly, SAMs are assessed in terms of their "transformative potential" to create an alternative, ecologically sustainable and socially just food system. Whether or not this is an excessively ambitious and unrealistic yardstick is taken up below. As an eloquent example, consider the research agenda set out by Patricia Allen and her colleagues for their study of 37 alternative agrifood initiatives (AFIs) in California:

> Our central question concerns the "tectonics" of these initiatives. To what degree do they seek to create a new structural configuration – a shifting of plates in the agrifood landscape – and to what degree are their efforts limited to incremental erosion at the edges of the political-economic structures that currently constitute these plates? That is, are they significantly *oppositional* or primarily *alternative*?
>
> (Allen *et al.* 2003: 61, original emphasis)

Their analysis then develops a narrative of decline as socially progressive oppositional politics give way to the contemporary entrepreneurial "turn" to localism. Looking back over three decades, these authors suggest that

> where in the early years AFIs combined the search for alternatives with a direct critique of existing industrial agricultural practices … the loss of this structural critique and the rise of a political culture of entrepreneurialism appear to have left these organisations with only neo-populism to explain the politics of their engagement.
>
> (Allen *et al.* 2003: 65)

This shift is explained by the weakening of the linkages between AFIs and "broader movements for labor justice and environmental regulation in the context of the neo-liberal revolution … after 1980" (ibid.: 65).

These new circumstances, it is argued, persuaded AFIs to downplay social justice demands and reframe their programs in terms of "the rights of consumers to choose alternatives, rather than their rights as citizens" (ibid.: 68). As a result,

> For many current California AFIs, changing the food system means increasing the diversity of alternative markets such that consumers have more choice, rather than making deep structural changes that could reconfigure who gets to make which kinds of food choices.
>
> (ibid.: 72)

This analysis drives home the point that the meaning of social justice has been transmuted from concern for an egalitarian society, particularly to redress exploitative labor relations and civil rights abuses – notably among California's migrant Latino workers – to more particularist local "questions of food access, urban community empowerment, and support for small farmers" (ibid.: 73).

Allen *et al.* (2003) illustrate this change of direction by analyzing the activities of several AFIs established in the late 1970s, including the Community Alliance with Family Farmers (CAFF), formed originally in 1978 as the California Agrarian Action Project:

> In the 1980s the Agrarian Action Project fought pesticide poisoning, organised victims and, with allies such as the United Farm Workers, provided the political pressure behind strong new regulation of pesticides by the state ... [in addition] it joined other organisations in a lawsuit against the Federal government to force the redistribution of large land holdings that benefited from government irrigation programs.
>
> (Allen *et al.* 2003: 66)

This oppositional stance gradually is overtaken in the course of the 1990s by an emphasis on

> farmer-to-farmer education (its Lighthouse Farms project), the Rural Water Impact Network (which seeks to protect water access for small farms), and its Biologically Integrated Orchards Systems initiative (which supports biological strategies for pest and fertility management...). Its urban manifestation is focused on alternative marketing pathways for small farmers, including farmers' markets and CSAs.
>
> (Allen *et al.* 2003: 67–68)

In this genealogy of Californian AFIs, the collective oppositional politics of social justice has been displaced by locally-focused programs to create entrepreneurial opportunities to enhance the economic reproduction of small farmers.

USDA regulation and the conventionalization thesis

The reconfiguration of sustainable agriculture movements discussed by Allen *et al.* (2003) from oppositional catalyst of social justice in the wider US food system to a localist, incremental politics of change adapted to the hegemonic notions of the market and consumer choice is closely paralleled and significantly reinforced by the institutionalization of a codified, USDA-regulated organic agriculture. From this perspective, national organic legislation removed any remaining obstacles to the rise of an organic *industry* and provided scope for corporate lobbying and related forms of insider "Beltway" politics that has left the organic agriculture *movement* in an embattled state.

Empirically, the rise of a mimetic organic provisioning system sharing the structural characteristics of its conventional industrial counterpart has been interpreted in terms of conventionalization and bifurcation. These theses envision a binary trajectory of structural change in organic agriculture, with the "mainstream" integration of large-scale, specialized producers contracted to supply national supermarket chains and organic stores, as well as international retailers, and a rump of holistic, "movement" farmers or "artisanal" growers engaged in direct selling in localized markets (Vos 2000; Guthman 2004a; Lockie and Halpin 2005). Many of these large-scale growers practice organic monocropping and are firmly in the grip of industrial appropriationism (Goodman *et al.* 1987), dependent on external inputs purchased from specialist suppliers in frank disregard for the ecological, philosophical, and ethical principles of sustainable agriculture (Rossett and Altieri 1997; Guthman 2004a).

In an early statement of the conventionalization thesis based on developments in California, Buck *et al.* (1997: 4, our emphasis) suggest that since "organic standards emphasise *inputs over processes*, conventional agribusiness firms are commandeering the 'organic' label and its associated price premiums by using only allowable inputs, but otherwise employing an industrial mode of agriculture which avoids the most costly sustainable agriculture practices." This argument echoes Buttel's (1993) insight that LISA-like technological approaches to organic practice can easily be integrated into the productivist model and would disempower holistic practitioners "farming in nature's image." In this analysis, regulatory capture of organic certification by agribusiness and its allies has marginalized progressive socio-ecological imaginaries. These earlier projects embraced not only agroecological practices, such as cover cropping, rotations, and biological pest control, but also non-exploitative labor relations and recognition of workers' civil rights, as Allen *et al.* (2003) make abundantly clear.

Although resisted by many activists, who favored the continuation of local, grassroots regulation, Tim Vos (2000 247) suggests that "at a certain moment in the mid-1980s ... the idea of instituting federal regulations for organic agriculture took hold, gaining influential advocates within the movement itself, and the legislative and political process began to go forward." This support had a twofold rationale that essentially arose as a *defensive* reaction to the sudden explosive growth and diversification of the organic market in the mid-1980s. Demand accelerated even more in 1990 with the food scare triggered by the TV program "60 Minutes" documenting the use of the carcinogenic growth-promoter, Alar, in apple cultivation. In these boom conditions, influential leaders were convinced that "a national standard needed to be established in order to alleviate consumer confusion about labelling ... (as) movement activists feared that opportunistic cheating ... was becoming more widespread" (ibid.: 247). Second, in a "climate of suspicion" that the USDA was "considering banning the term 'organic' altogether ... some leading members of the organic movement began lobbying members of congress, which ultimately led to the introduction by Senator Patrick Leahy of the Organic Foods Production Act (OFPA) into the 1990 Farm Bill" (ibid.: 247).

The OFPA initiated a consultative process by establishing a broadly-based civic advisory body, the National Organic Standards Board (NOSB), that was mandated to formulate the national standards or Rule and to make recommendations to the USDA. However, following this period of public consultation, when the provisions of USDA's National Organic Program Proposed Rule (NOPPR) were made public in December 1998 they were so far from the original

NOSB recommendations that they represented a travesty of organic production methods and its philosophic foundations. Furthermore, the NOPPR appeared to usurp the regulatory authority of NOSB to determine the synthetic materials on the National List. To the consternation of the organic movement, in what seemed to be a gratuitously provocative move by the USDA, the proposed National List of allowed inputs included genetically modified organisms, irradiation, and municipal sewage sludge or "biosolids" – the so-called "Big Three." As Tim Vos (2000: 247) observes, its language

> reads like a public repudiation of the organic tradition ... and seems almost openly condescending. It has been interpreted by organic activists as an apparent attempt to subvert the organic farming movement by calling into question its most basic premises.

As a result, the NOPPR drew heated opposition from the leadership and rank and file members of SAMs, not least concerned consumers encouraged to protest by natural food stores. In an impressive display of public participation, the USDA had received almost 300,000 comments by April 1998, a record number for a federal legislative proposal.

These protests against the "Big Three" ended in a resounding victory for grassroots mobilization, but the furore caused by their proposed inclusion effectively confined the debate on the NOPPR to the terrain of allowable inputs, drowning out more progressive voices and advocates of a *process* approach to organic certification (cf. Vos: 248–249). Furthermore, in his account of public hearings on the NOPPR, Vos (2000: 249, our emphasis) notes that many participants objected that the rule "disallows any additional language or label that differentiates a product *or claims higher standards than the generic USDA seal* ... (which) sets a virtual ceiling on organic standards (and other alternative farming practices)." This sense of profound disempowerment is captured at a public hearing on the NOPPR in Seattle, Washington, where one small farmer comments that "in reading through the proposed rule, I find it all garbage ... It does not allow us to take the high road. It caps the standards at the USDA level, which are very low" (ibid.: 249). These objections, reinforced by fears for the credibility of the "organic," have found an outlet in the food re-localization movement and its initiatives to go "beyond organic," as we discuss below. Despite these discontents, however, the NOSB has survived its contentious beginnings to provide an invaluable public forum and rostrum for the organic movement, resisting the sustained efforts of the Organic Trade Association, representing some 1,700 businesses, to abolish civic governance of the synthetic materials allowed on the National List, as we discuss in Chapter 8.

As we have already seen, the technocentric nature of federal regulation plays a vital causal role in the conventionalization thesis and is deployed by Buck *et al.* (1997: 8) to suggest that USDA certification underlies "a bifurcation among organic growers...," with this dualism being even more pronounced in marketing and distribution activities. As a result, small growers are relegated to the "economically marginal distribution channel" of direct marketing, exemplified by farmers' markets and CSAs, since they are unable "to meet the volume, timing and quality requirements of intermediaries, especially as retailing and wholesaling become increasingly integrated" (ibid.: 12–13). In their view, "local and direct marketing arrangements ... are effectively *default choices* for growers with few resources" (ibid.:14, our emphasis).

This influential early reading of California organic and its value as a generalizable model has been heavily scrutinized and qualified (cf. Guthman 2004a, 2004c). Thus Lockie and Halpin (2005) observe that the apparently straightforward theses of conventionalization and bifurcation take scale as the proxy for "industrial" and "artisanal" or "movement" producers and presume that this binary reflects radically different agroecological practices and social relations without interrogating the empirical, normative, and ideological assumptions that underpin this claim. Indeed, the thrust of Guthman's (2000, 2004a) empirical analysis of the agronomic and labor practices of organic growers in California and their ideological commitments is to demonstrate that this is patently *not* the case. Rather, her findings suggest that key variations in the use of agroecological farming practices are explained not by scale and grower commitment but "mostly ... (are) related to crop specificities and the availability of efficacious technologies and inputs to deal with crop-specific problems" (Guthman 2000: 265).

Without following this lead and disentangling these conflations of scale and practices empirically, as Lockie and Halpin (2005) also do in the Australian case, it is clearly unwarranted to *assume* that "artisanal" maps directly on to more progressive, movement-oriented politics and polycultural agroecological practices, and that "industrial" equates with both the economic behavioral and conservative ideological elements of the conventionalization thesis. This question of the *coherence* between different communities of practice and their modes of governance is explored further in Chapter 8.

Similar questions arise in populist agrarian discourses that portray re-localization in symbiotic terms, with the iconic "family farm" as the cement holding together "independent" rural communities to create the last line of defence against the corrosive effects of industrial food systems. Framed as "cultural brokers" who draw consumers and producers together in local "foodsheds," "the unexamined category of artisanal production ... introduces a range of implicit assumptions about the structural and ideological basis of food production" (Lockie and Halpin 2005: 287). Even though their social reproduction is inextricably enmeshed in capitalist market relations, it is implied "that smallholder agriculture is less commoditised and its proponents more committed to the preservation of community, tradition, environment and other non-market values" (Lockie and Halpin 2005: 287). These normative assumptions embedded in food re-localization discourse raise contentious questions about the room for maneuver producers can find within the agroindustrial dynamics of commodification processes, agricultural property markets and, notably in California, dependence on seasonal, undocumented, and typically non-unionized immigrant labor (cf. Guthman, 2004a). As we suggest below, such discursive strategies can be seen as a "boundary politics" to differentiate eco-social spaces where non-market values retain some weight in interactions between producers and their local customers (cf. Sage 2003; DuPuis and Block 2008).

Re-localizing food provisioning: positions and debates

Critiques of the conventionalization, mainstreaming, and bifurcation of organic agriculture, taken up later by popular writers (cf. Pollan 2001, 2006), reflect a growing scepticism in some academic circles about the transformative capacity of alternative food networks and their standing as precursors of an equitable, democratic, and socially just food system (cf. Allen 2004; Guthman 2004a). This disenchantment with the lack of concrete progress in addressing social justice goals extends to efforts to re-localize food provisioning based on direct market-ing, "Buy Local" campaigns, and regional labels of origin that increasingly have become the focus of food activism following the disappointments of federal organic regulation. In this section, we look at several controversies and debates generated by the strong differences now emerging in academic scholarship regarding the promise and progressive credentials of re-localization initiatives, extending our earlier discussion in Chapter 2.

We will suggest that these debates have brought marked political and analyt-ical cleavages out into the open. First, they have revealed a sharp divide between advocates of collective social change and those activists who would style them-selves as incrementalists and pragmatists (cf. Kloppenburg *et al.* 1996; Hassa-nein 2003; Hinrichs 2007). A second, related fault-line, exposed by the pointed exchanges in the farm-to-school (FTS) debate, has formed around the characteri-zation of alternative food institutions as exemplars of individualistic, market-based neoliberal ideologies of social change. In turn, these differences have drawn attention to the limitations of the concept and praxis of social justice in food re-localization projects, prompting demands that these be extended to embrace race, ethnicity, gender, and rights of citizenship rather than being con-fined mainly to economic equality.

As we have seen, Allen *et al.*'s (2003) seminal statement of these critiques contrasts the original progressive goals of AFNs, often still articulated in mission statements, with the priorities and concrete results of their current activities. In other words, the practices of new institutional forms of food re-localization fall significantly short as prototypes of more equitable food access and wider under-standings of social justice. Although often only implicit, this vein of "realism" in US scholarship is based on perceptions of AFNs as narrowly partisan, sectional-ist organizations whose fundamental, overarching aim is to ensure the economic viability and social reproduction of farmers and local food interests. This critical lens also has deconstructed contemporary expressions of the long tradition of ideological agrarianism, arguing that the framing of the family farm in neopopu-list rhetoric as the repository of community moral values can be read as a sec-tionalist discourse of economic livelihood.

Although it does not adopt a livelihoods perspective explicitly,[2] Patricia Allen's (2004) comprehensive social justice critique of sustainable agriculture and local food movements fits readily into this approach. That is, "alternative agrifood practices" serve almost exclusively to enhance the social reproduction of farmers. While acknowledging that alternative agrifood movements and institutions respect democratic principles, Allen (2004: 148, our emphasis) suggests that "*in other ways ... (these) ... reproduce a long-standing privileging of the priorities of only one group of those who labour in the agrifood sector – farmers.*" This leads to the broader charge that alternative agrifood movements tend "to privilege farmers as agents of change, the rightful beneficiaries of that change, and the savants who know what is to be done and how to do it. Most alternative agrifood advocates see farmers as the central figures" (ibid.: 150). As she demonstrates, this pre-eminence is strongly buttressed by the coherence of agrarian neopopulist "story lines" (Hajer 1995) articulated by alternative farming organizations, and their skill in constructing discourse coalitions to support family farm livelihoods in changing economic and political circumstances.

This emphasis on economic reproduction makes the simple but key point that the success of re-localization initiatives depends on the existence of markets that are sufficiently robust to generate producer rents that can sustain local farm livelihoods. In this context, Julie Guthman's (2004a) account of California organic agriculture can be interpreted within the framework of value chain analysis (Kaplinsky 2000), tracing the rise of the *organic* as a barrier to entry and source of economic rent and their subsequent competitive erosion as organic products enter the mainstream and are codified. She goes on to analyze the impacts of federal regulation on the distribution of these rents, the ensuing changes in industry structure and grower practices, and how these have undermined the agrarianist organic vision.

As Guthman (2004a) observes, direct marketing in local food systems developed in part as a response to these competitive dynamics. These initiatives, notably farmers' markets, CSAs, and "beyond organic" certification, can be seen as strategic attempts to re-establish barriers to entry to maintain producer rents, particularly by smaller producers excluded from the mainstream (Sligh and Christman 2003; Brown and Getz 2008a). Of course, in some instances, ethical and ideological motivations, such as food security for low-income households, also underpin these institutions, but their *sine qua non* is the capacity to sustain economically viable farm livelihoods (cf. Guthman *et al.* 2006).

The emphasis in LFNs on labels of origin and territorial certification to create and protect rent-rich activities also mirrors current practices in manufacturing sectors, which prioritize the more intangible elements in the value chain, such as brand names and other forms of intellectual property (Kaplinsky 2000: 127). The local, post-organic labelling and certification schemes now emerging in the USA are exemplified by the activities of Protected Harvest, a third-party certifying non-governmental organization (NGO), the national "Buy Fresh, Buy Local" campaign launched in 2002 by the FoodRoutes Network in partnership with local organizations (Allen and Hinrichs 2007), and new combined organic and fair trade labelling and certification systems being proposed by the Domestic Fair Trade Association and the Organic Consumers Association (Brown and Getz 2008a).

These initiatives represent and promote conventions of quality based on "narratives of place" and expressions of product identity formed by repeated social interaction between actors in localized markets (Ponte and Gibbon 2005: 13). However, although these "new economic spaces" arising at the intersection of place and livelihood may be glossed as local control, local development, or even "resistance" in LFN narratives, they embed very specific power dynamics and distributive patterns (cf. Hinrichs 2003; DuPuis and Goodman 2005).

These dynamics are central to the work of Patricia Allen, Julie Guthman and others that is now bringing unexamined dimensions of alternative food networks (AFNs) and re-localization projects under critical scrutiny. By focusing attention on the social relations of production and consumption and their embedded inequalities, these scholars interrogate the social meaning of constructs widely used in the analysis and advocacy of AFNs, such as "community," "foodshed," "resistance" to corporate food power, and "transformative potential" (cf. Kloppenburg *et al.* 1996; Hendrickson and Heffernan 2002; Lyson 2004; Feagan and Henderson 2009). In the following sections, we focus on the debates triggered by the analysis of FTS programs as forms of neoliberal governance, and calls to recognize and eradicate the raced nature or "whiteness" of re-localized, alternative food networks.

Re-localizing school food: the farm-to-school (FTS) debate

The background to this debate that flared like a meteor across rural and agro-food studies in 2006 concerns whether or not ethical consumption or other market-based movements can achieve meaningful social change in societies where neoliberalism is hegemonic. The agnostic position is that a consumer politics based on individual consumer choice reinforces the ideologies, subjectivities, and governmentalities of neoliberalization, notably by absolving the state of its regulatory functions and its universalistic commitments to the social welfare of its citizens. In the USA, this view has been propagated vigorously in recent work not only on FTS lunch programs (Allen and Guthman 2006) but also alternative food projects (Allen *et al.* 2003), combined organic and "labor" labelling initiatives (Guthman 2004a, 2004c, 2007; Brown and Getz 2008b), "Buy Local" schemes (Allen and Hinrichs 2007; Hinrichs and Allen 2008), agro-food activism in California (*Geoforum* 2008, Themed Issue), and the anti-GM movement (Roff 2007). Broadly speaking, this vein of critical analysis seeks to establish "how neoliberalisation incorporates, co-opts, constrains, and depletes activism" (Bondi and Laurie 2005: 395).

Allen and Guthman (2006: 408–409) argue that national school lunch public entitlement programs, for all their faults, such as the influence of commodity interests and outsourcing, "came with a certain guarantee of equal access" and "have been regulated with the broad public benefit in mind," reflecting their origins in the formative years of the welfare state. In contrast, FTS projects to localize school food provisioning, with support from private foundations and NGOs to supplement their access to core public funding, "have emerged in highly idiosyncratic ways and ... in the absence of standard, sustained support ... communities and (school) districts with the greatest resources – personal, political, financial – are most likely to develop into the most successful and longest-lasting programs" (ibid.: 408).

There certainly is a case to answer here and it is reasonable for Allen and Guthman (2006) to suggest that FTS activists focus their efforts on reforming the procurement practices institutionalized in the national school lunch program. Yet these activists would respond that this is indeed precisely the rationale for localized FTS initiatives working within existing institutions and whose demonstration effects are already evident in federal legislation and appropriations, as Allen and Guthman in fact recognize (ibid.: 405). The main bone of contention seems to be that FTS projects are local in scale, address national issues only indirectly "from the ground up," and are unevenly distributed geographically. This unevenness prompts Allen and Guthman (2006: 405) to argue "that this idiosyncratic site specificity is reflective of neoliberal approaches to providing services and is one of the key ways that FTS diverges from the uniform, national traditional school food program."

In other words, this divergence on the issue of strategic scale is used to support a much larger and far more contentious argument about the direction, forms and praxis of food politics. Thus Allen and Guthman (2006: 411) portray FTS programs as exemplars of neoliberalization, castigating their "embrace (of) consumer choice as the primary form of governance," their "framing ... in terms of the rights of children to have choices rather than ... rights to nutritious foods" and the assumption that "change will come through changes in taste and consumer education." This emphasis on consumer choice "reinforces the idea that social change is simply a matter of individual will rather than something that must be organized and struggled over in collectivities" (ibid.: 412; cf. Bernstein and Campling 2006b).

In short, Allen and Guthman (2006) categorically equate meaningful politics with collective action and national mass movements focused on the state. This reductive criterion is then used to discredit activist organizations that pursue market-based modalities of social change for their "collusion" in reproducing the logics of neoliberalization "as if they are ... naive victims of neoliberalism and/ or ingénues in their political encounters" (Bondi and Laurie 2005: 400). As Barnett (2005: 400) pointedly observes, this type of dismissive, reductionist critique is profoundly disempowering and reifies neoliberalism as a "hegemonic" project, while indulging the intellectual consolations of "unveiling the real workings of hegemonic ideologies in a characteristic gesture of revelation" (cf. Castree 2006).

However, if the state-centric politics of universalism that "Allen and Guthman seek to recover ... is ideologically and materially foreclosed" in the present conjuncture, as Alan Rudy (2006: 423) argues, then "what is to be done?"

In response, Kloppenburg and Hassanein (2006: 420) acknowledge "…that we are embedded in an overarching neoliberal structure that shapes and constrains action in various ways. At issue is what to do within these confines." In their view, this challenge is sidestepped by Allen and Guthman, for whom

> there appear to be few options worth pursuing. the power of capital is such that the actions of activists and advocates rebound to the "the almost inevitable production of neoliberal forms" (Allen and Guthman, 2006: 410) … perhaps because they can see no plausible alternatives themselves, they offer no concrete proposals for what might be done to change things.
>
> (Kloppenburg and Hassanein 2006: 420)

These polemics go to the heart of the tensions between those scholar-activists who doubt the capacity of myriad alternative food initiatives to coalesce into a mass movement that will build an equitable and socially just food system and others for whom the reconstruction of conventional food provisioning demands a pragmatic, incremental approach involving a gamut of different organizational forms, mechanisms, and instruments at diverse sites on multiple scales. Defending this incrementalist position, Kloppenburg and Hassanein (2006) argue that

> engagement with and action in the world is how we learn. The struggle illuminates more than it obscures. The FTS movement, like other progressive and emancipatory movements, does need to think more creatively about how to conceptualize the alternative institutional designs that will provide the vehicle for non-reformist reforms. But if what some call "real utopias" are to be achieved, it is the actions we actually *take* now that must prefigure and engender these possibilities.
>
> (Kloppenburg and Hassanein 2006: 420–421, original emphasis)

In these constrained political economic conditions, as Kloppenburg and Hassanein (2006) argue, political resistance is about making incremental gains "within" the consumerist model and its neoliberalized framings (cf. Bondi and Laurie 2005). The merits of political pragmatism are revealed in Sonnino's (2010: 37) case study of school food reform in two deprived areas in the UK, which supports her view that the interplay between localism and devolved (neoliberal) public food procurement "should be assessed in the concrete." She demonstrates that sustainable practices and more equitable outcomes can be achieved at this devolved scale and argues that "neo-liberal values and governance contexts do not necessarily disempower and immobilise the local" (ibid.: 28).

This emphasis on the diversity of local experience and the importance of "what works" on the ground also emerges in a recent analysis of two FTS programs in Pennsylvania (Bagdonis *et al.*: 2009). Of course, local success stories do not directly address the issue implicit in Allen and Guthman's (2006) agnosticism of whether and how these prefigurative forms can be moulded into a cohesive social movement to reconfigure conventional structures of food provisioning. By the same token, as we argued in Chapter 3, it is unacceptably reductive to propose that the only progressive food politics is a mass movement politics and to reject incremental market-based social change out-of-hand on ideological grounds.[3]

Appropriately, we turn from these macro-level issues to the rising disquiet about the *nature* of the social change promoted by food re-localization projects and calls for wider, more inclusive understandings of social justice.

The "whiteness" of food re-localization

Although now emerging in its own right as a specific theme of the US food re-localization literature, arguments that local networks of producers and consumers are predominantly "white" racialized projects in power, privilege, and ambition previously were subsumed by more general critiques of their social elitism, reactionary particularism and nativism (Allen 1999; Hinrichs 2000, 2003). Nevertheless, the ways in which sustainable agriculture mirrored its conventional counterpart in marginalizing people of color, as well as its related neglect of issues of hunger, class, gender, and the rights and living conditions of farm workers, were identified in several early studies (cf. Allen and Sachs 1991, 1993). More often, however, rather than being the explicit object of study, the "whiteness" of local direct marketing projects was imputed from empirical analyses of their demographic composition as defined by class, gender, income, and education (cf. Guthman 2008b). For example, a study undertaken in 2001 of the 14 CSAs established in the Central Coast region of California refers euphemistically to "the limited demographics" of the people participating in these networks (Perez *et al.* 2003: 4). Estimating that CSA members form a mere 0.2 percent of the region's population, the

> survey results suggest that these members are similar to other CSA shareholders nationwide: they tend to be European-American (90 per cent), highly educated, and middle-to-upper income (66 per cent have a household income of $60,000 or more). Members represent a relatively narrow proportion of the Central Coast population, where only 51 per cent of the people are European-American and the median income is below $45,000.
>
> (Perez *et al.* 2003: 2)

Although survey respondents were not asked about racial or ethnic identity, a similarly pronounced degree of socio-economic differentiation and an exclusive, largely European–American, demographic profile also emerge in Hinrichs and Kramer's (2002) study of a pseudonymous CSA, Midwest Growing. Furthermore, although ways were devised to subsidize the membership of lower-income households, these largely failed to

> broaden participation by other relevant components of class, such as occupational or educational status ... despite its conscious attention to social

inclusion, this local food system project remained a bastion of what we might call the educated, professional class.

(ibid.: 83–85)

The authors conclude that "the community features of this project in 1997 were driven most actively by middle-income, college-educated people, suggesting that the parameters, colors and tastes (to stretch the metaphor) of the CSA experience were set by this group" (Hinrichs and Kramer 2002: 85–86).

These studies amply document the economic, social, and ethnic difference and privilege firmly embedded in alternative food networks. Yet, as we suggested in Chapter 2, the "unmarked category" of whiteness and its naturalization in the institutional forms of these middle-class food politics is seldom called out explicitly. This situation is now changing as scholars focus directly on the racial character of the material practices and discourses of alternative food movements (Slocum 2006, 2007; Guthman 2008a, 2008b; see also Holloway 2007).

In one case study, Slocum (2006: 330) draws on her experience and participant observation of efforts to create a community food security coalition in Central New York to argue that these organizations "do not connect the dots among white privilege, institutionalized racism, their community work and the larger food system." She adds:

> these groups extol the virtues of community and self-sufficiency in a manner that obscures the racist, classist and gendered features of the food system, past and present. Preliminary findings reveal that community food strategizing, priority making and alliance building do not recognize or act on the intersections of race, class and gender in the food system.
>
> (Slocum 2006: 330)

Julie Guthman (2008b: 387) approaches the whiteness of alternative food spaces by exploring the cultural politics behind the rhetorical injunction: "If only people knew where their food comes from…," with its corollary that this knowledge "would necessarily trigger a desire for local, organic food and people would be willing to pay for it." Informed by the theoretical literature on the geography of race, she argues that such rhetoric and its cognates are

> illustrative of the color-blind mentalities and universalizing impulses often associated with whiteness. Moreover, much alternative food discourse hails a white subject to these spaces of alternative food practice and thus codes them as white. Insofar as this has a chilling effect on people of color, it not only works as an exclusionary practice, but *it also colors the character of food politics more broadly*.
>
> (Guthman 2008b: 388, our emphasis)

These mentalities and impulses are given substantive content by Guthman's (2008b) analysis of qualitative answers by managers of California CSAs and farmers' markets to questions about their "inclinations to implement practices that might encourage participation of people of color in these markets" (ibid.: 391). In summarizing these responses, she suggests that they

> represent various ways in which lack of knowledge or the "right" values is seen as the barrier to broader participation in alternative food institutions … [but] it is an old trope to attribute structural inequalities to cultural differences or lack of education … Specifically, managers portray their own values and aesthetics to be so obviously universal that those who do not share them are marked as other. These sorts of sensibilities are hallmarks of whiteness.
>
> (Guthman 2008b: 393)

Guthman (2008b: 395) concludes by arguing that these institutions "need to think about how to use the privileges of whiteness in antiracist practice" (cf. Slocum, 2007).

In a second paper covering much the same theoretical terrain, Guthman (2008a: 432) lists reasons why scholars and food security activists increasingly contend that alternative food movements have neglected the question of privilege and failed to address "the lack of access to and affordability of fresh, healthful food in communities of color," including those inhabiting urban "food deserts" (cf. Alkon, 2008). Supported by her own and co-authored research, Guthman (2008a: 431) argues that alternative food institutions "have tended to cater to relatively well-off consumers," are focused on securing "market opportunities and decent prices for farmers" and, "with some exceptions," are located in "areas of relative wealth … (that) for the most part … are also 'white' spaces." She also suggests that most FTS programs, "unless heavily subsidized by private foundations or the public sector … are developing in relatively white, affluent school districts" (cf. Allen 2008).

This indictment provides disturbing evidence of what we have called the social justice critique of AFNs and reflects deep-rooted disillusion with "the current menu of putatively transformative projects" and the "very limited politics of the possible" (Guthman 2008a: 437–442). It is also a rallying cry to food activists to recognize and extirpate the racism of privileged white food practice and its cultural codings. Research into the raced aspects of alternative food institutions and their discourse is just beginning but these first analyses expose the unacknowledged possessive investments in racial privilege and the narrow limits of their "emancipatory" claims of social justice. In the light of this discussion, Guthman (2008b: 388, our emphasis) is surely right to urge adoption "of *a less messianic approach* to food politics."

Mainstreaming alternative food

The corporate mainstreaming of organic and local food in the USA provides further reasons to accept this suggestion. In many respects, the US experience can be seen as the template for similar processes occurring in the UK and Western Europe. Each case has strong specificities, of course, but current developments in the USA nevertheless may foreshadow the future of organics and AFNs more generally.

We have already emphasized several leading features of US mainstreaming processes, notably the transfer of regulatory power from a hybrid private–public form to highly centralized federal control, the simplistic operational understanding of organic as input substitution, and the heightened vulnerability of barriers to entry and premium prices to competition and rent-seeking. These "rules of the game" favor large-scale specialist grower–shippers since organic monocropping and contract production dovetail seamlessly with conventional structures of processing and distribution, accentuating agricultural intensification and the concentration of organic production.

As Guthman (2004a: 166) documents in the case of California, economic rents have been "displaced elsewhere in the chain of provision or whittled away completely." Niche products that once enjoyed premium prices, such as salad mix or "yuppie chow," have been dramatically scaled-up and reduced to low-margin *commodity* status and market power is now concentrated in the hands of large grower–shippers in the Salinas Valley, such as Earthbound Farm/Natural Selection Foods, which has an estimated 74 percent share of the organic packaged salad market (Guthman 2003; Fromartz 2006). In turn, unable to resist these relentless downward pressures on prices, smaller-scale growers have turned to "yet to be commercialized crops" (Guthman 2004a: 167), such as heirloom tomatoes, direct selling or are going "beyond organic."

This consolidation and concentration of organic production structures has been accompanied and forcefully shaped by parallel tendencies in the sectors of organic processing and distribution. These downstream changes have been researched by RAFI-USA (Sligh and Christman 2003) and more recently by Philip Howard (2009a, 2009b). In their review of concentration in the US organic industry, Sligh and Christman (2003: 17) suggest that organic companies "have grown in two ways: initially by increasing markets for their product lines, especially during the explosive organic growth of the late 1990s; and secondarily by acquisition of other companies and brands." With the acceleration of this process of horizontal integration, pioneering organic firms, in turn, have themselves become targets for take-overs, mergers, and strategic alliances by the giants of conventional US and global food processing, such as General Mills, ConAgra, Cargill, Archer Daniel Midland, Kraft, Dean Foods, Kellog, and the French dairy conglomerate, Groupe Danone (Howard 2009a). Of course, in practice, these processes now are occurring simultaneously but it is useful here to separate them analytically.

Sligh and Christman (2003) use thumbnail company histories to illustrate these different growth trajectories. Thus the "largest organic farmers' cooperative in the US" – the Coulee Region Organic Produce Pool Cooperative based in Wisconsin – and its "Organic Valley" brand is taken as the exemplar of market expansion via the internal diversification of its product lines (ibid.: 18). The growth of market power by acquisition is illustrated by Earthbound Farm/Natural Selection Foods in the fresh produce sector and by the Hain-Celestial Group, whose aggressive buy-outs since the mid-1990s have created "the largest processor of organic and natural foods in the world" (ibid.: 17). Horizon Organic Dairy, on the other hand, has achieved its 70 percent share of the US organic milk market by combining the two growth strategies, diversifying from its initial product base in organic yogurt and buying out numerous local and regional dairies and their brands, including the Organic Cow of Vermont (ibid.: 19–20).

As we saw in Chapter 5, Horizon took over Rachel's Organic in the UK before suffering a similar fate in 2004 at the hands of Dean Foods, "the largest fluid milk producer in the United States and one of the five largest in the world" (Sligh and Christman 2003: 20). In activist circles and popular accounts, some agribusiness acquisitions have come to symbolize the organic movements' fall from grace and the concomitant rise of "Big Organic," such as the take-over by General Mills of Cascadian Farm/Small Planet Foods in 1999, followed by the marketing of an organic Cascadian Farm TV dinner (Pollan 2000, 2006), and Hain-Celestial's purchase in 2003 of Acirca and "the historic Walnut Acres brand" (Sligh and Christman 2003: 17).

As these examples illustrate, the huge conglomerates of US and global food processing have deployed classic industrial strategies of horizontal integration – take-overs, partnerships, and own-label organic product lines – to quickly gain market share in rapidly expanding sectors of organic food manufacturing. Investigating the repercussions of the USDA's draft national organic standard in 1997, Howard (2009a: 16) estimates that ten of the 30 largest North American food processing companies by sales value acquired organic brands and their marketing discourse in the following decade. Interestingly, "few of these giant processors identify these ties on product labels, a practice that is sometimes described as 'stealth ownership'" (Howard 2009b: 2; cf. Sligh and Christman 2003). Howard (2009a: 24–25) also notes "the explosion of private label or own-label brand organic foods … introduced by the top 30 supermarket chains." He goes on to observe that the "success of private label organics…" is stimulating these chains "to expand their offerings, with Loblaw and Safeway now carrying more than 300 different products" (Howard 2009a: 26). On this evidence, US supermarkets are rapidly catching up with their UK and European counterparts in their share of the retail market for organics.

These same strategies also have been widely used to consolidate the wholesale distribution of organic products to retail outlets in the USA. Sligh and Christman (2003: 24) identify United Natural Foods (UNF) and Tree of Life, the largest distributor of organic foods globally and owned by a Dutch conglomerate, Koninklijke Wessanen, as the "only two national distributors of natural and organic foods in the United States … these two giants handle about 80 per cent of the market." As an indication of how scale and industrial concentration can go hand-in-hand across sectors, "UNF links the largest organic food manufacturers – such as its largest single supplier Hain-Celestial – with retail outlets, such as its largest single buyer Whole Foods Market" (ibid.: 23).

These changes in market scale accompanying industry consolidation are constricting the marketing pathways open to smaller organic growers, including direct sales, such as those in farmers' markets and to local restaurants, as well as to retail food stores and cooperatives. Thus Sligh and Christman (2003: 23) see the latter as "a disappearing option relative to large retailers ... as large chains (such as Whole Foods Market) have shifted to regional warehouse systems for most of their purchasing." Scale and produce volume similarly are significant factors in the purchasing decisions of specialized grower–shippers, processors and distributors, making it increasingly likely that producers will be locked into contract production, mirroring conventional supply chain relationships, or be excluded from these pathways altogether (ibid.: 23). These same patterns of structural change characterized by the growing concentration of organic production and sales value, contract production, and the narrowing of direct marketing options are beginning to emerge in the UK, as we discussed in Chapter 5.

These dynamic, interactive tendencies have fuelled the expansion of organic food sales, with conventional supermarkets taking a growing share of this \$20 billion market, which has increased from less than 1 percent of total US food sales in 1998 to about 3 percent in 2006, according to estimates by the Organic Trade Association (Howard 2009a, 2009b). Although the three main marketing channels all expanded in this period, conventional supermarkets increased their market share at the expense of both natural and organic food stores and direct outlets, with farmers' markets and CSAs accounting for less than 5 percent of organic food sales (Howard 2009a).

The entry of Wal-Mart, the world's largest grocery chain, into this market in 2006 suggests that the shares of the two minority marketing channels will be eroded even more rapidly in the future. Wal-Mart's aim to limit the price differential between its organic and conventional product lines is a further reason to agree with Philip Howard (2009a: 27) that trends toward industrial concentration will be difficult to slow or reverse, particularly since "with the current USDA control of the term 'organic' ... regaining social movement influence over the industry appears unlikely."

The relatively faster growth of conventional supermarkets, now propelled by Wal-Mart, is particularly worrying news for natural and organic supermarket chains, which accounted for 48 percent of organic food sales as recently as the year 2000 (Sligh and Christman 2003: 25). Indeed, these authors represent these stores as the "core channel" of organic marketing and emphasize the "dominant presence" of Whole Foods Market (WFM) and Trader Joe's. With its leadership of the *organic* supermarket sector, WFM has become a dark and potent icon of "Industrial Organic" in popular and academic accounts (Pollan 2001, 2006; Fromertz 2006; Paumgarten 2010; Johnston 2008; Johnston *et al.* 2009). In part, this is because the rise of WFM, just one of many early pioneering companies in the 1980s, coincided with the reconfiguration of organics from a social movement with local roots into an industry serving the national market and beyond. Leaving a trail of takeovers, including the buy-out of major rival Wild Oats Marketplace for US\$565 million in 2008, WFM has grown from its Dallas origins in 1980 into a national chain of almost 300 stores with sales approaching US$8 billion (Paumgarten 2010). But WFM also owes its notoriety among organic activists to the libertarian, antiunion politics of its founder, John Mackey, an outspoken apologist for free-market organics.

Drawn by this iconic status and claims by WFM that consumers shopping at its stores can "make a difference," Josee Johnston (2008: 239) suggests that the mainstreaming of organics by WFM, Wal-Mart, and other chains "in part ... reflects how corporations have responded to the rise of ethical consumption activism, and its effective politicization of food issues in the public imagination." In an empirical case study of her local WFM supermarket, Johnston (2008: 250) challenges the implicit marketing message "that one can shop 'responsibly' at the store without sacrificing taste or convenience." Deploying discourse analysis, she deconstructs this framing of "ethical consumption as a seamless shopping experience" (ibid.: 250) to expose its contradictions – individual self-interest, inequality, and unsustainability – and reject the portrayal of WFM as an ethical actor.

In a subsequent paper, Johnston *et al.* (2009: 512) extend this analysis by mapping the contours of the "corporate-organic foodscape," where corporations use a "locally scaled" marketing esthetic, "particularly themes of food being rooted in a 'local' place, with connections to 'real' producers," to conceal their standard, unreconstructed production and distribution practices.[4] Drawing on a discourse and content analysis of the top 25 global food processors who have acquired smaller organic brands in North America, they suggest that this esthetic reflects the popularity of food democracy themes and "food democracy projects," such as farmers' markets, CSAs, and food box schemes. This analysis reveals

> the marketing of corporate organics consistently draws on food democracy images and narratives, connecting products to a particular locale and family farms, and highlighting a "personal" history behind the brand while obscuring spatially-dispersed commodity chains and centralized ownership structures.
>
> (Johnston *et al.* 2009: 512)

Their analytical framework recalls that of Callon and Wilkinson discussed in Chapter 5 as they reject "a simple story of co-optation ... (and) advocate a dialectical approach that recognizes a dynamic relationship between market actors and social movements ... and sees the corporate-organic foodscape as a hybrid entity drawing from movement themes while using market mechanisms" (Johnston *et al.* 2009: 511).

If we leave aside the strong similarities in North America and Western Europe of what Johnston *et al.* (2009: 510) call "the corporatization of organics," the really distinctive features of the US case spring from the institutional shift to centralized codification and inputs-based regulation. As we have emphasized, this change gave free rein to political lobbying, putting federal regulatory institutions under intense corporate pressure to weaken organic standards (Jaffee and Howard 2010). These strands weave the central thread that runs through the recent history of organics in the USA, from its activist origins and local roots to corporate mainstreaming and counter-movements going "beyond organic."

This degree of exposure to corporate influence sharply distinguishes the USA from the European Union (EU). Thus Gibbon (2008) finds that agribusiness has played a negligible role in the regulatory process, from enactment of the first EU regulation in 1991 and subsequently through a protracted cycle of amendment, repeal and its eventual replacement in 2007. In his view, "the main dynamic ... has been a techno-political rather than an economic one ... (and) essentially the same parties have been central to it throughout, namely, EU (and) Member State officials and experts and politicians from the organic movement" (ibid.: 578).

Some observers are in little doubt that industry has risen to a dominant position over the US regulatory process at the expense of the organic movement. Thus Jaffee and Howard (2010: 10) cite Guthman's (2004a: 312) observation that "the threat that agribusiness would dilute the meanings and practices of organic agriculture has in some respects already been borne out." In support, they add that "the major battles over organic standards arguably have already been fought and settled, although ... skirmishes continue." Others are more hopeful that the political strategies of civic market engagement can maintain the vitality of AFNs as both social movements and markets. These contrasting interpretations of the present conjuncture emphasize the critical salience of the ongoing struggles over civic participation in the governance of organics at local and national scales, as we see in the following two chapters.

Conclusion

This chapter has followed the trajectory of sustainable agriculture movements from the idealism and militancy of the back-to-the-land visionaries in the 1970s to the fringes of the mainstream in the 1980s and the institutionalization of an organic industry dominated by corporate interests and the giant globalized conglomerates of the industrial US food system. Buttressed by recent US scholarship, we have argued that the inputs-based federal codification of organics has played a pivotal role in this industrial reconfiguration and its accompanying trends of market consolidation and concentration as "Big Organic," subverting the original socio-ecological vision of sustainable, locally-scaled, and equitable food provisioning. In these circumstances, the "retreat" into localism and civic agriculture of direct selling, although widely lamented as a betrayal of its militant origins, can be seen as both a livelihood survival strategy and a way of retaining some latent capacity for change. However, analyses of the entrepreneurial ethos of these civic forms and the "whiteness" of food re-localization initiatives pointedly indicate that much reflexive political work needs to be done if this promise is to be credible.

The survival, to use the USDA lexicon, of "direct-to-consumer food marketing" against the forces of corporate mainstreaming can be interpreted analytically within the socio-technical regime perspective as "niche renewal" (Smith, 2006), as we saw in the UK case in Chapter 5. Yet there are few grounds to believe that this enclave of civic agriculture – farmers' markets, CSAs, farm-to-school programs, pick-your-own farms – poses any kind of competitive threat to the "incumbent" regime of "Industrial Organic," not to mention the wider conventional provisioning system. That said, the activism portrayed by the numerical proliferation of these forms is impressive. The number of farmers' markets has grown from around 100 in the 1960s to 5,274 in 2009, CSAs from a mere handful in the late 1980s to over 1,400 in 2010, and FTS programs from two in 1999–97, 400 in 2004 to 2,095 by 2009 (Martinez *et al.* 2010). Using Census of Agriculture data to chart the growth of "direct-to-consumer" marketing, the USDA (2009) estimates that sales rose by 105 percent in the decade 1997–2007, more than double the 48 percent increase in total agricultural sales in the same period.[5] Nevertheless, even when total US agricultural sales in 2007 are adjusted to a more comparable basis by excluding non-food crops and farm commodities not normally marketed directly to consumers, the share of direct sales is still only 0.8 percent.

While this base can be seen as a platform for further growth, the susceptibility of "local food" to corporate appropriation, as demonstrated by the marketing esthetic propagated by Wal-Mart, WFM, and others (Johnston *et al.* 2009), indicates that dimensions other than "place" alone, at least simply as provenance, are needed to establish its alterity (cf. DeLind 2011). This gives added importance to forging initiatives that heed Guthman's (2008a: 442) concern about "the very limited politics of the possible" and try to move beyond the cultural politics of white privilege and power. This will require wider, more inclusive conceptualizations of alterity that effectively embrace social justice, citizenship, and democratic governance, themes we will now explore in Chapters 8 and 9.

8 Resisting mainstreaming, maintaining alterity

Introduction

As we saw in the previous chapter, a heated political exchange occurred in the pages of the academic journal *Agriculture, Food and Human Values* following Patricia Allen and Julie Guthman's (2006) characterization of farm-to-school (FTS) programs as neoliberal. In essence, the authors contended that this attempt to change food provisioning in schools championed individual responsibility and private initiative at the expense of broader ideas of social justice. In response, Jack Kloppenburg and Neva Hassanein (2006: 417) defended FTS programs, arguing that recognition of such food movement initiatives is essential if we are to understand "the achievements and potentials of such approaches." For Kloppenburg and Hassanein, food movements are examples of governance fashioned from the ground up through experience, new practices, engagement, and experimentation. While they do not use the concept in their argument, discovering workable rules of governance through grassroots initiatives is a form of prefigurative politics, a way to try out new ways of living as a precursor to larger social change. To Guthman and Allen, on the other hand, the FTS emphasis on local governance reflected not change at all, just neoliberal politics as usual.

Our reflexive approach takes both points of view seriously, recognizing what alternative food network (AFN) politics has accomplished but also understanding the limitations of this approach to changing our food system. Simply said, the question of "what is to be done" about our food system is insufficient without a reflexive look at what the alternative food movement has done to try to change this system. Viewed through a reflexive lens, we see that AFNs are both representative of the current neoliberal political regime while also being an experiential, prefigurative social movement creating innovative processes of collective learning and grounded practices in particular places.

This chapter therefore extends the analysis of AFNs beyond praise and critique in hopes of providing a third approach to alternative food politics. Authors like Guthman and Allen may well consider our approach too laudatory while Kloppenburg and Hassanein may view it as not sufficiently appreciative of food movements. However, as we do academic work on food politics, we continually ask ourselves: "What is our work for?" By promoting this third, more reflexive, point of view, we hope that we can help pave the way to more effective, vibrant, and resilient AFN political strategies.

The following sections describe different ways in which alternative food movement actors have managed to establish alternative economies that maintain an existence separate from the mainstream economy. Through these new economies, people engage in alternative ways of living that resist mainstreaming. Taken alone, neither recognition nor critique is an adequate framework for understanding how food movement actors build these new economies. How then do we create a way of seeing alternative economies like AFNs as both strong forms of resistance as well as limited forms of politics?

To begin, we need to think about both of these approaches as models of economic life. Those who focus on the achievements of food movements take more of a network view of social life in which people make new worlds by coming together, not as communities bound by similar values but as actors with different, and sometimes contradictory interests who nevertheless end up working together to create their social and material worlds. Using several case studies, we will show how both networks and boundaries are part of what it takes to create new economies and new ways of life.

Those who take a more critical perspective focus on social interactions as ways in which people set themselves apart from others. People often accomplish this kind of "distinction" (Bourdieu 1984) through the creation of boundaries and territories. However, in the hands of elites these tools can help create new economies that preserve resources for the few, using these boundaries to increase their access to resources and privileges. Other times, these boundaries become the "weapons of the weak" (Scott 1985), that enable those who are less powerful to protect what they have.

Alternative economies are, therefore, powerful but not intrinsically egalitarian. They are unfixed; that is, they are always open to question. It is this "unfixedness" that makes it necessary to keep food systems in the larger, ongoing civic conversation about making a better world, with the "better" defined differently and reflexively by different people. It is the process of building this world despite our different worldviews that makes the dynamics of alternative economies so complex, and so powerful. We see reflexivity as the political practice that can make the power of alternative economies manifest in a more inclusive and livable world.

As we have argued throughout this book, AFNs that focus on forging communities of shared values are intrinsically inegalitarian, because they are based in a single worldview. We describe this kind of politics as romantic, recalling the romantic movements of the nineteenth century, where change is seen in didactic terms as based on a personal conversion to new values and then changing others' consciousnesses to become members of a community that shares these values.

Romantic alternative food movements attempt to implement modes of governance rooted in the values and ideals inherent in these communitarian visions and values. From the communitarian perspective, boundaries – such as the

"100-mile diet" and "buy fresh, buy local" – and networks – such as local food policy organizations – define and refine shared ideals. However, a politics based on shared values tends to discourage participatory deliberation and different points of view and can instead increase inequality. Here boundaries and networks tend to create an "us" vs. "them" situation in which "us" becomes an exclusive group that works to preserve a distinct status over others. Once eating gets mixed up with morality, shared food values become superior moral precepts. The fixedness of communitarian approaches to food systems undermines the civic nature of alternative economies and, as described in Chapter 7, makes these alternative systems susceptible to capture by the mainstream economy.

There are, however, reflexive ways to utilize boundary and network tactics to create a more egalitarian politics that goes beyond the romantic. Reflexivity is anti-romantic; that is, it is a politics that rejects the idea that there is such thing as an ideal life. A reflexive approach is dry-eyed about ideals and understands that each set of values derives from a specific social context. This does not mean the ideals are wrong; they are part of how people define themselves: one's ideals are the passions that motivate and inspire. However, idealism becomes dogmatism when idealists impose their ideals on others and insist that these represent the right way, the perfect way of life. According to the romantic way of thinking, social change is prescriptive and involves teaching others "the way" to live. A reflexive, unromantic approach to alternative food systems respects multiple definitions of the good life and good eating. Practitioners of reflexive food politics work to change the world via public engagement through civic modes that embrace different perspectives and worldviews without imposing a "frame" of "shared values" on others.

An academic perspective that sidesteps both recognition and critique of AFNs serves to move alternative food politics in this more reflexive direction. From this perspective, we ask: "How do more egalitarian alternative economies get made? How were such economies created and maintained in the past? What is the future of these economies?" We begin with a historical example to shed light on the existence of past alternative economies, ones that existed long before current food movement efforts. In this first case study, we consider the artisanal grass-fed dairy system and its century of coexistence with a more intensive and industrialized dairy system in order to understand how alternative economies persisted in the past, even in the face of mainstreaming. Inspired by an earlier form of local civic politics, the establishment of local market milksheds early in the twentieth century provides an interesting perspective on the use of boundary-making as a tool to maintain a necessary separation between two economic systems.

Next, we look at contemporary cases to show that alternative food economies persist not just by keeping economies apart but also by bringing people together around the making of material life and the design of specific objects in the world (Hess 2007). Organic food regulation is an alternative mode of governance that requires public, civic processes of group reflection for the resolution of boundary and design conflicts. The second and third case studies therefore show how the

National Organic Standards Board (NOSB) resolved two such boundary and design conflicts in organic regulation. These case studies provide contemporary examples of processes that maintain boundaries between conventional food systems and alternatives to the mainstream,[1] and illustrate the ways in which alternative food system actors have successfully used both boundary-making and object design in the creation of alternative economies (Shove *et al.* 2007).

Creating the protective boundaries of milksheds

Developed in the 1930s, milk market order legislation exemplified local boundary protection at work. At that time, two dairy production systems coexisted: market milk dairies that fed cows in the barn, and smaller "hill farms," often more remote from the cities. Known as "summer dairies," these smaller, lower-cost grass-feeding operations supplied mainly local, artisanal cheese and butter plants, whereas market milk dairies were part of food chains connected to larger milk processors. However, during the spring flush, grass-fed milk tended to "leak" from the artisanal dairy system into the higher-value fluid market milk system, undercutting prices and the ability of barn-fed dairy farmers to cover their higher production costs. In the late 1930s, Congress facilitated the continued existence of both systems by setting guidelines to define specific bounded "milksheds" that separated fluid milk and manufacturing milk production. These guidelines created a new economic boundary between the two types of dairying.

This territorialization of dairy production could not have happened without a civic politics. Fluid milk producers convinced federal officials to use their powers to define the boundaries between local fluid milksheds around cities and the outlying cheese-producing regions. Market order boundaries therefore protected both the artisanal and the industrial milk system, enabling both economies to coexist through much of the twentieth century.

The boundary between the two systems eventually eroded once the fluid milk system was in a position to compete and gain control of markets. Eventually, industrial processors began making cheese and other dairy products around cities as a way to absorb surpluses arising in the fluid milk market. Pasture-based dairy agroecological practices remained only in those areas distant from the fluid milk market – such as parts of Wisconsin and Minnesota.

The politics of boundary struggles between these two agroecological systems illustrates the complexity of localization as a strategy to protect alternative economic systems from mainstreaming. Strong boundaries between the two types of dairy economies eliminated or tempered competition between them. This enabled them to coexist with different agroecologies and farming "styles," and gave them the freedom to participate in different food chains, from producer to consumer. Scholars of "market segmentation" who have studied other industries, like textiles (Piore and Sabel 1984), argue that strongly segmented markets can shield certain market participants from competition and create conditions for the existence of multiple economies. Boundaries are therefore powerful governance tools that can constrain or allow particular forms of economic behavior in a society. As is evidenced by this example, localized boundary maintenance does not necessarily create more just, healthy, or sustainable food systems. However, boundaries do protect certain economic actors, and their system and practices, in particular contexts, which makes them strong tools to maintain alternative economies (Hess 2007).

In the next section, we will examine how AFN actors have forged modes of governance that allow people to come together and create new, alternative objects such as organic food. We will look at two case studies of decisions made by the NOSB, a civic body mandated to make recommendations about the design of organic food. NOSB recommendations led to the allowance of certain non-organic substances in organic food and to the definition of organic milk as milk from grass-fed cows. Both of these decisions involved a more civic mode of governance, in which the object – organic food – was the product of consumer–producer dialogue about what this object should be.

Networks and the design of objects

One way in which people come together is through the design of objects. When Langdon Winner asked many decades ago, "do objects have politics?" he brought the question of politics to material life (Winner 1980). Since then, a number of scholars, primarily in science and technology studies, have focused on objects and the politics of their making. For example, Bijker and colleagues (1989) note that today's common bicycle is the product of many years of contested design battles, with producers responding to pressure from various user groups to make the bicycle that would serve user needs (Bijker *et al.* 1989). Law and Callon (1992) and Callon (1992) studied the ongoing design, and eventual failure, of a particular fighter plane project, demonstrating that the designers could not satisfy the various agendas of user groups supporting the project. Feminist scholars have shown how particular producer and user interests made a now common cancer screening – the pap smear – the "right tool for the job" (Casper and Clarke 1998). These cases indicate that design of the material world of objects comes about through resolving political contests between producers and users, as different groups with different goals seek to influence the shape – and re-shape – of particular objects.

In other words, politics is inherent in the design process, as a particular set of network actors undertakes to shape a nascent object into a stable form. From this perspective, social change involves networks of people coming together to design new forms of material life. People who look at social change in these terms tend to reject the notion of creating boundaries as a strategy, and instead think of networks as "topologies" (Mol and Law 1994) or "fields" (Rheinberger 1997) in which design politics can take place. The community around a particular economy is not about exclusion but about how different interests come together and interact around the design of a particular object or project, forming network links and flows between them (Marston *et al.* 2005).

Scholars who take a network perspective likewise do not treat boundary maintenance as a tool to protect the existence of an alternative network. Instead they are more interested in what they call "boundary objects" (Bowker and Star 2000), where objects and concepts transcend the agendas of particular networks and, in so doing, bring them together.[2] Rather than seeing networks as coming together based on shared values, actors collaborate despite differences in values and worldview. It is the contested object that causes them to come together, and each network approaches the object with its own distinct interests and values. The object of concern is then shaped by the various actors, sometimes sharing values and goals and sometimes in contestation. Scholars looking at collaborative networks often focus on interdisciplinary networks of scientists working together. They examine the way a dispersed set of worldviews and interests develops into a collaborative political alliance – an actor network – that moves objects into new forms (Pinch and Bijker 1984; Oudshoorn and Pinch 2003).

David Hess (2007) has studied alternative political networks and how they create "alternative" objects that are linked to social movements. He distinguishes "technology and product-oriented" social movements, in which business interests form alliances to design and implement alternative technologies and economies, from anti-technology social movements, such as those against genetically modified organisms (GMOs) and biotechnology. The technology/product-oriented and anti-technology movements are clearly linked, but each has its own political practices and concerns. To some extent, they conflict in their opinions of what objects should look like, but they complement each other because they cause design change and move design practice in particular directions.

Hess (2007) describes the process of contestation over the form of particular objects as "object conflicts" and has argued that the world of organic food is a space in which object conflicts regularly take place. In his history of the organic food movement, Hess (2005) uses a historical perspective to demonstrate that conflicts over the definition of "organic" have changed and evolved over time in tandem with organic social movements. Organic conflicts began with an emphasis on reducing pesticide use in the 1940s, moved to resistance against a globalized, industrial corporate agriculture in the 1990s, and now focus on current issues of health and social justice. In other words, the civic discourse around organic food has changed in the last decades and, as a result, the food has changed as well. Hess also shows how these technology and product-oriented social movements tend to bifurcate. This bifurcation exists today between "complementary" objects, such as Whole Foods supermarkets, which work within the mainstream system, and "radical" objects, such as food coops, that seek to maintain their existence as an alternative system. Unlike Guthman (2004a) and other critics, Hess maintains that the development of complementary and radical organic objects can occur in tandem and that the existence of complementary objects does not necessarily lead to the conventionalization of radical alternatives.

Object conflict: two case studies

The idea of an object conflict is a productive point of departure from which to understand and analyze conflicts over organic standards that have taken place in the last decade. Conflicts over particular organic products illustrate the civic discussion around the meaning and maintenance of alterity in the face of mainstreaming threats. For example, the NOSB, a standing citizen advisory board comprised of farmers, consumers, certifiers, scientists, industry representatives, environmentalists, and other stakeholders, provides a national arena for civic conversation over the design of organic food. The NOSB hears testimony and makes recommendations about what should and should not be legally defined as organic. The United States Department of Agriculture (USDA) then makes decisions, taking NOSB recommendations into account, or not (Vos 2000).

The NOSB recently made recommendations over two controversial issues concerning the design of organic food. First, Arthur Harvey, a Maine blueberry farmer, sued the USDA, charging that it did not follow the legislative mandates in the Organic Foods Production Act (OFPA). Second, members of the organic dairy industry complained about the implementation of organic rules related to pasture-grazing in organic milk. The rest of this chapter will show how the NOSB resolved these issues by both creating clear boundaries between organic and non-organic objects and by bringing user interests together in the design of organic food.

The Harvey case[3]

Arthur Harvey, an organic product grower, certifier, and consumer, filed a lawsuit against the USDA in 2002 (*Harvey* v. *Veneman* 2002). He alleged that USDA's organic standards (Final Rule 2000) contained provisions that were not consistent with the OFPA. The OFPA mandated the creation of the National Organic Program (NOP), charged with implementing national standards for organic production.[4] It also charged the NOP with creating the NOSB, an advisory board to make recommendations concerning the design of these standards. In particular, the NOSB has been responsible for recommending which non-organic substances should be included on the National List of Allowed and Prohibited Substances in organic production ("The National List").

In *Harvey* v. *Veneman*, Arthur Harvey, an organic blueberry producer, charged that the NOP was not implementing the national standards consistent with the OFPA. While his challenge involved a number of different aspects of the NOP rules, we will focus here on two counts: First, Harvey argued successfully that the OFPA specifically prohibited the use of any *synthetic* substances in organic food processing, while the USDA had allowed processors to use some synthetic substances (such as pectin and baking powder). Second, he charged that the USDA left inadequate time for NOSB notice, comment and periodic review when it decided to allow *non-organic* substances onto the National List of Allowed and Prohibited Substances. This treatment of synthetic and non-organic substances, Harvey charged, was in violation of OFPA-established procedures. The appeals court agreed with Harvey on these points and the NOSB therefore began a process of notice and review for determining which synthetic and non-organic substances could be used as ingredients accounting for up to 5 percent of a food labeled "organic."

As processed food corporations entered the organic market, the National List became an arena of contention between large industrial organic producers, who favored flexible standards in determining what could be added into food labeled "organic," and smaller organic farmers and processors, who wanted to maintain strict standards. Increasingly the large corporations petitioned for the inclusion of various processing additives and non-organic products when these were not "commercially available" in organic form. Harvey argued that processors could interpret USDA regulations as a "blanket exemption" that would allow them to use non-organic substances in certified organic products if they were "not commercially available in organic form" (*Harvey* v. *Veneman* 2005). He claimed that "commercial unavailability" was not a valid reason to allow individual organic processors to use a given non-organic substance. The court agreed with Harvey and issued a declaratory judgment mandating clearer USDA guidelines and greater restrictions on the use of non-organic agricultural products. The court demanded that the USDA follow the OFPA-established procedure of submitting each non-organic ingredient to the NOSB for review. The NOSB would then review each ingredient and make recommendations as to which substances should be included on the National List.

Harvey also charged that allowing synthetics into production contradicted the plain language of the OFPA stating that certified processing operations "shall not, with respect to any agricultural product ... add any synthetic ingredient during the processing or any postharvest handling of the product" (7 USC 6501–6523, 1990). The court agreed, finding that the law explicitly forbade the introduction of synthetic additives into production processes. The USDA was therefore pressed to resolve the inconsistencies between the OFPA (no synthetics allowed) and the standards in practice (some synthetics used).

These rulings disturbed leading organic market actors, including USDA regulators, the NOSB, the Organic Trade Association (OTA), certifiers, farmers and consumers represented by the growing Organic Consumers Association (OCA). Each of these actors had different opinions concerning various aspects of the decision. Interested parties disagreed on whether to amend the OFPA in Congress or to resolve the conflict through the NOSB deliberation process (see Cummins 2005).

The OTA, representing the interests of larger organic processors (many of whom are large food corporations, like Kraft, that have purchased a number of smaller organic processors), responded by going directly to Congress and lobbying members to draft legislation that would reverse parts of the Harvey ruling, which the OTA described as a "court ruling [that] found a few technical inconsistencies between the 1990 organic law and the final standards" (OTA 2005a). OTA lobbyists slipped their legislation, now broadly known as the "OTA Rider," into the Agriculture Appropriations Act of 2006 at the last minute without deliberation, and it was signed into law on November 10, 2005. With no opportunity for public input or broad Congressional debate, the OTA Rider altered the OFPA to the extent that the court's decision on synthetic substances in organic was overturned. In effect, this eliminated the basis of Harvey's argument against the inclusion of synthetic substances on the National List, thereby permitting their inclusion, subject to regulatory review.

In addition, the OTA Rider authorized the Secretary of Agriculture to bypass public review and use expedited procedures for the inclusion of non-organic agricultural substances on the National List in the event of an "emergency." The OTA Rider legislation, in this case, defined "emergency" as an economic emergency for large-scale processors that were unable to source adequate organic inputs. Since these "emergency procedures" are still in effect and have yet to be defined or used, they left open the possibility of adding substances to the National List without a public review process. Thus not only has the OTA Rider nullified Harvey's successful court challenge to the use of synthetic materials in organic foods processing (count three), but has also potentially changed the USDA mode of governance of the boundary between organic and non-organic commodities.[5] Those who claim that the lengthy process of public review causes economic "market disruption" can now override the OFPA's original intent, which was to legitimize standards between producers and consumers through public deliberation. Should large-scale processors successfully claim economic market disruption – inability to compete and profit in the alternative food economy – they can continue to conventionalize AFNs. As we will see in Chapter 9, industrial agriculture actors design modes of governance that legitimize market disruption claims. Alternative economies are then forced to function according to the profit logics of industrial economies, rather than by alternative logics that leave industrial actors out of the alternative network.

This political maneuvering by the OTA was widely condemned by consumers and many producers. Producers recognized that these actions could jeopardize the legitimacy of the organic industry. Alternative economies rely on valuations other than price; they are "civic" in that they must include deliberative civic processes to craft legitimate public decision making (Lyson 2004). In alternative economies, civic discourse, legitimacy, and added value are intrinsically intertwined. Therefore, the lack of public deliberation was a threat to the survival of this alternative economy.

The Harvey lawsuit was one of a set of challenges to the lack of public deliberation in "National List" procedures. An earlier challenge had come from the former chairman of the NOSB, Jim Riddle. In 2004, he had written an open letter to the Secretary of Agriculture asking the NOP to restore "due process" in standards setting (Riddle 2004: 1). Citing several examples, Riddle argued that the USDA had insufficiently incorporated NOSB and public input when deciding whether certain substances should be placed on the National List. Riddle (2004: 1) wrote: "I urge you to ensure that the NOP actually do what it is supposed to do under the OFPA and require that proper administrative procedures be followed when new policies, letters, and directives are formulated and new technical advisory panels are contracted."

During the legal contests around the Harvey case, organic food and agriculture groups, called "Friends of the Court," also supported NOSB's important role in maintaining a deliberative mode of governance. They argued that the

OTA Rider threatened the survival of the organic industry by undermining the status of the NOSB as an arena for ongoing civic discussion about the object conflicts around organic food. In the media, the OCA decried the OTA Rider as a "sneak attack" and saw the authorization of "emergency procedures" as an explicit challenge to an inclusive, alternative mode of governance. Organic food actors such as these understood that alternative food economies rely on civic, deliberative processes. In the Harvey case, the court decision in favor of Harvey compelled the USDA to follow the "due process" that Riddle argued for in his letter (*Harvey* v. *Veneman* 2005). The Harvey controversy therefore illustrates a struggle between those who define organic by using a mainstream standard – a set of fixed rules – and those who define of organic through the deliberation of an alternative and civic mode of governance.

In an interview with a Maine newspaper, Harvey characterized his challenge to the USDA as a move to benefit small farmers rather than the "factory farmers" who were rapidly entering the organic market for the profits associated with the high value produce (Cavallaro 2002).[6] Harvey argued that less powerful actors who adhere to an ecological, process-oriented definition of organic should have a stronger voice in the market's construction. The OTA, on the other hand, supported a more standards-based industrial logic of mainstream organic actors. Rather than seeing organic as operating under a different mode of governance founded on civic processes, the OTA viewed the "alternative" organic market and the larger "conventional market" as inherent competitors for the consumer's dollar: "Market led growth is only possible if organic farmers and processors compete on level ground with non-organic farmers and processors" (OTA 2005b). OTA executive director, Katherine DiMatteo, argued that the standards should not be opened up to public debate. Instead they should "remain intact to minimize disruption and marketplace confusion and to protect the growing marketplace for organic farmers" (ibid.).

Consequently, following the Harvey rulings, the OTA worked on what they called "a discreet, very limited, legislative action" that would restore their fixed notion of "strong organic standards" (OTA 2005c). While this action did not incorporate public perspectives, their lobbying was certainly supported by some very key political figures. According to the *New York Times* (Warner 2005: 1), Abigail Blunt, wife of then interim House majority leader, Representative Roy Blunt, lobbied on behalf of Altria (an umbrella corporation then including Kraft Foods and Phillip Morris, parent companies of a number of organic food processing firms) and alongside the OTA to get the OTA Rider passed. Though this was not necessarily the sole reason for the passage of the OTA Rider, Blunt's lobbying helped stifle Congressional debate by moving the organic discussion into a closed-door committee meeting. Iowa Democratic Senator Tom Harkin decried the committee's action on the Senate floor:

> behind closed doors and without a single debate, the Organic Foods Production Act was amended at the behest of large food processors without the benefit of the organic community reaching a compromise. To rush

provisions into the law that have not been properly vetted, that fail to close loopholes, and that do not reflect a consensus, only undermines the integrity of the National Organic Program.

(quoted in OTA Members/Arnold *et al.*/Center for Food Safety 2005: 3)

For large food businesses, organic is a niche market, regulated by a fixed and stable set of standards, and designed to create a kind of extra-profitable "brand." Yet, for smaller and less profit-driven actors in the organic economy, the survival of organic as a distinct alternative market represents more than a profitable brand. The organic economy's list of actors is long and their needs are varied and at times dissonant. Organic producers seek to maintain their livelihoods, consumers seek to maintain their health, and social movement actors seek to maintain equality, environmental sustainability, and community resilience. The struggle to define organic shows that its survival as an alternative economy concerns more than just money. It is about maintaining the legitimacy of an alternative economy, the credibility of which depends on open deliberative civic processes in which these alternative food system actors address whether and how the market will meet these extra-economic needs. The OTA tried to obscure the necessity of a deliberative mode of governance for organic, failing to recognize that the only way for alternative economies to maintain their legitimacy is through ongoing civic discourse.

These examples show that the creation of legitimate organic products entails ongoing negotiation of organic modes of governance. The boundaries that separate a legitimate organic object from a non-organic or synthetic object and the process by which the object is defined (under what jurisdiction: legislative, legal court, or government agency?) and who is allowed to participate in civic deliberation over the organic object (consumers? processors? farmers?) will remain under public scrutiny and subject to civic discussion (see also Ingram 2007). The design of the organic object has therefore occurred in multiple jurisdictions, including the USDA, court cases, Congress, and the media. At the level of agency jurisdiction, the NOSB has represented many actors in the organic food system: farmers, certifiers, processors, retailers, scientists, environmental advocates, and consumers. It has power to shape the definition of the market boundary through recommendations as to what to include on The National List. Yet, the power of the NOSB has also been continually contested. As we have seen, frustrated in the courts and the powers these confirmed for the NOSB, the OTA turned to Congress to pursue its interests. The OTA Rider most clearly demonstrates industrial actors' rejection of civic modes of governance under NOSB processes.

Yet, NOSB's role as an arena of civic discussion in the design of organic objects remains. In response to these legislative and court actions, the USDA called for a public comment period and NOSB hearings on industry petitions to include substances on the National List. Accordingly, the NOSB held hearings and examined technical data and public comments to recommend the addition or exclusion of particular non-organic substances on the National List.[7] Organic food system stakeholders large and small participated in both the comment period and at the NOSB public hearings. Rather than using the "emergency power" given to them by the OTA Rider, the USDA initiated civic deliberations over the National List, a move that was central to maintaining the legitimacy of the organic boundary object.

As a result, industrial organic actors were forced into public deliberative discussion of extra-economic factors besides their concern about competition with the conventional food sector. Organic processors went so far as to request the inclusion of over 600 non-organic minor ingredients on the National List. In order to quickly move through the National List review process for each of the 600 substances, and meet legislated deadlines, the USDA initially determined that a public comment period of a mere seven days would be sufficient. In this one week, the USDA received approximately 1,250 public comments, many expressing concern about the less-inclusive mode of governance demonstrated by the extremely short public comment period. In response, the USDA extended the public comment period to 60 days. During this period the USDA received petitions from industry wishing to continue the use of non-organic agricultural products and collected public comments on the in/exclusion of these ingredients. The NOSB also held public hearings where interested individuals had the opportunity to speak.

The following case illustrates how the NOSB hearings provided a civic arena in which producers and users contested and designed new forms of organic objects.

Inulin/fructooligosaccharides (FOS)

The dialogue in the public hearings around the inclusion of FOS provides an understanding of the process of deliberative public review that the NOSB carries out to determine whether or not to include particular substances on the National List. This case of object conflict reveals that the design of organic objects involves both boundary work and the design of organic substances as material objects. Additionally, the analysis of the micropolitics of object design and boundary maintenance shows how governance processes can create or damage consumer trust. This case study demonstrates that the maintenance of a legitimate organic object depends upon a mode of governance that allows for public negotiation of the boundary around it and the design of the material organic object.

FOS are non-organic/additive nutraceutical ingredients that, according to advocates, increase calcium absorption when consumed in yogurt. In her testimony, nutritionist Coni Francis of Stoneyfield Farms painted dark pictures about the downside of removing FOS from organic food. In her gloomy warning against its removal, she alluded to the prevalence of digestive diseases in the USA, as well as calcium deficiency among children: "Now, if we think that those of us who are in our 50s and 60s are looking at an issue with osteoporosis, I am very frightened about what's going to happen when these children reach their

30s and 40s" (Francis 2007). This calcium deficiency story, so familiar to milk industry promoters, was consistently used to justify the inclusion of this substance on the National List.

Including nutraceuticals that are not organic on the National List because of their health benefits did not go uncontested. NOSB Member, Jim Riddle, distinguished organic foods from "functional foods" and nutraceuticals, arguing that the consumption of organic food is not based on the idea of a medical "cure" for pathological eating practices. He commented: "I think that the side effects of a poor diet are not necessarily the responsibility of organic agriculture" (Riddle 2007). Functional foods and nutraceuticals often play a role similar to medicine in claims of preventing or correcting the effects of poor nutrition. Organic food system actors, on the other hand, represent organic food as an inherently healthy alternative to non-organic food rather than a corrective or preventative. This disagreement brings to light the contest between a more functional and nutraceutical definition of "good food" – one that brings consumer health and curative powers – and the definition of organic, which has focused on a definition of "good food" based on agroecological production processes.

In the end, the NOSB recommended adding FOS to the National List, based on claims of its functional health benefits. As the interim final rule states: "The inclusion of this non-digestible carbohydrate is thought to promote a more favorable intestinal microbial composition which may be beneficial to human health" (7 CFR Pt. 205). But using health claims as a basis to add a non-organic ingredient to the National List clearly involves a significant rupture of boundaries. In this case, a "functional food/nutraceutical" input definition of healthy food overrode the definition of organic food – food created through pesticide-free, sustainable agricultural growing processes. Other exempted ingredients, such as non-organic fish oil, were also allowed because their ingestion increases omega-3 fatty acids in the product. In this case, the functionality of the food as an input has trumped the more agroecological, process-based definition of health commonly associated with the organic object.

While this may seem like a defeat of organic philosophy in the creation of the organic object, it also reflects how civic processes create objects based on different, and somewhat contradictory, interests and worldviews. Whether the NOSB will continue to allow non-organic substances on the National List because of their status as functional foods is uncertain. Because the substances on the National List must undergo periodic review, the conflict between those who see good food in functional terms and those who see good food as coming from agroecological processes will, hopefully, continue to be a matter of public debate.

The NOSB hearings on the National List also challenged the boundary between synthetic and non-synthetic ingredients. At the March 2007 NOSB public hearings, NOP personnel noted that they began their review of ingredients by trying to make a strong definitional distinction between synthetic and non-synthetic ingredients, as well as between agricultural and non-agricultural ingredients. Eventually NOP staff abandoned their efforts to clearly define each of these categories. Consequently the boundaries between synthetic versus non-synthetic and agricultural versus non-agricultural are somewhat ambiguous and NOSB board members remain unsure of how to classify certain ingredients. For example, one board member asked regarding flavorings:

> When does an organic essence stop being agricultural, after how many cuts and splits? You know, where do we draw a line and so we'll be looking for industry expertise such as yours to help us determine when does something stop being agricultural and become non-agricultural through the distillation process.
>
> (NOSB Hearings 2007: 349)

These definitional struggles blurred "natural" and "artificial," categories that gave rise to the birth of the organic movement (Vos 2000), adding yet another layer of complexity to boundary struggles between organic and non-organic. Tellingly, the NOSB member asked industry members to define the boundary between the natural and the artificial because he believed industry had the scientific knowledge necessary to make the distinction. However, as we will see in Chapter 9, boundary definitions require processes and decision making that extend beyond conventional scientific sources of knowledge.

The discussion of FOS also raised the question of other potential effects of the ingredient. As the discussion developed, it surfaced that FOS is not only a nutraceutical but also a preservative. As the Stoneyfield Farm representative noted, they had decided to use FOS as an ingredient

> because it improves the product, as far as now we are shipping more product further. And when it gets handled, you have more whey separation, and so forth. And because of the added benefit of the calcium absorption. With so much competition on the shelves right now, in natural and in mass market, we are much deeper into mass market now, that having, if you have choice between two markets and one says on it, increases calcium absorption by 30%, that's a very important claim for our, you know, it's an important attribute for our consumers.
>
> (NOSB Hearings, March 27, 2007: 71)

In this comment, we see the link between the competitive advantage of longer-lasting produce that preservatives offer to mass markets, combined with nutraceutical health claims. In this way, the design of organic food as an object is restructured according to different network interests.

The organic pasture rule

As we discussed earlier, two kinds of dairy systems coexisted for much of the twentieth century following Congressional legislation in 1937 introducing milk market orders, boundary-setting rules that separated barn-fed and grass-fed operations and the prices they received. However, since the 1980s, the rise in consumer demand for organic milk has created a market for an entirely new object: milk that is created through a seasonal ecology – grass feeding – yet is produced year-round. Grass-fed fluid milk is a product of network design, in which users (milk consumers) insist on a particular production system that fits their idea of traditional farm agroecologies. But this consumer interest in grass-fed fluid milk draws on an imaginary production tradition. Pasture-fed dairying has been based on the ecology of grass which, in most regions, is a seasonal crop. Therefore, most grass-based dairy systems have produced milk seasonally for manufactured products, such as cheese and butter.

The struggle over the role of grass-feeding in organic milk production has been contentious ever since the establishment of the NOP. During the controversy, the trade journal, *Progressive Dairymen*, noted that the organic dairy industry "has been working to secure clarification on organic milk production standards for years."[8] The USDA's notice of rule-making stated that its action was "a result of comments, complaints and noncompliances."[9] As a result, the USDA proposed a Livestock Access to Pasture Rule in October, 2008 and finalized that rule in February, 2010.

This rule mandates that cows producing certified organic milk must have a specific percentage of pasture-grazed grass as part of their diet. The two years of negotiations between the time of the proposed and the final rule brought most actors into agreement as to minimum national pasture requirements of 30 percent dry matter and at least 120 days of pasture-feeding a year. But two parties: Straus Family Creamery and Aurora Dairies, took strong positions against the rule during the negotiation process.

The Straus–Aurora joint lobbying effort represents the ultimate example of a strange bedfellow scenario in the politics of organic. Albert Straus is one of the pioneers of organic dairying. Straus Family Creamery, which milks a few hundred cows and buys milk from two other small local dairies, was the first certified organic dairy company west of the Mississippi. Straus' local Bay Area following is intense, and a number of his consumers submitted comments to the USDA on the proposed rule defending Straus' position. Straus does not take issue with the fact that the ruling asks for a certain percentage of a cow's diet to come from pasturing *per se*. However, his dairy is located in the Marin Agricultural Land Trust, and regulated by the California Regional Water Quality Control Board, whose water and land use quality requirements he must observe. Cows on pasture during the California Coast's severe winter rainstorms can be tough on watersheds, due to agricultural runoff. Straus's operation exists in this fragile environment only because he works closely with local environmental officials on agricultural runoff issues.

Straus' political partner in this contest produces milk at the other end of the organic spectrum. Aurora Dairy, which operates mega-dairy farms in semi-arid Texas and Colorado environments, supplies the milk for many large supermarket private organic milk brands, such as Wal-Mart, Safeway, and Costco. Grazing thousands of cows is clearly a headache, and in the past Aurora has violated organic dairy rules to such an extent that even the Bush Administration's lenient USDA was compelled to take action: in 2007 it sanctioned Aurora for violating the existing and loophole-ridden pasture requirements. Own-label supermarket brands seek to make organic milk more affordable, and Aurora is an ideal supplier for such supermarkets. To maintain low-cost operations, Aurora and other large-scale organic dairies have tended to shift the focus away from defining organic milk as grass-fed and toward a "pesticide-free" feeding standard. However, in so doing, these large-scale dairies have challenged the prevailing grass-fed consumer definition of organic milk.

Woes unite foes, and Straus and Aurora found themselves lobbying together, with Aurora clearly benefiting from Straus' higher reputation. The agroecological and industrial organic dairy operations found themselves on the same side of the fence as they argued the same point: pasture is complicated and costly and pasture rules should be more flexible. Yet they did so for different reasons and based on different agroecological organic dairy farming systems.

"A sustainable agro-ecosystem maintains the resource base upon which it depends," states agroecologist Steve Gliessman (Gliessman 2006), meaning that the operations of a sustainable agricultural production system must fit the context of its particular bioregion. This is certainly true when it comes to pasture; the number of days of available green grass in any one place depends on soil, water, weather, elevation, and a number of other factors that vary from one region to the next. Yet the proposed organic rule set a national floor for the amount of pasturing that an organic cow must have, regardless of a region's agroecological circumstances. In the end, there was some flexibility in the final ruling. The number of days and amount of dry matter consumed in pasturing were set as a floor, with dairies submitting plans indicating how much pasture was possible in their particular environment. Yet, ironically, this flexibility, which Straus argued for in order to deal with local environmental issues, opened a door for Aurora to minimize its grass-feeding and thereby to survive and compete – on price – with more agroecological dairy farms.

The argument for lower pasture requirements did not go unchallenged. Mark Kastel, of Cornucopia Institute, a non-profit with a mission "to empower farmers – partnered with consumers – in support of ecologically produced local, organic and authentic food" lumped Straus and Aurora together as villains in his critique of "rogue farms." The Cornucopia website questioned Straus' motives. For example, a San Joaquin Valley organic dairy farmer, who sells his milk to a competitor of Straus, alleged on the Cornucopia website that Straus's cows see a lot less pasture than is required under the rule.[10]

Cornucopia's critique of Straus' operations focused on the farm's methane digester, a technology that allows manure to be converted into energy without polluting local water sources. Cornucopia has presented the digester as evidence that Straus does not pasture his cows. Collecting manure to fuel the system is only possible when cows are confined, and fueling the digester is the only way to pay for the system (Wright 2001). Albert Straus denied that the methane digester proved that he was not pasturing his cows, defending his position on the

Straus Family Creamery website. He asked customers to imagine the challenges he must meet to fulfill local land trust and Regional Water Quality District agreements in the ecologically-sensitive and heavily open-space-regulated Marin Headlands. Ironically, the San Joaquin farmer who criticized Straus pastures his cows on irrigated alfalfa, a much more intensive form of agricultural land use, where "pasture" is more of a crop, a very different agroecology from the one in which Straus produces his milk: the ecologically-sensitive and recreational-intensive spaces of the Marin Headlands. The irony here is that this more intensive form of organic dairying, based on irrigated alfalfa, is better suited to the pasture requirements of the National Organic Rule. Yet, it is not in line with the consumer imaginaries of grass-fed milk in which cows could run on sylvan hills. Both pasture-based and irrigated alfalfa-based organic dairies serve the Bay Area milk market. But the irrigated alfalfa dairy and Straus' pasture-based dairy represent two agroecologically different systems, with very different ecological challenges and opportunities.

Once again, as with FOS, consumer demand shaped the meaning of organic milk in the contests over the design of this object. The USDA noted several times in the rulemaking process that their definition of organic milk was the product of various consumer surveys, such as one by Whole Foods, showing that consumers identified organic dairy production with grass-fed cows.[11] Unlike most conventional commodities, consumers had power over how organic milk was produced and thereby influenced the design of organic production systems, even if, in the end, these systems do not always fulfill consumer imaginaries of what this production system should look like.

Why do consumers have this power over the design of organic foods? Because consumers must perceive organic products as legitimate to be willing to pay a premium for them, especially when organic milk is often twice the price of conventional milk. They want to know that their imaginaries of organic milk production coincide with how that milk is actually produced. They continue to challenge the organic rules to live up to their production imaginaries. Producers, for their part, are thereby forced to design agroecologies not just to fit local environmental resources but also to meet consumers' pastoral fantasies. Fulfilling these fantasies is part of what is necessary to maintain organic milk prices. Correspondingly, if customers begin to feel that some organic companies are not meeting their production imaginaries, they become less willing to pay more for the organic product.

Yet, in many ways, the consumer imaginary of grass-fed milk is unrealistic. Consumers see grass-fed milk production as a return to nature when it is in fact a system that has never before existed in nature. As noted above, grass-fed dairying is intrinsically seasonal – that is, unless production is based on ecologically-intensive feed crop ecologies, such as irrigated alfalfa, often situated in areas with scarce water resources, such as California's Central Valley. Ironically, to meet consumer fantasies about the nature of organic milk, producers end up scrambling to conform to consumer imaginaries rather than working to create agroecological processes that are sustainable and make sense in terms of natural limits. Furthermore, as the Straus–Aurora political partnership demonstrated, national rules for grass-fed organic dairying ignore differences in bioregional agroecologies, creating a one-size-fits-all organic practice when in fact organic milk production is intrinsically linked to local agroecologies.

Consumers who want producers to fulfill their pastoral and personal health imaginaries should know that the notion of "consumer trust" in civic economies is agroecologically tricky. In civic markets, producers are sometimes forced to try to meet unrealistic consumer demands in terms of ecology, locality, animals, farmer-to-farmer, farmer-to-consumer, and farmer-to-government relationships. If consumers want the organic system to continue, they must understand the agroecologies behind organic production as reality and not as romantic pastoral imaginaries. If consumers really want to know "where their food comes from" – and if they want their milk produced through truly agroecological practices – they need to realize that agroecologies are contextual, and part of that context is political. Yet, the fact that organic farmers and organic consumers sometimes have conflicting political interests is likely to make producers fear an open, civic discourse with consumers about organic production agroecologies.

By the same token, if organic dairy farmers want to maintain their market, honest and trustworthy communication with consumers about their local contexts will be their best marketing tool. Media accounts express consumer suspicion that "the corporate takeover of organics, some say, is eroding the ethic that many take for granted as they throw an organic zucchini into the grocery cart" (*St Louis Post-Dispatch*, March 4, 2007: A1; see also Sassatelli and Scott 2001). Producers and consumers will need to be reflexive about their political interests and the degree to which they share production imaginaries. The organic food system as an alternative economy will only survive if consumers and producers participate in a public deliberative process that openly acknowledges these political and agroecological complexities.

Conclusion: the civic-ness of scales and networks

The Harvey and Pasture Rule cases provide strong examples of why the creation of a legitimate, or credible, organic object requires "civic" modes of governance. Modes of governance created through open, deliberative, public processes are most likely to take account of the different kinds of justice discussed in Chapter 2. Civic markets, like alternative fair trade markets, often foment contentious public political debate about setting market boundaries. The discourse may cover any number of questions regarding the design of alternative economies, including: who can participate in the market and who cannot; who is "conventional" and who is "alternative"; is the alternative defined by local politics (Napa wines or French *terroir*), process (such as biodynamics), object conflicts (such as what is artificial or natural), consumer productive imaginaries (such as their idea that cows should be on pasture), or actual market venue (such as who gets space in the local farmers' market or the local food co-op). In this way, boundary-setting is open to question and competition. While these contested categories may not elicit perfect solutions, the underlying roots of the struggles and contradictions become clear and open to public conversation.

The notion of a certain kind of credibility is necessary to civic processes – forging a legitimacy that creates economic value. This kind of economic legitimacy combines economic ideas about value with Weber's idea of legitimate authority and substantive action (Weber 1947). This concept indicates that consumers will participate in alternative economies if they believe that the object is legitimately alternative; that is, it carries a certain non-exchange value not present in the conventional form. If the consumer believes claims that the object is legitimately better, they will pay the higher, premium price for that object. Boundary work therefore is a kind of creation of "distinction" (Bourdieu, 1984) that gives credibility and authority to the object created and to the creator of that object. Without the creation of boundaries for alternative commodities, consumers will eventually lose trust in the producers of those commodities and cease to pay the premiums that maintain these alternative economies. In effect, alternative economies, including organics, would cease to exist without civic processes that establish the legitimacy of alternatives. Yet, the creation of that legitimacy involves civic struggles over the design of the organic object through ongoing civic discussion.

Needless to say, both the mainstream organic sector and the alternative organic market depend on the legitimacy value of organic to survive. Those in the alternative market might argue that mainstream organic depends on the legitimacy value of the alternative system and in some ways "preys" on that value-creation. Yet, the civic-ness of political debate over the design of organic food precludes the complete takeover of organic production systems by mainstream producers. In the debate about boundary setting and the creation of the organic object, the industrial food processors tend to support a static, un-civic standards-based definition of organic. These companies discourage civic, democratic practices around the maintenance of an organic food sector, undermining open, deliberative processes of organic alternative market creation. But, as soon as organic production systems become entirely conventional, they will be completely de-legitimized and consumers will cease to pay more for these products. Without accepted claims to legitimacy as a truly alternative object, the organic food production system would disappear. As the Harvey case study has shown, this anti-democratic definition of organic threatens the credibility of this alternative market, and therefore threatens the long-term viability of organic food systems.

In other words, the organic movement will never just be about the creation of standards. It will always be a civic conversation, with and between consumers, farmers, food businesses, and regulatory institutions. Once we admit that fact, sustainable farming systems will have a much better chance of meeting and overcoming the credibility challenge from those who seek to undermine this alternative food system.

9 Sustainable agriculture as knowing and growing

Introduction

Even if boundary making and network designing does succeed in creating viable and persistent alternative economies, the question remains: "Why is the existence of alternative economies important?" After all, these economies seldom account for more than a few percentage points of a mainstream world economy that remains mired in unsustainable production systems. In this chapter, we will argue that alternative economies, and the ability to create new economies that can survive outside of the mainstream, are more important than the percentages of economic life they represent. They are important because we will not be able to solve the problems of the future without them. We are on a new economic horizon where we will need to think about and create environmentally sustainable forms of economic life. Alternative economies may provide valuable signposts to the creation of a more sustainable mainstream economic future.

Mainstream economies in their current form will not be able to meet our sustainability challenges. Increasingly, we will need to take the lessons that we have learned in alternative economic systems as ways of thinking about changes to the mainstream economic system. While we need to use boundaries to protect alternative systems from cooptation into the mainstream, we will increasingly need to make hybrid systems to incorporate more alternative practices into the mainstream, thereby realizing the prefigurative potentials of alternative systems. However, to do this, we must create networks not only to design things differently, but also to think differently about how we go about designing our material world.

This chapter therefore will look at the making of one specific alternative commodity – organic strawberries – as requiring not just new boundaries and new design networks but also new ways of knowing. Organic strawberry production is a very tiny part of the entire food production system. However, it provides an example of how one small network of actors has struggled to know one alternative form of production in the face of a stubbornly unchanging conventional production system. In particular, this case will illustrate how difficult it is to go about *knowing* sustainable processes. We will show that the problem is not simply about people being stuck in blinkered ways of thinking – paradigms.

People who are attempting to create more sustainable ways of producing food sometimes work in the realization that their ways of knowing limit the options for creating a sustainable future.

However, this case makes clear that actors seeking to design new objects also are hampered by their embedded position in particular knowledge institutions. Knowledge institutions, in this case, scientific research centers and universities, base their legitimacy on particular knowledge production practices as the legitimate creation of "truth" (Stassart and Jamar 2008; Vanloqueren and Baret 2009). Yet the grower clients of these institutions work within a different set of knowledge practices that do not necessarily follow the same rules. This case will show how a set of scientists and growers struggled to create a source of knowledge that melded both kinds of knowledge practices. Over a period of two years, scientists from the University of California (UC) and the United States Department of Agriculture (USDA) met with California organic strawberry growers to assemble organic strawberry production knowledge into a manual that would be published by UC. We will follow parts of their conversations in meetings, supplemented by interviews with the scientists involved, to show how these organic system production actors went about trying to know how to grow organic strawberries. By looking closely at their struggles, we will learn a great deal about how we will need to produce knowledge in the future, if we are to build a more sustainable mainstream economy.

This case study will show that creating sustainable knowledge is tricky; the kinds of knowledge that are or are not legitimate differ according to your position in the knowledge production system. In particular, sustainable production systems challenge the legitimacy of mainstream scientific knowledge in ways that mainstream scientists who study organic agriculture are now beginning to acknowledge. Certainly, the scientists in the conversations below were strongly aware of *what* they did not know and *how* they did not know it. Yet, these scientists were also aware of the restrictions as to which knowledge was legitimate within their institution. The organic growers, for their part, see, share and produce knowledge in ways that are not legitimate in mainstream scientific institutions. They have their own way of producing and legitimizing knowledge that is not always compatible with scientific modes of production but "does not need to be justified" by those modes.

Knowledge about sustainable production processes is particularly tricky because sustainability is not a fixed concept, a set of ideals to which we can turn. As we described in Chapter 8, organic production is only possible if it exists in a civic economy of public discourse about what is, and what is not, organic. Sustainability is a broader concept but is equally civic in nature. Ever since the word "sustainability" entered popular parlance, people have been struggling to define this concept. How do we know what practices and products are sustainable? As we have argued throughout this book, the answer is not to set up an ideal, fixed idea of what alternative or sustainable economies should look like. Instead, we must answer the "how" question, to think about alternative economies as indefinable but ongoing civic processes which require democratic participation of all economic actors in order to survive in a mainstream world. To do this will require "unfixing" knowledge as well.

If (when) the mainstream world becomes environmentally, economically and politically untenable, an understanding of how to build these unfixed forms of economic life will be vital. This chapter is essentially a search for clues as to where we might turn. We therefore examine the following conversations between farmers and scientists about how to grow organic strawberries because we have a much larger project in mind than whether or not organic strawberry production systems are possible. We see the conversations about the creation of an organic strawberry production manual as giving us hints about how we will need to go about knowing, and creating new, sustainable economies in the future. In particular, rather than answering the unanswerable question: "What is a sustainable economy?," we will have to meet the larger question: "How do we know sustainability?" This chapter therefore seeks to throw light on the "how" question.

Sustainability and ways of knowing

Ongoing discussions about the nature of sustainability reflect broader transformations in the conceptualization of knowledge and understanding. What is the nature of knowledge? This question is increasingly important in scholarly conversations, and scholars have made numerous attempts to characterize knowledge in more comprehensive ways that go beyond technical, scientific knowledge. Some argue that scientific ways of knowing produce the only knowledge, "the way things are that is independent of us and our beliefs about it – an *objective* fact of the matter" (Boghossian 2007). This formal kind of knowledge is independent of context and cumulative, characterized by an accumulation of technical information (see, for example, Jamison and Lau, 1982). Gibbons *et al.* (1994) characterize this kind of knowing as "Mode 1." Mode 1 science begins from the position that scientific discoveries are disciplinary, investigator-driven and rely on formal, traditional science training that seeks to capture and portray universal truths as stable and objective.

The realization that sustainability is an intrinsically indefinable concept coincides with increasing recognition that knowledge production comes about in many different ways. Conversations about knowledge have shifted focus from technical information as intransigent truth to an examination of the knowledge practices – "modes" – we use to create new understanding (Barad 2007). New work in the fields of technological innovation, philosophy of science, business management, and education have therefore accepted that there are ways of producing new knowledge other than science, often called "Mode 2" knowledges. These ways of knowing are contingent on context and exist only insofar as they are "in use" – that is, applied through subjective experience and intersubjective practices. Gibbons *et al.* (1994) describe Mode 2 knowledge as that which is always in the making. From this perspective, the production of Mode 2 sustainable knowledge is experiential, processual, social, tacit, contextual, transdisciplinary, open to different worldviews, collaborative, practice-based, and informal (Martens 2006; Luks and Seibenhuner 2007; Brand and Karvonen 2007). Thought processes are not seen as separate from other forms of human activity but rather as integral to them. This leads to a more dynamic and de-centered view of knowledge creation as emergent and historically "contextualized," based in practice and distributed across agents and artifacts (Shove *et al.* 2007; Gibbons *et al.* 1994).

From this perspective, sustainable innovations – technologies and practices – will come from collaborative design processes that involve actors with different worldviews working together. They will not come from defining a single vision of sustainability, like a "sustainability blueprint" or a plan. Instead, it will involve different "how" processes in which people work through their differences as they make decisions about the design of a product or practice. For example, Nonaka and Peltokorpi (2006) studied engineers involved in designing the batteries, brakes, and electrical systems of the Toyota Prius and found that they had very different ontological viewpoints about how the world worked. Nevertheless, these engineers succeeded by adopting particular group processes that enabled them to work with their differences as they made decisions. In the end, these engineers designed a better car without creating a single, shared view of the "best" car.

As with other kinds of design, how people work to design a more sustainable agricultural production system is contingent on recognizing and working with different ways of knowing. A manual, however, like a blueprint or a plan, is a fixed technical document. This case study considers how university researchers put together such a manual while recognizing and attempting to work with more contextual kinds of knowledge.

Our case study observations are based on notes from a series of meetings in which university extension and research staff worked with organic growers to collect currently known information about producing organic strawberries. Interviews with key scientific research staff supplement and expand upon the meeting notes. The strawberry manual meetings focused on the creation of a template of instructions for interested current and potential organic strawberry growers. Creating the template involved determining and listing the crucial activities that growers should undertake during each month over the lifecycle of the strawberry crop.

The organic strawberry manual case study involves a closer look at how tensions between ways of knowing are contested and negotiated within this system, and between this system and the dominant system of strawberry growing in the region: the chemically intensive conventional system. In both the "what counts" and "how do we know" discussions below, we ask: Who is expected to know? Where is this knowledge born and how is it disseminated to others? Why is it important to know other ways of growing strawberries? What do we know and what do we not know about growing organic strawberries? If the knowledge requires the transformation of the production system, does it still count as knowledge? How do we negotiate competing sets of knowledges, and what happens when these ways of knowing are irreconcilable?

Vignette 1: what counts as knowledge?

Exactly what is known about organic strawberry growing is impossible to dis_
cuss without referring to the 2005 ban on methyl bromide that was added to the
1987 Montreal Protocol on Substances the Deplete the Ozone Layer in 1990.
Methyl bromide is a soil fumigant that has been central to the intensive, and
highly profitable, strawberry system that has existed for several decades on the
California coast. The advent of methyl bromide soil fumigation transformed
strawberries from a seasonal and regional fruit, often grown on local truck farms
around most cities, to an intensive, long-season monocrop, grown primarily in a
few California coastal valleys. Fumigated strawberry systems, along with new
cultivars developed by the UC to take full advantage of the nearly year-long
springtime weather in this region, enabled California coastal growers to produce
strawberries – and consumers to eat them – over much of the year. Fumigation
permitted months of high yields, enabling California strawberry growers to dominate markets with cheaper fruit most of the year, thereby out-competing local
truck farms even in spring (Wells 1996). The density, intensity, and length of
production in this system exposes this delicate fruit to a long list of diseases and
pests. This type of production system is only possible if the soil is fumigated to
make a kind of "clean room" for the crop. With the rise of the fumigated production system, therefore, the national market share of California strawberries rose
from 58 percent in 1970 (Bertelsen 1995: 24) to 83 percent in 2000 (National
Agricultural Statistics Service 2002).

Methyl bromide, however, also depletes ozone and was banned in 2005 by
international treaty, the Montreal Protocol. This treaty was signed originally to ban
chlorofluorocarbons and is widely considered the most successful environmental
treaty in existence (Benedick 1998). Unlike chlorofluorocarbons, the "drop in"
alternative to methyl bromide has proven to be elusive. The strawberry manual
meetings occurred as the deadline for the ban was becoming critical and alternatives were uncertain. Since 1995, more than $300 million has been spent on
research for alternatives to methyl bromide (Reifsnyder 2010). However, most of
this research money has gone to chemical alternatives that simply replace this
fumigant with another, so that the system remains intact. Yet, unlike many other
sectors that have discovered workable alternatives to methyl bromide, the strawberry industry has remained dependent on this chemical (Reifsnyder 2010).

Also, unlike chlorofluorocarbons, the Montreal Protocol rules for methyl
bromide were negotiated later in the treaty process and allow for exemptions due
to economic impacts. Industries that can demonstrate significant economic disruption due to the ban can request "critical use exemptions" (Gareau and DuPuis
2009). Therefore, while calling for more government research funding for alternatives, conventional strawberry growers depend upon – and continue to lobby
for – critical use exemptions. Although the amount allowable diminishes from
year to year, in essence these exemptions allow growers to continue to use
methyl bromide to grow strawberries, because there is no "technically reasonable alternative" that does not cause economic disruption to the industry.

The group of scientists and farmers who met to create an organic strawberry production manual were interested in showing that organic was a viable alternative to the system of growing strawberries with methyl bromide. Organic strawberry growers and researchers claim that we *do* know how to grow strawberries, and the creation of a manual sought to prove this to be the case. In the media, in extension and organic non-profit research communications, and in academic journal articles, organic strawberry growers and researchers present more sustainable alternatives as viable options. They highlight organic strawberries growing on their university test plots as proof that it works and studies showing strong profit margins from organic strawberries.

On the other hand, even those involved in looking for alternatives have realized that it is difficult to create a system that is as intensive and profitable as the methyl bromide-based system. "The products that we have just don't do the job," one industry representative stated.[1] When talking about the conventional vs. the organic system, even those who research organic alternatives will often also agree with conventional growers that "no one" knows how to grow strawberries organically in a way that can promise the profits of the conventional system.

But is knowing the organic system a matter of creating *more* knowledge? Is the problem with organic that there is not enough scientific research accumulated to give us an alternative system? What if what we do know does not count? What counts in strawberry production is not just whether or not you can grow strawberries without methyl bromide – after all, strawberries were grown for centuries without it – but whether you can grow them as profitably as you can with methyl bromide. As one researcher put it: "There are no biological methods available that growers think are economically doable.... There are bio-controls, and we work with all those that are commercially available, but nothing works as well as methyl bromide. Nothing works as well." For example, growers and researchers know that intercropping strawberries with broccoli cuts down on soil pathogens, performing to some extent the fumigation work done by methyl bromide (Subbarao *et al.* 2007). However, it is evident that this system is less profitable. According to UC Davis cost of production studies, broccoli brings in a return of approximately $680 per acre while strawberries bring in approximately $2,600 per acre. Farmers are therefore unwilling to devote a growing season to broccoli, especially if they are paying land rents that are based on the per acre returns expected from strawberry production.

In addition, strawberry production, while being one of the most profitable, is also one of the most risky production systems of the high-value California specialty crops (Wells 1996). Methyl bromide lowers this risk by shifting the risk burden on to those who are protected by the ozone layer. Organic growing has greater risk because maintaining agroecological balances is trickier than "nuking" with chemicals, threatening the high investment per acre necessary to grow this crop. Organic growers therefore take on more risk. In the world of conventional strawberry growing, any knowledge that involves more risk is not really knowledge.

Therefore, researchers and organic growers "know" how to grow organic strawberries, but they do not know how to grow them in a way that provides the kind of relative guarantee – the type of super-productivity, super-reliability and super-profit – that the current chemical-based system provides, and which is required for growers to meet the high cost of strawberry growing. Because the year-round strawberry system is dependent on certain weather conditions found only in certain parts of the California coast, this land is scarce and rents expensive. While the practices of intercropping and rotating land in and out of strawberries are known to resolve soil pathogen problems, they lower profits. The Montreal Protocol allows the continuation of methyl bromide use if an industry experiences significant "economic disruption" without it. Thus knowing how to produce strawberries without methyl bromide means knowing how to produce the same profits with the alternatives. As a result, organic practices are given no room in the pool of knowledge of conventional strawberry growers. "Knowing" in this case therefore involves knowing within the context of the current conventional strawberry system, current risk sharing, and the rules of an international environmental treaty.

Efforts to reduce methyl bromide use have included using other chemicals in the fumigant mix, such as chloropicrin and telone. The California Department of Natural Resources recently approved the use of methyl iodide as a replacement for methyl bromide. These alternatives do not deplete ozone. However, once again, they do shift risk burdens. Methyl iodide is particularly problematic by most scientists' assessments. While, like methyl bromide, it is acutely toxic – in fact more so – methyl iodide does not move quickly into the upper atmosphere, away from where it is applied.[2] This makes it more risky in terms of local exposure. A turn to methyl iodide for fumigation therefore shifts risks from the ozone layer to local environments and people (Erikson 2008).[3]

Researchers hoped that creating a manual would give growers all the information necessary to produce organic strawberries profitably and reliably enough to count as "real" knowledge. They also wanted to demonstrate that organic strawberries practices point to viable alternatives that would alleviate the need for extensions to the use of methyl bromide.

Scientists studying sustainable alternatives to conventional strawberries therefore build upon current conventional production systems. They recognize that growers know these systems best. "Conventional farmers have expertise I don't have," one researcher stated. "I use them as a tool for information so we can design a system." Conventional farmers have the practice-based knowledge of day-to-day production in the California coast context that research and extension personnel lack. However, by building on conventional methods researchers are "locked in" to the conventional system.

Yet, these scientists recognize the limitations of this perspective and try to understand issues beyond the lock-in of intensive strawberry production. One problem here, over and above the economic context, is posed by nature: organic strawberry growing requires environmental factors and processes that differ from conventional production. For example, organic production practices often involve rotation and the finding of pest-predator balances, and it is not simply a question of replacing chemical inputs with organic inputs. This introduces another kind of "unknown" besides lack of profitability. There is also the "unknown" in terms of practices not known, and perhaps not knowable according to formal, scientific ways of knowing, the kind of tacit forms of knowing described by Gibbons *et al.* (1994) as "Mode 2" knowledge.

In the following discussion, scientists and growers consider what can be put into the strawberry manual about edge or "trap" crops of alfalfa that some growers have used to attract lygus bugs away from strawberry plants. Trap crop planting is a practice that has been shown to help manage pests, but knowledge about the effectiveness of trap cropping in strawberries is not firmly established with peer-reviewed scientific data.

Research – We can't put in suppositions like trap crops. People are saying this works, but beats me.

Extension – That's tacit knowledge. We can't put it in.

Research – I wasn't saying that. If we have the data, we can put it in.

Extension – We can probably label this – "The Tacit Knowledge Box."

The legitimacy of a scientific institution depends on the reproducible validity of what it claims as "facts." If scientific authorities claim a fact that turns out not to be reproducible, the legitimacy of that institution suffers. Agricultural scientists are in the process of experimenting with trap crops in strawberries, but, when this discussion took place, the results of these experiments had not been reproduced enough to make this practice a legitimate "fact" in agricultural research institutions. The agricultural scientists involved in creating the strawberry manual were very much aware of the matter of institutional credibility: if the UC publishes anecdotes as facts and the facts later are not confirmed, the legitimacy of the institution is diminished.

However, the mission of UC extension is to give the growers as much information as possible, within their institutional constraints. The members of the meeting recognize and are trying to communicate this other kind of knowledge that is not the same as "proven" scientific knowledge found in the rest of the manual. They know they cannot mix such knowledge with that which is legitimized by scientific verification processes involving reproducible results published in peer-reviewed journals. Therefore, they resort to a different form of presentation in the manual, putting it in a "box" where knowledge sits that is known but not "known" in the sense that it has not been verified by formal scientific methods.

What to do with this kind of knowledge continually emerged in the manual meetings, particularly over the issue of trap crops. The following is another discussion about edge or "trap" crops that illustrates this negotiation over how to disseminate this kind knowledge, once again with a process of marking a particular fact as a specific kind of knowledge in the manual, separating it out into what the meeting members begin to call a "Farmer John Box."

Grower – XX just talked about oak trees. Do we have anything on [trap crops].

Extension – We may have enough diversity in our field to not have to do that.

Grower – One guy doesn't mow down.

Extension – When do we have enough data to recommend? We need to get that knowledge systematized.

Grower – For example: eucalyptus trees do something to air currents. Downside is shading of crops.

Grower – Wind break or wind filter?

Grower – Maybe you can put this in the Farmer John anecdotal box, to understand that kind of outside info. That's what farmers do around their pickups. I put a lot more store in what a farmer says than what a researcher says. If you have the two, what I do is ask farmers whether the research works in the field.

Extension – There are some ways in which we can keep the creativity of this.

Researcher – The credibility, we have to deal with that.

Extension – Organic growers are carrying a big burden of observational knowledge. Local knowledge and ecological heterogeneity makes all the difference, 10 to 20 miles.

In this discussion, grower vs. researcher knowledge, and observational vs. experimentally-proven knowledge gets immersed into the larger question of credibility vs. creativity. The following discussion, in which a piece of information moved from the realm of the tacit to a "solid recommendation," shows how knowledge moves around, or not, from one realm to the other. The discussion is about the rise of a particular pest and the use of an organic anti-microbial agent to keep that pest under control. In this case the scientific legitimation of the knowledge is the deciding factor that transforms tacit knowledge into inside fact.

Grower – We've had big problems in XX for the first time in Southern California this year.

Extension – Why?

Grower – Changes in cropping patterns. The hosts are around longer. The ground was in tomatoes until recently. I tried to XX area.

Extension – How did XX work out?

> Grower – We had a low population. Did good. You need to do it with a low population.
> Extension – We put down XX in hot spots.
> Grower – Rates?
> Extension – Based on XX's research.
> Researcher – We have a report to look at.
> Extension – It's a solid recommendation from the literature.

In another discussion on predators, field information was supported by data disseminated not around pickups but at a scientific conference.

> Extension – Do you use [a beneficial predator]?
> Grower – No I don't.
> Researcher – I heard of [another beneficial predator].
> Grower – Really?
> Extension – I saw some paper on this in Washington.

In these discussions, we see a tension between growers with a certain set of knowledge they find most credible (pickup talk between growers about what works in the field), and research and extension staff with a different set of knowledge that they find most credible (what has been published or presented at scientific conferences, with peer-reviewed data behind it). The knowledge is not completely transferable between the worlds of the researchers, where knowledge is legitimized in certain specific ways, and the worlds of the growers, who have other criteria – informal proof in the field – for judging the legitimacy of knowledge about strawberry growing.

While sometimes a scientific paper can move knowledge from one realm to the other, much grower knowledge is not open to Mode 1 scientific proof because it is a product of specific practices that cannot be formalized because they are so contextual. This struggle over what-there-is-to-know about strawberry production shows how researchers' work can become mired in competing sets of knowledge embedded in institutional hierarchies, local knowledges, conventional production systems, organic production systems, and local agroecologies. Researchers are thus torn between what they are expected to know in their own institutional context and what their clientele – the growers – want them to know. The researchers therefore try to "manage" growers' knowledge expectations and mediate these expectations in relation to the scientifically verified knowledge expected of researchers in their organization.

In addition, scientifically legitimate research practices do not always produce knowledge useful to growers. "If the results are mediocre, there's no farmer exchange," noted one researcher. Extension is then in a position where farmers expect extension to know what they do not know. There is a risk in raising grower expectations by claiming that a certain project is going to yield useful information. When such a project fails to produce anything useful, it threatens the legitimacy of extension as an effective institution. Growers expect extension to test various growing practices and products and to report on what works. If this type of knowledge work is not productive, extension and the research institutions that employ them face challenges to their legitimacy.

In California, much government agricultural research is supported by commodity associations funded by growers through a system of "check-offs," a levy on sales that commodity association growers vote into place to support agricultural research. When commodity producers lose confidence in agricultural extension research, they begin to complain about paying this levy. A number of commodity groups have been questioning check-offs (Eldridge 2003), consequently, the tension between growers' expectations and extension's knowledge production work can lead to actions that threaten the future of extension as an institution. This reflects a larger set of contradictions between the risky returns to government knowledge work and citizen expectation that government work will lead to solid results.

Characterizing sustainable knowledge

Scientific practice and expertise rose with the establishment of modern agricultural universities and state-funded scientific laboratories charged with increasing agricultural production and farmer income (Colman 1963; Danbom 1979). In this formative period, public agricultural scientists imagined "agricultural knowledge" as invented in the laboratory and flowing from scientist to farmer. The extension agent, a role also associated with agricultural universities, disseminated scientific knowledge as advice on agricultural practices (Jones and Garforth 1997). Administrators of this type of conventional, modern agricultural information system designed the dissemination of this formal, scientific knowledge through "the pipeline model" of information flow (Clark 2002; see also Freire's (1970) concept of "banking"). Social scientists working within this perspective would study the diffusion of this centralized pipeline knowledge flow, in which "innovation" created in the university would spread out to the agricultural practitioner. In this knowledge production model, the "innovative" farmer was the one who was an "early adopter" of technology created in the university through laboratory processes (Geisler and DuPuis 1989). The term "extension," therefore, explains the direction of knowledge flow extended from the center of knowledge into the receptive minds of farmers.

Under this system, agricultural problems become characterized as a "gap" in scientific laboratory-based work, which demands more research work to create, cumulatively, larger amounts of context-free formal knowledge that can then flow out from the center (Latour 1987; Murdoch and Clark 1994). In the pipeline model, extension works by increasing the flow of "expert" knowledge to the grower, perhaps customizing it to particular circumstances.

Many farmers have resisted this model of knowledge production or learning (Hassanein 1999; DuPuis 2002; Danbom 1979). In some agricultural states, like Wisconsin, farmers historically have pressured the state for a more partnership-like model of learning between farmers and extension in which knowledge flows in both directions, from and to farmers (Hassanein 1999; DuPuis 2002).

More recently, this partnership model has re-emerged and a number of researchers have attempted to re-capture the "lost" knowledge and preserve older, local agricultural production systems (Sumberg *et al.* 2003; Altieri 1999; Kloppenburg 1991; McCorkle 1989). Some scholars have documented the imperialist and colonial motivations behind the promotion of "scientific" agriculture based on the dissemination of Western technologies (Gilmartin 1994; Thrupp 1989). Like the coercion of indigenous populations to adopt Western cultural practices, imposition of models of knowledge production based on the diffusion of modern scientific agricultural methods have forced farmers to abandon local sets of knowledge and replace them with knowledge approved by external powers.

The local knowledge turn was a necessary antidote to agricultural development perspectives that presented local knowledge as "backward" and misinformed. This new approach gave due credit to local knowledge sets, which are often "contextually rational," learned responses by farmers and often effective in minimizing local risk (Vanclay and Lawrence 1994; Chambers *et al.* 1989). Additionally, researchers have found that farmers' traditional risk-reduction strategies often involve the preservation of ecological diversity (Altieri 1995, 1999).

However, if knowledge is not just a one-dimensional system, *neither* modern *nor* traditional, but a variety of systems that include *both* context-free (formal) *and* contextual (tacit) ways of knowing, then the question about local knowledge is reframed from a static retrieval of something lost to a different and dynamic way of knowing. This reframing of knowledge toward a more dynamic perspective opens up the possibility of innovation, as well as the re-capture of lost knowledge. As previous chapters have shown, conventional forms of thinking have bifurcated agricultural production into dichotomies of good vs. bad (or modern vs. traditional) and knowledge as separating the true from the false, or the old from the new. In contrast, a relational modes of knowledge perspective does not deny scientific, technical knowledge but rather places it in context with other forms of knowledge. That is, acknowledging the contextuality and diversity of knowledge forms opens up new ways of looking at sustainable practices (Nowotny *et al.* 2001). Rather than fixed as scientific or local, the Mode 2 perspective allows us to see knowledge as multiple and mutable, and thereby understand knowledge production in – and out – of context.

Yet how to characterize multiple ways of knowing remains largely undeveloped. Many describe differences in ways of knowing from a historical perspective: knowledge changes over time, as in traditional to modern knowledge or in terms of Kuhnian paradigms. From the Kuhnian perspective, only one dominant knowledge paradigm can exist at any one time. Kuhn argues that accepted knowledge changes when its advocates are persuaded of the irrelevance of the old paradigm, leading to a shift that makes room for new, relevant knowledge. Those who treat organic production as a form of knowledge through the historical lens argue that organic knowledges are "locked out" because of a "productivist paradigm" that emphasizes increasing yields as the scientific focus in private and public agricultural research (Vanloqueren and Baret 2009; Stassart and Jamar 2008).

Those who take the multiple knowledge perspective see Kuhn's notion of paradigm as a somewhat restrictive view. Different ways of knowing can coexist without having to compete for dominance. A variety of knowledges can exist together. Because organic agriculture depends on a more agroecological, and therefore place-based, context, it tends to be more tacit and situated. Industrial agriculture, on the other hand, tends to be based on a more codified, universal, and mobile (Latour 1987) form of knowledge. Universities, as the name indicates, typically teach more universalized forms of knowledge, and are centers of formal knowledge using pedagogies that depend on the knowledgeable expert instructor as "the sage on the stage" filling recipients with new knowledge and diffusing rigorously-proven research into the world (DuPuis *et al.* 2011.

Yet the organic strawberry manual conversations above show that while organic researchers realize that the current system locks them into formal modes of knowing, they also recognize the existence and value of tacit, contextual knowledge. The strawberry manual discussions reveal that researchers recognize and are struggling to disseminate both kinds of knowledge. While this willingness to disseminate all kinds of knowledge meets the expectations of growers, it violates the expectations of the scientists' own institution because scientific institutions are considered to be effective if they provide scientific, universalizable, peer-reviewed knowledge. Growers, for their part, therefore challenge the validity of the university's universal knowledge mission when they say that they trust tacit, grower-to-grower knowledge more than researchers' knowledge.

Because their own institutional legitimacy requires a certain process of peer-review and empirical, data-based support for their arguments, researchers work within the tension between scientific and tacit knowledge. From a scientific knowledge perspective, the problem is a lack of knowledge, a need to fill the cup of knowledge more fully, to bridge a knowledge gap, in which not enough time and/or money has been spent collecting enough data. The problem then becomes a "not enough knowledge" and therefore a "not enough support for gathering knowledge" problem. From this perspective, the "not enough knowledge" problem parallels the "not enough yield" problem and the "not enough profit" problem. From the viewpoint of conventional agriculture, the problem is one of quantity. From the Mode 2 perspective, the problem is one of kind.

However, there is further issue in terms of recognizing tacit knowledge in an institutional setting. Since tacit knowledge does not lend itself to scientific testing, there is no way for researchers to justify tacit knowledge within the current university structure of peer review and data collection. As a result, they need to put this knowledge in a "box" – a "Farmer John Box" in this case – as something knowable but not credible according to university research standards. In fact,

Farmer John boxes do not appear in the final manuscript of the strawberry manual. This is more than what Vanloqueren and Baret (2009) refer to as "lock-in." Researchers are not locked into particular ways of knowing. They understand that there are other ways of knowing out there. They tried to incorporate these different kinds of knowledge production and dissemination within their institutional communication systems, but such knowledge is not legitimately "knowable" within their institution. Their knowledge production is locked in to their membership of particular institutions where tacit knowledge cannot be internally legitimized. In these circumstances, lock-in is not the result of a dominant knowledge paradigm but of a dominant institutional protocol for knowledge production. Lock-in is not a problem in researchers' heads but in their knowledge context, the modes of knowing that legitimize their identities as scientists. Tacit knowledge is not unknowable because there is no definition of "what" tacit knowledge is. The research scientists and growers could recognize tacit knowledge when they saw it. The problem was "how" to know this knowledge.

This leads to the question: how do researchers work with multiple ways of knowing, given these institutional restrictions? The next set of organic strawberry meeting conversations will look at this question.

How do we know organic?

The idea of a growing manual exemplifies the dissemination of formal, codified knowledge, particularly through the use of "templates" as a tool. Organic agriculture, because it works with local agroecologies, is more contingent and contextual, depending on the kinds of knowledges that do not lend themselves to templates (Hassanein and Kloppenburg 1995). Nevertheless, the members of the strawberry manual team were struggling to codify contingent knowledge through the production of templates. A standardized template describing a form of organic production intrinsically entails negotiation between local and centralized knowledge systems.

The problem of mediating between growers' local knowledges and a centralized, standardized description of organic strawberry growing is evident in the following strawberry meeting discussion, which describes when to begin monitoring for a particular pest and its predators. This conversation involved one grower relating to the group his wish to know more about pest cycles. Many of the larger growers have strawberry land both on the Central Coast and in Southern California, thereby extending their ability to supply the market throughout the year. Although much of Southern California's strawberry land is rapidly going out of production, due in part to suburban encroachment, university researchers want to create a state-wide manual. To this end, they encouraged growers to make regional comparisons, asking *where* and *when* particular knowledges are true.

One grower asks about the appearance of a [beneficial predator] in an organic researcher's test plots: "Do you have a (natural area)? A nursery?" The researcher replies: "We're not absolutely sure we found the first XX nymph yet. But we have plenty of adults."

> Grower – It's the second week in March in this area.
> Extension – Suction samples in January?
> Extension – That's what we (extension) do.
> Researcher – For research use.
> Extension – What is the historical biofix?
> Extension – End of March
> Grower – For this area, for San Diego, we start earlier.
> Grower – We don't have much lygus in Southern California. It's a non-issue. Our fresh crop is done by then.
> Grower – As soon as we've got green areas in the hills, I don't worry. When the hills get dry, they come down, when it gets warmer.
> Extension One – We might want to put temperature for mite growth.

A grower is noting the natural signals to look for before he needs to worry about a particular pest in a particular place. The extension worker understands that not all farmers have the same climate and tries to translate the information into a universal measurement: a temperature. Because this is a state-wide template and California has many climates, there is some discussion about how to adjust the template for Southern and Northern California strawberry growing regions. The mostly larger farmers who grow in multiple regions talk about the differences between their southern acreage and their northern acreage. They are very much aware of the differences in the climates they are working with. At the beginning of the conversation above, there is also a discussion of how researchers know about pests and the presence of beneficials using suction samples.

The question of how to disseminate knowledge also plays a role in legitimizing particular pieces of information. This becomes apparent in the following discussion about the usefulness of monitoring insect eggs. The discussion revolved around the issue of how to communicate what a new grower should look for in terms of these incredibly small objects.

> Grower – Is there value in considering eggs?
> Extension – Lygus eggs – no one wants to look for them. Predator eggs – if we find one I know that help has arrived. Some are too small to find. There are pictures of eggs in the IPM manual.
> Grower – I like that.
> Grower – How about a poster?
> Grower – A poster might be good. Of beneficials.
> Extension – We had one ten years ago. We could revive it.
> Grower – In the format of a calendar.

In this case, the growers and extension are working together to figure out the best way to communicate ecological knowledge to a wider audience of growers. Extension's role is to make knowledge universal and thereby make it "mobile" in Latour's terms; that is, by removing it from context so that it can be spread to growers in general. Organic growers work by knowing their own context, the balances and imbalance in their own systems. However, they also hope to bring in new information from the outside to improve their systems and, in this case, they are willing to share their information with others who seek to grow organic strawberries. The manual discussions reflect these differences in roles, but also the attempts by participants to overcome these differences. In the above discussion, they are attempting to communicate different practices in different places at different times as a calendar with pictures. But there are also discussions about context-specific knowledge that cannot be understood universally, and thus cannot fit into templates for a universal manual. Once again, however, the group attempts to communicate as much as possible.

Also, many organic strawberry growers produce on lower rent, hillier, and less fertile land than their conventional counterparts. As one researcher observes, they are "not in the high-rent strawberry district. This helps to keep costs down, but they also have to know-how to grow in those areas." One of the many challenges of growing on this less-fertile, hilly, and erodible land is the multiplicity of microclimates that exist in the Central Coast region. Local knowledge of one's own place of production therefore is particularly important in this case, making the creation and use of a template especially difficult for farmers in these areas.

Finally, growers repeatedly referred to the agroecological uniqueness of their individual fields and how they learned the specifics of their particular growing place by using their own place-based agroecological strategies. Manual discussions would often entail researchers trying to make generalizations for the manual while growers would interrupt with comments, like, "not at my place." One grower describes how he gets to know his own field:

> The food chain is the crux of it. I'm working with XX. He has a whole new way of looking at the field – don't walk – sit down and watch the food chain – watch the cycle of life going on in the field, ... the food source, not intervening with it. Like with white fly, if you spray it, it explodes. But I am impacting it, balancing the food chain.

How do we know?

As the strawberry manual process illustrates, university agricultural extension staff, charged with diffusing centralized knowledge, are unsure how to deal with contextual, tacit, and emergent organic knowledges important to organic production processes. In interviews, university staff indicated that they had explicitly designed the manual process as working in partnership with growers, to overcome the limitations of the pipeline model. Yet, simply creating a participatory model of knowledge production was not enough. Participants were still constrained by their institutional knowledge contexts.

The knowledge-production partnership approach arose during the 1980s, when people began to question the notion of central science institutions, such as universities, as the sole source of knowledge (Nowotny *et al.* 2001). This skepticism of scientific knowledge in agriculture occurred in the context of general disillusionment with science. Certain agricultural social scientists echoed public concerns by questioning the "myth" of science in agricultural development, some rejecting it strongly (cf. Norgaard 1988). The public then began to deconstruct previously strong beliefs in the relationship between centralized authority and social improvement (Morgan and Murdoch 2000).

Experience-based approaches to knowledge have largely contributed to newer theories of learning. Based on the works of Piaget and Montessori, educators in the 1960s and 1970s began to reject the idea of learning as a process of memorizing static categories. They replaced their support of rote memorization with experiential learning based on problem-solving and project-centered pedagogies. In other words, researchers in educational institutions have long realized that experience is a form of knowledge. The challenge has been how to teach that kind of knowledge in formal institutions that were organized to de-contextualize and universalize knowledge (DuPuis *et al.* 2011). Communities have traditionally granted these institutions legitimacy according to their production of codified knowledge that lends itself to generalization over multiple contexts.

Universities are currently undertaking the challenge of creating knowledge to promote environmental sustainability. However, as illustrated by the strawberry manual conversations, sustainable knowledge is often contextual, tacit, and proliferative. Yet, in the university context, legitimate knowledge requires a form of dissemination, such as a manual, that contains knowledge created in the university and verified through the process of peer review. If sustainable knowledge tends to be more contextual, how will universities, designed to spread knowledge from the center, work with sustainable knowledge? Will university institutions truly produce and disseminate the type of knowledge needed to create a more sustainable world if the process requires stepping outside of institutional protocols? Organic agriculture researchers in university institutions grapple with these questions on a daily basis.

The fatal attraction of technical knowledge

However, sustainable knowledge is not as bounded and dichotomous as the above discussion indicates (Murdoch and Clark 1994). Researchers, extension workers, and organic farmers that attended the template meetings collaborated to strategize, negotiate, and stretch the boundaries between the two systems, with great reflexivity. In one meeting conversation, participants resisted the rigid requests of manual leaders to specify the exact number of pests counted prior to a predator release: "People are looking for the number. 'What's the number'? What's the number?'" But people with experience in the field know where they feel comfortable. "You don't have to justify what you do to anyone," stated one participant, summarizing the conversation. Another grower agreed that counting is not the key. "We counted mites for a long time. We don't look at numbers, we look at trends." Here, growers' ways of knowing "in the field" come up against scientists who need numbers in order to move the knowledge from the field into the manual. Growers are resisting putting their knowledge into a number because they recognize that is not how they go about making their decisions about predator–prey balances.

In the manual conversations, both growers and scientists recognized that the question "when to release beneficials" in organic production systems echoes the "when to spray pesticides?" question in conventional systems. "Beneficials" are organisms, generally insects and microbes, that prey on agricultural pests. In organic systems, beneficials are sometimes released in fields to help control pests. However, organic growers prefer to see beneficials as not something you add to the field to create balance, but instead as a self-proliferating part of a well-managed organic system. Throughout the strawberry manual conversations, both growers and scientists tended to portray the release of beneficial organisms as a result of failing to keep the predator–prey balance. In the case of release, the solution is a type of intervention to stem a pest problem that represents a failure to maintain a balance. Jokes about releasing beneficials disparaged this practice as an organic strategy, often playing on the ways in which the decision was similar to the "spray and pray" conventional system. These jokes indicated an overall agreement between scientists and growers that organic agriculture should rely more on cultural practices and soil maintenance to prevent problems from happening in the first place. Once participants started to discuss problem interventions, "spray and pray" as a metaphor continued to resurface as "release and pray": an analog.

Yet, in the "when to spray, when to release" discussion, growers expressed a nostalgia for the predictability of pest control and yield that the conventional alternative provides. However, they tempered this nostalgia by admitting that conventional predictability is based on following specific directions – "reading the label" – which growers saw, in itself, as a limited choice. One grower explained how his idea of predictability differed from the conventional mode. Instead of relying on label directions, he explained that he wanted predictability based on his experiential observations about the environment of his production system: "I would feel more comfortable if I knew more about the natural cycle of pest populations, so I can act early. For a predator, release timing is crucial." This grower also debated the usefulness of a pest monitoring service: "Monitoring service info takes time to get to you," compared to a more useful kind of systemic knowledge: "whereas understanding natural cycles gives one an ability to act quickly." In these conversations, growers tended to compare the practice of intensive observation as a form of control to the predictability of either "the numbers" or chemical inputs as different kinds of control.

On the other hand, while disparaging the kind of Mode 1 technical knowledge that is more typical of conventional production systems, both scientists and growers sometimes expressed a wish that organic production systems could work according to this measurable, predictable, less risky kind of knowledge, what Max Weber referred to as "rational" knowledge. For scientists, this more rational form of technical knowledge represented the kind of knowing that is legitimate within their institution and easy to communicate in a manual. For growers, rational Mode 1 knowledge provides a predictability, and a concomitant lowering of risks, that is not typical of organic production systems. Both growers and scientists recognize the attractiveness of this sort of knowledge, while also understanding that organic systems do not work along these lines. In other words, there is a constant tension between formalized, institutional knowledges that rely on universalization and contextual knowledges based in experiential practice.

How do we create modes of governance that enable scientists and growers to work creatively within the tension between formal and contextual knowledge practices? So far, studies of organic vs. conventional knowledge systems have tended to focus on categorizing differences between "sustainable" knowledge and "conventional" knowledge. This process of distinguishing and defining categories is problematic since it ignores the dynamic, everyday processes that are involved in the creation and negotiation of the world. Recent studies using Latourian actor-network and feminist symbolic interactionist theories (Clarke and Montini 1993) open up the black box of dichotomization in studies of knowledge to show that the terms "conventional" and "sustainable" are actively negotiated on a day-to-day basis (Latour 1987). The strawberry manual conversations show that scientists and growers are working together within these tensions and that a different kind of knowledge production is emerging from these efforts to understand agroecological cycles.

This hybridization is becoming increasingly apparent in the ways that conventional agriculture has taken up some parts of the organic production system. As one extension agent stated during the meetings: "The chemical companies are moving from calendar spray to count and spray." While organic growers disparaged acting according to "the numbers," the move from calendar-based decision making to count-and-spray involves a hybridization between rational and contextual knowledge in which numbers do not come from a context-free calendar but from the actual production field. Users of conventional knowledge are therefore reacting to sustainable knowledge by discovering ways to hybridize their practices.

Conclusion

From a theoretical framework that sees knowledge production and learning as an everyday, dynamic, experiential activity, one begins to care less about categorizing knowledge as sustainable by definition versus conventional by definition. Instead, one can focus on the relevant actors creating knowledge, and how they negotiate the understanding of these categories. Chapter 8 introduced the notion of relational ontologies as a way of seeing the world as "worlds," according to different relationships. From a relational point of view, we can see that there are multiple ways of producing knowledge. But our current institutions maintain their legitimacy by acknowledging only certain knowledge practices as capable of producing truth, thereby locking members into particular ways of knowing. The question then becomes, can we design new modes of governance as mechanisms to formalize more complex relational worlds that can acknowledge and work with multiple ways of knowing? Can we protect the autonomy of different ways of knowing while making the boundaries between them more leaky, enabling more hybridization between the systems?

Yet, rationalized industrial agriculture is more predictable and therefore less risky, at least for individual growers' profits. We may "know" how to grow organic strawberries, but we will never be able to know in a way that matches all of the capabilities of the conventional system, in terms of its guarantees. The challenge of creating sustainable production systems, like organic strawberry production, will always involve people working within these tensions.

Part IV

Globalizing alternative food movements

The cultural material politics of fair trade

Starbucks, Cadbury, Tesco, Sainsbury's, McDonald's, Kraft, Sara Lee, Unilever, Wal-Mart/Asda, Albertson's, Chiquita, Dunkin' Donuts. What does it mean that these corporations – in addition to one of the most boycotted company on the planet, Nestlé – all source and sell fair trade goods? Asked another way, what does it mean that a nascent charity-led, global-justice movement selling fair trade handicrafts through catalogues and dusty second-hand shops is now intimately connected to some of the largest and most dubious food multinational brands in existence? Furthermore, what does it mean that Cafédirect – a fair trade company begun by the likes of Oxfam, Twin Trading, Traidcraft, and Equal Exchange – now has upwards of 10 percent of the UK's coffee market as its fifth largest coffee brand (Cafédirect 2011)? Similarly here, what does it mean that supermarket shelves are stuffed full of fair trade cakes, wines, rum, melons, bananas, grains, nuts, avocados, and sugar in addition to the early triumvirate of fairly traded coffee, tea, and chocolate?

The chapters that follow this brief introduction to the fourth and final section of the book examine these questions through the lens of the fair trade movement as an expression of a contemporary globalized alternative food network (AFN). In particular, these chapters draw on research and writing on fair trade movements and markets in the USA, UK, and EU to explore how this sense of *fairness* was conceived and calculated and how it has been put into practice *differently* overtime. This exploration provides interesting insights into the core themes animating the engagement with AFNs in this book: the changing knowledge regimes around fair trade, its shifting cultural materialities of consumption/production places and spaces, the changing meanings and markets for fair trade and, overall, its bid to create alternative political economies of development and consumption as related to food.

More broadly, we explore the cultural, material, and political implications of the globalized *marketization* of an ethics of care that is at the heart of fair trade networks (FTNs). In this, we bring to the fore some of the more subtle themes of this volume in its engagements with the politics of consumption – and of ethical consumption, more specifically – and the growing moral economies of (alternative) foods. In analyzing these implications, we work to cut through, as well as take a different cut through, the debates about fair trade, ethical consumption and the politics of consumption that have seemingly raged across the social sciences of late (cf. Adams and Raisborough 2009, 2010; Barnett *et al.* 2005; Clarke *et al.* 2007; Goodman 2010; Goodman *et al.* 2010; Guthman 2007; Lyon 2006; Raynolds 2009). We see the specific debates on ethical consumption as overly polarized, overly theorized, and down-right vague in parts. On the one hand, it is argued that consumption "singularities" get worked up into "collectivised politics" by enlisting "ordinary people into broader projects of social change" through their purchase of more ethical/moral goods (Barnett *et al.* 2005: 39). On the other hand, Guthman (2003, 2007, 2008a) argues that ethical and other forms of "politicised consumption" (cf. Clarke 2008; see also Barnett *et al.* 2011) work to privatize, individualize, and responsibilize consumers into voluntarily solving the economic, social and environmental problems that litter the landscapes of food, farming, and neoliberal capitalism writ large.

As painted in these debates, this is what might be called the "paradox of ethical consumption": the choice of organic and fair trade food empowers *ordinary* acts of consumption and these same acts can create the *extra-ordinary* by saving us (and Others), seemingly, from ourselves, As Micheletti and Stolle (2008: 750) put it in the context of the politics of the anti-sweatshop movement, "capitalism is helping capitalism to develop a face of social justice." Thus, for some, the private vice of shopping has the very real potential to become a politicized public virtue, while for others public virtue and politics are becoming problematically entrenched as the privileged vice of a few shoppers and self-reflexive foodies.

If we wish to more fully understand FTNs as a globalized AFN, as instances of ethical consumption and as offering an ethics of care across space and place, we need to know how these networks are materialized and governed in and through *practice*. This starts from the recognition that an ethics of care is relational in its crafting, development, and articulation (McEwan and Goodman 2010), especially in the context of food (Kneafsey *et al.* 2008). But, specifically with respect to FTNs, we need to ask relational to what and how and, in addition, why do these relationships matter in the material, political, and moral senses? One key set of relationalities fully embedded in fair trade is that between fair trade's ethics of care and the cultural economic logics of the market within which it operates. Indeed, the slogans that fair trade operates "in and against the market" and/or "in the market but not of it" (Taylor 2005) need to be reassessed and rearticulated in the current climate of its mainstreaming. Focusing on the practice of fair trade – how it is realized as a socio-material *thing* embedded with a multiplicity of ethical/moral meanings – brings to light how the logics of the market work to shape the particularized and bounded trajectories of the ethics of care and ethical consumption singularities embedded in fair trade goods. In this respect, the "turn to quality" in the form of "better tasting" fair trade commodities has not only become entangled very quickly with the Bourdieuian sense of "taste" as expressions of discerning distinction, but has operated as a form of governance that dictates, structures, and bounds how and why fair trade's relationalities are developed, maintained, and have shifted over time.

Understanding the practices of FTNs – how its ethics of care is materialized, governed, and made "durable" (Latour 1991) in particularized ways for particularized reasons – requires moving beyond the narrow confines of the sites of fair trade consumption (Varul 2008; Hudson and Hudson 2003), its ability to create ethical consumer subjects (cf. Barnett *et al.* 2005), the critiques of food labels as voluntaristic/private regulatory regimes (cf. Guthman 2007), as well as more opaque philosophical treatments of fair trade (Watson 2006, 2007). Indeed, to explore the practices of FTNs we must deploy a theoretical/conceptual lens that takes on and expands the "social life of things" to incorporate a sort of "material life of things" that engages with the relationalities of the material *and* social life of FTNs (Appadurai 1986; see also Bakker and Bridge 2006; Cook 2004; Jackson 1999, 2000; Mansfield 2003a, 2003b). In particular, the co-produced entanglements of the material requirements/expressions and discursive tropes of quality in fair trade have fundamentally altered its "moral economy" – and, as we would also argue, its politics – in far-reaching ways.

Exploring the shifting and circulating culture of fair trade in the changing texts, discourses, and images of its networks is crucial to grasping its "thingness" practice. These analytical moves might be overly annoying to some (Bernstein and Campling 2006a, 2006b; Goss 2004, 2006; Hartwick 2000) or not a focus for others (cf. Raynolds *et al.* 2007; Lyon and Moberg 2010). What we propose, then, is an understanding of the practices of FTNs as a kind of *cultural material politics* that incorporates the "analysis of the nature, culture, and political economy" of fair trade foods (Freidberg 2003b: 6; see also Carolan, 2011). The chapters that follow explore the cultural, material and political implications of the commodification and marketization of an ethics of care in the networks of the globalized AFN that is currently fair trade.

Historicizing fair trade: of movements, markets, and the quality turn

Fair trade has a long, fascinating, and complex history that spans upwards of six decades and encompasses much of the globe. Started by a host of religious and secular solidarity organizations such as Ten Thousand Villages and Equal Exchange in the USA, Oxfam and Christian Aid in the UK, GEPA in Germany and Max Havelaar in the Netherlands, much of the story of fair trade has already been recounted in various forms (cf. Anderson 2009a, 2009b; Bacon 2010; Fridell 2007; Kleine 2005; Levi and Linton 2003; Littrell and Dickson 1999; Nichols and Opal 2005; Raynolds *et al.* 2007; Renard 1999, 2003, 2005; Rice 2001; Schmelzer 2010; Zadek and Tiffen 1996; see also Trentmann 2007, 2010), one of the earliest being Barrett-Brown's (1993) book *Fair Trade: Reform and Realities in the International Trading System*. These early "movement-oriented" (Jaffee 2007: 205) alternative trading organizations (ATOs) had, as Barrientos *et al.* (2007: 52; see also Leclair 2002) put it, "a vision of greater social justice and fairer trade, but from different origins." This vision involved reversing the historical injustices of global markets and reconfiguring the structures that created these injustices by channeling trade through alternative markets that work against the conventional economic global order (Jaffee 2007: 27–28). For one key early ATO, Twin Trading in the UK, this meant trading on " 'non-capitalist principles' with the intentions of creating jobs, improving the quality of work and reinforcing the labor movement" (Barrientos *et al.* 2007: 53).

Volunteer-staffed world-shops (see Goodman and Bryant, in press) – still very important in the fair trade movement in Europe today – and catalogues of handicrafts and bad-tasting coffees were at the front-line of the early fair trade movement. For many activists, in addition to the economic and livelihood benefits to producers, the key was the educational opportunities that allowed alternative and fair trade to "put a face on commodities" (Jaffee 2007: 14) by having small producers "telling their stories" to consumers and the public (Ten Thousand Villages cited in Barrientos *et al.* 2007: 53). In this small-scale "age of innocence" of fair and alternative trade, the ethics of care in these networks was created, fostered, and articulated by the committed relationships developed among the small producer cooperatives, activist non-governmental organization (NGOs) and ATOs and committed consumers of these early fair trade handicrafts and foods. In our lexicon, "coming home to eat" meant moving across distances to make connections between the lifestyle and livelihood "homes" of producers and consumers through the intermediaries of the handicraft and world-shop, the holiday catalogue, and members of solidarity/charity NGOs.

Yet, throughout its evolution, there has always been a tension between the movement's "solidarity strand" and its "economic development strand" (Jaffee, 2007: 28). This tension has stretched very much to the breaking point as the market has grown, fair trade has gone mainstream and, specifically, with the growing inclusion of food multinationals. Indeed, today in the USA in particular, many of the early fair trade organizations and companies who have maintained and defended their "100 per-center" status, are vehemently opposed to the involvement of large supermarkets and retailers such as Starbucks in FTNs. This sort of acute split in the US movement has been somewhat blunted in the UK and European Union (EU) as many activists were *behind* some of the first and most successful fair trade brands, such as Cafédirect as we see below, that have themselves moved into the mainstream. But even in the UK, this split in the movement and in wider civil society is still apparent, as vividly expressed by the policy director of Baby Milk Action: "To give a fairtrade mark to Nestlé ... would make an absolute mockery of what the public believes the fairtrade mark stands for" (Jaffee 2007: 220).

There are several key *moments* in the history of fair trade movements and markets which have facilitated its current market standing and popular appeal today.[1] The first was the development of Fairtrade Labelling Organisations International, or FLO, which worked to centralize and consolidate the separate national fair trade standards, certification regimes, and institutions throughout Europe and the USA. This was done to make the meaning of "fair trade" trustworthy and transparent for producers but especially for its current and (most importantly) potential consumers. Yet, as explored in the subsequent chapters, these rules of the game not only established a consistent set of meanings behind the fair trade mark to foster its global credibility, but also created boundaries around who could be *in* and who was *out* of the fair trade game and its globalized and rapidly marketizing networks.

The second key moment involved the US-based campaign, generated by the activists at Global Exchange in San Francisco, to get Starbucks to source and sell fair trade coffees. Jaffee (2007: 200; see also Jaffee 2010 and Jaffee and Howard 2010) calls this a watershed moment with "activists [getting] most of what they had hoped for – yet, at the same time, also much less." In fact, this was a sweetheart deal from the US fair trade certifying institution Transfair USA in that Starbucks was able to negotiate down the amount of fair trade coffee they were required to supply in their stores. Additionally, by selling fair trade, Starbucks not only came into direct competition with the early fair trade innovators who had painstakingly developed the model and market and who were committed to selling *only* fair trade goods, but also was able to benefit from the "halo effect" gained by having fair trade sold by its *baristas*. This was one of the first high profile cases in which big players are persuaded to dip their toe into the fair trade waters as a way of increasing the volume of fair trade supply and sales. This tactic, through direct action as well as closed-door negotiations, has become *de rigueur* in much of the fair trade movement in the UK.

A third key moment involves the development of Cafédirect and Divine/Day Chocolate in the UK.[2] Both were what might be called "collective entrepreneurial ventures" which were started and supported by solidarity and faith-based global justice NGOs with the specific hope of breaking into the mainstream. Both companies have achieved this quickly and effectively, propelled by their growing presence on the shelves of supermarkets and in smaller, more local shops. The importance of their success cannot be underestimated given their powerful branding of fair trade, their growing economic and market presence in the UK and the supply chains that they have created and developed. We explore these points more fully in Chapter 11 on the shifting materialities of FTNs.

The fourth important moment in the evolution of fair trade involves the development of own-label fair trade goods, most predominantly by UK supermarkets led by the Co-op. Barrientos and Smith (2007: 103; see also Smith, forthcoming) make the following observation about the implications of the growth of own-label branded fairly traded goods for FTNs:

> Supermarket own brand Fair Trade has brought it further into the ambit of the more conventional agrofood system and potentially enhanced the power that supermarket buyers can exert within Fair Trade networks. This is compounded by an anomaly in the FLO system that allows supermarkets to use the FLO mark on their own brand products without having to become a licensee, due to the fact they outsource packing and labeling. Since supermarkets are therefore not necessarily bound by Fair Trade rules and regulations, their suppliers are potentially being exposed to the types of practices and pressures that exist in conventional production networks.
>
> (Barrientos and Smith 2007: 103)

Similar to some of the outcomes of the Starbucks activism above, own-label brand fair trade in the UK has set up further competition between established, movement-oriented fair trade companies and the powerful agents of supermarkets and allowed the latter to garner ethical credibility through the fair trade halo effect. Most importantly own-label branding has not only opened up novel fair trade supply chain pathways but has also shifted the meanings of fair trade as historically developed and established by its original supply networks.

The final moment we discuss here is one that cuts across and is implicated in all of the above moments: the move in FTNs to develop fair trade specifically as a product of *quality*. The logic here is that if fair trade could get out of its niche by moving beyond the core of its so-called solidarity consumers to capture new consumers and, thus, greater market share, more "development" for those farmers in FTNs would ultimately result. In short, moving fair trade into the mainstream by accentuating its quality characteristics would increase sales, expand the market, and generate greater revenues for small farming communities to improve their livelihoods *even more*. Also, the route into the mainstream seen by those in FTNs was to develop and position fair trade goods as quality products that were simultaneously both "better tasting" and a mark of "better taste"; that is, to make fair trade goods more *palatable* while accentuating their cultural material "qualities" of *distinction*.

This drive for higher quality and a better taste/tasting product, the poles around which FTNs currently revolve, has had multiple and simultaneous implications for the cultural material politics of fair trade. As described in the following chapters, fair trade's discursive tactics and its material supply chains have gravitated toward more normalized commodity- and market-ness with the focus on increasing sales, quality, and taste. In the realms of the shifting discourses surrounding fair trade, the once ubiquitous image and descriptions of the fair trade farmer have been successively replaced by the images of quality drawn from touristic landscapes and endorsements by fair trade celebrities and the current emphasis on the "tools of the trade", such as baskets, shovels, and hand clippers used by fair trade producers. Farmers have now essentially gone *virtual* to be placed online where consumers can more fully and easily learn about the benefits that fair trade brings to them. At the same time, due to a multiplicity of different mainstreaming processes at work in FTNs – one of the most important being the growth of own-label brand fair trade lines by supermarkets described above – fair trade supply chains are now much more diverse, varied, and circuitous than the original direct relationships between producing communities and consumers that were core to the earlier practices of the fair trade model.

In essence, as fair trade has mainstreamed and become more marketized, there has been a *de-centering* of the historically-contingent characteristics and meanings embedded in FTNs. "Fairness" in fair trade networks – as expressed in FTN's desire to be more "care-full," transparent, direct, and connecting – has been discursively and materially *overtaken* in the drive to have fair trade taken seriously as a set of products of taste and quality. This is at the heart of fair trade's "Faustian bargain": mainstreaming has allowed market share to grow and thus brought more development, but at the price of shifting the cultural material politics of fair trade away from its original grounding in transparency, direct producer/consumer relations, and global justice. As a result, it is in danger of becoming just another product on the shelves and/or in the brand lines of the very same corporations its moral economy was set up to resist and subvert from its inception.

The following chapters tell a set of tales about the contradictions and paradoxes inherent in the success of FTNs through the increasing commodification and marketization of the ethics of care and moral economy embedded in fair trade goods. It is a cautionary tale that, at its most general, explores the benefits and drawbacks of organizing and pursuing care for Others and Other places through the market. This is what Shamir (2008, 14) calls a "market-embedded morality" that dissolves "the distinction between market and society [by] encod[ing] the 'social' as a specific instance of the 'economy'." More specifically, these chapters engage with the shifting, discursive, and material practices that simultaneously open up but also bound FTNs, open up but also bound its embedded moral economy and ethics of care, and open up but also bound the ethical consumption possibilities and singularities as fair trade has moved into the mainstream and been taken up by corporate brands, and now has become a brand in its own right.

We can buy and consume an ethics of care and a particular kind of monetized and commodified global justice in the form of mainstreamed fair trade even more than ever now, but at what cost to the cultural material politics of its original vision for small producers, Northern consumers and the "right" ways that global trade and moral economies should be articulated? Should the means of *doing* fairer trade, an ethics of care and the cultural material politics of a moral economy in FTNs matter just as much as, if not more than, the ends of a much expanded market, increasing sales and more development? Are there perhaps, even Other ways of doing FTNs – possibly foreshadowed by the growing trend of cooperative ownership FTN schemes being taken up and spread by some fair trade companies? Do these offer new and interesting pathways to *defend* the moral economic structures and possibilities of fair trade? It is toward exploring and engaging with these questions about the contemporary governance of FTNs and their potential futures that we now turn.

10 The shifting cultural politics of fair trade

From transparent to virtual livelihoods

One of the key components of the practice of fair trade is the set of visual and textual imaginaries it creates and circulates throughout its networks. Acting as a set of semiotic intermediaries situated between consumers, fair trade organizations, and companies and producers, these imaginaries have gone through substantial shifts over time as fair trade has moved into the mainstream and worked to extend its market. As these imaginaries have changed in parallel with its bid to become a high quality set of goods, the cultural politics of fair trade has undergone changes: most notably the historical commitment to transparency as one of the cornerstones of fair trade has started to slip and/or been transferred to other outlets in interesting and potentially compromising ways. Put another way, the imaginaries that create the "spatial dynamics of concern" embedded in fair trade's moral economy have ebbed and flowed as its positioning as a quality item "good" enough for supermarket shelves has taken hold, but also as one marketing campaign has given way to another over the repositioning of the brand.

Most specifically, the knowledge networks of fair trade – namely, who is producing it, how and what it means to their livelihoods, what its consumption contributes to – that originally circulated on its packaging have given way to images of landscapes, celebrities advocating fairer trade and now, more recently, to the tools of fair trade production. Fair trade growers and their livelihood narratives have moved into the virtual spaces of fair trade company and organization websites – as well as becoming part of the stories being told about fair trade by supermarkets and other multinational corporations (MNCs) – and these changes have altered the historical knowledge regimes at the base of fair trade networks and movements in significant ways.

This chapter explores the shifting cultural politics of fair trade in the visual and textual narratives it tells about itself, the knowledge it attempts to impart to consumers and the ethics of care it tries to foster through these narratives and, ultimately, consumer purchases. Indeed, this more historical and cultural materialist approach provides a richer understanding of how fair trade has tried to develop multiple and/or different "subjects and spaces of ethical consumption" (Barnett *et al.* 2005) over time as its markets, messages, and moralities have been (re)articulated and (re)envisioned.

The politics of animating fair trade networks

The narratives and related growth in fair trade market and marketing networks, let alone its material supply networks, have certainly not remained static and so any analysis of fair trade's bid to articulate the subjects of ethical consumption must fundamentally recognize and account for this fact from the outset. In other words, if fair trade is to be held up as an example of both ethical consumption and a "new form of political action," as Barnett *et al.* (2005) argue, it is essential to support this characterization with a detailed exploration of how the mainstreaming of fair trade, its deeper marketization, and more commercial imperatives have changed these ethico-political practices.

The tale being told here should not be seen as one whereby fair trade underwent some sort of ethical and political "immaculate conception" that then led to a fall from grace the instant that the first fair trade commodities started to be stocked at supermarkets. Rather the stories related here attempt to reflect a more subtle and complex historical and cultural economic account. Thus, on the one hand, this analysis is at least partially sensitive to the fact that fair trade is a product of, and also reinforces, the current socio-economic moment of neoliberal consumerist politics in which it is embedded. On the other hand, this account recognizes that fair trade is *also* a product of the specific but evolving governance and institutional networks that articulate what it is and should be. In other words, the mainstreaming success of fair trade and the processes and/or forces behind this should be seen as being enmeshed in – and contributing to – the generic cultural and political ethos of neoliberal, consumerist capitalism. At the very same time, it is, however, important to recognize fair trade has its own specific history in the structures, trajectories, and outcomes of its networks, the most crucial of which is to generate more funds for producer cooperatives.

So, the mainstreaming and deeper marketization of fair trade is tied intimately to the broader and deepening penetration of commodification and marketization of all aspects and forms of life, society, and social relations. This extends to various forms and/or materialities of nature (cf. Castree 2003b) or its conservation (cf. *Antipode* 2010), various modalities of care (cf. McEwan and Goodman 2010 and *Ethics, Place and Environment* 2010) and other "affects" more widely (cf. Ilhouz 2007; Lorimer 2007). Thus, the *Zeitgeist* of "shopping for change" (Littler 2009; see also Johnston 2008) leads from but also creates the cultural economic space for, and gives power to, consumerism and consumer choice. This promotes, in turn, the generation of value through market signals for "off the shelf" purchases of a better environment and more progressive development, and all of this within easy time and spatial reach if done during the weekly shopping.

The powerful pathways to change through fair trade were described in unequivocal terms by the executive director of the Fairtrade Foundation in the UK:

> What works so well is that, although we are putting a spotlight on the negative, there is a positive solution to hand which everybody can be a part of. You don't have to wait for Government to move; you don't even have to

wait for companies, because you can push them into acting by buying these products. So you've got all these NGOs, the church groups, and the community-based organizations – but the really fantastic thing about Fair-trade is that you can then go shopping!

(Observer Food Monthly 2006)

Here, consumption, in the form of "developmental consumption" (Goodman 2010) and the conscious consumerist choice to pick more progressive and/or environmentally and socially friendly products over others is a major – if not the most important – pathway to saving the environment and caring for Others available today.

Finally, one of the key attributes and expressions of this commodification and marketization of environment and development, and of the more specific trends of shopping to change the world through a politics of consumerist choice, has been the flourishing of private and voluntary regulatory standards and certification schemes (Barham 2002; Conroy 2007; Getz and Shreck 2006; Guthman 2007; Steinbrucken and Jaenichen 2007). In the light of this chapter, it is important to recognize the expansion and growing power of labeling schemes that work to signal to consumers they are trustworthy in that their label and/or logo denotes certification by a third-party to a set of production standards such as organic, bird-friendly, or fair traded. Conceptualized as "immutable mobiles," "translation devices" and "boundary objects" (Latour 1993; see also Berlan and Dolan 2011; Goodman and Goodman 2001), labels work to carve out a market niche and thereby earn higher prices, create meanings in and around progressive goods and provide a quick "knowledge-fix" (Eden *et al.* 2008a, 2008b) for consumers about the qualities of these commodities. In short, caring commodities not only must articulate their caring qualities to consumers – and the very fact that care can be and is commodified in its material substance – but must do so in a way that invites their purchase through an often richly adorned and information-rich, label-led "switching on" of the consumerist politics *of* choice and choice *for* politics through the acts of shopping.

Fair trade thus has its own particular way of translating and articulating this circulating culture of choice-led, conscious consumerism – and so its own trajectories and evolution fostered by the actors, organizations, and businesses at its center. At the same time, fair trade has fundamentally influenced what choice-led, conscious consumerism is and looks like in the UK, Europe, and USA. We call this the "fair trade effect" and it is taken up more fully in Chapter 12. For now, suffice it to say that the importance and impact of fair trade on the wider processes and constitution of consumerist politics through its mainstreaming and its economic, social, and political success is hard to underestimate.

What events or characteristics are historically or structurally unique to fair trade in its evolving successful move into the mainstream? Of many, we highlight several important points here. First, the economic structures at the base of the fair trade model – a minimum price floor as a safety mechanism and the price premium dedicated to the producers' community development – are arguably the most far-reaching and innovative aspect of fair trade networks. Even given the massive difficulties and concerns of divining a suitable livelihood wage in the minimum price and the problematic transfer of the fair trade premium into community development,[1] the fair trade model nevertheless works to translate the social relations of care into the economic terms of the minimum price and price premium.

In the fair trade model, care and, furthermore, development, are commoditized and subsumed into the exchange-value of fair trade goods. At the same time, care and development, in the form of this exchange-value, then become part of the use-value of fair trade goods. Here, in a way, the use-value of fair trade commodities is not just the utility of the items to be consumed – the coffee to be drunk, the chocolate to be enjoyed, the banana to be eaten. Use-value also derives from the utility of that fair trade commodity to foster livelihood and community development. Moreover, the "labor" of fair trade consumers in the form of choice – the physical, mental, and/or emotional work entailed in putting a fair trade good into one's shopping basket over other items – is as equally valuable as the actual labor that goes into growing, processing, and shipping fair trade coffee beans, cocao, and bananas.[2]

Here not only are consumers setting the care/development use-value of fair trade commodities loose through the labor of their purchases, they are able to access an additional use-value aspect of fair trade goods: the creation of the moral and ethical self through the displayed performances of buying fair trade products. As Barnett *et al.* (2005: 41) argue in summing up their analysis of ethical consumption articulated in the specific example of Transfair:

> insofar as ethical consumption involves an explicit marking of commitments, then governing the consuming self depends on various sorts of performative practice associated with being an ethical consumer (e.g. shopping, giving, wearing, eating, drinking, displaying, protesting).
>
> (Barnett *et al.* 2005: 41)

For these authors, all of this goes into the making of the subjectivities and identities of ethical, fair trade consumers. Furthermore, if one digs even deeper into their arguments (see Clarke *et al.* 2007), a further use-value of fair trade comes to the fore: this is the ability of fair trade non-governmental organizations (NGOs) and related charities to translate the increasing size and growth of the market in fair trade commodities into an important and elevated voice on such matters as trade and development policy. These organizations speak to policy makers and the media in the name of consumers/concerned citizens and, presumably, the larger the market, the stronger the voice and more space fair trade (and other) NGOs have in which to influence policy decisions and progressive politics more broadly.

This brings us back to our opening point about the commodification of care in fair trade, since what we have here is the further and deeper economization of the voice of consumers/citizens and indeed, politics more broadly, as Shamir

(2008) details in his work on "market-embedded morality" and ethics. Indeed, part of what this says is that politics will only have a voice if it can be backed up by consumers, who must be aggregated into a market-share and so give lobbying power to NGOs and charities. In short, these actors are able to gain access to politics, politicians, and the media by virtue of this voice of the consumer-citizenry. One corollary, of course, is that those who do not buy these care-full commodities do not contribute to market share and so, on these terms, do not register as a voice nor set of political concerns.

Yet, and particularly in the work of Clarke *et al.* (2007), most of these afore-mentioned arguments remain theoretical ones: they have yet to be fleshed out in empirical detail about how, *specifically*, fair trade NGO and charity revenues translate into actual political power, an elevated voice or even policy changes. These are very compelling and indeed intuitively logical arguments to make, yet the evidence for this kind of translation of consumption choice into politics and policy has yet to be demonstrated in any sort of real way, for example, by shifting UK trade or international development policy in a certain direction as a consequence of the market growth of fair trade goods.

In summary, the main point we are arguing here is that the literal and figurative "buying in" to the moral economies of fair trade, whether by consumers or MNCs, has been facilitated through the commodification of care and its ability to turn human and community development into an economic expression of exchange/use value embodied in the form of fair trade goods. Following from this, there is then the (theoretical) potential to turn these individualized consumptive acts into a collective politics and collectivized voice that can shout for more progressive national and international policies in the context of development, the environment, and fairer trade more generally.

Fair trade consequentialism and the quality turn

The second point we would emphasize about the historical development and mainstreaming of fair trade, is what might be referred to as a form of beneficial mutualism that operates at a number of different levels for the actors involved in its networks. On the one hand, there has been a temporal component to this: at just about the time supermarkets were looking to improve their image because of a series of negative reports about anticompetitive behavior, as well their growing control and concentration of the food supply in the UK, fair trade activists and businesses, such as Cafédirect, were actively courting supermarkets to sell fair trade goods, and vice-versa. Thus, supermarkets and later MNCs, like Nestlé and Cadbury, would benefit from the so-called halo effect of selling fair trade goods while fair trade companies and the broader movement would be provided space in which to grow their sales and expand their brand exposure to a new set of more conventional consumers.

On the other hand, the structural and governance regimes of fair trade also have worked to enable this mutualism. In particular, for the likes of supermarket own-label fair trade goods or the branded lines of fair trade products of MNCs, corporations are able to merely license the use of the fair trade logo. As a result, all the hard work involved in setting up the more direct and shortened trading relationships, longer-term contracts, direct relations with the producers, and processing of the goods – each typically a part of the original set of rules under which fair trade first operated – is pushed downstream on to other actors engaged in fair trade sourcing (see Jaffee 2007). In short, supermarkets and/or MNCs wanting to enter the market found it a simple matter to obtain the fair trade logo and thus take advantage of this halo effect. Nevertheless, many fair trade companies and activists rejoiced at these first mainstreaming moves of fair trade as sales went up and new consumers were reached as fairly traded lines were added to the product portfolios of supermarkets or MNCs.

This is really at the crux of the mainstreaming of fair trade and explains why so many advocated this as the direction to take: the more sales are made, the more the market grows, the more development goes back to producers, and the more economic and social support they get to improve their lives and livelihoods. Thus, in some ways, it does not matter who sells or how fair trade is sold as long as sales revenues rise and more money is going to producers. Of course, what does matter is whether or not standards groups like FLO can resist any watering-down of existing fair trade standards in the face of pressure from MNCs which, to a large extent, though with some exceptions, has been the case up to now.[3] In short, more sales equals more development in fair trade networks, regardless of whether it is being sold through a single line of fair trade goods by Nestlé or Cadbury or through the networks of Cafédirect or any other "100 percent" fair trade company.

Here, a sort of *ethical consequentialism* has taken hold in fair trade. This has been facilitated by the consumerist model of development situated at its core and by the fact that many fair trade companies either are owned outright by MNCs, such as Green and Blacks, or are run by former heads of MNCs and/or are populated by MBAs and marketing experts rather than activists (see Ballet and Carimentrand 2010; Bezencon and Blili 2009; Davies 2008; Davies *et al.* 2010; Fridell 2009).[4] Indeed, when a leading member of a charity organization heavily involved in fair trade was asked in an interview (2007) if he was concerned at all about the sale of fair trade through the likes of Nestlé, he answered with a resounding and uncompromising "no," citing many of the points being made here about the positive correlations between increasing sales and development. In essence, the ends of more development, principally because of the governance structures of fair trade but also its ability to fend off total control by MNCs, have worked to justify the means of mainstreaming, supermarket partnerships and lines of fair trade goods supplied by some of the world's most competitive and powerful MNCs.

Third, in the UK at least, the decision to take fair trade mainstream was at the base of the founding directives and business plans of both Cafédirect and Divine Chocolate. This happened at or about the same time that supermarkets such as the Co-op, followed by Tesco and others, decided to bring fair trade onto their market shelves through their own-label branded fair trade goods. This strategy meant that fair trade goods needed to become more attractive to consumers beyond the activist core who had supported it from the beginning of its market development. Thus the decision was taken to market fair trade as a product of "quality" – one of distinction based on taste as well as perception through its presentation with associated marketing imagery. Fair trade thus began to trade on brand reputation, taste and distinction as much as, or even more than, its ethics and qualities of embedded care. Of course, this decision has had huge implications for supply chains since this marketing strategy called for an almost overnight improvement in the quality of coffee and other fair trade goods, as well as much greater supplies of fair trade commodities. These points are taken up in greater detail in the next chapter, while the implications for the evolution of fair trade's cultural politics are explored more fully below.

Fourth, through this shift to a quality product, fair trade has been at the fore-front of developing the possibilities of internet technologies as a way to make interactive connections between consumers and fair trade producer communities. Colloquially known as the growing trend of "clicktivism," going virtual with fair trade activism (Kleine 2005, 2010) and, more broadly, sustainable consumption (Hinton 2011; Hinton and Goodman 2010), builds on the ability of the internet to "defetishize" commodities (Miller 2003). In agro-food networks, the internet has been used as a way for consumers to, for example, get to know their veget-ables and/or sheep they are buying and eating (Holloway 2002; Kneafsey *et al.* 2008). Specifically, as other images of quality have taken over in fair trade net-works, farmers, their livelihoods and their confessional stories about fair trade have gone online in interesting and potentially transgressive ways designed to connect consumers with the actual producers and farms providing their fair trade goods.

Thus, the once vaunted transparency of fair trade networks – a transparency defined by showing consumers where their fair trade coffee comes from and how it contributes to the livelihoods of the farmers – has moved into the virtual spaces of the internet in ways that could simply not be deployed on coffee bags and jars, supermarket shelves, and advertisements. These virtual knowledge net-works of transparency in fair trade seem set to characterize much of the future of fair trade.

Traffic in things, traffic in care: the making of fair trade's moral economy

One of the key points articulated in these chapters is that the ethics of care embedded in fair trade networks through the processes of commodification, in short, fair trade's moral economy, is a function of both the specific economic structures of the fair trade model and the discursive and visual *cultural econom-ies* that accompany and work to construct these networks. But these cultural eco-nomies of fair trade are much more than just simply there to market fair trade goods: as semiotic intermediaries situated in between consumers and producers of fair trade goods, they are, in essence, *indispensable* in creating the meanings of fair trade good as caring consumption and ethical development. In addition, they also work to articulate the emotional, moral, and material difference of what fair trade is and does to consumers and potential consumers. In this respect, the material networks and specific economic "conventions" of fair trade (Raynolds 2000, 2002, 2009; Raynolds *et al.* 2007; Renard 2003, 2005; Whatmore and Thorne 1997) only really get it so far: they can certainly bring these items to supermarkets and consumers to be bought and sold. Yet, without the discourses and images surrounding fair trade – whether that be a farmer testimonial, the fair trade certification logo, or a fair trade celebrity as part of a wider campaign – consumers would be hard pressed to know or see the difference that the fair trade difference makes and can make.

These fundamental connections among commodities, cultures, and mater-ialities have been explored by geographers and others through work on the "social lives" and "traffic" in things (Appadurai 1986; Cook 2004; Jackson 1999), as well as commodity cultures, networks, circuits, and chains (see Jackson 2002; Cook and Crang 1996; Crang *et al.* 2003; Hughes 2000, 2001; Hughes and Reimer 2004; Watts 1999).[5] In particular, this work has highlighted, in a very broad sense, how the production and migration of various forms of knowledge within commodity networks is a crucial element to their creation and function (Hughes 2000). That this knowledge is often particularly geographic in nature should come as no surprise given concerns about the continuing globalization of food networks and the growing interest in where our food is coming from (Jackson 2010) and what development it is supporting.

In their innovative work on food geographies, Cook and Crang (1996: 142) detail the kinds of knowledge they see making up food commodities' geographic imaginations: the contextualized use of food by consumers (their "settings"), how foods move in commodity systems (their "biographies"), and where they come from (their "origins"). While these three knowledges are provisioned in fair trade networks, other knowledges also are made visible and moved within these networks. On some products and in some outlets, though at lower satura-tion levels than just a few years ago, these additional knowledges consist of the redesigned fetish of producers' place-based and politicized livelihood struggles. Thus, what has been called fair trade's "political ecological imaginary" (M. Goodman 2004) tells consumers how the commodity works but also, and most importantly, demonstrates the progressive effects of their act of consumption on the particular community that grew what they are eating. It is this imaginary that attempts to rally and energize consumers to be morally reflexive, what Probyn (2000: 32) refers to as "wearing one's stomach on one's sleeve," and literally buy-in to the politics of fair trade and alternative development.

Yet, it is these imaginaries and knowledges about fair trade networks – its bid for a semiotic transparency to make the ethical and care-full connections between consumers and producers – which have not remained consistent. Indeed, they have been replaced or rendered opaque as other imaginaries and sets of knowledges have come to construct different meanings in fair trade networks. As a consequence, the virtual spaces of website imagery and text have taken on this "knowledge dissemination" role by opening up new and much broader and richer spaces in which to engage consumers with the political ecological imaginary of fair trade. Here, "clicking on a face" of a fair trade producer takes consumers or others through to the literal (but also partial) world of these producers using photo-essays of their lives and livelihoods and extensive testimonials in ways that are impossible in other marketing materials like labels and advertisements. The place of transparency and knowledge provisioning in fair trade has moved to the web as this very same transparency was made opaque by the drive for quality in fair trade markets. Of course, this virtualization of farmers and fair trade knowledges has its own problems as well as potential possibilities in further cultivating fair trade networks. Nevertheless, the web provides a significant new setting for the provisioning of knowledge about commodities and, indeed, food commodities more broadly.

In six movements: the embodiments of fair trade ... at least up to now

So, how have the imaginaries and knowledge regimes of fair trade shifted as it has moved into the mainstream and become a product of quality and what does this mean for fair trade's cultural politics of, among other things, transparency, connection, and care? We conceptualize these shifts in six separate visual and textual "embodiments" of what fair trade is and is about. As such, these embodiments are cumulative and have built up over the years as new campaigns and marketing strategies have been introduced to the sector. Fair trade's embodiments are thus multiple and often occur in parallel to each other. This is especially so today as their power to capture the media and marketing space has changed over time with a perceived need to continue to manage these embodiments and imaginaries in order to maintain and attract more fair trade consumers. Yet, each has its own implications for the practices of fair trade as an ethical connectivity of care between producers and consumers. We take each of these six embodiments in turn below.

Fair trade's political ecological imaginary, its (re)fetishization and transparency

The initial and earliest embodiment of fair trade includes the creation, deployment, and dissemination of what we are calling its political ecological imaginary: a visual and textual "thick description" of the producers' lives and livelihoods as written in the very faces, bodies, words, and farms of the farmers themselves.

Thus, in examples drawn from Goodman (2004, (1)900), a farmer with the famous Kuapa Kokoo cooperative in Ghana explains:

> We rely on the money we get from cocoa for everything: for food, clothes, medicines, and school fees.... Kuapa Kokoo pays all its farmers a fair price

for their crop, in cash, and on time. I am very happy: since I joined Fair Trade I can afford to send my children to school.

Consumer testimonials are also common, as the UK's Fairtrade Foundation relates:

> Emily Eavis drinks a lot of coffee. But coffee didn't arouse her passion till she met Fairtrade-registered coffee farmers in the Dominican Republic. "It was incredibly eye-opening. You arrive here, and you realise that the whole system is completely imbalanced".... Emily was most struck by "how simple it could be for consumers in the UK to change things. All we need to do is to be aware of the problem."
>
> (M. Goodman 2004: 900)

These images and discourses were very much front and center on coffee bags and chocolate bars, on the in-store/charity-shop marketing materials, and in advertisements in the media. The political ecological imaginary, as we have it, serves several crucial functions and has a number of important effects in fair trade networks.

First, this initial embodiment in the earliest fair trade networks has a pedagogical function in teaching consumers the difference that the fair trade difference makes. The knowledge regime – or better yet, educational regime – of fair trade networks is the key to educating consumers in the "what," "where," "who," "why" and "how" of the practices of fair trade. This educational regime, through its connectivity, as we argue below, is also crucial for the encouragement of the self-governance and identity-making processes of consumers as "fair trade consumers" specifically and/or as "caring individuals" and/or "ethical consumers" more broadly (cf. Barnett *et al.* 2005; see also Dubuisson-Quellier and Lamine 2008).

Second, the provisioning of knowledge in this initial embodiment is about the development and encouragement of a semiotic connectivity between fair trade consumers and fair trade producers. Seeing fair trade farmers and hearing their testimonials about how fair trade has improved their livelihoods is a powerful set of devices designed to articulate these production/consumption connections. These connections of care create a kind of "solidarity in difference" between producers and consumers. That is, while encompassing and utilizing the situated cultural, economic, political, and power differences between producers and consumers, fair trade looks to transcend these differences with a move toward a more social justice-like vision of equality in "the good life" (Smith 1997).

In this way, fair trade seeks to expand the everyday experiences of care and responsibility to include the "needs of distant strangers" (Corbridge, 1998) through the everyday-ness of eating, drinking, and situated commodity production. In these narratives of fair trade, its embedded and commoditized ethics of care is materialized across the spaces of globalization in a moral economy encompassing a politics both of recognition and redistribution (cf. Fraser 1999).

The spatial dynamics of concern in fair trade networks, one that works to connect the distant places and spaces of production and consumption, offers up a moral economy that is as much discursive, visual, and indeed, emotional and cognitive, as it is material in the provisioning of the fair trade premium, its minimum prices and more direct trade relations.

Third, taking this embodiment further, fair trade's knowledge regime and connections of care seek to make its networks semiotically transparent. This works in conjunction with the original material and economic transparency of fair trade networks that proposed to do business differently by making the terms of trade in fair trade supply chains available to the public: who is buying from whom, at what price and under what conditions. Focusing on this semiotic transparency in fair trade networks as we do here, producers as well as consumers are made to "(re)appear" by being painted in the light of labels and marketing materials.

In somewhat more theoretical terms, some have argued that this transparency in fair trade networks "de-fetishizes" these commodities in that it "peels away" the veil of who produced what and how that haunts all commodities in capitalist market relations (Hudson and Hudson 2003). In other words, the social relations of production (and consumption) are made known and knowable to fair trade consumers on and around the very bodies of fair trade commodities and this becomes a powerful selling point for these goods. Yet what actually occurs is more of a "re-fetishization" of fair trade goods by deploying an esthetic that creates further cultural and economic surpluses for fair trade networks in the displayed livelihoods of fair trade farmers, their farms, and worked upon natures.[6] In the words of Cook and Crang (1996), actors in fair trade networks, from producer cooperatives to fair trade NGOs and businesses, have "seized" the fetish in the bodies and livelihoods of producers to facilitate development that might otherwise not happen without consumer interest and their purchases.

At the very same time, however, a more worrying process is set in train, namely, the deeper commoditization of people and place in the form of farmers' livelihoods with all its consequences. That is, greater competition based on one's development narrative and livelihood, the need to have a narrative and marketable livelihood to sell, and thus the deeper embedding of uneven development in the processes of economic growth of fair trade networks (Goodman 2010; Guthman 2007; Johnston 2002; Lyon 2006; Scrase 2010; Varul 2008; see also Castree 2001). Here the commodification of difference can make a difference but one that is characterized and confined by the dictates of the market relations in which fair trade networks are entangled.

Quality landscapes/landscapes of quality and the "logo-ization of care"

The second embodiment of fair trade is situated directly at the center of its move into the mainstream and desire to be viewed as a "quality" product. Indeed, early on, much like organic foods, fair trade suffered from an image problem: that of poor taste and of poor or inconsistent quality. For example, some of the earliest fair trade coffees were rather hard to drink, thus only the most committed and core solidarity buyers bought fair trade coffee and other early fair trade items. As a key player in the UK fair trade coffee industry put it in an interview, "in the early days, Oxfam would basically sell anything." Thus the drive to develop fair trade as a set of quality branded products of distinction and good taste, led very much by the coffee sector, occurred in parallel with the mainstreaming of fair trade. Indeed, for some companies, selling and marketing fair trade goods as a quality item has overtaken much of the moral economy embedded in fair trade. In the same conversation, the informant stated the following:

> We're not the ethical brand they have on their shelves, we are another brand and sure we're ethical ... but we are a brand just like Kellogg's.... So there is definitely the changing focus to premium foods and fair trade second because that is how we see ourselves being, competing under mainstream against the big players, we differentiate on quality and price.
>
> (Interview, fair trade marketing manager, 2003)

While insisting that "we are fair trade at our core," he presented one of their newest fair trade lines by arguing that "it's a great tasting product, and, you know, that's what we are selling it on. It's on quality; it's not on fair trade." Another interviewee from an organic, fair trade chocolate company put it succinctly: "I think with [our company], taste is the first thing, and then the fact that it's organic and then the fact it's ethical."

Thus, in many ways, much of the first embodiment of fair trade is now moot, especially on the labels and main marketing materials in the coffee and chocolate sectors in the UK. Indeed, in order to develop "premium looks" of quality as a marketeer at a major UK fair trade coffee brand put it, the farmers were removed in favor of a newer and second embodiment: that of dazzling and more "touristic" images of sunsets/sunrises, spectacular mountainsides, and coffee trails, as well as world-famous landscapes like Machu Picchu, the latter less known for its coffee than for the iconic Incan ruins perched at its apex. The problem, as an interviewee observed, was that the images and descriptions of farmers and their livelihoods became "too" ethical and "fair trade," and thus too closely associated with those earlier perceptions of the poor quality of these goods. As he stated:

> There's not a picture of a smiling farmer on the front and there is a reason for that because that would be very fair trade and very ethical, and you go, "oh look," you know, "farming" ... but that scares consumers.
>
> (Interview, fair trade marketing manager, 2003)

The connective and meaning-full transparency of fair trade networks had become a liability in the rapidly mainstreaming spaces of fair trade quality. Here, then, are the beginnings of the opacity and muddling of the discursive transparency of fair trade. No longer were consumers able to engage with communities' livelihood struggles, however superficial this interaction might be, as depicted on a coffee bag through these earlier semiotics of transparency of the conditions of production and consumption. Instead, the fair trade logo – now recognized by 72 percent of UK adults in a recent survey (Fairtrade Foundation 2011) – has become a kind of visual proxy for the relations developed in previous fair trade narratives and has taken on greater meaning in these shifting cultural politics.[7] That is, in the absence of the previous images and voices of farmers, it has now become an emblem of trust embodying both a pedagogical function – "You see the logo and you know it is about care and development" – and a semiotic connective role – "The logo connects me to poor farmers." Mainstreaming, the drive for quality and this growing "logo-ization" of fair trade are obscuring these articulations of care, connection, and transparency that formed the base of fair trade's historical activism.

In particular, the semiotic transparency and knowledge regimes, so much an established part of fair trade networks, became muddled through this simultaneous "sexing-up" and logo-ization of care that greased the pathways for the mainstreaming of fair trade. Concomitantly, it allowed these newly crowned good tasting/high quality networks to build on and contribute to the further marketization of care and development and the wider precepts and dictates of neoliberal societies as *the* way to do care and development. The promotion of these new semiotic cues of taste and quality as the use-values in fair trade has displaced those of care, connectivity, and development, which have now been re-embedded in the much less transparent but even *more* meaningful form of the fair trade logo.

In an interesting twist to this story, it has actually been the likes of Nestlé and Tesco who have taken up the mantle of fair trade's bent for semiotic transparency by going somewhat "old school" and using the first embodiment of the political ecological imaginary. In short, both Nestlé's "Partners' Blend" and Tesco's own-label branded fair trade coffees – through the use of both the image of poor farmers and the tag line of "Coffee that helps farmers, their communities and the environment" in Nestlé's case – arguably are more transparent than the goods sold by the dedicated fair trade coffee company of Cafédirect. In some ways, Nestlé in particular already had the reputation for quality and so needed to push its "care" and "connectivity" credibility more than anything else contra other fair trade goods. Either way, that the likes of Nestlé and Tesco are more semiotically transparent than dedicated fair trade companies is quite a bitter mouthful and is worthy of much further consideration and engagement than can be done here.

The celebritization of fair trade, Chris Martin and the "="

The third cumulative embodiment of fair trade includes the growing list of television, movie, and other media celebrities engaged in stumping for fair trade.[8] As the turn to quality has continued to evolve and sediment, the growing disassociation with producers' livelihoods and the retreat from transparency has been further accentuated by the marketing of fair trade through celebrities. Three particular instances of this stand out in the UK, all either concocted by or attached to Oxfam, the Fairtrade Foundation, and/or Fairtrade Fortnight.[9] First, there was the "dumped-on" celebrity campaign which launched this new embodiment (Goodman 2010).[10] Published fully in the *Observer Magazine* (Siegle 2004) and then in dribs and drabs in other parts of the UK media and on Oxfam's "maketradefair.com" website, the point was to

> illustrate a story. A story about how poor farmers are being 'dumped on' every day by rich countries and rich companies and about how you can change this by joining the Big Noise petition to make trade fair. If we all join together and make a big enough noise politicians and corporate bosses will have to listen.
>
> (maketradefair.com, 2006)

The second instance involves photographs and celebrities again, but instead of having goods dumped on them, different foods were placed in various celebrities'[11] mouths bringing a new level of performativity to fair trade media. This culminated in a photo exhibit at a London gallery and write-up in the *Observer Food Monthly*:

> It's the new black – or rather, the new blue, green and black [the colours of the Fairtade logo]. Fairtrade, with its funky but strangely impenetrable logo, has become fashionable.... Last year it was voted "best of the superbrands" in a poll to mark the launch of the Superbrands 2005 handbook – beating AOL, BT and The Times as the one that has excelled in its field.
>
> (Purvis 2006)

The third instance involves the enrolment by Oxfam of Chris Martin, the lead singer of the British band, Coldplay. Clearly not just the "other half" of Gwyneth Paltrow, nor only the frontman for a band that has sold over 30 million albums and has multiple Emmys; rather, he is quite convinced about fair trade: "If Beyoncé sells hair products, I can sell fairer trade as that is what I believe in" (Siegle 2004). Taken to talking about fair trade and being photographed with "dumped" food, Martin has shifted this to another level by wearing fair trade shirts and, more interestingly, by writing "maketradefair.com" on his piano and then his hand. As fair trade has become a brand and the maketradefair.com campaign began to spread to a wider audience, he turned into simply writing – with a nod to the Artist-Formerly-Known-as-Prince – an "equals" (i.e., "=") symbol on his hand.[12] This then progressively becomes the fourth embodiment of fair trade: its earlier images, voices, and stories of poor producers working themselves out of poverty through fair trade has been reduced to a mere equals sign. Thus, as these third and fourth embodiments of fair trade have taken hold, the semiotics of what fair trade is and is about have progressed from poor producers' livelihoods, to the fair trade logo, to celebrities, to a "=" on the hand of a rock star. This has been accompanied by a shift in who can speak about fair trade and how this can be done. Indeed, as Martin has put it – in a rather astounding statement for a musician – "Nobody has to listen to me as long as they can see me." Celebrities, logos, symbols, and landscapes are overtaking fair trade's previous ethos of transparency and constructing a much less rich visual and textual language around the producer/consumer relationship on which fair trade's material structures are built.

Thus, abandoning transparency and meaningful imaginaries in its drive for market growth, fair trade is compounding its ambiguities. As more celebrities such as Chris Martin continue to colonize the media and marketing space for fair trade, fair trade consumption becomes a set of stories and images made for and told to our rich and northern selves and less about those (always limited) stories and images of poor Others that at least carry the possibilities of building ethical networks of care. This "mirror of consumption," as one might have it, works to disassemble any opportunity to develop those connections with producers and the potentially collectivist political and knowing subjects of fair trade consumers. In other words, if all we see is celebrities talking about and supporting fair trade, consuming these commodities becomes more about being like that celebrity – and thus our "ordinary" and "extraordinary" selves – than it does about making connections to poor producers and their marginal and marginalized livelihoods, wherein lies at least the opportunities to develop consumption as a form of knowable and engage-able "politics in an ethical register" (Clarke *et al.* 2007).

The biggest worry is that with the celebritization of both development and fair trade more specifically, we are entering a veritable house of mirrors that works to reflect more of our own selves back to our own selves than it does to shine light on the global spaces of poverty, inequality, and injustice that are displayed, in however limited ways, on coffee bags and websites. This house of mirrors might work to squeeze out the growing ethics of care in networks like fair trade in favor of a cosmopolitan celebritization that could easily slip into more hollow spectacles than material change.

Connected labor/hidden voices

A fifth embodiment of fair trade specifically involves a recent relaunch and repackaging of most of Cafédirect's coffee, chocolate, and tea lines. These imaginaries, like the celebrity landscapes of quality in earlier embodiments, include a set of visuals of the celebrity tools of the trade in images of hand clippers, woven baskets, hand scoops, shovels, small-scale processing machines, machetes, and scales. In this way, Cafédirect builds on the earlier images of quality, but does so in a way that starts to bring the labor of the farmers and cooperatives back into the framing of what fair trade is and does. Here is a set of re-fetishized images of tools that provide an echo of the labor and a sort of phantom presence of the farmers, but avoids the "un-quality" of the actual farmers, growers, and pickers.

Yet, there are further, indeed, multiple, layers to be read in this newer imaginary. On the one hand, there is a sort of resuscitation of a connection to the growers and a form of transparency in these tools and their "ordinary" materialities and evocation of the labor involved in harvesting and processing these goods. On the other hand, a kind of distanciation is maintained without the specificities of who is actually wielding these tools, and it is one that carries a kind of generic form of labor speaking to (perhaps) the tools used by *all* fair trade farmers, and so there is the sense in these visuals that fair trade supports a multiplicity of poor farmers, their communities, and community development. Thus, in this implied semiotics of support for the multiplicity of the missing farmers and their communities who wield these tools, there is a sort of "extraordinariness" being conveyed here. That is, these hidden multiplicities in conjunction with consumers' purchases are contributing not only to the creation of high quality networks of fair trade goods but also to the development and care of producers' livelihoods. Knowledge circulating in and on these goods is of the dis-embodied labor of the farmers and practices of fair trade harvesting which, since it is dis-embodied and generic adds to its capacity to articulate the power of fair trade to be about more diffuse forms of community development. In this way, it reveals how consumers' purchases help to enable these tools to be put in action to facilitate the high quality goods they are consuming and the fair trade networks that bring them to their place of purchase.

This embodiment is an extension of the quality landscapes and celebritization described above in that it maintains and even further develops the muddled transparency and care-full sets of connections created in the first embodiment of fair trade networks. But it does so in a very interesting fashion: these tools stand in for the labor, efforts, and indeed bodies of farmers and their communities, but they do so in such a way that suggests a connection, albeit of a "phantom" sort, to fair trade farmers. Ultimately, this embodiment is one that is actually about and maintains the dis-embodiment of fair trade farmers and their livelihood places and spaces, and does so through the form of the spectacles of labor seen in the tools of the trade of fair trade farmers and their communities. It is up to the final embodiment discussed here – in the virtual spaces of the internet – to make these connections and the faces and places of fair trade visible and knowable after a fashion to consumers and web-surfers alike.

The virtualization of livelihoods, labor, and care

The final embodiment of fair trade here goes back to the original political ecological imaginary in fair trade's initial embodiment: that of the farmers, their lives, livelihoods, farms, and communities but it does so in the "virtual" environment of the internet. Fair trade, in a sense, is being semiotically "re-placed" back into the bodies and places of producing communities as performed and practiced in the online forum of the webpages of Cafédirect and the UK's Fairtrade Foundation. Interestingly the "un-quality" of farmers and their livelihoods has gone virtual, yet in such a way that it does not take away from the quality that fair trade goods have built up over the last few years. Virtual farmers and their phantom labor are "safe," while "real" (albeit as re-fetishized) farmers – at least on the packages of the largest fair trade companies – are not.

For Cafédirect, there is an obvious tie in with their tools campaign and, when one accesses the Cafédirect website, each product line is associated with a different packaged tool and we are given an image of a particular farmer using that implement and text about fair trade in their own words. For example, underneath their main, overarching message of: "We are the growers and you can taste it," there is an image of Mugisha Pauson, a tea picker from Uganda with the tea-picking basket full of freshly picked tea leaves on his back. The following words from him are placed next to his picture:

> I like my work – I pick tea and put it in my basket. Believe it or not, I can smell the quality tea leaves. Cafédirect has helped our community by giving us a fair price, so now I pick the tea with a big smile.
>
> (Cafédirect 2011)

We are then encouraged to click through to another page dedicated to fair trade tea with further images, testimonials, and descriptions of the tea, as well as more information about the company's relationship with the cooperative that produces their tea. This is similar across the dozens of other product lines that Cafédirect sells and markets: numerous rich images are related to the tools on the actual product packaging, with testimonials from the growers and their communities alongside Cafédirect's descriptions of the various products, festooned with key words such as flavor, body, fresh, full-bodied, mellow, fulsome, lush, fertile, and of course delicious.

The Fairtrade Foundation provides us with something similar in their ability and desire to have us "meet the producers." One of their main tabs across the top of their webpage is entitled "Producers," where a click will take us to a list of the various fair trade products they certify in the UK. Here we can click on the names of particular producers and their cooperatives, some products having more than one farmer, some only having one, some only with the name of the cooperative. Once there, we are encouraged to read the testimonials of the fair trade farmers or descriptions of the cooperatives, their history and/or how they have benefited from fair trade. The Fairtrade Foundation provides many more images and visuals of farmers and their cooperatives, as well as much longer and involved histories and/or testimonials from farmers and growers compared to Cafédirect. This is an even greater and much more involved form of thick description that is enabled through the platform of the web in which images, texts and documents can be linked, expanded and lodged in ways beyond what can be done on packaging or marketing material.

The development of these web spaces and virtual farmers in fair trade networks has somewhat solidified the locations for the circulation of these different types of knowledge about fair trade through these different embodiments. In short, fair trade packaging carries the message of the high quality of fair trade products, and the media conveys messages of "emulation," "popularity" and "credibility" through the use of fair trade stars. But the voices of actual farmers in actual communities are silenced through the mirror-like qualities of celebrities, their voices on fair trade websites being resuscitated, brought to the foreground and given space to appear. In other words, fair trade packaging is about quality, fair trade celebrities are about awareness and sales, and fair trade websites are about knowledge, connection, and transparency.

Fair trade websites allow for a much more fully-formed sort of transparency and perhaps one that was situated at the core of fair trade from its beginnings. But here too, like the first embodiment, there is a kind of re-fetishization of farmers, their livelihoods and their "quality" labor, in addition to a coincident and further commodification of these things in the body of fair trade goods. Thus, in the case of fair trade websites, the internet is less about de-fetishization per se (see Miller 2003) but rather a very crafty and carefully staged de-fetishization *and* re-fetishization in the name of providing knowledge and information about fair trade products in order to sell them and their version of market-based care. Indeed, not only are growers able to tell their own stories in their own voices – a move that should perhaps be celebrated to some extent – but they are doing it in order to sell their story and livelihood and, of course, fair trade products they are associated with. The difference is that they are now doing it more in the language of the quality and taste of these products.

Finally, in parallel with the knowledge-rich content that the web provides to fair trade networks, two concerns stand out. First, the power relations, even on the web, remain in the hands of consumers in that transparency and the abilities to achieve it are one-sided. Consumers get to "see" producers and farmers but producers have few opportunities to see who is buying their products, how and why, even further embedding what Wright (2004; see also Lyon 2006) has problematized as a sort of "one-way vision" of the transparency of fair trade networks. Second, while the web seems to open up one particular if wider pathway to transparency and/or knowledge in fair trade networks, it might be closing down or indeed *actively* close down others. Since this information is being provided on the internet and not at the point of sale, the sort of immediacy in the connection between producers and consumers is lost (if it was ever there, but it certainly was the intention from the early days of fair trade).

Fair trade websites thus have created new forms of intention and care, in that consumers or those interested in fair trade must make the trip to certain websites rather than just a trip down a certain aisle while doing the shopping. While transparency might be facilitated by the information-rich environments of the web, the ability to access these virtual spaces is not spread evenly across consumers.

Conclusion

This chapter has explored the changing cultural material politics of fair trade in its shifting semiotic regimes of knowledge and their practices as FTNs have moved into the mainstream. The move to fair trade as a quality product has had extensive implications for FTNs' knowledge regimes as they have turned more opaque, been muddled but also, in parallel moves, gone online to reclaim the historical transparencies of fair trade. Moreover, we have argued here that formulations of fair trade as an instance of ethical consumption need to extend their analytical gaze beyond these shifts in FTNs' bids to develop the subjects and spaces of ethical consumption. A fuller understanding of these processes brings to light the commodification of care and responsibility in FTNs, as well as revealing that this is the center-piece of neoliberal approaches to the problems of market-led development. In order to build on this discussion, the next chapter examines the material implications of this quality turn in FTNs as a way to more fully flesh out the cultural material politics of contemporary fair trade movements and markets.

11 The price and practices of quality

The shifting materialities of fair trade networks

Introduction

What are the materialities of quality in agro-food networks? What are the materialities of ethical consumption in the specific context of food? In other words, how do quality and ethical consumption *work* and how are they practiced in terms of their cultural material politics of food? This chapter explores these questions in relation to the shifting materialities that arise as a result of the mainstreaming of fair trade networks. The material *effects* of the move of fair trade to a quality product and of the increase in market share for fair trade as ethical consumers bought into it, should perhaps be seen as good things: more sales mean that more development is being funded and supported in fair trade producer communities throughout the world. As we saw in the last chapter, these changes have muddied the semiotics surrounding fair trade. Furthermore, however, as this chapter argues, this quality turn and mainstreaming have also triggered significant shifts in the materialities of the processes that bring fair trade products to the market, in the UK in particular, and make them available to the ethical consumers who support, choose, buy, and consume these products (cf. Barnett *et al.* 2005).

Agro-food literatures have focused strongly on the conceptualization of quality food networks and provided valuable case material on the processes of the re-connection of consumers, producers, and food (cf. Kneafsey *et al.* 2008). Typically, we have very good snapshots of what quality or alternative food networks look like at a particular moment in time – for such projects as community supported agriculture (CSAs)/box schemes (Kneafsey *et al.* 2008; Clarke *et al.* 2008), farmers' markets (D. Goodman 2010; Kirwan 2004; Holloway and Kneafsey 2000, 2004), short food supply chains (Ilbery and Maye 2005b) and "ecological entrepreneurship" (Marsden and Smith 2005; Sonnino and Marsden 2006). However, there are far fewer explorations of who wins or loses and/or *why* this might be the case across particular production/consumption sectors over time. In short, much less attention has been given to the material implications of these shifts to quality foods, especially the effects on supply chains and the farmers themselves. That said, current research and writing, building on key past and related work (e.g., Cook 2004; DuPuis 2000; Jackson *et al.* 2009;

McMichael 1994; Mintz 1985; Watson and Caldwell 2005), has turned to explorations of what might be called a *political economy of food quality* that is beginning to uncover the important historical trajectories and scalar/geographical differences of quality in food networks (Busch 2000; Freidberg 2003a, 2003b; D. Goodman 2004; Guthman 2004a, 2004c; Harvey *et al.* 2004; Mansfield 2003a). One of the key strands of this research, at least in the context of this chapter, is a more specific focus on the processes and effects of the *globalizations* of quality for such goods as organic and fair trade foods (Bacon 2005, 2010; McEwan and Bek 2009; Mutersbaugh 2002; Raynolds 2004; Renard 2003, 2005).

In engaging with these recent contributions, it is becoming clear that analyses of quality in food networks must recognize that while quality distinction can open up new markets and pathways for alternative foods, it can equally close down access for those who are unable to produce a certain quality or set of qualities in their foods. In alternative food networks (AFNs) such as organic agriculture, exclusion is achieved through the "barriers to entry" that production standards and certification requirements erect for participants in these markets (Guthman 2004c; Mutersbaugh 2002). Clearly, geography, too, plays an obvious part in the case of place-based products of *terroir* since those outside its territorial boundaries are unable to claim the quality rights or benefits of that particular place (Barham 2003; Feagan 2007; M. Goodman 2011).

Yet, one of the key qualities of quality foods – having the organoleptic properties of being "good" or "better" tasting – can also act as a further barrier to entry in the construction of the "precious" (Guthman, 2004c) nature of many alternative foods. So, for example, it is very often argued that organic foods taste better than those produced by conventional agriculture (Guthman 2003; Selfa and Qazi 2005). This differentiation strategy is certainly evident with fair trade foods in the UK. As the last chapter highlighted, efforts to promote these goods as higher quality through their packaging and also, crucially, as better tasting have been at the forefront of the fair trade movement and markets for a while now. Thus, in fair trade networks, chasing good and/or better tasting supplies, and so goods of higher quality, has brought interesting and substantive changes to the supply chains and materialities of these networks. In the case of fair trade, the quality distinction thus not only (re)connects consumers, producers, and their food in explicitly moral economies but can also maintain or erect *dis-connections* through standards and, most importantly here, taste.

The exploration of this quickly growing *tyranny of quality* is therefore crucial given what is at stake for producers and their communities hoping to participate in fair trade networks: those farmers and communities without the right "quality," typically the most marginalized and disadvantaged farmers on the worst soil, for example – and the ones for whom fair trade has been designed to support – are often excluded from access to fair trade networks and markets. Producers and producer cooperatives thus face a double set of barriers to entry: fair trade's standards and certification governance scheme *and* the ability to meet the quality standards established for these networks. Fair trade coffees, for example, must not only be certified as fairly traded, but must now also conform to the increasingly demanding taste requirements that circulate in fair trade supply chains.

The mainstreaming of fair trade, and the strategic decision to promote its quality and qualities of taste, has put the fair trade movement in an ambivalent position: its moral economy must conform to the pragmatic "moralities" of markets. In other words, such moral economies have to follow the market-embedded logics of expansion, sales, and marketing if they are to continue to grow. Over time therefore fair trade has experienced twin pressures to expand: those related to the generic characteristic of being in a market – which were accentuated as it mainstreamed – and the movement-derived pressures to expand in order to sell and thus provide more development.

The key point here is that the decision to take fair trade into the mainstream has brought material requirements that create *new* ethical quandaries for the con-struction of its supply chains. In short, the consequentialism of fair trade that ini-tiated and also very much supported its mainstreaming is now complicating and challenging some of the core principles at the base of its moral economy. As we emphasized in Chapter 10, the "market-ness" that bounds and governs fair trade now also works to bound its alternative and ethical characteristics that, in turn, define its moral economy. With fair trade's mainstreaming pragmatism, it is more "in" the market than "against it" and very much less "not of it" (Barrett-Brown 1993; Raynolds 2002; Taylor 2005). Indeed, being "in the market" – and following the requirements this imposes – now very much governs what fair trade is and can do at the moment.

Yet the growing literature that situates fair trade in the wider context of ethical consumption so far has failed to address these complications of fair trade and its moral economy (cf. Barnett *et al.* 2005, 2010; Malpass *et al.* 2007; Pykett *et al.* 2010). Indeed, little of the writing that uses fair trade as a specific example of ethical consumption gets at how fair trade actually currently works and/or is practiced in more political economic terms, which, if examined closely, might call current conceptualizations of ethical consumption into question.[1] In the fol-lowing paragraphs, we explore several points about ethical consumption and analyses that illustrate and articulate its contours using the example of fair trade.

First, one of the key propositions in recent discussions of ethical consumption is that all acts of consumption are enmeshed in what are called the "ordinary ethics" of peoples' everyday lives (Barnett *et al.* 2005). On this argument, non-governmental organizations (NGOs), such as fair trade organizations, engage with and make connection to these ordinary and everyday ethics through their campaigns and marketing materials that then provide consumers with a way to act on their everyday ethics by choosing to buy fair trade products. Yet, whose ordinary ethics are these, and who decides what is "ordinary" and what is "ethical" in terms of consumption? How is this "ordinariness" developed and framed and why is consumption privileged as the site for the expression of this ordinariness? More specifically, what is this ordinariness that fair trade is tapping into in order to develop and put its ethics of care in train across places and space? For example, in Fair Trade Networks (FTNs), the ordinariness of providing and ingesting good or even better tasting goods seems to be at odds with the moralities of the supply chains that bring them to ethical consumers. Current accounts of ethical consumption fail to get to grips with these issues and questions by ignoring the social, cultural, and political economic contexts, and their spatial specificities or differences, around which ordinary ethics are, have been or can be developed, deployed, or brought into being.

Second, most of the research and writing on ethical consumption has been at the level of the consumer/commodity interface and/or theorizations of these entanglements and the generalized politics of ethical consumption more broadly. Here, with the help of NGO campaigns and ethical consumer guides, consumers govern themselves to act-at-a-distance to promote development or stave off environmental disaster through their "collectively individualized" acts of ethical consumption. Yet, what happens *in between* the production and consumption of these goods matters and matters in ethically-contingent ways as much as the "forward" effects (i.e., identity creating and articulating) of ethical purchases made by ethical consumers. Indeed, in most of the work on ethical consumption, little is said about the social or, better yet, ethical *lives* of the goods being consumed or about the social relations that bring these goods to the store shelves for ethical consumers to be able to choose.

Moreover, what about the ethical issues related to *where* these items are bought and sold? Selling fair trade goods through Oxfam and Christian Aid catalogues and at churches and worldshops is quite different than doing the same at some of the ethically-dubious supermarkets that now corner the market for fair trade goods. Similarly, how does buying fair trade chocolate from Nestlé or fair trade bananas sourced through Chiquita complicate the "ordinary" ethics of ethical consumption or, indeed, the ethical social life of these fair trade goods? Individualized and/or collectivized consumption acts might appear to be ethical at the level of NGO marketing, consumption choice and their supply chain effects. Then again, perhaps not if one considers their contemporary supply chains and places of purchase. At the very least, these issues should be examined in the light of a more fully fleshed-out accounting of the social life of the goods in question.

Overall, the shortcomings of work on ethical consumption can be traced to its overtly *specific* – albeit instructive and theoretically-innovative – focus on consumption, consumer self-governance, identities, and assumptions about consumer politics to the detriment of a more broadly defined materialist and practice-oriented perspective that works to understand ethical commodity networks and their effects up *and* down supply chains. Thus, the geographies of ethical consumption do not simply begin at the sites of the upward and outward effects of consumption, nor do ethically-consumed goods come from nowhere: they are fundamentally embedded in the socio-material relations of markets, as well as those socio-material relations that, in this case, define what fair trade is, does and should be.

The sections below explore aspects of the socio-ethical life of fair trade under the contemporary pressures of mainstreaming. This discussion calls on research on major actors in fair trade supply chains in the US, UK, and Europe – fair trade businesses, NGOs, retailers, suppliers, and certifiers – as well as fieldwork carried out in Costa Rica and the Dominican Republic over a period of about ten years.[2] We identify emerging trends in fair trade supply networks that reveal how it is beginning to work in the shadow of the pragmatic consequentialism and market-led morality that now holds sway in the provisioning of fair trade. We draw out the implications of these trends in terms of producer access to fair trade networks, shifts in the balance of power and the pressures they are imposing on long-standing governance structures that defined what fair trade was supposed to be about. We look first at the impacts that supplying fair trade for supermarkets and multinational corporations (MNCs) – one of the main characteristics of its mainstreaming – has had on fair trade supply chains and networks responding to demands for sufficient quantities of high quality fair trade goods.

Growing markets, shifting supply chains and "decentering" directness

One of the foundational principles of fair trade has been the development and maintenance of more direct trade routes between producers, importers, and consumers. The idea was to not only provide a more direct semiotic connection, as we saw in the last chapter, but also reduce the number of "middle-men" along the supply chain in order to allow a greater share of the value of the fair trade good to remain with the farmers and producer communities. At the same time, this directness provided greater scope to develop more immediate and durable social relations between the producer communities and importers, allowing each to invest more in that relationship, whether in terms of commercial concerns or those of care, and so provide longer-term investments in the health of each others' livelihoods, communities, and businesses. Barrientos and Smith (2007: 109; see also Raynolds and Wilkinson 2007) call this the "relational coordination" of fair trade whereby "…transactions are undertaken through regular direct contact and sustained notions of solidarity and trust." Thus part of fair trade's moral economy was about making it more "human" as well as "humane" and bound up in relations of care and responsibility as an antidote to the "facelessness" and "placelessness" of the conventional food system and its abstracting of socio-economic relations.

Yet, for a number of reasons, the requirement, and, indeed, ability to have direct trading relations began to slip as the mutual interest of supermarkets, MNCs, and fair trade organizations in mainstreaming fair trade products intensified. Supermarkets and MNCs require reliable and uninterrupted supplies of goods to sell and in the early phase of mainstreaming it was hard to establish and maintain consistent quantities of fair trade goods. The ability to ensure a consistent supply at sufficient quality was one of the key conditions fair trade had to meet in order to gain access to supermarkets and be sourced by MNCs. This imperative resulted in supermarkets, such as the Co-op, pushing to have their already existing suppliers such as Ffyfes, the massive MNC banana supplier, registered as able to handle supplies of fair trade goods.[3] The same has happened with Chiquita and Dole, two MNCs whose ethical standing is even more dubious and who are also now registered to supply fair trade bananas across Europe and especially to Sainsbury's in the UK, who is a 100 percent fair trade banana retailer (Fairtrade Foundation, 2006).

With the introduction and use of MNCs in fair trade supply chains, the ability to trace where and by whom fair trade goods are being produced has become much more muddled. Furthermore, the development of supermarket own-label fair trade has resulted in supply networks unique to fair trade, in that the products are much like any other sourced by supermarkets. Here a kind of generic pool of fair trade goods has emerged that is very much detached from the distinct producer cooperatives growing and selling fair trade goods, again reducing material and semiotic directness and traceability.[4] Smith and Barrientos (2005: 196; see also Robinson 2009) describe it this way:

> In the case of supermarket own brand fair trade products, these are increasingly sourced through category managers (as part of modular value chain governance). Category managers are agents or large suppliers that are contracted to supply a range of items within one product category (e.g., "salads" or "citrus fruit"). Fair trade products may be treated by the supermarket as no different from any other product in a particular category. The category manager is usually responsible for the relationship with producers, ensuring that they deliver according to the supermarket's standards, and the supermarket may have little direct contact with individual producers.

In a more recent piece of writing, they articulate this growing distanciation even more forcefully:

> Direct contact between supermarket buyers and Fair Trade producers is rare. Some supermarkets actively resist relationships being developed between supermarket buyers and producers by rotating staff frequently between product sectors, which makes it difficult to take a process approach in line with the development objectives of Fair Trade producers.
>
> (Barrientos and Smith, 2007: 119)

Interestingly, they see these growing relationships between fair trade and supermarkets as a potential "good" in that the governance and ethical characteristics of fair trade might actually work to influence supermarket supply chains for the better:

> [S]ome supermarkets, especially those with lower market share and eager to differentiate themselves amongst more exacting consumers, are keen to pursue strong direct relationships with the producers of their own brand goods. This has a greater synergy with the relational commitments of fair trade. For these supermarkets fair trade may facilitate dialogue and increased awareness of the producer's position, and foster a more equitable balance of

power in the trading relationship. The potential for fair trade to transform governance of supermarkets' own brand chains may therefore come down to company values and strategies.

(Smith and Barrientos 2005: 196)

Unfortunately, beyond the possible effects of fair trade on supermarkets, much of this seems to be wishful thinking; either way, the key point here is that novel supply chains and markets are being opened up for fair trade producers in interesting, far reaching, yet also troublingly complex ways.

When direct relations *are* being established between supermarkets, MNCs and fair trade producers, these more often than not are developed with some of the largest and/or more well-established fair trade cooperatives. This is exemplified by Cadbury's deal with Kuapa Kokoo in Ghana, which is reputed for the high quality of its "tasty" fair trade cacao and is one of the largest fair trade cooperatives in existence.[5] Such deals, given the known quality, established reputation, experience, and infrastructure of the cooperative, typically ensure the consistent supplies and qualities demanded by the large corporate players now engaged in fair trade networks and markets.

These trends have several important implications. First, it must be recognized that there is now a multiplicity of fair trade networks across a diversity of supply chain pathways. This is articulated in Figure 11.1 which shows this growing range of the different types and pathways of supply chains that now characterizes fair trade networks.

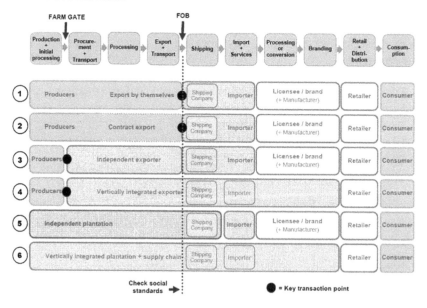

Figure 11.1 New Fair Trade Supply Chains. Multiple pathways define FTNs but also, in many and growing cases, work against the transparency and directness that has defined fair trade as an AFN (source: Twin Trading).

These new pathways in most cases have been developed for and by supermarkets and MNCs in partnership with fair trade retailers, businesses, and standards organizations in order to allow these actors to obtain stable and more diversified supplies of fair trade goods. These changes, as already argued, have opened up markets for some but at the price of "de-centering" the historically-embedded directness that earlier had so distinguished fair trade from conventional trade relations.

A second implication is that quality in fair trade networks has quickly come to mean *stable quantity* as much as good tasting, creating yet another barrier to entry and/or another requirement for producers in order to retain their status as a fair trade supplier. Third, Fairtrade Labelling Organizations International's (FLO's) role has expanded from the global governance of fair trade standards and certification to take on a powerful sort of "beneficent intermediary" function with respect to supply chains. FLO is being asked by suppliers and retailers in the global north to provide them with connections to and/or relationships with suppliers in the global south.[6] Thus, many of the specific supply chains for fair trade goods that make up the generic ones described in Figure 11.1 have been crafted and made viable by FLO through its own social networks with producers, suppliers, and retailers.

Indeed, both FLO and supermarkets have been able to create and define fair trade markets in their own ways, FLO through its abilities to connect the "sourcers" of fair trade with the "sourcees," and supermarkets by expanding existing fair trade markets for products like bananas, cacao, and coffee and developing new ones for fresh fruits and other goods. In fact, as one of FLO's head of standards related in 2003, it was actually supermarkets that wanted the development of fairly-traded fruits and vegetables and so they pushed FLO to not only develop standards for these products but also to identify suppliers capable of meeting their quality and volume requirements. Thus, in one of the interesting twists to FTNs, both FLO and supermarkets have become new intermediaries working between producers and consumers in ways that would have been inconceivable in the early days of fair trade – and playing the kind of role that early fair trade networks worked to resist.

Fourth, we would argue that this de-centering of the directness of fair trade militates against fair trade's desire for transparency in its networks, whether semiotic transparency in providing knowledge to consumers or material transparencies of where and how fair trade goods are grown. Tesco's own-label fair trade coffee is a great example of this: on the front of the label is a (presumably fair trade) farmer picking coffee – demonstrating their awareness of the importance of these semiotic/visual connections in fair trade – but on the side of the jar is the statement: "Any photograph used on this pack is simply representational and may not depict the actual Fairtrade farms or farmers who supplied this product." In addition, Percol's fair trade coffee label states unequivocally that it is a "product from multiple countries" so dispelling any confusion that their product comes directly from a particular place or producer group. In short, these goods are simply "fair trade" and the FLO logo on the front of the product no longer means that they come from a particular place, from a particular set of farmers, and/or support a particular type of development.

For companies like Cafédirect, the fair trade logo has taken on the semiotic weight and work that used to be carried by the images of farmers – who are now mostly virtual. In other words, it really is the fair trade name and logo that "stands-in" for what used to be conveyed directly on fair trade goods. Here, as consumers, we are asked to trust fair trade *even more* now in the absence of the semiotic images of its moral economy. Alternatively, we can shift our eyes and ears to the important fair trade websites that are now articulating these connections, this direct-ness and knowledge about fair trade quality, producers and their livelihoods.

Finally, in an interesting outcome, this de-centering of directness has provided space for fair trade companies, such as Cafédirect, to re-claim the original parameters of directness in fair trade as a way for them to maintain and build up their own market niche. Cafédirect's "Gold Standard" on its products provides the assurance that the good comes directly from specified producers and that this relationship allows the company to return an even larger share of the value to the producer communities in question. Vis-a-vis other fair trade goods from other companies or supermarkets, the Gold Standard implies that Cafédirect goes beyond fair trade in some ways, whereas, in reality, it hews to the original fair trade guidelines of building long-term partnerships, mutual responsibility, and relations of trust, care, and knowledge – as well as taste – in the products that it certifies and sells.

These developments are producing a growing bifurcation in the fair trade market. The "super" fair trade goods of companies like Cafédirect, simply by reasserting many of the original tenets of FTNs, are becoming differentiated from "bulk" fair trade goods supplied to other companies and/or supermarkets for their own-label lines that are obtained from the open and much more untraceable fair trade market. This re-claiming of directness, beyond Cafédirect's Gold Standard, has quickly become one of the qualities alongside taste that is currently defining important parts of fair trade networks.

The ethico-material implications of quality in fair trade

But what more has the specific turn to quality as taste wrought directly and indirectly in fair trade networks? Again, we focus here on recent trends in order to engage with the fair trade sector more fully and provide a more macro overview of supply chains and their novel requirements and shifts under the new mainstreamed regime of quality in fair trade networks.

There is little doubt that the shift to being a quality product has grown the fair trade market: the strategy of becoming better tasting and better looking made fair trade more appealing to large retailers and, thus, more consumers. On the other hand, this focus on taste has begun to exclude from fair trade networks those producers and producer cooperatives who are unable to meet the quality and taste requirements of the respective fair trade good markets.[7] These are typically the poorest farmers working the poorest and most marginal lands who, most often because of this, are unable to provide the right quality for fair trade networks.

Similarly, some of the most resource poor cooperatives also are excluded because they lack the organizational infrastructure needed to meet the accounting and governance standards required by FLO: they can be left by the wayside in the push to grow fair trade markets. These new standards for producer cooperatives include the payment of upwards of $3,500 for FLO certification as fair trade *and* the ability to demonstrate that they have a fair trade market available for their products.[8] A more informal standard includes the growing need to be certified as organic as well as fair trade – which is as costly, if not more so, than the fee for fair trade certification – for the often food-anxious and environmentally concerned consumers of Europe. While all three of these standards are more a function of the quantitative growth of fair trade markets through mainstreaming rather than tied directly to issues of quality, these more recent barriers to entry are creating a further set of complications that in many ways disturb fair trade's established credentials as a moral economy but also its characterization as an instance of ethical consumption.

The growing salience of quality has further effects, accentuating the sort of structural disconnections enforced in fair trade due to taste and quality standards but also opening up possibilities for those able to meet these requirements. One significant effect, for example, is the tendency for fair trade buyers to stay or go with those producer cooperatives and suppliers that they already know. This kind of "benevolent concentration" is not based on economies of scale but rather the socio-economic relations set in train by fair trade's mainstreaming. In other words, when expanding existing lines of fair trade goods or developing new lines, fair trade businesses and importers rely on the cooperatives with whom they already have close working relationships or source from more well-known quality fair trade suppliers.[9] The same is true for the development of new fair trade businesses: they tend to source from known suppliers who already have the capacity to produce to the quality and quantity standards they require for whatever product they wish to sell. As a result, those cooperatives with the best and most hardy business-oriented operations – typically those cooperatives with the longest history of support from development NGOs – and those who innovated and established themselves early on have better access to both existing and new markets.

This is certainly the case with fair trade cacao where CONACADO from the Dominican Republic and Kuapa Kokoo from Ghana have become *the* major players in the global trade of fair trade cacao (see Berlan and Dolan 2011). Both had early and extensive engagements and support from a number of development NGOs, good connections to fair trade networks in the North, a reputation for the high to excellent quality of their supplies and with thousands of members in their respective cooperatives.[10] Thus, going with "who you know" or "who is known," which are typically the most well-established and largish cooperatives, is much easier than having to support and work with smaller, less-established and more shaky cooperatives. Structural integrity in fair trade networks is not only leading to new and interesting instances of competition, as in the case of organic coffee networks (cf. Mutersbaugh 2002), but is also beginning to de-select for the hard work of developing relations with new, smaller and the most marginal, relatively unknown producer cooperatives (cf. Barrientos and Smith 2007).

Thankfully, these trends are *also* being resisted and countered by FLO and development NGOs that work with fair trade cooperatives. FLO in particular, along with the UK's Twin Trading, have quality improvement programs that support cooperatives either wishing to get into fair trade or those already in fair trade but attempting to improve their product quality. The role of FLO and many development NGOs therefore has shifted over time: they are now in the business of quality arbitration and support since, as they are keenly aware, taste and quality equate to more market opportunities, more sales and more development. Accordingly, FLO and these NGOs have had to become particularly entrepreneurial in outlook and operation in order to meet these taste/quality requirements and so keep up with the expanding markets demanded by large retailers, MNCs, and importers. These pressures and trends, we would argue, are slowly but *fundamentally* chipping away at not only the "relations coordination" of fair trade but also the core relationalities of care built up between the North and the South through fair trade's moral economy.

Conclusion: the de-centering of fairness?

Whereas the last chapter focused on the implications of quality and mainstreaming in the context of the consumer and the semiotics of fair trade, this chapter has explored the shifting trends in the governance of fair trade supply networks provoked by these changes. In short, getting into and maintaining access to fair trade supply chains and networks is no longer based on the marginality of livelihoods – although this motivation is clearly still there – but rather is dictated heavily by the quality and quantity supply chain requirements associated with the processes of mainstreaming. The same conundrum applies to size in fair trade networks now: while support is still given to some of the smallest and most marginal cooperatives and farmers, the trends embedded through fair trade's mainstreaming are excluding many of these due to a lack of quality or suppliers following "the lines of least resistance" by going *back to* or *with* some of the largest and most well-established cooperatives. These latter cooperatives are quickly building up their competitive advantage based on quality, quantity and, in a way, their brand as a cooperative, in order to have better access to new and existing fair trade networks and the capacity to innovate by developing new product lines, bringing in new producers or achieving organic certification.

Given its embedded and growing market-oriented focus and governance, fair trade is quickly proving to be a "better deal" for some producer cooperatives than others – by building up their capacity (see Raynolds *et al.* 2004) – and creating internal competition among producer cooperatives on a global scale. At the same time, new centers of power are emerging as FLO, supermarkets and,

MNCs develop novel supply chains and erect new barriers to entry for new, small and under-supported producer cooperatives. In essence, fair trade's more "mature" market status and its need and, indeed, desire to hew to the moralities of markets is not just de-centering the historical semiotic and material directness of fair trade markets but also its semiotic expressions and materialities of fairness as well.

Put another way, the pragmatics and consequentialism that has developed with the mainstreaming of fair trade seems to be complicating not only its core "fair trade-ness" but also its expression as an instance of ethical consumption. Here, the politics of ethical consumption must be seen as part and parcel of the ethical supply chains that bring forth these ethical consumer goods and they are as material as they are social. It is the cultural material politics of fair trade, and their fundamental relationalities, that need to be better understood to tell more full-fledged stories about what ethical consumption does, how it does it and the sorts of politics it can and does create. More broadly, ethical consumption is as much about market moralities and the specificities of their governance as it is about moral markets, moral economies, and the moralities embedded in and facilitated by ethical consumer choices.

Thus, the ordinary ethics invoked by fair trade in a desire, ability, and choice to care for Others, such as fair trade cooperatives, is contingent on the supply chain ethics, moralities, and political economies of fair trade in its contextualized and seemingly now increasingly structured and market-bounded governance regimes. The quality, quantity, and taste requirements of fair trade make its invocation of ordinary ethics more specific and indeed more complicated, contradictory, complex, and contextualized than work on ethical consumption has so far either uncovered or been willing to admit. Yet, this social life of fair trade goods under the pressures of mainstreaming raises a point that is much more fundamental: Geography matters – as does the cultural material politics of space and place – in fair trade and ethical consumption networks and it matters in substantive and important ways that extend much beyond the spatialities and political effects of consumption, ethical or otherwise, in the global North.

12 The practices and politics of a globalized AFN

Whither the possibilities and problematics of fair trade?

As a globalized Alternative Food Network (AFN), fair trade has come a long way from its much more radical yet rather humble socio-economic origins. As one of its key goals, with wide support from within the fair trade movement and embedded in its working ethos, the mainstreaming of fair trade has brought not only massive and rapid growth, creating a worldwide market worth €3.4 billion in 2008 (FLO 2011) but also concentrated sales in supermarkets, at least in the UK. For example, Sainsbury's claims to be the world's largest retailer of fair trade goods (surpassing Wal-Mart) with sales in 2009 topping £218 million and one in every four pounds spent on fair trade in the UK going through their stores (Mortimer and Baker 2010; Thomas 2010). Yet, all of this – albeit while generating substantially more revenue for development in FTNs[1] – has been accompanied by a marked shift in the cultural material politics of fair trade through significant changes to the discursive and visual semiotics of the knowledge regime that makes the connection between production and consumption. At the same time, fair trade supply chains have been transformed by supermarket and multinational corporation (MNC) involvement and the parallel need for better quality items.

These processes, events, and outcomes provide the context for the critical question provoked by mainstreaming: what kind of moral economy is now being articulated by fair trade? Critically, this assessment must come to grips with the consequentialism that has taken hold of its ethico-political practice and is manifested in the marketization and corporatization that now seem to be the guiding principles governing the business and movement-related decisions in Fair Trade Networks (FTNs).

As the last two chapters have argued, this is a consequentialism – referred to by some observers as fair trade's strategic and/or instrumental pragmatism (e.g. Herman 2010; Barnett et al. 2005; Taylor 2005) – that complicates key parts of the ethico-political vision and, indeed, the very "politics of the possible" embedded in fair trade. These complications similarly must be brought out more explicitly in the kind of one-to-one mapping of fair trade onto instances of ethical and sustainable consumption that is beginning to emerge in the literature on fair trade and ethical consumption networks. Indeed, if anything, the mainstreaming of fair trade and its shifting cultural material politics should make us reconsider (anew) what sorts of "ethical subjects," "ethical consumption singularities" and "collectivized individual politics" are being forged, articulated and supported through FTNs as they are currently embodied and put into practice.

Much of this current research argues from an understanding of a model of fair trade that no longer holds much water either discursively or materially. These contributions advance abstract theoretical and conceptual generalizations that, as yet, have been unable to grasp the impacts of the mainstreaming drive toward quality-led marketization. Moreover, they also fail to move much beyond the realm of the consumer in their understanding of the materialities of contemporary ethical consumption/fair trade networks. Yet the discursive and material contexts of fair trade, each fundamentally and relationally geographic in constitution and outcome, *do matter* and matter to how fair trade is governed and to its ethical and material precepts and outcomes. All of this matters not only to the lifestyles of ethical consumers and their ability to make themselves into ethical subjects through the power of choice, but also to the very livelihoods of some of the most marginal and disenfranchised primary commodity producers, their families, and their communities caught up in the continuing throes and uncertainties of the processes of neoliberal globalization now defined by the deepening marketizations of sustainability.

In this chapter, against the backdrop of mainstreaming and continuing expansion of FTNs, we reflect on some of the wider politics, trajectories, and meanings of fair trade markets and movements. This will help us to consider what the future might hold for FTNs but also ethical/sustainable consumption and globalized AFNs more broadly. We do this in three sections. First, we explore what FTNs as currently practiced might mean for the "doings" and politics of the "good foods;" that is, those foods, food networks, and food actors working for progressive social and environmental change, that inhabit global AFNs.[2] Second, we assess the implications of mainstreaming and the relative success of FTNs for the politics, process, and outcomes of what might be called "neoliberal sustainabilities," which fair trade should perhaps be considered as a hybrid or variant thereof. Finally, we examine some of the potentially interesting alternatives within fair trade that might buffer the effects of its mainstreaming and marketization, as well as offering up other interesting models of doing fair trade. We end with some speculative reflections on the futures of fair trade, ethical consumption, and globalized AFNs and articulate questions for further investigation.

Contemporary fair trade networks, good foods, and globalized AFNS

The mainstreaming achievements of fair trade demonstrate that it is among the most successful instances of good food "net-working" (Whatmore and Thorne 1997). Yet, what does this success, its outcomes and its enabling processes mean? How does this experience constrain what fair trade is and, perhaps, can become under contemporary governing regimes of neoliberalism? First, the current cultural material politics of fair trade reveal that knowledge and place – and here the knowledge of the places of production – have become much less important to the functioning of FTNs as AFNs. In short, the *terroir* of fair trade, communicated by its semiotics of people and places of production as a form of connective know-ledge, alternativeness, and difference-making, now figures much less prominently than the new signifiers of quality, taste, and the generics of the fair trade logo.

A more media- and marketing-friendly "spectacle-ization" of fair trade has taken hold with the embodiment of its politics into the figures of celebrities – with all the aforementioned potential benefits and drawbacks here – and onto the media- and medium-rich spaces of the web. In this way, the websites of fair trade companies and non-governmental organizations (NGOs), as well as super-markets and MNCs, have become the place where the geographies of "caring at a distance" (Barnett *et al.* 2005) are now being crafted and crafted in interesting and possibly useful and far-reaching ways. One of the original tenets of fair trade – strong direct connectivities between production and consumption – has retreated to the realms of various marketing niches.

Second, mainstreaming has redirected the politics of the possible away from the transformation of the inequalities in the structures of global trading that was at the core of the early politics of fair trade to a possibilism *defined by market expansion* for fair trade goods. While the latter is without doubt laudable, expan-sion only works for those producers who can furnish goods in the "right" quanti-ties and with the "right" qualities and taste, as determined by Fairtrade Labelling Organizations International (FLO), local fair trade development NGOs, fair trade businesses and, now increasingly, MNCs and supermarkets. More than ever before, the possibilities for change embedded in fair trade seem to be circum-scribed by what is marketable, sellable, and accessible rather than the much harder sell of structural change. Very crucially, this mainstreamed fair trade movement has abandoned key discursive spaces where the more normalized and negative practices of supermarkets and MNCs could be taken to task. On several occasions recently, the Fairtrade Foundation in the UK has come to the defence of the likes of Nestlé and Cadbury's – among other powerful Big Food players – in the media having accepted their overtures to source and sell fair trade goods.

However, this slippery slope of an increasingly marketized politics of the possible works to re-entrench core/periphery inequalities that are still very pronounced. Such a politics asks very little of people beyond changing their shopping habits (Johnston 2002) and so also reinscribes the power of consump-tion and consumers in FTNs often to the detriment of other forms of action and/ or other actors in good food networks (but see Clarke *et al.* 2007). Thus while consumers are encouraged to think that social and economic justice for small farmers is only a shopping trip away, the transformative "alternativeness" of FTNs has been diminished by the drive to marketize and corporatize this very same economic and social justice. Bluntly, fair trade has been wildly successful as a market – putting the supposed tension between market and movement far behind it (Jaffee, 2007) – but less so as a transformative social movement.

In this particular mainstreamed moment, the social change fostered by pur-chasing the good foods of FTNs is restricted to what is achievable within the narrow confines and parameters of a neoliberal, market-led system. This system is much better at expanding these existing markets for change – and again for those particular consumers and producers endowed with the right qualities – rather than organizing and supporting the kind of radical and transformative change that confronts corporate power, the power we have ceded to particular classes of consumers and the inequalities that make up much of the world as we currently know it.

Third, even in good food networks such as fair trade, supermarkets and MNCs are "too big to ignore" and so their involvement and role in shaping good foods is both inescapable and inevitable if networks wish to be successful at marketing goods in the name of ethical consumption, care, and responsibility. Clearly, the pragmatics of this make sense, particularly for FTNs who needed to move beyond the early committed consumers of charities and faith-based groups, but this cements the role of these immensely powerful institutions as key players not only in fair trade and sustainability discourses but also in their material networks.

Increasingly, these powerful actors are in the position to sell us sustainability – and here this sustainability cannot be merely dismissed as "green-" or "fair-washing" since FTNs have specific, real-world impacts on producers' livelihoods. Yet, even at the best of strategic times, it is hard for fair trade activists to swallow this sales pitch when many of the selfsame multinationals have a long history of exploitative and unsustainable practices and figured prominently in the "rogues' gallery" of the fair trade movement. Indeed, for some activists, Nestlé's involvement has become a breaking point in the process of mainstreaming given its past problematic transgressions and political economies. Thus groups like Baby Milk Action are actively calling for boycotts of fair trade in general and the Fairtrade Foundation in particular. The consequentialism in fair trade and, in particular, the *need* for this consequentialism to support communities in the global South, really hits home in the context of the continuing and ever growing power of supermarkets and MNCs as the distributors of good foods in an era of market- and consumerist-led sustainability.

Fourth, the two preceding chapters, as well as the work of Clarke *et al.* (2007), highlight the fundamentally crucial role that development, consumer, and activist NGOs have played in the trajectories of FTNs since their inception. This role has many different facets, ranging from their early engagements with producer cooperatives and use of their power to convert individualized purchases into collective action and/or NGO viability (Clarke *et al.* 2007) to the hybrid NGO/business/activist operations of fair trade certifiers and companies. Thus, in a way, fair trade is less about ethical consumption, consumers, and the act of purchasing/shopping *per se* and more or as much about what we might call "ethical activism" which, in the parlance of Clarke *et al.* (2007), might be called "ethical collectivization." Here then, as Whatmore and Thorne (1997) detailed so long ago, it is the relationalities between ethics, consumers, NGOs, and producers that are paramount in FTNs rather than simply the isolated figure of the ethical consumer, who is outside of the social, economic, cultural, and material relations that bring these networks into being. In short, the past and current activities of fair trade and many other related NGOs are central to these relationalities (Barnett *et al.* 2005).

Finally, there is now what we are calling the "fair trade effect," whereby fair trade, because of its market success and cultural cache, has become one of the most important if not *the* model of how to do development and save Others and their environments. From the likes of Product (RED) (Richey and Ponte 2008; Ponte *et al.* 2009) to Charity:Water,[3] the processes and successes of FTNs have served as an incredibly important "pedagogic" function for other NGOs, charities, and development organizations interested in harnessing the power of consumers, commodification, and marketization to right the wrongs of globalization and underdevelopment. Indeed, with respect to food specifically, the success of fair trade has brought with it the development of fair trade "like" and/or fair trade "lite" labels – the final classification depending on one's perspective – such as the private standards label developed by Starbucks, the Rainforest Alliance seal of approval and the Utz Kapeh label (see Bacon 2005). In short, the fair trade effect and its continuing legacy suggests that the model of attaching a series of social, environmental, and development-related guarantees to a particular commodity not only has succeeded in demonstrating the utility of this model but also has caused it to expand into other market sectors and niches constructed around the selling and buying of sustainability literally off-the-shelf in supermarkets, clothing stores, and websites. Fair trade has not only pioneered this market-led movement but embedded it in our collective consciousness as *the* normalized way to go about making a better world.

Neoliberal sustainabilities and the good foods of fair trade

Given the preceding discussion of the mainstreaming of fair trade, the statements about fair trade "being in the market, but not of it" or, indeed, "against it," are now in need of serious reformulation – qualification and caveats will no longer do. Here, we wish to argue that fair trade is one of the key variants of what might be called "neoliberal sustainabilities." That is, sustainability is pursued through processes of voluntary action by institutions, corporations, and consumers, whose ethical choices across goods, services, and good causes build a market by commodifying eco-social sustainabilities. Consumption, consumers, and their ethical selves are the pivots around which all of these processes turn (cf. Guthman 2007). Following Clarke *et al.* (2007), NGOs, such as the Fairtrade Foundation in the UK, perform the absolutely crucial role not only of marketing to consumers to gain their eyeballs and wallets, but also of collectivizing these individual purchases for political purposes and to achieve politicized power through consumer choice (see Clarke 2008; Sassatelli 2004, 2006; Sassatelli and Davolio 2010).

Thus, the ability of NGOs to be "political" – to speak to the media, politicians, and wider civil society about their concerns to reduce trade inequalities and poverty – comes from the size of the market for these ethically-consumed goods, such that market size for fair trade goods, for example, acts as a sort of proxy for the level of concern about these issues in civil society. In these processes, then, one of the new pathways into the realms of the political is based on products, goods, and their purchase by wider concerned publics. Through their powers of collectivization or aggregation, NGOs can equate purchases and market size with political interest in a particular cause, and speak for and articulate these commodified politicized concerns to those in power. Thus, fair trade should perhaps be rebranded as "in the market" and, fundamentally, "*using it*" as a way to gain political power under the wider aegis of the processes of neoliberal sustainabilities.

One way to see this is as a sort of "coming of age" of alternatives and activism in and under the auspices of a neoliberal world. Good food and other development-related causes similar to fair trade can now operate like any other political lobby: by drawing on the power of their combined consumer/citizen/ economic constituencies, they are able to gain traction in the politics of food, trade, and development-related issues. This resembles the power of MNCs to lobby the State based on their economic status and ability to speak for their shareholders, in addition to their consumers. Ethical consumerism and neoliberal sustainabilities have, in one sense, worked to level out parts of the political playing field – at least discursively[4] – from one fully dominated by MNCs and other powerful capitals and institutions. Here, then, is another reason to work to sell more fair trade products insofar as more sales represent greater market power for fair trade NGOs and thus more political power.

Yet the political voice and indeed politics of fair trade is much more muddled than these theorizations of political consumption would lead one to believe, especially given the mainstreaming of fair trade into the brands of MNCs. In short, instead of simply speaking for consumer citizens and, one would suppose, poor farming communities, fair trade is now also in the business of speaking for those MNCs involved in fair trade networks. So, it is not just that the discursive spaces of critique of those in power in international trade regimes are beginning to slip away. It is also that the collective political voice of the fair trade movement now speaks for powerful MNCs, including some previously charged with unethical practices, *in addition* to the collectivized singularities of ethical consumers and poor farming communities. That the politicized fair trade interests of Nestlé and Chiquita now stand alongside those of poor farming communities in Nicaragua, Kenya, and the Caribbean seems a world apart from the politicized aspirations of a social movement devoted to transforming the structures of trade that these MNCs very much had a hand in creating and exploiting.

In neoliberal sustainabilities, then, there is a kind of market-led, consumer-oriented pathway to political visibility and power and which, in the case of fair trade, also funds development and livelihoods. At a more general level, a politics that works through processes of commodification creates insuperable problems for those issues that do not lend themselves to commodification for sale through careful and ethical means. In short, what gets commodified gets saved (cf. McAfee 1999) in a way that works to embed competition, marketization, and entrepreneurialism as the keys to these new forms of neoliberal activism. Thus, in the markets structured by neoliberal sustainabilities, not only is the collectivizing power of NGOs incredibly important but so too is their power to articulate winning causes and the winning aspects to these causes.

As a result, how NGOs craft the messages and articulate specific causes when reaching out to the ordinary ethics of ethical consumers (Barnett *et al.* 2005) becomes crucial. In other words, in order to create an ethic of care for distant others, NGOs selectively choose the messages and images from the global South that are projected back to prospective ethical consumers and hopefully forge enduring connections. These "spatial projections" need much more contextualization, engagement, and exploration if we are to gain a better understanding of the markets constructed by NGO political activism (cf. Fligstein 1996). Specifically, how do the discursive and material knowledges selectively filtered and projected on to these markets work to activate particular aspects of the ordinary ethics of ethical consumption? This question deserves far more attention than it has received in the literature.

At the same time, neoliberal sustainabilities work to inscribe and fully embed the continuing and, indeed, growing power of consumers and consumption. But even here the arguments about the role of choice, ordinary ethics, and care at a distance as deployed in the discussions of ethical and political consumption (Clarke *et al.* 2007; Clarke 2008) are not convincing. Our point is that it is not just the choices made by ethical consumers that set the politics of consumption in motion, but rather that this power of ethical consumption turns on the *ability* to choose. Taking this further, in neoliberal sustainabilities, the market determines which producers can enter, which NGOs, causes or concerns can be commodified and so can "make it," as well as who can participate specifically as ethical consumers based upon the requisite range of abilities, such as knowledge, access, and the simple economic ability of being able to buy in to these networks. Thus, voting with one's money and being able to contribute to the politics of political consumption involves much more than the processes of "articulating the subjects and spaces" of ethical consumption (Barnett *et al.* 2005).

Looking toward the future

Fair trade, ethical consumption and good foods as globalized AFNs are undergoing rapid and important changes, not least in the spaces of the global recession, food security crises, and climate change. In this final section, we explore some interesting trends in the doing of FTNs and suggest some areas for further investigation across FTNs, ethical consumption, and global AFNs.

Fair trade futures and politics

The mainstreaming of fair trade does not seem to be slowing down and where the market and its networks go from here is clearly of interest. While consequentialism seems to have won the day, it is crucial to investigate the specificities, detailed processes, and spatial outcomes of FTNs to gain a better understanding of their impacts on both the lifestyles of ethical consumers and the livelihoods of those in and out of FTNs. In this context, it would be especially interesting to explore the differences across different types of fair trade goods beyond the relatively well-researched sectors of coffee and bananas.[5] What will further pragmatism, strategic planning, and consequentialism in FTNs look like and, most importantly, how will the increasing presence of MNCs and supermarkets affect these pathways, processes, and politics? Moreover, how will this "corporate citizenship" work in tension with "consumer citizenship" and the citizenship of fair trade NGOs as mainstreaming is bedded down even more, new product lines are brought on board and consumer awareness grows or, possibly, even begins to contract?[6]

Here, we highlight four areas and potential future developments in fair trade and its politics that are particularly worthy of engagement. The first is the role of alternative ownership schemes – the two most famous being Divine Chocolate in the UK and Agrofair from the Netherlands[7] – in either directing or working to buffer the kind of corporatization at the center of fair trade's mainstreaming. In these two cases, the producers and their cooperatives have an ownership stake in the company and so they seem to have direct involvement in the direction of corporate travel and also have a real line to democratic representation within the corporation. This is a different and important form of partnership seemingly beyond that embedded in normal fair trade relationships and has the potential to influence any move toward a reworking of the alternative natures and promises of fair trade. It will be interesting to see whether or not this mutualistic cooperative and tied model of ownership can mitigate aspects of fair trade's mainstreaming or perhaps work to deepen this process but in a way that is more distributive and possibly less overtly competitive than now appears to be the case.

The second area is the rapid development of the institutional sector in fair trade markets, which is attracting the interest of movement activists and merits further study (Gendron *et al.* 2008). In this sector, choice by and for consumers is taken out of the equation since fair trade becomes *the only* coffee, tea or other item supplied at a business, university, or government agency. These supply networks also have the potential to develop more stable buying/selling relationships between these institutional buyers and fair trade companies, suppliers and producers. One very direct link is with the UK's "fair trade town" movement – now numbering 500 or more – where the criterion for membership is an undertaking that a certain proportion of goods sold within the city or town limits must be certified as fair trade (Malpass *et al.* 2007; see also Pykett *et al.* 2010). While there is little direct evidence, this movement seems to be one reason that fair trade sales have remained steady or even grown (Clarke 2010; Smithers 2010) during the current recession that has seen the sales of other caring goods like organic foods decline, as we noted in Chapter 5.

One question for further investigation concerns whether or not these new "institutional citizens" will become supermarket-like and so drive the development of even more bulk supplies of fair trade. Alternatively, these new institutional citizens and their supply networks might provide a new and relatively large stage upon which the more classic characteristics of fair trade's directness and solidarity can begin to flourish again and so work to reassert themselves. In addition, how might we theorize these growing institutional networks and the nature of their collectivized choice regime in the context of ethical consumption and its cultural material politics more broadly? In short, how is institutional citizenship different from, or similar to, that of consumer and corporate citizenship, and how are we to analyze this question in the context of the neoliberal sustainabilities that seem to define the current era of progressive (good food) politics?

Third, how are we to understand the backlash – if, indeed, there is one – to the mainstreaming and, in particular, the corporatization of fair trade? The "100 per-center" fair trade companies in the USA have certainly made it known that they are uncomfortable with the corporatization and special dispensation of retailers like Starbucks (Jaffee 2007), but what do consumers – whether of fair trade or more conventional stripes – think? Some of the largest and most disturbing fault-lines developing in fair trade are those provoked by Nestlé's sourcing and sale of fair trade certified products. Baby Milk Action was one of the original organizations active in the campaign to boycott the marketing of Nestlé baby formula to the global poor. It is now at the forefront of efforts to organize a similar boycott of fair trade because of the ethical conflicts they see between fair trade and the Nestlé corporation.[8] One of their key concerns is that, given the present governance structures of fair trade, a single product line can be taken in isolation and certified as fair trade rather than the certification process extending to the whole company and its range of economic activities. How this and other forms of tension in fair trade markets and movements might play out certainly merits more sustained investigation.

A fourth and final suggestion is the need for much deeper engagement with the virtualization of fair trade, its relationships and fair trade farmers in the spaces and places of the internet. Such virtualization has moved to the forefront as the preferred mode of expression of fair trade's moral economy of connection. Moreover, use of the internet to convey the forces of transparency in good food and ethical consumption networks is quickly becoming *de rigueur* as the way progressive food and many other politics are being articulated. How the tools of the internet are used to make FTNs even more interactive and transparent is key here, although the limitations of access, types, and processes of transparency and of interaction must be front and center of further research. For example, is it possible for video content from producers to be supplied on fair trade websites to bring even more voice and "reality" to the connections of producers and consumers? Indeed, can consumers be brought into the conversation and contribute their voice and/or transparency to these networks to allow producers to see who is consuming their goods and in what ways? Is this even something that producers would care to have provided to them by fair trade movements and would consumers be interested in constructing this more "two-way" version of transparency in FTNs?[9]

Moreover, could the ordinary ethics of consumers and of connection in FTNs go "real time" to facilitate more ordinary connections between producers and consumers through the technologies of webcams, comment boards, blogs, and websites that facilitate these instantaneous connections, at once making them more spectacular as well as more mundane? We see the possibilities here as interesting and perhaps empowering but also limited and limiting in their political economies and materialities as much as their technologies and technological optimism. Either way, online activism and connectivities like these around neoliberal sustainabilities are seemingly only set to grow. The accompanying opportunities, barriers, and problematics, as well as the complexities they might hold for FTNs and ethical consumption, deserve serious scrutiny.

Ethical consumption futures

Understanding ethical consumption, today, must be as much about its material incarnations, practices, and materialities as its theorization. Indeed, theorizing about ethical consumption has, in a sense, run ahead of considerations of its material dimensions and their implications for livelihoods and lifestyles within these networks. Moreover, if fair trade is any indication, it should be recognized that "doing politics in an ethical register" (Clarke *et al.* 2007) is as much about market-based inequalities in both the realms of consumption and production as it is about empowerment, day-to-day contributions to social change and an ethics of care across distance. How these dialectics of inequalities – the promotion of socio-economic justice through the processes of embedded inequalities of consumption, ethical or otherwise – play out in the materialities and supply chains of ethical consumption networks needs further engagement and critical analysis. The study of ethical and/or sustainable consumption can and should become a very broadly materialist project in the spaces of their theorization and conceptualization.

In the context of the moralization of the economic and the parallel economization of the moral (cf. Shamir 2008), future research needs to draw out more fully the implications of this growing "economization" of citizenship, care ethics, politics, and political representation that are said to be embedded in ethical consumption (cf. Clarke *et al.* 2007; Seyfang 2005, 2006; Jacobsen and Dulsrud 2007; Harrison *et al.* 2005; Lockie 2009; Quastel 2008). As we have argued throughout this chapter, ethical consumption as a form of progressive politics sits directly at the center of neoliberal sustainabilities and so is entangled in the commodification, individualization, and marketization of the wider social problems of poverty, inequality, and ecological destruction. In ethical consumption networks, is there a point of transition where processes of individualization give way to processes of collectivization? Do these entanglements and the questions they raise even matter as long as financial resources are being generated for the causes and politics of creating fairer trade, for example? Or is there a metric other than NGO receipts and market size for fair trade against which we can measure success?

Finally, Clive Barnett's recent work on ethical consumption gives tantalizing hints of a neglected yet potentially significant area of research (Barnett 2009, 2010a, 2010b; Barnett and Land 2007). That is, the tensions between the empowering abilities of knowledge about food and Others versus its debilitating role in overwhelming our actions such that we feel we cannot do anything about anything. Arguments for greater transparency vis-à-vis consumers lie right at the heart of fair trade networks and their online strategies of connection but there is little or no consideration of the tension between empowerment and a disabling information overload in these semiotics of transparency that work to educate consumers. An understanding of these changing politics of knowledge is critical as the internet and online advocacy become increasingly significant in food and wider progressive politics.

Conclusion: globalized AFN futures

This chapter has explored a wide array of issues arising from the mainstreaming of fair trade and the limitations of market-led ethical consumption in addressing the market-created inequalities of the globalized food system and catalyzing broadly-based social change. Can other models of success in the mainstreaming of alternatives be articulated that are not accompanied by corporatization? If not, are there "alternatives to the alternatives" (Goodman 2010) that might work at other scales and that are less about transnational relations of care and responsibility and more focused on local, endogenous change, as in the case of such food rights movements as Via Campesina (see Patel 2007)?

This prompts the further question of whether there are any spaces for a sort of "re-movementization" of fair trade networks, perhaps through institutional supply networks and mutual forms of supply chain organization. Can fair trade and its market success be taken as a new starting point in the politics of food that works to overcome its drawbacks without the triumphalism of regarding mainstreaming as the pinnacle of alternative-ness in food provisioning? Change in FTNs is much more than a matter of simply opening up more markets for more and more products: it must involve working to remove structures of inequality in international trade.

Fair trade has shown that a globalized network for economic and trade justice knows how to marketize and market itself very well. But can marketization be redirected to *turn*, or perhaps *return*, ethics and morality into more transformative processes and provide spaces of social transformation and not just further ethical consumption possibilities?

13 Concluding thoughts

This book has traced the contested growth and continuing struggles to develop alternative networks of food provisioning and fair trade in Western Europe and the USA. These struggles have branched out in different directions, in large part to circumvent or "flow around" the corporate challenge of mainstream assimilation that threatens to undermine their alterity and subvert their social agendas. We have explored this challenge in organics, locality products, local foods, and fair trade and the efforts of social movements to defend their political imaginaries and keep alive their hopes of making different worlds of food and everyday practice.

There are close parallels and tangencies between this discussion and recent work on alternative or "diverse economies" in the fields of human and economic geography. This work was galvanized by Gibson-Graham's (1996: 11) classic deconstruction of the *master narrative* of capitalism and their insistence on the significance of "a plurality and heterogeneity of economic forms" co-habiting with capitalism, and not merely those like household production that lie outside the social relations of capital (Lee 2010). This pluralism is central to their diverse economies project to counter the hegemonic representation of capitalism as "co-extensive with the social space" (Gibson-Graham 2008: 3).

But coexistence in the mainstream circuits of capitalism has its own dangers and contradictions – discursive, material, and political. Most of the alternative economies created by the social movements discussed in this book are fiercely contesting the spaces found *within* this world of capitalist markets in order to secure their social reproduction and disseminate their values. In terms of Gibson-Graham's (2005: 13) schema of the different ways of organizing the labor process and "the production, appropriation, and distribution of surplus," the majority of enterprises – organic farms, locality food firms, and fair trade producers – would be described as " 'alternative capitalist' businesses with an environmental or social ethic." The question then is how do social movements define a path that avoids "selling out" to capitalist conformity and yet provides the economic security to perform and propagate these ethical values effectively?

As we have seen, responses to this question are the source both of the diversity and complexity of alternative economic forms and the heated exchanges in activist and academic circles on the gaps between movement discourse and practice, exemplified here by the mainstreaming of fair trade and organics. Such dissonance is aggravated by well-founded fears that movement values are being assimilated and diluted by corporate production and retailing practices. This is why John Wilkinson (2009: 20) believes that relations between markets and social movements will remain in a state of "permanent tension," which he characterizes as a "dialectics without synthesis." On the other hand, by using conventional means for alternative ends, these movements have achieved significant behavioral change and material gains. For example, by (re-) capturing rural space for sustainable agriculture – enacting Lefebvre's "trial by space" – and bringing a greater measure of social justice to international trade by expanding the market for fair trade sales by producer cooperatives in the global South.

Do such gains define and circumscribe the "alternative worlds" that are attainable by market-embedded social movements? Certainly rising sales of organic and fair trade goods by such giants of global food as Wal-Mart, Tesco, Carrefour, Nestlé, and Starbucks provide both a mechanism and a metric of "successful alterity." Yet the heavy and ubiquitous presence of these giants unquestionably is collapsing the boundaries between the "alternative" and "conventional." This erosion of difference has dulled the cutting edge of political consumption insofar as such corporate outcomes are seen to represent the "politics of the possible" (cf. Goodman *et al.* 2010). Quantitative gains in rural acreage and sales revenues achieved via corporate assimilation are a pallid reflection of the radical political imaginaries that inspired earlier generations of organic agriculture and fair trade activists.

Little wonder, then, that critical analyses of alternative food politics are drawing increasing attention to the disjunctures between foundational values, movement discourse, and the practice of organic agriculture, direct marketing, and fair trade. Claims that these movements are "transformative" and "prefigurative," for example, are now being assessed in the harsh light of experience stretching over four decades or longer. These assessments are contributing to growing concern and disenchantment with market-based movements, beginning with the critique of organic agriculture, particularly in the USA, as scholars became aware of the "conventionalization" and "corporatization" of this sector and the more limited access of lower-income groups to organic food (Buck *et al.* 1997; Guthman 2000, 2004a; Allen 2004; D. Goodman 2004; Johnston *et al.* 2009).

These unequal consumption relations have many expressions, often intertwined, including well-to-do Slow Food supporters (Gaytan 2004), local food advocates or *locavores* (DeLind 2011), seekers of social distinction, and individualistic responses to the perceived health threats of industrial foods involving a "resigned, fatalistic environmentalism," a general phenomenon that Andrew Szasz (2007: 2–6) calls "inverted quarantine." A related critique, again focusing on the USA but relevant to the entrepreneurial "turn" in Western Europe, warns against the dangers of widespread economic reductionism that myopically privileges market potential, commercial performance, and farmer livelihoods. Such reductionism, it is argued, is distancing the local food movement from "its systemic roots" in context-specific, place-based practices, values, and processes of civic empowerment (DeLind 2011: 3).

As we have seen, this question of limited social access recently has been calibrated to focus more pointedly on the exclusionary, white cultural politics of alternative food movements. This critique extends an earlier indictment of the unjust, racialized production relations in organic agriculture to the spaces of direct marketing – farmers' markets, community supported agriculture (CSAs)/ box schemes, farm-to-school programs. These spaces are constituted, it is argued, by close "connections among property, privilege and paler skin" (Slocum 2007: 7). Whether or not the legacy of white privilege can be transformed into effective antiracist practice is a huge question hanging over the future of alternative food movements, and one that calls for different sensibilities and in some cases "a politics of listening, watching and not always helping" (Guthman 2008a: 443).

We have recognized the force of these critiques and related concerns throughout this book but, rather than "throw the baby out with the bathwater," we have also chosen to give weight to the achievements and potential of alternative food and fair trade movements. In the case of the USA, for example, we have highlighted the significance of boundary politics and object conflicts in obstructing the totalizing ambition of industrial corporatized organic. As we emphasized in Chapter 8, open, deliberative processes of civic governance are the fulcrum of these struggles to defend the legitimacy of the organic and its alterity as an alternative or diverse economy.

Clutching at straws or straws in the wind?

Returning to the question posed earlier, does the mainstream "corporatization" of their values describe the limits of the attainable for market-based social movements? There is evidence to suggest that in fact this is the case. Equally, the evolving strategies of these embedded actors, including vertical integration by fair trade producer cooperatives, such as Day/Divine Chocolate, the expansion of institutional fair trade purchasing and the remarkably diverse proliferation of alternative food projects suggest that we have not yet reached the endgame. Some critics are unimpressed by these social dynamics, arguing that these local food initiatives, in reality, are doing the work of neoliberalism by propagating its entrepreneurial ideology and individualistic subjectivities and governmentalities. As Gibson-Graham (2010: 125) observe, this critique is the "latest incarnation" of the master narrative of capitalism that makes collective action both futile and complicit, much like consumer politics in Marx's framework of commodity fetishism.

However, small groups of local people, cognizant or not of their putatively neoliberal subjectivities or the consolations of intellectual critique, continue to experiment and strive for what they see as greater empowerment by adopting a politics of practice: of attempting to remake the world as they find it in the places they inhabit. In the UK, a proliferative and processual politics of practice is central to the work of the Making Local Food Work (MLFW) campaigns and the Transition Network. A politics of practice, and therefore the praxis of politics, also underlies the accelerating growth and eclectic range of mutual forms of social enterprise organizations and community-owned food projects, as we emphasized in Chapter 6.

This emerging and diverse social economy of food, nurtured in the beginning by state and charitable funding, opens up political opportunities to create possible worlds beyond the reach of heavily market-embedded movements. In many respects, whether as civic governance in the USA or community-led mutual enterprise in the UK, these new initiatives are reinventing and revitalizing the socially embedded roots of their predecessors (cf. DeLind 2011). That is, returning to their origins, they are *de-centering the economic* – as profit-making and other related market constraints – and *restoring the social* to the forefront. With hierarchical expansion through the market (and its vulnerability) no longer paramount, movements putting the social first can respond to a different imperative: growth by replication.

This second, more recent trajectory builds on the economic pluralism of the first generation of alternative food organizations and potentially extends the material gains these market-embedded forms have achieved. Taken individually, initiatives that define the new social economy of food – cooperatives and community enterprise, for example – make a difference to only a relatively small handful of people in particular places. Yet to see only particularism ignores the multiplier effects of these projects in disseminating new ways of knowing, growing and organizing food using *horizontal* networks of knowledge sharing and learning. These networks have some interesting parallels with the social process methodologies of farmer-to-farmer movements in the global South (Holt-Jimenez 2006; Rossett *et al.* 2010; see also Hassanein and Kloppenburg, Jr 1995).

Network processes of knowledge transmission are the catalyst for expansion by horizontal replication that demonstrates "the power of a 'politics of ubiquity' to enrol local projects in building new worlds" (Gibson-Graham 2010: 126). This politics and its material local impacts interrogate the rather dismissive arguments of some prominent economic geographers, who regard the political symbolism of these "diverse (local) economies" as an achievement in itself, whether or not this leads to "the construction of materially effective and socially widespread 'spaces of hope' " (Lee and Leyshon 2003: 193; see also Lee *et al.* 2004). "It is this potential of 'alternative' economic geographies to demonstrate *a proliferation of possibilities, as much as their prospective material power*, which endows them with such political significance" (Lee and Leyshon 2003: 195–196, our emphasis). This point is restated more recently by Andrew Leyshon (2010: 122), who observes that: "by thinking the economy differently, we can see that what on the surface may appear to be a series of inconsequential small acts ... actually draw attention to the real limits to capital. So while resistance may be hard work, may suffer as many retreats as advances, it is by no means futile."

A politics of ubiquity is not content simply with political symbolism, nor should it be. Instead, it is important to recognize that the collective action behind these seemingly "inconsequential small acts" can have cumulative, possibly radical, effects on the social control of food provision. This book is part of this conversation and we have found hopeful political geographies as well as "materially effective" alternative economic geographies. At the same time, as Lee and Leyshon (2003: 196) remind us, "their relationship with the 'other' – the mainstream – remains unavoidable, ambivalent, unequal and full of contradiction."

We acknowledge this complex relationship and its contradictions – and here we would again highlight the social injustice of the many excluded and "missing guests at the table" set by alternative food and fair trade movements. Equally, we acknowledge the ambition to change the material, ethical, and political foundations of how we live our lives in the world. We have therefore tried to strike a balance in this book between critique and constructive analysis of the problems facing those working to change the place of food in our lives, practices, and politics.

Notes

3 Bridging production and consumption: alternative food networks as shared knowledge practice

1 Murdoch and Miele (1999: 481) do note that consumer awareness of, and interest in, more natural and traditional products "derives not only from questions of taste (which might be linked, as in Bourdieu (1984), to questions of social identity) but, more prosaically perhaps, to questions of health and safety."

2 In agro-food studies, a focus on women's labor in the private sphere is seen most clearly in Jane Dixon's (1999) "cultural economy" reformulation of commodity systems approaches to production–consumption relationships.

3 In this respect, ironically, studies on the consumption side of Tovey's (1997) divide are regarded as exemplary for "the ways in which they simultaneously deal with the symbolic aspects of domestic consumption and the structural and material parameters within which consumers operate and meanings are made" (Crewe 2000: 279, original emphasis).

4 As we see in Chapter 7, a closely related theme in the literature on organic agriculture *qua* organized social movement concerns the growth of a mimetic organic sector – "Big Organic," "Organic, Inc." – that shares the attributes of its corporate industrial counterpart. This has generated a vigorous debate on the "conventionalization thesis" (Guthman 2004c; Lockie and Halpin 2005) that has spilled over into popular writing on food (cf. Pollan 2001, 2006; Fromartz 2006). For a critique of this thesis and its conceptual foundations and a defence of organic agriculture as a worthy alternative to conventional provisioning, see Lockie *et al.* (2006).

Part II Alternative food provisioning in the UK and Western Europe: introduction and antecedents

1 Other influences on "radical rural" movements from the 1990s, too many to discuss individually, include radical green networks, such as Earth First!, involved in antiroad building campaigns and anti-GM protests (Doherty *et al.* 2003; Doherty 1999; Wall 1999), The Land is Ours organization and its offshoot, Chapter 7 (Halfacree 1999; Reed 2008), and Farmers for Action (Doherty *et al.* 2002; Reed 2004).

2 Although not examined here, the Agenda 2000 reforms were part of the EU enlargement negotiations with Central and East European countries.

3 The varied influence of national context on the implementation of modulation and the RDR, and the points of resistance to more progressive models of rural development, emerge strikingly in the case of the UK (Falconer and Ward 2000; Rutherford 2004; Ward and Lowe 2004) and France (Buller 2004).

4 The modest proposals of the European Commission for a recent mid-term review of the CAP, the so-called 2008 Health Check, were watered down during the final negotiations in November 2008, resulting in little headway in the reform process. The share

of Pillar I (Market and Income Support) was 81 percent in 2008, with 19 percent allocated to Pillar II (Rural Development), which is co-financed by Member States. With food security concerns now becoming paramount following the intense episode of global food inflation in 2007–08 and another bout of rapid price increases in 2010–11, further decoupling of direct income support payments from production is increasingly being challenged, as we discuss in Chapter 6.

5 The 1989–93 reforms of the Structural Funds identified Objective 5b regions as those with fragile rural economies and Objective 1 areas as lagging agricultural regions, whose GDP per capita was 75 percent or less than the EU average. The rural areas of northern Finland and Sweden later were designated as Objective 6 regions (Ray 2000). On the origins of EU regional policies and the evolution of the Structural Funds as the main channel of implementation, see Audretsch *et al.* (2009).

6 Only local communities in Objective 1, 5b, and 6 regions were eligible for LEADER II funds, whereas LEADER+ was extended to all rural areas.

7 According to Ilbery and Kneafsey (2000: 319), "the key distinction between PDOs and PGIs ... is that the geographical link must occur in *all* stages of production, processing and preparation for a PDO and at least *one* for a PGI." Numerous technical details of these geographical indications, including difficulties of EU harmonization and their relationship to the WTO/TRIPS agreement, are discussed in Barjolle and Sylvander (2000).

4 Rural Europe redux? The new territoriality and rural development

1 The eight indirectly-elected regional assemblies were abolished in 2010 and their executive functions transferred to the Regional Development Agencies.

2 Maye and Ilbery (2007) refer to Lord Haskin's review of rural policy delivery and the 2004 Rural Strategy published by the Department of Environment, Food, and Rural Affairs (DEFRA). Winter (2006) notes that this rescaling process is full of reversals and far from being unidirectional. See also Ward and Lowe (2007) on rural development policy under New Labour.

3 This collective shorthand expression refers mainly to the case studies published in Theme Sections and Special Issues of *International Planning Studies* 4(3): 1999; *Sociologia Ruralis* 40(2): 2000, 40(4): 2000, and 41(1): 2001; and *Environment and Planning A* 35(4): 2003.

4 According to a 2001–03 survey of organic marketing initiatives (OMIs) in 19 European countries, supermarkets "play an increasingly important role (nearly 55 percent of the total) as a sales channel for OMIs" (Sylvander and Kristensen 2004: vi). This share exceeds 70 percent in Austria, Denmark, Finland, Sweden, and the UK (ibid.: 37). For further discussion, see Chapter 5.

5 Further evidence of the "hybridity" of locality and local food networks comes from studies of agricultural diversification in the East Midlands (Clark 2005) and the networking practices of "alternative" food producers in the West Midlands of England (Watts *et al.* 2007).

6 These entanglements recently became something of a *cause célèbre* in the case of Rhodda's Cornish clotted cream, exposing the strange rationality of mainstream supply logistics and confirming Rhodda's credentials as a locality product. A tub of clotted cream on sale at a branch of Tesco's in Redruth, just two miles from the Rhodda creamery, is first transported to the Tesco regional distribution center in Avonmouth near Bristol, before being shipped back to Redruth, a round trip of 340 miles. Rhodda's also makes next-day deliveries as far afield as Norfolk and Scotland (*Guardian* September 4, 2010).

7 As these lines imply, convention theory has been widely used to analyze the transition from local to locality food. For a semiotic approach to quality construction, see Brunori (2007).

8 According to a recent press report, there are roughly 62,000 social enterprise organizations employing 800,000 people and contributing £24 billion to the UK economy
   (*Guardian*, January 27, 2010).
9 An idea of the diversity and complexity of the institutional landscape of this local food
   economy in the UK can be gleaned by consulting some "movement" websites. For
   example, www.makinglocalfoodwork.org, www.sustainweb.org, www.soilassociation.
   org, www.foodcoops.org, www.growingcommunities.org, www.transitiontowns.org,
   and www.plunkett.co.uk. Local, community-centered food networks in the UK are discussed in greater detail in Chapter 6.

5 Into the mainstream: the politics of quality

1 In the UK food retailing sector, this segmentation can be seen in the divisions between
   more up-market retailers, such as Waitrose, Sainsbury, and more recently, Tesco,
   "value" supermarkets – Asda (Wal-Mart) and Morrison's – and discounters like Aldi,
   Lidl, and Netto. There is now more overlap between these categories as all retailers
   have introduced and expanded "value for money" lines to prevent loss of market share
   in the current recession.
2 Imports account for an estimated 50 percent of sales in the UK market for organic
   products.
3 Perceptions that the wide margins between farm-gate prices and retail prices in the UK
   are due to the abuse by supermarkets of their oligopsonistic buying power have
   prompted two statutory inquiries into food retailing by the Competition Commission
   since the late 1990s, with inconclusive results in each case (Competition Commission
   2000, 2008).
4 Unlike Riverford, the Abel and Cole website is not forthcoming about the provenance
   of its boxes nor its supply chain relations other than to say that they source seasonal
   British produce.
5 Clarke *et al.* (2007) provide a general case history of Riverford Organic Vegetables
   from its origins as a family-run dairy farm in Devon to its more recent business
   development.
6 In fact, several supermarkets have paid it the supreme compliment by running box
   schemes of their own at some point, with mixed results. Of course, with online delivery
   from Tesco, Sainsbury's, Waitrose, and the internet food retailer, Ocado, for example,
   consumers can "make up" their own individual box scheme (Moya Kneafsey, personal
   communication).
7 Wilkinson (2010: 107) uses the case of Unilever to illustrate the efforts of food processors and retailers to dominate the "origin" and "artisan quality" sector in order to
   appropriate "place" and the rents it can generate. This giant corporation "provides an
   interesting case because its strategy reveals a possible marketing weakness in *appellation* products – the rigidity of their production processes in the light of market segmentation. Unilever has developed a line of traditional olive oils including ingredients not
   permitted for *appellation* products, such as aromas and special tastes, which permit the
   targeting of specific consumer segments (www.unilever.com). Whether this proves to
   be a market advantage over *appellation* products remains to be seen."

6 Changing paradigms? Food security debates and grassroots food re-localization movements in the UK and Western Europe

1 The coincidence in September 2010 of food riots in Maputo, the capital of Mozam-
   bique, and Russia's decision to extend its ban on grain exports for a further year was
   eerily reminiscent of events in 2006–07. The continuing precariousness of the global
   food security situation was underlined in early 2011 when the FAO announced that its
   benchmark index of agricultural commodity prices had exceeded the levels reached in

the 2006–08 crisis. Commentators expect prices to remain at or above these levels and inflationary pressures to continue, provoking further political instability in poorer countries (see, for example, *Financial Times* 6 January, 2011).

2 For all the current concern with geophysical constraints on food production, it is well to remember that poverty and inequality are longstanding structural causes of food insecurity and malnutrition in the global South.

3 Representative examples include Defra (2006; 2008; 2009a), The Strategy Unit (2008), Policy Foresight Programme (2008), Sustainable Development Commission (2009a), EFRA/House of Commons (2009a, 2009b, 2009c), and Ambler-Edwards *et al.* (2009).

4 Two recent reports emphasize the considerable potential of organic agriculture and community food enterprises in mitigating climate change and contributing to the transition to a more secure, low carbon food system. See Soil Association, *Soil Carbon and Organic Farming.* (2009b) and Making Local Food Work (MLFW), *Local food and Climate Change: The Role of Community Food Enterprises* (May 5, 2010).

5 The Chatham House report by Ambler-Edwards *et al.* (2009) fails to assess recent studies (cf. Badgley *et al.* 2007; Halberg *et al.* 2006) that dispute the "yields argument" marshalled against organic agriculture, although this is a notably difficult and contentious field. See the comments in June/July, 2009 on the Food Climate Change Network website (www.fcrn.org.uk) on the report commissioned by the Soil Association from the Centre for Agricultural Strategy, University of Reading: *England and Wales Under Organic Agriculture: How Much Food Could be Produced?* For further discussion of the potential of organic agriculture to feed a world population of 9.5 billion in 2050 under different scenarios of yield, cropland, diet, and livestock systems, see CWF/FoE (2009) (see also IAASTD 2008).

6 Coincidentally, in late November 2009, the European Commission (EC) opened a public consultation to gather views for a revised approach to international agricultural development and food security in order to propose a policy framework for the EC and the EU Member States. See www.ukcds.org.uk/news-Public_consultation_on_food_ security.

7 Across the EU, Pillar I funding for 2007–13 is budgeted at €295 billion and €87 billion for Pillar II (IEEP, 2009a). The equivalent breakdown for the UK in 2007 was €3,950 million and €264 million, respectively (IEEP 2009b).

8 Caroline Spelman, Secretary of State for the Environment, Food, and Rural Affairs in the Con-Lib Dem coalition reiterated the orthodox UK position on CAP reform at the 2010 Oxford Farming Conference, stating that "Rising prices and rising global demand make it possible to reduce subsidies and plan for their abolition" (Spelman 2011).

9 Caroline Spelman, Secretary of Defra, is sceptical of what would amount to continued reliance on direct subsidies, observing: "I am wary of the proposal to 'green' Pillar I" (Spelman 2011).

10 While it is dangerous to speculate on the approaching EU budget negotiations and the future CAP, the EU Commission in November 2010 presented three options for further reform in 2013–20. Its preferred option indicates that direct payments to farmers would continue to absorb a significant share of CAP funding. A proposed ceiling on payments would possibly favor the "social agriculture" of smaller farms.

11 A more recent report (FAO 2010) provides separate estimates for the global dairy cattle sector and calculates that the output of milk and dairy products, processing and transportation, excluding meat production in these activities, accounts for 2.7 percent of global anthropogenic GHG emissions.

12 On the adjustment to lower dietary intake of meat and dairy products, the difficulties of making risk assessments for particular population groups and possible steps to meet deficiencies of key nutrients, see Millward and Garnett (2009).

13 Alarm about the commitment of the Con-Lib Dem coalition to consumer behavior change was triggered in July, 2010, when Health Secretary Andrew Lansley announced that he would solicit food industry funding to replace public expenditure for the Change4Life program set up by the recent Labour government to promote healthy lifestyles to reduce rising rates of obesity. In exchange for funding of this campaign, the new coalition is promising to take a "non-regulatory approach" to the food industry (*Guardian* July 8, 2010; Lang and Raynor 2010).

14 Organic sales at farmers' markets accounted for 9.5 percent of market turnover in 2008 (Soil Association 2009a).

15 These new legal forms with illustrative case studies are discussed in the Soil Association (2005). Further sources include MLFW (2009) and Woodin *et al.* (2010).

16 This "Big Society" rhetoric is accompanied by a specious localism that appears to promise decentralization and local devolution. Yet the Localism Bill published in December 2010 retains the central government's stranglehold on local authority financing, with grant support accounting for roughly 70 percent of local government funding. Under the Con-Lib Dem coalition's deficit-reduction policy, this grant support has been severely cut, which will mean, in many cases, that social enterprises and charities delivering local services also will face funding cuts, though these actors are supposedly key players in the "Big Society." Furthermore, rates of council tax, the largest single local source of revenue, have been frozen (see Cox 2010).

7 Broken promises?: US alternative food movements, origins, and debates

1 This and the next subsection draw on an earlier paper that gives an instrumentalist reading of the organic movement as a farmer livelihood strategy (Goodman and Goodman 2007). The dangers for local food movements of an economic reductionism that gives priority to market potential and commercial outcomes at the expense of context-specific, place-based values, behaviors, knowledges, identities, and deliberative democratic practices are discussed by DeLind (2011).

2 The livelihoods approach emerged in the literature on sustainable development, risk, and vulnerability (Chambers and Conway 1992; Blaikie *et al.* 1994; Chambers 1995) and more recent applications include poverty research (Murray 2001) and development geography (Bebbington and Batterbury 2001; Bebbington 2003).

3 The polarization of the FTS debate in the US neatly encapsulates the point made by Harris (2009: 55–56) that the choice of theoretical framing gives rise to very different readings of alternative food projects: as neoliberal logics and subjectivities or as new political opportunities. As he observes, "the reading of AFN activism as reproducing neoliberal subjectivities is *just one* reading, but it is *not the only reading possible*" (ibid.: 61, original emphasis).

4 WFM is piloting a more direct, transparent "local" marketing campaign under the slogan of "local-est," or local sourcing whenever possible, in the wealthy Californian town of Mill Valley north of San Francisco. A new WFM store reportedly will carry a range of local products from over 375 farmers, ranchers, and artisan food producers in the San Francisco Bay Area. WFM also offers financial support under the Whole Foods Local Producer Loan Program (Edible Marin and Wine Country 2010).

5 Evidence from 15 case studies of direct local food marketing chains in five US states indicates that farmers in these supply chains were not committed exclusively to one type of marketing but instead used a variety of outlets, including farmers' markets, CSAs, buying clubs, roadside farm stands, and home delivery, as well as sales to grocery stores and restaurants (King *et al.* 2010).

8 Resisting mainstreaming, retaining alterity

1 These discussions include syntheses of previous pieces DuPuis has done with colleagues Brian Gareau, Daniel Block, and Sean Gillon (DuPuis and Gareau 2008; DuPuis and Gillon 2009; DuPuis and Block 2008), her own work on perfect politics (DuPuis 2002) and on sustainable knowledges (DuPuis *et al.* 2011), as well as the work of co-authors and others, as part of a larger project to reflexively understand alternative food systems.

2 Michel Callon calls this bringing together of people and things – or "actants" – in a collaborative network "translation." Translation brings together these actants into a joint effort of network-building despite differences in material characteristics (for objects), interests, or worldviews (for people).

3 This case study is part of a larger look at the Harvey lawsuit with Sean Gillon (2009).

4 Initially, Harvey lost on all counts. However, he appealed the decision. On January 26, 2005, a Maine Appellate court ruled for Harvey on three of the nine counts (counts 1, 3, and 7) he had brought against the USDA (Harvey v. Veneman 2005).

5 Analysis of the OTA Rider by Paula Dinerstein, Harvey's attorney: "What the rider does is amend the portion of OFPA which limits the National List to substances proposed by the NOSB, to permit the USDA Secretary to develop emergency procedures to designate for the National List agricultural products not commercially available in organic form for a maximum one year period. This would be the first time that the duty to evaluate and recommend substances for the National List would be removed from the NOSB."

6 Harvey's official standing in the court was as a consumer, but he often spoke as a producer when talking to the press.

7 The list is divided into several parts: (1) Synthetic substances allowed in agricultural production (e.g., ethylene for fruit ripening); (2) Non-synthetics not allowed in production (e.g., arsenic and tobacco dust); (3) Synthetics allowed and prohibited in livestock production (e.g., aspirin is allowed, strychnine is not); (4) Non-agricultural, non-organic, non-synthetic substances allowed in organic food processing (e.g., yeast); (5) Non-agricultural, non-organic, synthetic substances allowed in organic food processing (e.g., cellulose used as an anticaking agent and ascorbic acid); and (6) Non-organically produced agricultural products allowed as up to 5 percent of the ingredients in certified organic products (e.g., non-organic hops). Substances in the latter category, namely non-organic agricultural products, are allowed in a certified organic product when their organic counterpart is not "commercially available." Products can be certified as organic when at least 95 percent of their ingredients are organic. Thus, non-organic agricultural products deemed unavailable in organic form (and added to the National List) can comprise up to 5 percent of certified organic products, unless the product is labeled as "100 percent organic," in which 100 percent of the ingredients must be certified organic.

8 Accessed at www.progressivedairy.com/index.php?option=com_content&view=article&id=803:0607-pd-organic-dairy-industry-approaches-life-with-harveyq&catid=99:past-articles. This article was submitted by Horizon Organic, which was originally associated with one of the most controversial organic mega-dairies.

9 Federal Register Vol. 73, No. 207, October 24, 2008. Agricultural Marketing Service 7 CFR Part 205 National Organic Program (NOP) – Access to Pasture (Livestock) Proposed Rule.

10 www.cornucopia.org/2010/01/organic-family-dairies-being-crushed-by-rogue-factory-farms/.

11 For example, USDA officials mentioned these surveys in both the proposed and final pasture access rule.

9 Sustainable agriculture as knowing and growing

1 Barry Bedwell, President of the California Grape and Tree Fruit League, quoted in the *Sacramento Bee*, February 22, 2010.
2 Acute toxic exposure has immediate effects as compared to chronic exposure, which has effects that only manifest over the long term.
3 Strangely, very little of the $200 million in public funding for alternatives has been devoted to methyl iodide. The research on this chemical has been almost entirely private, undertaken by the Japanese company that owns iodine mines, and much of the work by the US Environmental Protection Agency to register the chemical as an alternative to methyl bromide has been kept secret (Erikson 2008). As a result, the chemical of which there is least public knowledge is the one that conventional growers are asking to use. What public research does exist indicates that methyl iodide is more effective than methyl bromide in terms of pest, disease, and weed control (Zhang *et al.* 1997; Hutchinson *et al.* 2000).

Part IV Globalizing alternative food movements: the cultural material politics of fair trade

1 For other discussions centered on the mainstreaming of fair trade, see Boersema (2009), Hira and Ferrie (2006), Low and Davenport (2005, 2006), Moore *et al.* (2006), Raynolds (2009), Reed (2009), Tallontire (2006), Taylor *et al.* (2005), and Wilkinson (2007).
2 For more on these companies specifically, see Doherty and Meeham (2006) and Doherty and Tranchell (2005) for Day Chocolate, and Tallontire (2000) and Davies *et al.* (2010) for Cafédirect.

10 The shifting cultural politics of fair trade: from transparent to virtual livelihoods

1 For much further discussion on this point, see Berlan and Dolan (2011) and Dolan (2007, 2008, 2010).
2 This, of course, is also in conjunction with the already "sunk costs" of the previous and continuing performative labor of fair trade NGOs, churches, charities and businesses designed to promote and sell fair trade to a wide and wider audience.
3 For more on this point specifically, see Jaffee (2010) and Jaffee and Howard (2010).
4 The mantra to grow markets at any cost has taken hold in the USA in a much bigger way with Transfair USA and its CEO Paul Rice, as Dan Jaffee (2007, 2010) has described in several of his works on the topic.
5 Curiously, the growth of research on "global production networks" (Coe *et al.* 2008) seems to avoid engaging with this more "culturalist" work – that is, exploring the connections and relationalities of production and consumption networks and cultures – and so seems more of a step backward or at least sideways than a novel way to engage with shifting and established economic geographies of the global landscape, particularly that related to agro-food (Goodman 2011).
6 For critical takes on this re-fetishization, as well as alternative interpretations of what is being argued here, see Lyon (2006), Varul (2008), Carrier (2010), and Herman (2010).
7 For more on fair trade marketing from a number of different angles, see Golding (2009), Golding and Peattie (2005), Le Mare (2007) Linton *et al.* (2004) Low and Davenport (2004, 2009), Moore *et al.* (2006), and Wright (2004, 2009).
8 For more general treatments of the celebritization of both the environment and development, see Boykoff and Goodman (2009) and Goodman and Barnes (2011).
9 This is two weeks of a fair trade media blitz spearheaded by both Oxfam and the Fairtrade Foundation. See www.fairtrade.org.uk/get_involved/fairtrade_fortnight/fairtrade_fortnight_2009/default.aspx.

10 Celebrities here included UK and global stars such as Chris Martin, Colin Firth, Thom Yorke, Antonio Banderas, Minnie Driver, and Alanis Morissette and more regionally specific celebrities from Australia, Africa, and other parts of the globe.

11 These included mainly UK celebrities like Anita Roddick from the Body Shop and media stars such as Harry Hill, Jon Snow, Vic Reeves, Fearne Cotton, Gail Porter, and Lenny Henry.

12 Both of these moves of writing on his hand were Martin's way of circumventing the censoring of the "make trade fair" shirts he would wear in televized appearances in both the UK and the USA. With the message and symbol on his hand, it was impossible for the message to be blurred out and so it became his rather ingenious way of continuing to get the message over and show his commitment to fair trade and fair trade markets/movements.

11 The price and practices of quality: the shifting materialities of fair trade networks

1 The key exception to this is Catherine Dolan's excellent work on Kenyan FTNs in which she gets specifically at these complications of "representation and reality" (Dolan 2007, 2008, 2010; see also Berlan 2011; Berlan and Dolan, 2011). Recent anthropological and geographical work on FTNs (e.g., De Neve *et al.* 2008; Luetchford 2008; Lyon 2007a, 2007b; Lyon and Moberg 2010; Lyon *et al.* 2010; Moberg 2005; Mutersbaugh and Lyon 2010; Shreck 2002, 2005; Wilson 2010; see also Le Mare 2008) has started to interrogate the "on the ground" complications of FTNs in ways that usefully inform analyses of ethical consumption.

2 In what follows, wherever possible, the interviews where this information came to light are referenced; in some instances, total anonymity was promised so more generalized points are made or indicated. Moreover, much of this research was carried out in the context of the fair trade coffee and cacao markets and supply chains, but also more generally around fair trade movements and markets. Nevertheless, while this may seem to color the specific details and arguments here, the general points about the role of quality and supply stand when looking across the whole of the fair trade sector and in other commodities beyond coffee and cacao, which may have different specific supply chain routes.

3 Interview, supply chain manager, Co-op (2003). For more on the Co-op and its fair trade strategies see Doherty (2008).

4 This point was articulated across several interviews with supply chain certification and standards managers at FLO (2003).

5 Interview, Twin Trading (2003).

6 Interview, head of standards, FLO (2003).

7 This sort of exclusionary practice was witnessed first-hand through research with one of the earliest fair trade cacao exporting cooperatives in Costa Rica and several others in the Dominican Republic; this was also confirmed in an interview with the head of a US fair trade certifier in 2004 as something that happens in FTNs. For more on these issues more generally, see Arce (2009).

8 This last requirement of having to show a market makes sense from both the perspectives of FLO and cooperatives as it does neither good to certify or be certified as fair trade if the cooperative under question cannot sell their goods on the fair trade market. This is also a requirement of the various ISO standards under which FLO operates.

9 This point was articulated specifically in interviews with a leading UK fair trade coffee company as well as a UK fair trade standards organization.

10 For CONACADO, quality was something that was built up over the years and is actively pushed by the cooperative and the development NGOs involved in supporting its operations (Interview, CONACADO [2003]).

12 The practices and politics of a globalized AFN: whither the possibilities and problematics of fair trade?

1 The Fairtrade Foundation estimates that FTNs reach close to 7.5 million people in the developing world across 58 different countries (Fairtrade Foundation 2010) while FLO estimates that in 2008, €43 million went to producer communities to support development and community projects (FLO 2011).
2 For more on good foods, see Goodman *et al.* (2010).
3 See www.charitywater.org/.
4 Again, across the work of Barnett and his colleagues, there has been little in the way of showing the actual impacts of this political consumerism on, for example, trade and trade policy, rather than effecting its useful theorization.
5 There is, however, a number of important works that have already expanded into exploring other fair trade commodities and supply chains; key examples include Bassett (2010) Berlan (2008, 2011), Berlan and Dolan 2011), Binns *et al.* (2007), Hilson (2008), Lyon and Moberg (2010), McEwan and Bek (2009), Moseley (2008), Neilson and Pritchard (2010), Raynolds and Ngcwangu (2010), Raynolds *et al.* (2007), Scherer-Haynes (2007), and Shaw *et al.* (2006).
6 Similar issues and questions have been raised by Fridell (2009), Fisher (2009), Le Velly (2007), Smith (2008), Tallontire (2009), Walton (2010), and Wilkinson (2007).
7 Oké bananas from the USA, now branded under Equal Exchange, operates from a similar "cooperative ownership" model but one that involves ownership by those working for the company in the USA; for more on their interesting corporate structure, see www.okeusa.com.
8 www.babymilkaction.org/action/nestlefairtrade.html.
9 This might be a way to supplement the producer visits which are often a part of marketing campaigns of fair trade companies, certifiers, and NGOs during such events as the "Fair Trade Fortnight" in the UK.

References

Adams, M. and Raisborough, J. (2009) "What can sociology say about fair trade? Reflexivity, ethical consumption and class," *Sociology*, 42(6): 1165–1182.

Adams, M. and Raisborough, J. (2010) "Making a difference: ethical consumption and the everyday," *British Journal of Sociology*, 61(2): 256–274.

Agyeman, J. (2002) "Constucting environmental (in)justice: transatlantic tales," *Environmental Politics*, 11: 31–53.

Alkon, A. (2008) "Paradise or pavement: the social constructions of the environment in two urban farmers' markets and their implications for environmental justice and sustainability," *Local Environment*, 13(3): 271–289.

Allen, P. (1999) "Reweaving the food security safety net: mediating entitlement and entrepreneurship," *Agriculture and Human Values*, 16(2): 117–129.

—— (2004) *Together at the table: sustainability and sustenance in the American agrifood system*, University Park: University of Pennsylvania Press.

—— (2008) "Mining for justice in the food system: perceptions, practices and possibilities," *Agriculture and Human Values*, 25(2): 157–161.

Allen, P. and Guthman, J. (2006) "From 'old school' to 'farm-to-school': neoliberalization from the ground up," *Agriculture and Human Values*, 23(4): 401–415.

Allen, P. and Hinrichs, C. (2007) "Buying into 'Buy Local': engagements of United States local food initiatives," in D. Maye, L. Holloway, and M. Kneafsey (eds) *Alternative food geographies*, Oxford: Elsevier.

Allen, P. and Kovach, M. (2000) "The capitalist composition of organic: the potential of markets in fulfilling the promise of organic agriculture," *Agriculture and Human Values*, 17: 221–232.

Allen, P. and Sachs, C. (1991) "The social side of sustainability: class, gender and ethnicity," *Science as Culture*, 2(13): 569–590.

—— (1993) "Sustainable agriculture in the United States: engagements, silences and possibilities for transformation," in P. Allen (ed.) *Food for the future: conditions and contradictions of sustainability*, New York: Wiley.

Allen, P., FitzSimmons, M., Goodman, M., and Warner, K. (2003) "Shifting plates in the agrifood landscape: the tectonics of alternative agrifood initiatives in California," *Journal of Rural Studies*, 19(1): 61–75.

Altieri, M. (1995) *Agroecology: the science of sustainable agriculture*, Boulder, CO: Westview.

—— (1999) "The ecological role of biodiversity in agroecosystems," *Agriculture, Ecosystems and Environment*, 74: 19–31.

Alvarez, R. (2005) *Mangoes, chiles and truckers: the business of transnationalism*, Minneapolis: University of Minnesota Press.

Ambler-Edwards, S., Bailey, K., Kiff, A., Lang, T., Lee, R., Marsden, T., Simons D., and Tibbs, H. (2009) *Food futures: rethinking UK strategy*, London: Royal Institute of International Affairs.

Amin, A. (2002) "Spatialities of globalisation," *Environment and Planning A*, 34(3): 385–399.

Amin, A., Cameron, A., and Hudson, R. (2003) "The alterity of the social economy," in A. Leyshon, R. Lee, and C. Williams (eds) *Alternative economic spaces*, London; Sage.

Anderson, M. (2009a) " 'Cost of a cup of tea': fair trade and the British co-operative movement, C. 1960–2000," in L. Black and N. Robertson (eds) *Consumerism and the co-operative movement in modern British history*, Manchester: Manchester University Press.

—— (2009b) "NGOs and fair trade: the social movement behind the label," in N. Crowson, M. Hilton, and J. McKay (eds) *NGOs in contemporary Britain: non-state actors in society and politics since 1945*, London: Palgrave.

Anderson, M. and Cook, J. (1999) "Community food security: practice in need of theory?," *Agriculture and Human Values*, 16(2): 141–150.

Andrews, G. (2008) *The Slow Food story: politics and pleasure*, Montreal: McGill-Queen's University Press.

Antipode (2010) *Special issue on capitalism and conservation, Antipode* 42(3).

Appadurai, A. (1986) "Introduction: commodities and the politics of value," in A. Appadurai (ed.) *The social life of things: commodities in cultural perspective*, Cambridge: Cambridge University Press.

Arce, A. (2009) "Living in times of solidarity: fair trade and fractured worlds of Guatemalan coffee farmers," *Journal of International Development*, 21: 1031–1041.

Arce, A. and Marsden, T. (1993) "The social construction of international food: a new research agenda," *Economic Geography*, 69(3): 291–311.

Audretsch, D. B., Grimm, H. M., and Schuetze, S. (2009) "Local strategies within a European framework," *European Planning Studies*, 17(3): 463–486.

Bacon, C. (2005) "Confronting the coffee crisis: can fair trade, organic and specialty coffees reduce small-scale farmer vulnerability in northern Nicaragua," *World Development*, 33(3): 497–511.

—— (2010) "Who decides what is fair in fair trade? The agri-environmental governance of standards, access and price," *Journal of Peasant Studies*, 37(1): 111–147.

Badgley, C., Moghtader, J., Quintero, E., Zakem, E., Jahi Chapell, M., Aviles-Vazquez, K., Samulon, A., and Perfecto, I. (2007) "Organic agriculture and the global food supply," *Renewable Agriculture and Food Systems*, (22): 86–108.

Baffes, J. and Haniotis, T. (2010) *"Placing the 2006/2008 commodity price boom in perspective,"* Policy Research Working Paper 5371, Development Prospects Group Washington, DC: World Bank.

Bagdonis, J., Hinrichs, C., and Schafft, K. (2009) "The emergence and framing of farm-to-school initiatives: civic engagement, health and local agriculture," *Agriculture and Human Values*, 26(1–2): 107–119.

Bahro, R. (1986) *Building the green movement*, London: Heretic Books.

Bailey, I., Hopkins, R., and Wilson, G. (2009) "Some things old, some things new: the spatial representations and politics of change of the peak oil relocalisation movement," *Geoforum*, 41(4): 595–605.

Baker, P. (1990) "The domestication of politics: women and American political society, 1780–1920," in L. Gordon (ed.) *Women, the state and welfare*, Madison: University of Wisconsin Press.

—— (1991) *The moral frameworks of public life: gender, politics and the state in rural New York: 1870–1930.* New York: Oxford University Press.

Bakker, K. and Bridge, G. (2006) "Material worlds? Resource geographies and the 'matter of nature'," *Progress in Human Geography*, 30(1): 5–27.

Balfour, E. (1943) *The living soil*, London: Faber and Faber.

Ballet, J. and Carimentrand, A. (2010) "Fair trade and the depersonalization of ethics," *Journal of Business Ethics*, 92: 317–330.

Banks, J. and Bristow, G. (1999) "Developing quality in agro-food supply chains: a Welsh perspective," *International Planning Studies*, 4(3): 317–331.

Barad, K. (2007) *Meeting the universe halfway: quantum physics and the entanglement of matter and meaning*, Durham, NC: Duke University Press.

Barham, E. (2002) "Towards a theory of value-based labeling," *Agriculture and Human Values*, 19(4): 349–360.

—— (2003) "Translating terroir: the global challenge of French AOC labeling," *Journal of Rural Studies*, 19(1): 127–138.

Barjolle, D. and Sylvander, B. (2000) "Protected designations of origin and protected geographical indications in Europe: regulation or policy? Recommendations." *Final Report. PDO and PGI Products: Market, Supply Chains and Institutions.* FAIR 1-CT95–0306. Brussels: European Commission.

Barling, D., Sharpe, R., and Lang, T. (2008) *Rethinking Britain's food security: a research report for the Soil Association.* Centre for Food Policy, City University, London.

Barnett, C. (2005) "The consolations of 'neoliberalism'," *Geoforum*, 36: 7–12.

—— (2009) "Publics and markets: what's wrong with neoliberalism?," in S. Smith, R. Pain, S. Marston, and J. Jones (eds) *The Sage handbook of social geography*, London: Sage.

—— (2010a) "Geography and ethics: justice unbound," *Progress in Human Geography*, 35(2): 246–255.

—— (2010b) "The politics of behaviour change: how to make people act ethically (without them knowing it)," *Environment and Planning A*, 42(8): 1881–1886.

Barnett, C. and Land, D. (2007) "Geographies of generosity: beyond the moral turn," *Geoforum*, 38(6): 1065–1075.

Barnett, C., Cloke, P., Clarke, N., and Malpass, A. (2005) "Consuming ethics: articulating the subjects and spaces of ethical consumption," *Antipode*, 37(1): 23–45.

—— (2011) *Globalizing responsibility: the political rationalities of ethical consumption*, London: Blackwell.

Barratt-Brown, M. (1993) *Fair trade*, London: Zed Press.

Barrientos, S. and Smith, S. (2007) "Mainstreaming fair trade in global production networks: own brand fruit and chocolate in UK supermarkets," in L. Raynolds, D. Murray, and J. Wilkinson (eds) *Fair trade: the challenges of transforming globalization*, London: Routledge.

Barrientos, S., Conroy, M., and Jones, E. (2007) "Northern social movements and fair trade," in L. Raynolds, D. Murray, and J. Wilkinson (eds) *Fair trade: the challenges of transforming globalization*, London: Routledge.

Bassett, T. (2010) "Slim pickings: fair trade cotton in West Africa," *Geoforum*, 41(1): 44–55.

Bebbington, A. (2003) "Global networks and local development: agendas for development geography," *Tijdschrift voor Economische en Sociale Geographie*, 94(3): 297–309.

Bebbington, A. and Batterbury, S. (2001) "Transnational livelihoods and landscapes: political ecologies of globalisation," *Ecumene*, 8(4): 369–380.

Beck, U., Giddens, A., and Lash, S. (1994) *Reflexive modernization: politics, tradition and aesthetics in the modern social order*, Stanford: Stanford University Press.

Becker, H. S. (1997) *Outsiders: studies in the sociology of deviance*, Glencoe, Illinois: Free Press.

Belasco, W. (1989) *Appetite for change: how the counter-culture took on the food industry, 1966–1988*, New York: Random House.

Bell, D. (1997) "Anti-idyll: rural horror," in P. Cloke and J. Little (eds) *Contested countryside cultures: otherness, marginalisation and rurality*, London: Routledge.

Bellows, A. and Hamm, M. (2002) "US-based community food security: influences, practice, debates," *Journal for the Study of Food and Society*, 6(1): 31–44.

Benedick, R. (1998) *Ozone diplomacy: new directions in safeguarding the planet*, Cambridge, MA: Harvard University Press.

Benhabib, S. (1996) "Toward a deliberative model of democratic legitimacy," in B. Seyla (ed.) *Democracy and difference: contesting the boundaries of the political*, Princeton: Princeton University Press.

—— (2002) *The claims of culture: equality and diversity in the global era*, Princeton, NJ: Princeton University Press.

Benn, H. (2009) Online. Available www.defra.gov.uk/corporate/ministers/speeches/hilary-benn/hb090106.htm (accessed September 14, 2009).

—— (2010) www.defra.gov.uk/corporate/about/who/ministers/speeches (accessed February 1, 2010).

Bensel, R. (1984) *Sectionalism and American political development, 1880–1980*. Madison: University of Wisconsin Press.

Berlan, A. (2008) "Making or marketing a difference? An anthropological examination of the marketing of fair trade cocoa from Ghana," *Research in Economic Anthropology*, 28: 171–194.

—— (2011) "Good chocolate? An examination of ethical consumption in cocoa," in J. Carrier and P. Luetchford (eds) *Ethical consumption: social value and economic practice*, New York: Berghahn.

Berlan, A. and Dolan, C. (2011) "Of red herrings and immutabilities: rethinking fair trade's ethic of relationality among cocoa producers," in M. Goodman and C. Sage (eds) *Food transgressions*, Aldershot: Ashgate.

Bernstein, H. and Campling, L. (2006a) "Review essay. Commodity studies and commodity fetishism I: Trading Down," *Journal of Agrarian Change*, 6(2): 239–264.

—— (2006b) "Review essay. Commodity studies and commodity fetishism II: 'Profits with principles'?," *Journal of Agrarian Change*, 6(3): 414–447.

Bertelsen, D. (1995) *The US strawberry industry*, Washington, DC: Economic research Service, United States Department of Agriculture.

Bezencon, V. and Blili, S. (2009) "Fair trade managerial practices: strategy, organisation and engagement," *Journal of Business Ethics*, 90: 95–113.

Binns, T., Bek, D., Nel, E., and Ellison, B. (2007) "Sidestepping the mainstream: fair trade *rooibos* tea production in Wuppertal, South Africa," in D. Maye, L. Holloway, and M. Kneafsey (eds) *Alternative food geographies: representation and practice*, Oxford: Elsevier.

Bijker, W., Pinch, T., and Hughes, T. (1989) *The social construction of technological systems: new directions in the sociology and history of technology*, Cambridge, MA: MIT Press.

Blaikie, P., Cannon, T., Davis, I., and Wisner, B. (1994) *At risk: natural hazards, people's vulnerability, and disasters*, London: Routledge.

Block, D. and DuPuis, E. M. (2001) "Making the country work for the city: von Thunen's ideas in geography, agricultural economics and the sociology of agriculture," *American Journal of Economics and Sociology*, 60(5): 79–98.

Blond, P. (2009) "Rise of the red Tories," *Prospect*, 155: 32–36.

Boersema, J. (2009) "The urgency and necessity of a different type of market: the perspective of producers organized within the fair trade market," *Journal of Business Ethics*, 86: 51–61.

Boghossian, P. (2007) "Fear of knowledge: against relativism and constructivism," *Ars Disputandi*, 7: 1566–1599.

Boltanski, L. and Chiapello, E. (1999) *Le nouvel esprit du capitalisme*, Paris: Gallimard.

Bordo, S. (1993) *Unbearable weight: feminism, Western culture, and the body*, Berkeley: University of California Press.

Born, B. and Purcell, M. (2006) "Avoiding the local trap: scale and food systems in planning research," *Journal of Planning Education and Research*, 26: 195–207.

Bondi, L. and Laurie, N. (2005) "Introduction. Working the spaces of neoliberalism," *Antipode*, 37(3): 394–401.

Bourdieu, P. (1977) *Outline of a theory of practice*, Cambridge: Cambridge University Press.

—— (1984) *Distinction: a social critique of the judgement of taste*, London: Routledge & Kegan Paul.

Bowker, G. and Star, S. (2000) *Sorting things out: classification and its consequences*, Cambridge, MA: MIT Press.

Boykoff, M. and Goodman, M. (2009) "Conspicuous redemption? Reflections on the promises and perils of the 'celebritization' of climate change," *Geoforum*, 40: 395–406.

Bramwell, A. (1989) *Ecology in the 20th century: a history*, New Haven: Yale University Press.

Brand, R. and Karvonen (2007) *The ecosystem of expertise: complementary knowledges for sustainable development*. Online. Available http://ejournal.nbii.org/archives/vol.3iss1/0601–004.brand-print.hmtl (accessed January 25, 2010).

Brenner, N. (2001) "The limits to scale? Methodological reflections on scalar structurization," *Progress in Human Geography*, 25(4): 591–614.

Brewer, J. and Trentmann, F. (2006) "Introduction: space, time and value in consuming cultures," in J. Brewer and F. Trentmann (eds) *Consuming cultures, global perspectives: historical trajectories, transnational exchanges*, Oxford: Berg.

Brown, S. and Getz, C. (2008a) "Towards domestic fair trade? Farm labor, food localism and the 'family scale' farm," *Geojournal*, 73, 11–22.

—— (2008b) "Privatizing farm worker justice: regulating labor through voluntary certification and labelling," *Geoforum*, 39(3): 1184–1196.

Brunori, G. (2006) "Post-rural processes in wealthy rural areas: hybrid networks and symbolic capital," in T. Marsden and J. Murdoch (eds) *Between the local and the global: confronting complexity in the contemporary agri-food sector*, Oxford: Elsevier.

—— (2007) "Local food and alternative food networks: a communication perspective," *Anthropology of Food*, S2. Online. Available http://aof.revues.org/index6379.hmtl (accessed July 20, 2010).

Brunori, G. and Rossi, A. (2007) "Differentiating countryside: social representations and governance patterns in rural areas with high social density. The case of Chianti, Italy," *Journal of Rural Studies*, 23(2):183–205.

Brunori, G., Guidi, F., and Rossi, A. (2008) "On the new social relations around and beyond food: analysing consumers' role and action," paper presented at the Conference on Sustainable Consumption and Food, Arlon, Belgium, May, 27–30.

Bryant, R. and Goodman, M.K. (2004) "Consuming narratives: the political ecology of 'alternative' consumption," *Transactions of the Institute of British Geographers NS* 29: 344–366.

Buck, D., Getz, C., and Guthman, J. (1997) "From farm to table: the organic commodity chain in Northern California," *Sociologia Ruralis*, 37(1): 3–20.

Buller, H. (2004) "The 'espace productif', the 'theatre de la nature' and the 'territoires de developpement local': the opposing rationales of contemporary French rural development," *International Planning Studies*, 9(2/3): 101–119.

Buller, H. and Morris, C. (2004) "Growing goods: the market, the state, and sustainable food production," *Environment and Planning A*, 36: 1065–1084.

Bunting, M. (2009.) "The maverick ideas of red Toryism could give Cameron a potent edge," *Guardian*, February 9.

Burns, J. A. (1983) "The UK food chain, with particular reference to the inter-relations between manufacturers and distributors," *Journal of Agricultural Economics*, 34(3): 361–378.

Busch, L. (2000) "The moral economy of grades and standards," *Journal of Rural Studies*, 16(3): 273–283.

Busch, L. and Bain, C. (2004) "New! Improved? The transformation of the global food system," *Rural Sociology*, 69(3): 321–346.

Busch, L. and Juska, A. (1997) "Beyond political economy: actor-networks and the globalization of agriculture," *Review of International Political Economy*, 4(4): 668–708.

Butler, J. (1999) *Gender trouble: feminism and the subversion of identity*, Philadelphia, PA: Routledge.

Buttel, F. (1993) "The production of agricultural sustainability: observations from the sociology of science and technology," in P. Allen (ed.) *Food for the future: conditions and contradictions of sustainability*, New York: John Wiley.

—— (1997) "Some observations on agro-food change and the future of agricultural sustainability movements," in D. Goodman and M. J. Watts (eds) *Globalizing food: agrarian questions and global restructuring*, London: Routledge.

—— (1998) "Nature's place in the technological transformation of agriculture: some reflections on the recombinant BST controversy in the USA," *Environment and Planning A*, 30: 1151–1163.

—— (2000) "The recombinant BGH controversy in the United States: toward a new consumption politics of food?," *Agriculture and Human Values*, 17(1): 5–20.

—— (2005) "Ever since Hightower: the politics of agricultural research activism in the molecular age," *Agriculture and Human Values*, 22: 275–283.

Bynum, C. W. (1991) *Fragmentation and redemption: essays on gender and the human body in medieval religion*, New York: Zone Books.

Cafédirect (2011) http://brewing.cafedirect.co.uk/.

Callon, M. (1992) "The dynamics of techno-economic networks," in R. Coombs, P. Saviotti, and V. Walsh (eds) *Technological change and company strategies: economic and sociological perspectives*, London: Academic Press.

—— (1998) "Introduction: the embeddedness of economic markets in economics," in M. Callon (ed.) *The laws of the markets*, Oxford: Blackwell.

—— (1999) "Actor-network theory – the market test," in J. Law and J. Hassard (eds) *Actor network theory and after*, Oxford: Blackwell.

Camden Sustainability Task Force (2008) *Report on food, water, biodiversity and green spaces.* London Borough of Camden (CENV/2008/22), June 25.

Campbell, H. and Liepins, R. (2001) "Naming organics: understanding organic standards in New Zealand as a discursive field," *Sociologia Ruralis*, 41(1): 21–39.

Carolan, M. (2001) *Embodied food politics*, Aldershot: Ashgate.

Carrier, J. (2010) "Protecting the environment the natural way: ethical consumption and commodity fetishism," *Antipode*, 42(3): 672–689.

Casper, M. J. and Clarke, A. E. (1998) "Making the pap smear into the 'right tool' for the job: cervical cancer screening in the US circa 1940–95," *Social Studies in Science*, 28: 255–290.

Castree, N. (2001) "Commodity fetishism, geographical imaginations and imaginative geographies," *Environment and Planning A*, 33: 1519–1525.

—— (2003a) "Place: connections and boundaries in an interdependent world," in S. Holloway, S. Rice, and G. Valentine (eds) *Key concepts in geography*, London: Sage.

—— (2003b) "Commodifying what nature?," *Progress in Human Geography*, 27(3): 273–297.

—— (2004) "Differential geographies: place, indigenous rights and 'local' resources," *Political Geography*, 23: 133–167.

—— (2006) "From neoliberalism to neoliberalisation: consolations, confusions and necessary illusions," *Environment and Planning A*, 38: 1–6.

Cavallero, M., (2002) Lawsuit launched against the USDA over organic standards, *Maine Biz*, November 25.

CWF/FoE: Compassion in World Farming/Friends of the Earth (2009) *Eating the planet? How we can feed the world without trashing it.* Online. Available www.cwf.org.uk/resources/publications/eating_the_planet.aspx.

Chambers, R. (1995) *Poverty and livelihoods: whose reality counts?* Brighton: IDS.

Chambers, R. and Conway, G. (1992) "Sustainable rural livelihoods: practical concepts for the 21st Century," Institute of Development Studies, University of Sussex, Discussion Paper 296, Brighton: IDS.

Chambers, R., Pacey, A., and Thrupp, L. (1989) *Farmer first: farmer innovation and agricultural research*, London: Intermediate Technology Publications.

Childs, J.B. (2003) *Transcommunality: from the politics of conversion to the ethics of respect*, Philadelphia: Temple University Press.

Clancy, K. and Ruhf, K. (2010) "Is local enough: some arguments for regional food systems," *Choices* 25(1). Available www.choicesmagazine.orn/magazine/aticle.php?atricle=114 (accessed September 10, 2010).

Clark, J. and Murdoch, J. (1997) "Local knowledge and the precarious extension of scientific networks: a reflection on three case studies," *Sociologia Ruralis*, 37(1): 38–60.

Clark, J. R. A. (2005) "The 'New Associationalism' in agriculture: agro-food diversification and multifunctional production logics," *Journal of Economic Geography*, 5: 475–498.

Clark, N. (2002) "Innovation systems, institutional change and the new knowledge market: implications for Third World agricultural development," *Economics of Innovation and Technology*, 11: 353–368.

Clarke, A. and Montini, T. (1993) "The many faces of RU486: tales of situated knowledges and technological contestations," *Science, Technology and Human Values*, 18(1): 42–78.

Clarke, D. (2010) "The seduction of space," in M. K. Goodman, D. Goodman, and M.

Redclift (eds) *Consuming space: placing consumption in perspective*, Farnham, Surrey: Ashgate.

Clarke, N. (2008) "From ethical consumerism to political consumption," *Geography Compass*, 2(6): 1870–1884.

Clarke, N., Barnett, C., Cloke, P., and Malpass, A. (2007) "Globalising the consumer: doing politics in an ethical register," *Political Geography*, 26: 321–349.

Clarke, N., Cloke, P., Barnett, C., and Malpass, A. (2008) "The spaces and ethics of organic food," *Journal of Rural Studies*, 24: 219–230.

Codron, J.-M., Gireaud-Heraud, E., and Soler, L.-G. (2005) "Minimum quality standards, premium private labels, and European meat and fresh produce retailing." *Food Policy*, 30: 270–283.

Coe, N., Dicken, P., and Hess, M. (2008) "Introduction: global production networks – debates and challenges," *Journal of Economic Geography*, 8: 267–269.

Cohen, L. (2003) *A consumer's republic: the politics of mass consumption in post-war America*, New York: Random House.

Coleman, W. D. (1998) "From protected development to market liberalism: paradigm change in agriculture," *Journal of European Public Policy*, 5(4): 632–651.

Coleman, W. D. and Chiasson, C. (2002) "State power, transformative capacity and adapting to globalisation: an analysis of French agricultural policy, 1960–2000," *Journal of European Public Policy*, 9(2): 168–185.

Collins, P. H. (2000*) Black feminist thought: knowledge, consciousness and the politics of empowerment*, New York: Routledge.

Colman, G. (1963) *Education and agriculture: a history of the New York State College of Agriculture at Cornell University*, Ithaca, NY: Cornell University Press.

Competition Commission (2000) *Report on the supply of groceries from multiple stores in the United Kingdom*, London: HMSO.

—— (2008) *Report on the market investigation of the supply of groceries in the United Kingdom*, London: HMSO.

Conford, P. (2001) *The origins of the organic movement*, Edinburgh: Floris Books.

Conroy, M. (2007) *Branded! How the certification revolution is transforming global corporations*, British Columbia: New Society Press.

Conway, G. (1997) *The doubly green revolution – food for all in the 21st century*, London: Penguin Books.

Cook, I. (2004) "Trade," in S. Harrison, S. Pile, and N. Thrift (eds) *Patterned ground: ecologies of culture and nature*, London: Reaktion.

—— (2004) "Follow the thing: papaya," *Antipode*, 36(4): 642–664.

Cook, I. and Crang, P. (1996) "The world on a plate: culinary culture, displacement and geographical knowledges," *Journal of Material Culture*, 1(2): 131–153.

Corbridge, S. (1998) "Development ethics: distance, difference, plausibility," *Ethics, Environment and Place*, 1(1): 35–54.

Cox, E. (2010) *Five foundations of real localism*, Discussion Paper, Institute for Public Policy Research, November.

Cox, K. (2002) " 'Globalization,' the 'Regulation Approach,' and the politics of scale," in A. Herod and M. Wright (eds), *Geographies of power: placing scale*, Oxford: Blackwell.

Crabtree, T. (2009) "Local Food Links Ltd. Making good food affordable and accessible," presentation at the Conference on Making Local Food Work, Bristol, September 30. Online. Available www.makinglocalfoodwork.co.uk/conference.cfm (accessed October 20, 2009).

Crang, P., Dwyer, C., and Jackson, P. (2003) "Transnationalism and the spaces of commodity culture," *Progress in Human Geography*, 27(4): 438–456.

Crewe, L. (2000) "Geographies of retailing and consumption," *Progress in Human Geography*, 24(2): 275–290.

Cronon, W. (1991) *Nature's metropolis: Chicago and the Great West*, New York: W. W. Norton.

Cummins, R. (2005) *The organic consumer association's stance on the Arthur Harvey lawsuit and 2007 farm bill*. Online. Available www.organicconsumers.org/organic/harvey-farmbil.cfm (accessed March 17, 2006).

Cunha, A. and Swinbank, A. (2009) "Exploring the determinants of CAP reform: a Delphic survey of key decision-makers," *Journal of Common Market Studies*, 47(2): 235–261.

Curry Commission (2002). "Farming and food/a sustainable future," *Report of the policy commission on the future of farming and food*, London: UK Cabinet Office.

Dahl, R. (1961) *Who governs? Democracy and power in an American city*, New Haven: Yale University Press.

Danbom, D. (1979) *The resisted revolution: urban America and the industrialization of agriculture, 1900–1030*, Ames, Iowa: Iowa State University Press.

Daniel, A. (2009) "An alternative food future," in T. Pinkerton and R. Hopkins (eds) *Local food. How to make it happen in your community*, Totnes, Devon: Green Books.

Darton, A., White, P., Sharp, V., Downing, P., Inman, A., Strange, K., and Garnett, T. (2009) *Food synthesis review summary report: a report to the Department of the Environment, Food and Rural Affairs*, London: Defra.

Davies, I. (2008) "Alliances and networks: creating success in the UK fair trade market," *Journal of Business Ethics*, 86: 109–126.

Davies, I., Doherty, B., and Knox, S. (2010) "The rise and stall of a fair trade pioneer: the Cafédirect story," *Journal of Business Ethics*, 92: 127–147.

Davis, M. (1998) *Ecology of fear: Los Angeles and the imagination of disaster*, New York: Vintage Books.

Dean, M., 1999. *Governmentality: power and rule in modern society*, Thousand Oaks, CA: Sage.

Defra (2006) *Food security and the UK: an evidence and analysis paper*, Food Chain Analysis Group. London: Defra.

—— (2008) *Ensuring the UK's food security in a changing world: a Defra Discussion Paper*. London: Defra.

—— (2009a) *UK food security assessment: our approach*, London: DEFRA.

—— (2009b) *First Report from the Council of Food Policy Advisors*, London: Defra.

—— (2010) *Food: a recipe for a healthy, sustainable and successful future. Second Report of the Council of Food Policy Advisors*, London: Defra.

DeLind, L. B. (2002) "Place, work, and civic agriculture: common fields for cultivation," *Agriculture and Human Values*, 19(3): 217–224.

—— (2003) "Considerably more than vegetables, a lot less than community: the dilemma of community-supported agriculture," in J. Adams (ed.) *Fighting for the farm: rural America transformed*, Philadelphia: University of Pennsylvania Press.

—— (2011) "Are local food and the local food movement taking us where we want to go? Or are we hitching our wagon to the wrong stars?," *Agriculture and Human Values*, 28(2): 273–288.

De Neve, G., Luetchford, P., Pratt, J., and Wood, D. (eds) (2008) "Hidden hands in the market: ethnographies of fair trade, ethical consumption and corporate social responsibility," *Research in Economic Anthropology*, 28.

DeVault, M. L. (1994) *Feeding the family: the social organization of caring as gendered work*, Chicago: University of Chicago Press.

Di Maio, P. (2007) An open ontology for open source emergency response systems, Open Source Research Community. Online. Available http://citeseerx.ist.psu.edu/viewdoc/summary?doi=10.1.1.93.1829.

Dixon, J. (1999) "A cultural model for studying food systems," *Agriculture and Human Values*, 16: 151–160.

Doherty, B. (1999) "Paving the way: the rise of direct action against road building and the changing character of British environmentalism," *Political Studies*, 47(2): 275–292.

—— (2008) "A truly co-operative venture: the case study of co-operative food, a retailer response to fair trade," *Journal of Strategic Marketing*, 16(3): 205–221.

Doherty, B. and Meehan, J. (2006) "Competing on social resources: the case of the Day Chocolate Company in the UK confectionary sector," *Journal of Strategic Marketing*, 14: 299–313.

Doherty, B. and Tranchell, S. (2005) "New thinking in international trade? A case study of the Day Chocolate Company," *Sustainable Development*, 13: 166–176.

Doherty, B., Paterson, M., Plows, A., and Wall, D. (2002) "Explaining the fuel protests," Working Paper, School of Politics, International Relations and the Environment, Keele University.

Doherty, B., Plows, A., and Wall, D. (2003) " 'The preferred way of doing things': the British direct action movement," *Parliamentary Affairs*, 56, 669–686.

Dolan, C. (2005) "Field of obligation: rooting ethical sourcing in Kenyan horticulture," *Journal of Consumer Culture*, 5: 365–389.

—— (2007) "Market affections: moral encounters with Kenyan fair trade flowers," *Ethnos*, 72(2): 239–261.

—— (2008) "The mists of development: fair trade in Kenya tea fields," *Globalizations*, 5(2): 1–14.

—— (2010) "Virtual moralities: the mainstreaming of fair trade in Kenyan tea fields," *Geoforum*, 41: 33–43.

Dolan, C. and Humphrey, J. (2001) "Governance and trade in fresh vegetables: the impact of UK supermarkets on the African horticulture industry," *Journal of Development Studies*, 37(2): 147–176.

Dosi, G. and Nelson, R. (1994) "An introduction to evolutionary theories in economics," *Journal of Evolutionary Economics*, 4: 153–172.

Douglas, M. and Isherwood, B. (1978) *The world of goods*, London: Allen Lane.

Dowler, E. (2008) "Food and health inequalities: the challenge for sustaining just consumption," *Local Environment*, 13(8): 759–772.

Dowler, E. and Caraher, M. (2003) "Local food projects: the new philanthropy?," *The Political Quarterly*, 74: 57–65.

Dreher, R. (2006) *Crunchy cons: the new conservative counterculture and its return to roots*, New York: Three Rivers Press.

Dubuisson-Quellier, S. and Lamine, C. (2008) "Consumer involvement in fair trade and local food systems: delegation and empowerment," *GeoJournal*, 73: 55–65.

DuPuis, E. M. (2000) "Not in my body: rBGH and the rise of organic milk," *Agriculture and Human Values*, 17: 285–295.

—— (2002) *Nature's perfect food: how milk became America's drink*, New York: New York University Press.

—— (2004a) "Introduction," in E. M. DuPuis (ed.) *Smoke and mirrors: the culture and politics of air pollution*, New York: New York University Press.

—— (2004b) "From veils to chains to nets and scales: some notes on the strawberry commodity and the ironies of body and place," paper presented at the Conference on Trading Morsels, Growing Hunger, Decimating Nature, Princeton University, Winter, 2004.

—— (2007) "Angels and vegetables: a brief history of food advice in America," *Gastronomica*, 7: 34–44.

DuPuis, E. M. and Block, D. (2008) "Sustainability and scale: US milk-market orders as relocalization policy," *Environment and Planning A*, 40(8): 1987–2005.

DuPuis, E. M. and Gareau, B. (2008) "Neoliberal knowledge: the decline of technocracy and the weakening of the Montreal Protocol," *Social Science Quarterly*, 89(5): 1212–1229.

DuPuis, E. M. and Gillon, S. (2009) "Alternative modes of governance: organic as civic engagement," *Agriculture and Human Values*, 26(1): 43–56.

DuPuis, E. M. and Goodman, D. (2005) "Should we go to 'home' to eat? Toward a reflexive politics of localism," *Journal of Rural Studies*, 21: 359–371.

DuPuis, E. M. and Vandergeest, P. (eds) (1995) *Creating the countryside: the politics of rural and environmental discourse*, Philadelphia: Temple University Press.

DuPuis, E. M., Ball, T., and Mulvaney, D. (2011) "Teaching sustainability as 'how' not just 'what'," forthcoming.

DuPuis, E. M., Goodman, D., and Harrison, J. (2006) "Just values or just value? Remaking the local in agro-food studies," in T. Marsden and J. Murdoch (eds) *Between the local and the global: confronting complexity in the contemporary agri-food sector*, Oxford: Elsevier.

Dwyer, J. (2000) "European experience of promoting countryside products," unpublished report, Countryside Agency.

East Anglia Food Link, (2008) *Review of opportunities for supply chain brokerage*, Online. Available www.eafl.org (accessed October 20, 2009).

Eden, S., Bear, C., and Walker, G. (2008a) "Mucky carrots and other proxies: problematising the knowledge-fix for sustainable and ethical consumption," *Geoforum*, 39: 1044–1057.

—— (2008b) "Understanding and (dis)trusting food assurance schemes: consumer confidence and 'the knowledge-fix'," *Journal of Rural Studies*, 24(1): 1–14.

Eder, K. (1996) *The social construction of nature*, London: Sage.

Edible Marin and Wine Country (2010) "Notable edibles," Issue 6: 6.

EFRA: Environment, Food and Rural Affairs Committee/House of Commons, (2009a) *Securing food supplies up to 2050: the challenges faced by the UK. Volume I: Report, together with formal minutes*, London: The Stationery Office Ltd.

—— Environment, Food and Rural Affairs Committee/House of Commons, (2009b) *Securing food supplies up to 2050: The challenges faced by the UK. Volume II: Oral and written evidence*. London: The Stationery Office Ltd.

—— Environment, Food and Rural Affairs Committee/House of Commons, (2009c) *Securing food supplies up to 2050: Government responses*, London: The Stationery Office Ltd.

Eldridge, William Conner (2003–2004) *United States* v. *United Foods*: united we stand, divided we fall – arguing the constitutionality of commodity checkoff programs 56 Ark. L. Rev. 147.

Erikson, B. (2008) "Methyl iodide saga continues," *Chemical & Engineering News*, 86: 28–30.

Esteva, G., (1994) "Re-embedding food in agriculture," *Culture and Agriculture*, 48: 2–13.

Ethics, Environment and Place (2010) *Special issue on place geography and the ethics of care*, 13(2).

Etzioni, A. (1995) *The spirit of community: rights, responsibilities and the communitarian agenda*, New York; Fontana.

Evans, A. (2008) "Rising food prices: drivers and implications for development," Briefing Paper, Chatham House, London.

Fairlie, S. (2000) "The end of agriculture," *Ecos*, 21(3/4): 8–11.

Fairtrade Foundation (2006) Sainsbury's banana switch is the world's biggest ever commitment to fair trade. Available www. fairtrade.org.uk/press_office/press_releases_ and_statements/archive_2006/dec_2006/sainsbury's_banana_switch_is the_world's_ biggest_ever_commitment_to fairtrade.aspx.

—— (2010) Fair trade raisins from Afghanistan now. Online. Available www.fairtrade. org.uk/press_office/press_releases-and-statement/November/fairtrade_raisins_from_ Afghanistan_now_available.aspx.

—— (2011) 20 companies say "I do" to fair trade and fair mined gold. www.fairtrade. org/uk/press_office_releases_and_statements/February_2011/20_companies_say_i_ do_to_fairtrade_and_fairmined_gold.aspx.

Falconer, K. and Ward, N. (2000) "Using modulation to green the CAP: the UK case," *Land Use Policy*, 17: 269–277.

FAO: United Nations Food and Agriculture Organization (2006) *Livestock's long shadow – environmental issues and options*, Rome: FAO.

—— (2010) *Greenhouse gas emissions from the dairy sector: a life cycle analysis*, Rome: FAO. Online. Available www.fao.org/docrep/012/k7930e/k7930e00.pdf (accessed September 8, 2010).

Feagan, R. (2007) "The place of food: mapping out the 'local' in local food systems," *Progress in Human Geography*, 31(1): 23–42.

Feagan, R. and A. Henderson, A. (2009) "Devon Acres CSA: local struggles in a global food system," *Agriculture and Human Values*, 26: 203–217.

Fiddes, N. (1997) "The march of the earth dragon: a new radical challenge to traditional land rights in Britain?," in P. Milbourne (ed.) *Revealing rural "others": representation, power and identity in the British countryside*, London: Pinter.

Fine, B. (1995) "From political economy to consumption," in D. Miller (ed.) *Acknowledging consumption: a review of new studies*, London: Routledge.

Fine, B. and Leopold, E. (1993) *The world of consumption*, London: Routledge.

Fine, B., Heasman, M., and Wright, J. (1996) *Consumption in the age of affluence*, London: Routledge.

Fisher, E. (2009) "Introduction: the policy trajectory of fair trade," *Journal of International Development*, 21: 985–1003.

Fligstein, N. (1996) "Markets as politics: a political cultural approach to market institutions," *American Sociological Review*, 61: 656–673.

Fligstein, N. and Dauter, L. (2007) "The sociology of markets," *Annual Review of Sociology*, 33: 105–128.

FLO (2011) Facts and figures. Available www.fairtrade.net/facts_and _figures.0.hmtl.

Flynn, A., Marsden, T., and Smith, E. (2003) "Food regulation and retailing in a new institutional context," *The Political Quarterly*, 74(1): 38–46.

Fonte, M. (2006) "Slow food's presidia: what do small producers do with big retailers?," in T. Marsden and J. Murdoch (eds) *Between the local and the global: confronting complexity in the contemporary agri-food sector*, Oxford: Elsevier.

—— (2008) "Knowledge, food and place: a way of producing, a way of knowing," *Sociologia Ruralis*, 48(3): 200–222.

Food Ethics Council (2010) *Food justice: the report of the food and fairness inquiry*, Brighton, UK: Food Ethics Council.

Fourcade, M. and Healy, K. (2007) "Moral views of market society," *Annual Review of Sociology*, 33: 285–311.

Francis, C. (2007) Comments at National Organic Standards Board Meeting, Public Hearing, March 28, 2007.

Fraser, N. (1999) "Social justice in the age of identity politics: redistribution, recognition and participation," in L. Ray and A. Sayer (eds) *Culture and economy after the cultural turn*, London: Sage.

Freeman, C. and Perez, C. (1988) "Structural crises of adjustment: business cycles and investment behaviour," in G. Dosi, C. Freeman, R. Nelson, G. Silverberg, and L. Soete (eds) *Technical change and economic theory*, London: Francis Pinter.

Freidberg, S. (2003a) "Culture, conventions, and colonial constructs of rurality in south-north horticultural trades," *Journal of Rural Studies*, 19: 97–109.

—— (2003b) "Editorial. Not all sweetness and light: new cultural geographies of food," *Social and Cultural Geography*, 4(1): 3–6.

—— (2004) *French beans and food scares: culture and commerce in an anxious age.* New York: Oxford University Press.

Freire, P. (1970) *Pedagogy of the oppressed*, New York/Continuum.

Fridell, G. (2007) *Fair trade coffee: the prospects and pitfalls of market-driven social justice*, Toronto: University of Toronto Press.

—— (2009) "The co-operative and the corporation: competing visions of the future of fair trade," *Journal of Business Ethics*, 86: 81–95.

Friedland, W. H. (1984) "Commodity systems analysis: an approach to the sociology of agriculture," *Research in Rural Sociology and Agriculture*, 1: 221–236.

Friedmann, H. (1994) "Food politics: new dangers, new possibilities," in P. McMichael (ed.) *Food and agrarian orders in the world economy*, Westport, CN: Praeger.

Friel, S., Dangour, A. D., Garnett, T., Lock, K., Chalabi, Z., Roberts, I., Butler, A., Butler, C. D., Waage, J., McMichael, A. J., and Haines, A. (2009) "Public health benefits of strategies to reduce greenhouse gas emissions: food and agriculture," *The Lancet*, 374, Issue 9706: 2016–2025.

Fromartz, S. (2006) *Organic Inc.: natural foods and how they grew*, Orlando, FL: Harcourt.

Fuller, D. and Jones, A. (2003). "Alternative financial spaces," in A. Leyshon, R. Lee and C. Williams (eds) *Alternative economic spaces*, London: Sage.

Garcia, M. (2001) *A world of its own: race, labor, and citrus in the making of Greater Los Angeles, 1900–1970*, Chapel Hill: University of North Carolina Press.

Garnett, T. (2008). *Cooking up a storm: food, greenhouse gas emissions and our changing climate*, Food Climate Research Group, Centre for Environmental Change, University of Surrey, UK.

—— (2009) "Livestock-related greenhouse gas emissions: impacts and options for policy makers," *Environmental Science and Policy*, 12: 491–503.

Gareau, B. and DuPuis, E. M. (2009) "From public to private environmental governance: lessons from the Montreal Protocol's stalled methyl bromide phase-out," *Environment and Planning A*, 41: 2305–2323.

Gaventa, J. (1980) *Power and powerlessness: quiescence and rebellion in an Appala-chian valley*, Oxford: Clarendon Press.

Gaytan, M. S. (2004) "Globalizing resistance: slow food and local imaginaries," *Food, Culture and Society*, 7(1): 97–116.

Geels, F. and Schot, J. (2007) "Typology of sociotechnical transition pathways," *Research Policy*, 36: 399–417.

Geisler, C. and DuPuis, E. M. (1989) "From green revolution to gene revolution: what can we learn from new biotechnology strategies in the Third World," in J. Molnar and H. Kinnucan (eds) *Biotechnology and the new agricultural revolution*, Boulder, CO: Westview.

Gendron, C., Bisaillon, V., and Rance, A. (2008) "The institutionalization of fair trade: more than just a degraded form of social action," *Journal of Business Ethics*, 86: 63–79.

Geoforum (2008) *Themed Issue: agro-food activism in California and the politics of the possible*, 38(3): 1171–1253.

Getz, C. and Shreck, A. (2006) "What fair trade labels do not tell us: towards a place-based understanding of certification," *International Journal of Consumer Studies*, 30(5): 490–501.

Gibbon, P. (2008) "An analysis of standards-based regulation in the EU organic sector, 1991–2007," *Journal of Agrarian Change*, 8(4), 553–582.

Gibbons, M., Limoges, C., Nowotny, H., Schwartzman, S., Scott, P., and Trow, W. (1994) *The new production of knowledge: the dynamics of science and research in contemporary societies*, Thousand Oaks, CA: Sage.

Gibson-Graham, J. K. (1996) *The end of capitalism (as we knew it): a feminist critique of political economy*, Oxford: Blackwell.

—— (2005) "Surplus possibilities: postdevelopment and community economies," *Singapore Journal of Tropical Geography*, 26(1): 4–26.

—— (2006) *A postcapitalist politics*, Minneapolis: University of Minnesota Press.

—— (2008) "Diverse economies: performative practices for 'other worlds'," *Progress in Human Geography*, 32(5): 613–632.

—— (2010) "Author's response. Gibson-Graham, J. K. 1996: The end of capitalism (as we knew it): a feminist critique of political economy. Oxford/Blackwell. Classics in human geography revisited," *Progress in Human Geography*, 34(1): 123–127.

Gilg, A. and Battershill, M. (1998) "Quality farm food in Europe: a possible alternative to the industrialised food market and to current agri-environmental policies. Lessons from France," *Food Policy*, 23(1): 25–40.

Gilmartin, D. (1994) "Scientific empire and imperial science: colonialism and irrigation policy in the Indus basin," *The Journal of Asian Studies*, 53: 1127–1149.

Girou, S. (2008) "Collective farm shops and AMAP (French CSA) in southwest France: commitment and delegation on the part of producers and consumers," paper presented at the Conference on Sustainable Consumption and Alternative Agri-Food Systems, Arlon, Belgium, May, 2008.

Gliessman, S. R. (2006) *Agroecology: the ecology of sustainable food systems*, 2nd edn, Boca Raton, FL: CRC Press.

Golding, K. (2009) "Fair trade's dual aspect: the communications challenge of fair trade marketing," *Journal of Macromarketing*, 29(2): 160–171.

Golding, K. and Peattie, K. (2005) "In search of the golden blend: perspectives on the marketing of fair trade coffee," *Sustainable Development*, 13: 154–165.

Goldsmith, E. (1972) "Blueprint for survival," *The Ecologist*, 2(10): 1–43.

Goodman, D. (1999) "Agro-food studies in the 'Age of Ecology': nature, corporeality, bio-politics," *Sociologia Ruralis*, 39(1): 17–38.

—— (2001) "Ontology matters: the relational materiality of nature and agro-food studies," *Sociologia Ruralis*, 41(2): 182–200.

—— (2002) "Rethinking food production–consumption: integrative perspectives," *Sociologia Ruralis*, 42(4): 271–227.

—— (2003) "The quality 'turn' and alternative food practices: reflections and agenda," *Journal of Rural Studies*, 19: 1–7.

—— (2004) "Rural Europe redux? Reflections on alternative agro-food networks and paradigm change," *Sociologia Ruralis*, 44(1): 3–16.

—— (2010) "Place and space in alternative food networks: connecting production and consumption," in M. Goodman, D. Goodman, and M. Redclift (eds) *Consuming space: placing consumption in perspective*, Farnham, Surrey: Ashgate.

Goodman, D. and DuPuis, E. M. (2002) "Knowing food and growing food: beyond the production–consumption debate in the sociology of agriculture," *Sociologia Ruralis*, 42(1): 5–22.

Goodman, D. and Goodman, M. (2001) "Sustaining foods: organic consumption and the socio-ecological imaginary," in M. J. Cohen and J. Murray (eds) *Exploring sustainable consumption: environmental policy and the social sciences*, Oxford: Elsevier.

—— (2007) "Localism, livelihoods and the 'post-organic': changing perspectives on alternative food networks in the United States," in D. Maye, L. Holloway, and M. Kneafsey (eds) *Alternative food geographies: representation and practice*, Oxford: Elsevier.

Goodman, D. and Redclift, M. (1991) *Refashioning nature: food, ecology and culture*, London: Routledge.

Goodman, D., and Watts, M. (eds), (1997) *Globalizing food: agrarian questions and global restructuring*, New York: Routledge.

Goodman, D. and J. Wilkinson (n.d.) *Agro-food futures: towards a polyvalent agro-food system.* Unpublished paper.

Goodman, D., Sorj, B., and Wilkinson, J. (1987) *From farming to biotechnology: a theory of agro-industrial development*, Oxford: Blackwell.

Goodman, M. (2004) "Reading fair trade: political ecological imaginary and the moral economy of fair trade foods," *Political Geography*, 23(7): 891–915.

—— (2010) "The mirror of consumption: celebritization, developmental consumption and the shifting cultural politics of fair trade," *Geoforum*, 41: 104–116.

—— (2011) "Towards visceral entanglements: knowing and growing the economic geographies of food," in R. Lee, A. Leyshon, L. McDowell, and P. Sunley (eds) *The Sage companion of economic geography*, London: Sage.

Goodman, M. and Barnes, C. (2011) "Star/poverty space: the making of the development celebrity," *Celebrity Studies*, 2(1): 69–85.

Goodman, M. and Bryant, R. (in press) "The ethics of sustainable consumption governance: exploring the cultural economies of 'alternative' retailing," *Journal of Environmental Policy and Planning*.

Goodman, M., Maye, D., and Holloway, L. (2010) "Ethical foodscapes? Premises, promises and possibilities," *Environment and Planning A*, 42: 1782–1796.

Gordon, L. (ed.) (1990) *Women, the state and welfare*, Madison: University of Wisconsin.

Gorz, A. (1980) *Ecology as politics*, London: Pluto Press.

Goss, J. (2004) "Geography of consumption I," *Progress in Human Geography*, 28(3): 369–380.

—— (2006) "Geographies of consumption: the work of consumption," *Progress in Human Geography*, 30(2): 237–249.

Gottlieb, R. and Fisher, A. (1996a) "Community food security and environmental justice: searching for common ground," *Agriculture and Human Values*, 3(3): 23–32.

—— (1996b) "'First feed the face': environmental justice and community food security," *Antipode*, 28: 193–203.

GRAIN, (2008) *Seized! The 2008 land grab for food and financial security*, GRAIN Briefing, Barcelona. Online. Available www.grain.org (accessed October 15, 2009).

Gray, J. (2000) "The common agricultural policy and the re-invention of the rural in the European community," *Sociologia Ruralis*, 40(1): 30–52.

Gregson, N. (1995) "And now it's all consumption," *Progress in Human Geography*, 19(1): 135–141.

Grievink, J.-W. "The changing face of the global food industry," paper presented at the OECD Conference on the Changing Dimensions of the Food Economy. The Hague, February, 2002.

Guthman, J. (1998) "Regulating meaning, appropriating nature: the codification of California organic agriculture," *Antipode*, 30(2): 135–154.

—— (2000) Raising organic: an agro-ecological assessment of grower practices in California. *Agriculture and Human Values*, 17: 257–266.

—— (2003) "Fast food/organic food: reflexive tastes and the making of 'yuppie chow'," *Social & Cultural Geography*, 4(1): 45–58.

—— (2004a) *Agrarian dreams? The paradox of organic farming in California*. Berkeley: University of California Press.

—— (2004c) "The trouble with 'organic lite' in California: a rejoinder to the 'conventionalisation' debate," *Sociologia Ruralis*, 44(3): 301–316.

—— (2007) "The Polyanian way? Voluntary food labels as neoliberal governance," *Antipode*, 39(3): 457–478.

—— (2008a) "Bringing good food to others: investigating the subjects of alternative food practice," *Cultural Geographies*, 15: 431–447.

—— (2008b) "'If only they knew': color blindness and universalism in California alternative food institutions," *Professional Geographer*, 60(3): 387–397.

Guthman, J. and DuPuis, E. M. (2006) "Embodying neoliberalism: economy, culture, and the politics of fat," *Environment and Planning D: Society and Space*, 34: 427–448.

Guthman, J., Morris, A., and Allen, P. (2006) "Squaring farm security in two types of alternative food institutions," *Rural Sociology*, 71(4): 662–684.

Hajer, M. (1995) *The politics of environmental discourse*, Oxford: Clarendon Press.

Halberg, N., Alroe, H., Knudsen, M. T., and Kristensen. E. S. (2006) *Global development of organic agriculture: challenges and promises*, Oxford: Oxford University Press.

Halfacree, K. (1996) "Out of place in the country: travellers and the 'rural idyll'," *Antipode*, 28(1): 42–72.

—— (1999) "'Anarchy doesn't work unless you think about it: intellectual work and DIY culture," *Area*, 31: 209–220.

—— (2001) "Constructing the object: taxonomic practices, 'counter-urbanisation' and positioning marginal rural settlement," *International Journal of Population Geography*, 7: 395–411.

—— (2006) "From dropping out to leading on? British counter-cultural back-to-the-land in a changing rurality," *Progress in Human Geography*, 30(3): 309–336.

—— (2007a) "Back-to-the-land in the twenty-first century – making connections with rurality," *Tijdschrift voor Economische en Sociale Geografie*, 98(1): 3–8.

—— (2007b) "Trial by space for a 'radical rural': introducing alternative localities, representations and lives," *Journal of Rural Studies*, 23(2): 125–141.

Hall, S. (1989) "Introduction," in S. Hall and M. Jacques (eds) *New times: the changing face of politics in the 1990s*, New York: Verso.

Halweil, B. (2004) *Eat here: reclaiming homegrown pleasures in a global supermarket*, New York: Norton.

Hamlin, C. (1998) *Public health and social justice in the age of Chadwick: Britain, 1800–1854*, New York: Cambridge University Press.

Hand, M. and Shove, E. (2007) "Condensing practices. Ways of living with a freezer," *Journal of Consumer Culture*, 7(1): 79–104.

Haraway, D. (1991) "Situated knowledges: the science question in feminism and the privilege of partial perspective," *Feminist Studies*, 14(3): 575–599.

Harris, E. (2009) "Neoliberal subjectivities or a politics of the possible? Reading for difference in alternative food networks," *Area*, 41(1): 55–63.

Harris, F., Robinson, G., and Griffiths, I. (2008) "A study of the motivations and influences on farmers' decisions to leave the organic farming sector in the United Kingdom," in G. M. Robinson (ed.) *Sustainable rural systems: sustainable agriculture and rural communities*, Aldershot: Ashgate.

Harrison, R., Newholm, T., and Shaw, D. (eds) (2005) *The ethical consumer*, London: Sage.

Hartsook, N.C.M. (1983) *Money, sex, and power: toward a feminist historical materialism*, New York: Longman.

Hartwick, E. (2000) "Towards a geographical politics of consumption," *Environment and Planning A*, 32: 1177–1192.

Hartwick, E. R. (1998) "Geographies of consumption: a commodity-chain analysis," *Environment and Planning D: Society and Space*, 16: 423–437.

Harvey, D. (1985) *The urbanization of capital*, Oxford: Blackwell.

—— (1996) *Justice, nature and the geography of difference*, Oxford: Blackwell.

—— (2001) *Spaces of hope*, Berkeley, CA: University of California Press.

Harvey, M., McMeekin, A., and Warde, A. (eds) (2004) *Qualities of food*, Manchester: University of Manchester Press.

Hassanein, N. (1999) *Changing the way America farms: knowledge and community in the sustainable agriculture movement*, Lincoln: University of Nebraska Press.

—— (2003) "Practicing food democracy: a pragmatic politics of transformation," *Journal of Rural Studies*, 19(1): 77–86.

Hassanein, N., and Kloppenberg, Jr, J. (1995) "Where the green grass grows again: knowledge exchange in the sustainable agriculture movement," *Rural Sociology*, 60: 721–740.

Hatanaka, M., Bain, C., and Busch, L. (2005) "Third-party certification in the global agri-food system," *Food Policy*, 30: 354–369.

Hendrickson, M. and Heffernan W. D. (2002) "Opening spaces through relocalization: locating potential resistance in the weaknesses of the global food system," *Sociologia Ruralis*, 42(4): 347–369.

Henson, S. and Reardon, T. (2005) "Private agri-food standards: implications for food policy and the agri-food system," *Food Policy*, 30: 241–253.

Herbert, F. (1987) *White plague*, New York: Ace Books.

Herman, A. (2010) "Connecting the complex lived worlds of fair trade," *Journal of Environmental Policy and Planning*, 12(4): 405–422.

Herod, A. (1991) "The production of scale in United States labor relations," *Area*, 23: 82–88.

Herod, A. and M. Wright (eds), (2002) *Geographies of power: placing scale*, Oxford: Blackwell.

Hess, D. (2005) "Technology- and product-oriented social movements: approximating social movement studies and science and technology studies," *Science, Technology and Human Values*, 30: 515–535.

—— (2007) *Alternative pathways in science and industry*, Cambridge: MIT Press.

—— (2009) *Localist movements in a global economy: sustainability, justice and urban development in the United States*, Boston, MA: MIT Press.

Hightower, J. (1973) *Hard tomatoes, hard times: a report of the Agribusiness Accountability Project on the failure of America's LGU complex*, Cambridge, MA: Schenkman.

Hills, J. (2010) *Ends and means: the future roles of social housing in England*. London: Centre for Analysis of Social Exclusion (CASE), London School of Economics and Political Science.

Hillson, G. (2008) "Fair trade gold: antecedents, prospects and challenges," *Geoforum*, 39: 386–400.

Hinrichs, C. (2000) "Embeddedness and local food systems: notes on two types of direct agricultural market," *Journal of Rural Studies*, 16: 295–303.

—— (2003) "The practice and politics of food system localization," *Journal of Rural Studies*, 19(1): 33–45.

—— (2007) "Introduction: practice and place in the remaking of the food system," in C. Clare Hinrichs and T. Lyson (eds) *Remaking the North American food system: strategies for sustainability*. Lincoln, NB: University of Nebraska Press.

Hinrichs, C. and Allen, P. (2008) "Selective patronage and social justice: local food consumer campaigns in historical context," *Journal of Agricultural and Environmental Ethics*, 21: 329–352.

Hinrichs, C. and Kremer, K. (2002) "Social inclusion in a mid-west local food system project," *Journal of Poverty*, 6(1): 65–90.

Hinton, E. (2011) *Virtual spaces of sustainable consumption: governmentality and third-sector advocacy in the UK*, PhD Thesis, Department of Geography, King's College London.

Hinton, E. and Goodman, M. (2010) "Sustainable consumption: developments, considerations and new directions," in M. Redclift and G. Woodgate (eds) *The international handbook of environmental sociology*, Cheltenham: Edward Elgar.

Hira, A. and Ferrie, J. (2006) "Fair trade: three main challenges for reaching the mainstream," *Journal of Business Ethics*, 63: 107–118.

HM Government (2010a). *The 2007/08 agricultural price spikes: causes and policy implication*, London: HM Government.

—— (2010b) *Food 2030*, London: HM Government.

HM Treasury and Defra, (2005) A *vision for the Common Agricultural Policy*, London: HM Treasury and Defra.

Hodgson, G.M. (1997) "The ubiquity of habits and rules," *Cambridge Journal of Economics*, 21: 663–684.

—— (1998) "The approach of institutional economics," *Journal of Economic Literature*, 66(1): 166–192.

—— (1999) *Evolution and institutions: on evolutionary economics and the evolution of economics*, Cheltenham: Edward Elgar.

Hofstadter, R. (1955) *The age of reform: from Bryan to FDR*, New York: Knopf.

Holloway, L. (2002) "Virtual vegetables and adopted sheep: ethical relation, authenticity and internet-mediated food production technologies," *Area*, 34(1): 70–81.

Holloway, L. and Kneafsey, M. (2000) "Reading the space of the farmers' market: a case-study from the United Kingdom," *Sociologia Ruralis*, 40: 285–299.

—— (2004) "Producing–consuming food: closeness, connectedness and rurality," in L. Holloway and M. Kneafsey (eds), *Geographies of rural cultures and societies*, London: Ashgate.

Holloway, S. (2007) "Burning issues: whiteness, rurality and the politics of difference," *Geoforum*, 38(1): 7–20.

Holt-Jimenez, E. (2006) *Campesino-a-campesino: voices from Latin America's farmer-to-farmer movement for sustainable agriculture*, Oakland, CA: Food First Books.

Hopkins, R. (2008) *The Transition handbook: from oil dependency to local resilience*, Totnes, Devon: Green Books.

House of Lords, EU Committee, (2010) *Adapting to climate change: EU agriculture and Forestry. Volume I: Report.* London: Stationery Office Ltd.

Howard, P. (2005) "Consolidation in food and agriculture: implications for farmers and consumers," *The Natural Farmer*, Spring 17–20. Online. Available www.nofa.org (accessed October 13, 2009).

—— (2009a) "Consolidation in the North American organic food processing sector," *International Journal of Sociology of Agriculture and Food*, 16: 13–30.

—— (2009b) "Organic industry structure," Media N Online Journal, 5(3). Online. Available www.newmediacaucus.org/journal/issues.php?f=papers&time (accessed April 20, 2010).

Hudson, I. and Hudson, M. (2003) "Removing the veil? Commodity fetishism, fair trade and the environment," *Organization and Environment*, 16(4): 413–430.

Hughes, A. (2000) "Retailers, knowledges and changing commodity networks: the case of the cut flower trade," *Geoforum*, 31: 175–190.

—— (2001) "Global commodity networks, ethical trade and governmentality: organizing business responsibility in the Kenyan cut flower industry," Transactions of the Institute of British Geographers, 26: 390–406.

Hughes, A. and Reimer, S. (eds) (2004) *Geographies of commodity chains*, London: Routledge.

Hughes, A., Wrigley, N., and Buttle, M. (2007) "Organizational geographies of corporate responsibility: a UK–US comparison of retailers' ethical trading initiatives," *Journal of Economic Geography*, 7: 491–513.

—— (2008) "Global production networks, ethical campaigning, and the embeddedness of responsible governance," *Journal of Economic Geography*, 8: 345–367.

Humphrey, J. (2006) "Policy implications of trends in agribusiness value chains," *The European Journal of Development Research*, 18(4): 572–592.

Hutchinson, C., McGiffen Jr., M., Ohr, H., Sims, J., and Becker, J. (2000) "Efficacy of methyl iodide and synergy with chloropicrin for control of fungi," *Pest Management Science*, 56: 413–418.

IAASTAD: International Assessment of Agricultural Knowledge, Science and Technology for Development (2008) *Summary for decision makers of the global report.* Online. Available www.agassessment.org (accessed October 20, 2009).

IEEP: Institute for European Environmental Policy, (2008) *French Presidency ends on a whimper, rather than a roar*, CAP2020, December 12. Online. Available www.cap2020.ieep.eu/2008/12/12 (accessed September 25, 2009).

—— (2009a) *The future of rural development: the role of the CAP and the Cohesion Policy*, CAP2020, Policy briefing, No. 5, May. Online. Available www.cap2020.ieep.eu/2009 (accessed September 2, 2009).

—— (2009b) *Exploring policy options for more sustainable livestock and feed production*. Final report for Friends of the Earth, March.

Ilbery, B. and Kneafsey, M. (2000) "Registering regional speciality food and drink products in the United Kingdom: the case of PDOs and PGIs," *Area*, 32(3): 317–325.

Ilbery, B. and Maye, D. (2005a) "Food supply chains and sustainability: evidence from specialist food producers in the Scottish–English borders," *Land Use Policy*, 22: 331–344.

—— (2005b) "Alternative (short) food supply chains and specialist livestock products in the Scottish–English borders," *Environment and Planning A*, 37: 823–844.

—— (2006) "Retailing local food in the English–Scottish borders: a supply chain perspective," *Geoforum*, 37: 3523–367.

Ilbery, B., Morris, C., Buller, H., Maye, D., and Kneafsey, M. (2005) "Product, process and place: an examination of food marketing and labelling schemes in Europe and North America," *European Urban and Regional Studies*, 12(2): 116–132.

Ingram, M. (2007) "Disciplining microbes in the implementation of US federal organic standards," *Environment and Planning D: Society and Space*, 39(12): 2866–2882.

Jackson, P. (1999) "Commodity cultures: the traffic in things," *Transactions of the Institute of British Geographers N.S.*, 24: 95–108.

—— (2000) "Rematerializing social and cultural geography," *Social and Cultural Geography*, 1(1): 9–14.

—— (2002) "Commercial cultures: transcending the cultural and the economic," *Progress in Human Geography*, 26(1): 3–18.

—— (2010) "Food stories: consumption in an age of anxiety," *Cultural Geographies*, 17(2): 147–165.

Jackson, P., Russell, P., and Ward, N. (2007) "The appropriation of 'alternative' food discourses by 'mainstream' food retailers," in D. Maye, L. Holloway, and M. Kneafsey (eds) *Alternative food geographies: representation and practice*, Oxford: Elsevier.

—— (2010) "Manufacturing meaning along the chicken supply chain: consumer anxiety and the spaces of production," in M. Goodman, D. Goodman, and M. Redclift (eds) *Consuming space: placing consumption in perspective*, Aldershot: Ashgate.

Jackson, P., Ward, N., and Russell, P. (2009) "Moral economies of food and geographies of responsibility," *Transactions of the Institute of British Geographers, New Series*, 34: 12–24.

Jackson, T. (2004) *Motivating sustainable consumption: a review of evidence on consumer behaviour and behavioural change*, A Report to the Sustainable Development Research Network, Centre for Environmental Strategy, University of Surrey. Draft version, August 1.

—— (2009) *Prosperity without growth*. London: Earthscan.

Jacobs, J. (1961) *The death and life of great American cities*, New York: Random House.

Jacobson, E. and Dulstrud, A. (2007) "Will consumers save the world? The framing of political consumerism," *Journal of Agricultural and Environmental Ethics*, 20: 469–482.

Jaffee, D. (2007) *Brewing justice: fair trade coffee, sustainability and survival*, Berkeley, CA: University of California Press.

—— (2010) "Fair trade standards, corporate participation and social movement responses in the United States," *Journal of Business Ethics*, 92: 267–285.

Jaffee, D. and P. Howard 2010 "Corporate cooptation of organic and fair trade standards." *Agriculture and Human Values*, 27(4): 387–399.

Jaffee, D., Kloppenburg, Jr, J., and Monroe, M. (2004) "Bringing the 'moral charge' home: fair trade within the North and within the South," *Rural Sociology*, 69(2): 169–196.

Jamison, D. and Lau, L. (1982) *Farmer education and farm efficiency*, Baltimore, MD: Johns Hopkins University Press.

Jessop, B. (1997) "Capitalism and its future: remarks on regulation, government and governance," *Review of International Political Economy*, 4(3): 561–581.

—— (1998) "The rise of governance and the risks of failure: the case of economic development," *International Social Science Journal*, 155: 29–46.

—— (1999) "Narrating the future of the national economy and the national state? Remarks on remapping regulation and reinventing governance," in G. Steinmetz (ed.) *State/Culture*, Ithaca: Cornell University Press.

—— (2000) "The crisis of the national spatio–temporal fix and the tendential ecological dominance of capitalism," *International Journal of Urban and Regional Research*, 24(2): 323–360.

Johnston, J. (2002) "Consuming social justice: fair trade shopping and alternative development," in J. Goodman (ed.) *Protest and globalization*, Annandale: Pluto Press.

—— (2008) "The citizen–consumer hybrid: ideological tensions and the case of Whole Foods Market," *Theory and Society*, 37(3): 313–325.

Johnston, J., Biro, A., and MacKendrick, N. (2009) "Lost in the supermarket: the corporate-organic foodscape and the struggle for food democracy," *Antipode*, 41(3): 509–532.

Jolly, D. (1998) "Organics on the brink," *Information Bulletin*, no. 5, pp. 1, 16, Santa Cruz, CA.: Organic Farming Research Foundation.

Jones, G. and Garforth, C. (1997) "The history, development and future of agricultural extension," in B. Swanson and Claar, J. (eds) *The history and development of agricultural extension*, Urbana, Il: University of Illinois Press.

Kaltoft, P. (1999) "Values about nature in organic farming practice and knowledge," *Sociologia Ruralis*, 39(1): 39–53.

Kaplinsky, R. (2000) "Globalisation and unequalisation: what can be learned from value chain analysis?," *Journal of Development Studies*, 37(2): 117–146.

Katz, C. (2001) "Vagabond capitalism and the necessity of social reproduction," *Antipode*, 33(4): 709–729.

Keech, D. (2007) "Growth and ethics: conflict or complementarity in sustainable food enterprises," unpublished paper, London: The new economics foundation, September.

Keech, D., Alldred, S., and Snow, R. (2009) *Community Supported Agriculture. An analysis of seven community supported agriculture enterprises*, Bristol: Soil Association.

King, R., Hand, M., DiGiacomo, G., Clancy, K., Gomez, M., Hardesty, S., Lev, L., and McLaughlin, E. (2010) *Comparing the structure, size and performance of local and mainstream food supply chains*, Washington, DC: ERR-99, Economic Research Service, United States Department of Agriculture.

Kingsolver, B., Kingsolver, C., and Hopp, S. (2007) *Animal, vegetable, miracle*, New York: Harper Collins.

Kirwan, J. (2004) "Alternative strategies in the UK agro-food system: interrogating the alterity of farmers' markets," *Sociologia Ruralis*, 44(4): 395–415.

Kirwan, J. and Foster, C. (2007) "Public sector food procurement in the United Kingdom: examining the creation of an 'alternative' and localised network in Cornwall," in D. Maye, L. Holloway, and M. Kneafsey (eds) *Alternative food geographies: representation and practice*. London: Elsevier.

Kjeldsen, C. and Ingemann, J. H. (2009) "From the social to the economic and beyond?

A relational approach to the historical development of Danish organic food networks," *Sociologia Ruralis*, 49(2): 151–171.

Kleine, D. (2005) "fairtrade.com versus fairtrade.org: how fair trade organisations use the internet," *Interacting with Computers*, 17: 57–83.

—— (2010) "How fair is fair enough? Negotiating alterity and compromise within the German fair trade movement," in D. Fuller, A. Jonas, and R. Lee (eds) *Interrogating alterity: alternative economic and political spaces*, Aldershot: Ashgate.

Kloppenburg, Jr, J. (1991) "Social theory and the de/reconstruction of agricultural science: local knowledge for an alternative agriculture," *Rural Sociology*, 56(4): 519–548.

Kloppenburg, Jr, J. and Hassanein, N. (2006) "From old school to reform school," *Agriculture and Human Values*, 23(4): 417–421.

Kloppenburg Jr, J., Hendrickson, J., and Stevenson, G. W. (1996) "Coming into the foodshed," *Agriculture and Human Values*, 13(3): 33–42.

Kneafsey, M., (2000) "Tourism, place identities and local relations in the European rural periphery," *European Urban and Regional Studies*, 7(1): 35–50.

Kneafsey, M., Cox, R., Holloway, L., Dowler, E., Venn, L., and Tuomainen, H. (2008) *Reconnecting consumers, producers and food: exploring alternatives*, Oxford: Berg.

Konefal, J., Mascarenhas, M., and Hatanaka, M. (2005) "Governance in the global agrofood system: backlighting the role of transnational supermarket chains," *Agriculture and Human Values*, 22(3): 291–302.

Krippner, G. (2001) "The elusive market/embeddedness and the paradigm of economic sociology," *Theory and Society*, 30: 775–810.

Kymlicka, W. (1990) *Contemporary political philosophy: an introduction*, New York: Oxford University Press.

Lamine, C. (2005) "Settling shared uncertainties: local partnerships between producers and consumers," *Sociologia Ruralis*, 45(4): 324–345.

Lamine, C. and Deverre, C. "Is local (food system) beautiful?," paper presented at the Conference on Sustainable Consumption and Alternative Agri-Food Systems, Arlon, Belgium, May 27–30, 2008.

Lang, T. (2007) "Going public: food campaigns during the 1980s and early 1990s," in D. F. Smith (ed.) *Nutrition in Britain: science, scientists and politics in the twentieth century*, London: Routledge.

—— (2009a) Oral evidence to the House of Commons Environment, Food and Rural Affairs Committee. *Ensuring food supplies up to 2050: The challenges faced by the UK. Volume II: Oral and written evidence*, page EV19, January 28.

—— (2009b) "Reshaping the food system for ecological public health," paper presented to the Conference on Food Systems and Public Health: Linkages to achieve Healthier Diets and Healthier Communities. Airlie Center, Warrenton, Virginia, April, 2009.

—— (2010) "From 'value-for-money' to 'values-for-money'? Ethical food and policy in Europe," *Environment and Planning A*, 42(8): 1814–1832.

Lang, T. and Raynor, G. (2010) "Corporate responsibility in public health/the government's invitation to the food industry to fund social marketing on obesity is risky," *British Medical Journal*, 341: c3758.

Lang, T. and Wiggins, P. (1984) "The industrialisation of the British food system," in M. J. Healey and B. W. Ilbery (eds) *The industrialisation of the countryside*. Norwich: Geo Books.

Lappe, F. M. (1971) *Diet for a small planet*, New York: Ballantine.

Lappe, F. M. and Lappe, A. (2002) *Hope's edge: the next diet for a small planet*, New York: Jeremy P. Tarcher and Putnam.

Latour, B. (1987) *Science in action: how to follow scientists and engineers through society*, Cambridge, MA: Harvard University Press.

—— (1991) "Technology is society made durable," in J. Law (ed.) *A sociology of monsters: essays in power, technology and domination*, London: Routledge.

—— (1993) *We have never been modern*, Brighton: Harvester Wheatsheaf.

Lave, J. and Wenger, E. (1991) *Situated learning: legitimate peripheral participation*, Cambridge: Cambridge University Press.

Law, J. (1992) "Notes on the theory of actor-network: ordering, strategy and heterogeneity," *Systems Practice*, 5(4): 379–393.

—— (1994) *Organizing modernity*, Oxford: Blackwell.

Law, J. and Callon, M. (1992) "The life and death of an aircraft: a network analysis of technical change," in W. Bijker and J. Law (eds) *Shaping technology – building society: studies in sociotechnical change*, Cambridge, MA: MIT Press.

Lawrence, G. (2005) "Promoting sustainable development: the question of governance," in F. Buttel and P. McMichael (eds) *New directions in the sociology of global development*, New York: Elsevier.

Le Mere, A. (2007) "Fair trade as narrative: the stories of fair trade," *Narrative Inquiry*, 17(1): 69–92.

—— (2008) "The impact of fair trade on social and economic development: a review of the literature," *Geographical Compass*, 2(6): 1922–1942.

Le Velly, R. (2007) "Is large-scale fair trade possible?," in E. Zaccai (ed.) *Sustainable consumption, ecology and fair trade*, London: Routledge.

Leclair, M. (2002) "Fighting the tide: alternative trade organizations in the era of global free trade," *World Development*, 30(6): 949–958.

Lee, R. (2010) "Commentary 1. Gibson-Graham, J. K. 1996: The end of capitalism (as we knew it): a feminist critique of political economy. Oxford: Blackwell. Classics in human geography revisited," *Progress in Human Geography*, 34(1): 117–120.

Lee, R. and Leyshon, A. (2003) "Conclusions: re-making geographies and the construction of 'spaces of hope'," in A. Leyshon, R. Lee, and C. Williams (eds) *Alternative economic spaces*, London: Sage Publications.

Lee, R., Leyshon, A., Aldridge, T., Tooke, J., Williams, C., and Thrift, N. (2004) "Making geographies and histories? Constructing local circuits of value," *Environment and Planning D: Society and Space*, 22(4): 595–617.

Leitch, A. (2003) "Slow food and the politics of pork fat: Italian food and European identity," *Ethnos*, 68(4): 437–462.

Leitner, H. (2004) "The politics of scale and networks of spatial connectivity: transnational interurban networks and the rescaling of political governance in Europe," in E. Sheppard and R. McMaster (eds) *Scale and geographic enquiry: nature, society and method*, Oxford: Blackwell.

Leslie, D. and Reimer, S. (1999) "Spatializing commodity chains," *Progress in Human Geography*, 23(3): 401–420.

Levi, M. and Linton, A. (2003) "Fair trade: a cup at a time?," *Politics and Society*, 31(3): 407–432.

Leyshon, A., Lee, R., and Williams, C. (2003) "Introduction: alternative economic geographies," in A. Leyshon, R. Lee, and C. Williams (eds) *Alternative economic spaces*, London: Sage.

—— (2010) "Commentary 2. Gibson-Graham, J.K. 1996: The end of capitalism (as we knew it): a feminist critique of political economy. Oxford: Blackwell. Classics in human geography revisited," *Progress in Human Geography*, 34(1): 120–123.

Linton, A., Liou, C., and Shaw, K. (2004) "A taste of trade justice: marketing global social responsibility via fair trade coffee," *Globalizations*, 1(2): 2233–2246.

Lipsitz, G. (1998) (revised 2006) *The possessive investment in whiteness: how white people profit from identity politics*, Philadelphia: Temple University Press.

Little, J. (2001) "New rural governance?," *Progress of Human Geography*, 25(1): 97–102.

Littler, J. (2009) *Radical consumption*, Maidenhead: Open University Press.

Littrell, M. and Dickson, M. (1999) *Social responsibility in the global market: fair trade of cultural products*, Thousand Oaks, CA.: Sage.

Lobley, M., Fish, R., Butler, A., Courtney, P., Ilbery, B., Kirwan, J., Maye, D., Potter, C., and M. Winter (2009a) *Analysis of socio-economic aspects of local and national organic farming markets. Summary Report*, Centre for Rural Policy Research, University of Exeter. Online. Available http://centres.exeter.ac.uk/crpr/publications/index.htm (accessed May 5, 2010).

—— (2009b) *Analysis of socio-economic aspects of local and national organic farming markets. Main Report*. Centre for Rural Policy Research, University of Exeter. Online. Available http://centres.exeter.ac.uk/crpr/publications/index/htm (accessed May 5, 2010).

Lockie, S. (2002) "The invisible mouth: mobilising 'the consumer' in food production–consumption networks," *Sociologia Ruralis*, 42(4): 278–294.

—— (2009) "Responsibility and agency within alternative food networks: assembling the 'citizen consumer'," *Agriculture and Human Values*, 26: 193–201.

Lockie, S. and Collie, L. (1999) "'Feed the man meat': gendered food and theories of consumption," in D. Burch, J. Cross, and G. Lawrence (eds) *Restructuring global and regional agricultures: transformations in Australasian agri-food economies and spaces*, Aldershot: Ashgate.

Lockie, S. and Halpin, D. (2005) "The conventionalisation thesis reconsidered: structural ideological transformations of Australian organic agriculture," *Sociologia Ruralis*, 45(4): 284–307.

Lockie, S. and Kitto, S. (2000) "Beyond the farm gate: production–consumption networks and agri-food research," *Sociologia Ruralis*, 40(1): 3–19.

Lockie, S., Lyons, K., Lawrence, G., and Halpin, D. (2006) *Going organic: Mobilising networks for environmentally responsible food production*, Wallingford, UK: CABI Publishing.

Logan, J. and Harvey, M. (1987) *Urban fortunes: the political economy of place*, Berkeley, CA: University of California Press.

Long, N. (2000) "Exploring local/global transformation: a view from anthropology," in A. Arce and N. Long (eds) *Anthropology, development and modernities*, London: Routledge.

Lorimer, J. (2007) "Nonhuman charisma," *Environment and Planning D: Society and Space*, 24(5): 911–932.

Lotti, A. (2010) "The commoditisation of products and taste: slow food and the conservation of agrobiodiversity," *Agriculture and Human Values*, 27: 71–83.

Lovering, J. (1999) "Theory led by policy: the inadequacies of the 'New Regionalism' (illustrated from the case of Wales)," *Regional Studies*, 23(2): 379–395.

Low, W. and Davenport, E. (2004) "Has the medium (roast) become the message? The ethics of marketing fair trade in the mainstream," *International Marketing Review*, 22(5): 494–511.

—— (2005) "Postcards from the edge: maintaining the 'alternative' character of fair trade," *Sustainable Development*, 13: 143–153.

—— (2009) "Organizational leadership, ethics and the challenges of marketing fair and ethical trade," *Journal of Business Ethics*, 86: 97–108.

Lowe, P., Buller, H., and Ward, N. (2002) "Setting the next agenda? British and French approaches to the second pillar of the common agricultural policy," *Journal of Rural Studies*, 18(1): 1–17.

Luetchford, P. (2008) "The hands that pick the fair trade coffee: beyond the charms of the family farm," *Research in Economic Anthropology*, 28: 143–169.

Luks, F. and Siebenhuner, B. (2007) "Transdisciplinarity for social learning? The contribution of the German socio-ecological research initiative to sustainability governance," *Ecological Economics*, 63: 418–426.

Lyon, S. (2006) "Evaluating fair trade consumption: politics, defetishization and producer participation," *Journal of Consumer Studies*, 30(5): 452–464.

—— (2007a) "Fair trade coffee and human rights in Guatemala," *Journal of Consumer Policy*, 30: 241–261.

—— (2007b) "Maya coffee farmers and fair trade; assessing the benefits and limits of alternative markets," *Culture and Agriculture*, 29(2): 100–1122.

Lyon, S. and Moburg, M. (eds) (2010) *Fair trade and social justice: global ethnographies*, New York: NYU Press.

Lyon, S., Bezaury, J., and Mutersbaugh, T. (2010) "Gender equity in fair trade-organic coffee producer organizations: cases from MesoAmerica," *Geoforum*, 41: 93–103.

Lyson, T. (2004) *Civic agriculture: reconnecting food, farm and community*, Medford, MA: Tufts University Press.

McAfee, K. (1999) "Selling nature to save it?," *Environment and Planning D: Society and Space*, 7: 155–174.

McCorkle, C. (1989) "Toward a knowledge of local knowledge and its importance for agricultural RD&E," *Agriculture and Human Values*, 6(3): 4–12.

McEwan, C. and Bek, D. (2009) "The political economy of alternative trade: social and environmental certification in the South African wine industry," *Journal of Rural Studies*, 25: 255–266.

McEwan, C. and Goodman, M. (2010) "Place geography and the ethics of care: introductory remarks on the geographies of ethics, responsibility and care," *Ethics, Place and Environment*, 13(2): 103–112.

McLeod, D. (1976) "Urban–rural food alliances: a perspective on recent community food organizing," in R. Merrill (ed.), *Radicalizing agriculture*, New York: Harper Row.

McMichael, P. (ed.) (1994) *The global restructuring of agro-food systems*, Ithaca, NY: Cornell University Press.

—— (2000) "The power of food," *Agriculture and Human Values*, 17(1): 21–33.

McPhee, J. and Zimmerman, W. (1979) *Giving good weight*, New York: Farrar-Strauss-Giroux.

maketradefair.com (2010) ever felt dumped on? Online. Available www.maketradefair.org/en/index/php?file=dumped.htm&cat=1&subcat=2&select=2.

Malpass, A., Barnett, C., Clarke, N., and Cloke. P. (2007) "Problematising choice/ responsible consumers, sceptical citizens," in M. Bevir and F. Trentmann (eds) *Governance and consumption*, Basingstoke: Palgrave Macmillan.

Mansfield, B. (2003a) "Fish, factory trawlers and imitation crab: the nature of quality in the seafood industry," *Journal of Rural Studies*, 19(1): 9–22.

—— (2003b) "Spatializing globalization: a 'geography of quality' in the seafood industry," *Economic Geography*, 79(1): 1–16.

Mailfert, K. (2007) "New farmers and networks: how beginning farmers build social connections in France," *Tijdschrift voor Economische en Sociale Geografie*, 98(1): 21–31.

Marmot, M. (2010) *Strategic review of health inequalities in England post 2010 (Marmot Review) Final Report. Fair society, healthy lives*, London: University College London Research Department of Epidemiology and Public Health.

Marsden, T. (1997) "Creating space for food: the distinctiveness of recent agrarian development," in D. Goodman and M. J. Watts (eds) *Globalising food: agrarian questions and global restructuring*, London: Routledge.

—— (1999) "Rural futures: consumption countryside and regulation," *Sociologia Ruralis*, 39: 501–520.

—— (2004) "Theorising food quality: some key issues in understanding its competitive production regulation," in M. Harvey, A. McMeekin, and A. Warde (eds) *Qualities of Food*, Manchester: Manchester University Press.

Marsden, T. and Arce, A. (1995) "Constructing quality: emerging food networks in the rural transition," *Environment and Planning A*, 27(8): 1261–1279.

Marsden, T. and Smith, E. (2005) "Ecological entrepreneurship: sustainable development in local communities through quality food production," *Geoforum*, 36(4): 440–451.

Marsden, T. and Sonnino, R. (2006) "Beyond the divide: rethinking relationships between alternative and conventional networks in Europe," *Journal of Economic Geography*, 6: 181–199.

—— (2006b) "Alternative food networks in the South-west of England: towards a new agrarian eco-economy?," in T. Marsden and J. Murdoch (eds) *Between the local and the global: confronting complexity in the contemporary agri-food sector*, Oxford: Elsevier.

—— (2008) "Rural development and the regional state: denying multifunctional agriculture in the UK," *Journal of Rural Studies*, 24(4): 422–431.

Marsden, T. and Wrigley, N. (1995) "Regulation, retailing and consumption," *Environment and Planning A*, 27: 1899–1912.

Marsden, T., Banks, J., and Bristow, G. (2002) "The social management of rural nature: understanding agrarian-based rural development," *Environment and Planning A*, 34: 809–825.

Marsden, T., Flynn, A., and Harrison, M. (2000) *Consuming interests: the social provision of food*, London: UCL Press.

Marsden, T., Lee, R., Flynn, A., and Thankappen, S. (2010). *The new regulation and governance of food: beyond the food crisis?*, London: Routledge.

Marsden, T., Murdoch, J., and Morgan, K. (1999) "Sustainable agriculture, food supply chains and regional development," *International Planning Studies*, 4(3): 295–301.

Marston, S., Jones III, J., and Woodward, K. (2005) "Human geography without scale," *Transactions of the British Institute of Geographers*, 30(4): 416–432.

Martens, P. (2006) "Sustainability/science or fiction?," *Sustainability: Science Practice and Policy*, 2: 36–41.

Martin, P. (1990) "Trolley fodder," *Sunday Times Magazine*, November 4, London.

Martinez, S., Hand, M., Da Pra, M., Pollack, S., Ralston, K., Smith, T. Vogel, S., Clark, S., Lohr, L., Low, S., and Newman, C. (2010) *Local food systems: concepts, impacts and issues.* Online. Available www.res.usda.gov./publications/err97.

Maye, D. and Ilbery, B. (2007) "Regionalisation, local foods and supply chain governance: a case study from Northumberland, England," in D. Maye, L. Holloway, and M. Kneafsey (eds) *Alternative food geographies*, Oxford: Elsevier.

Meijering, L., Huigen, P., and van Hoven, B. (2007) "Intentional communities in rural spaces," *Tijdschrift voor Economische en Sociale Geografie*, 98(1): 42–52.

Menard, C. and Valceschini, E. (2005) "New institutions for governing the agri-food industry," *European Review of Agricultural Economics*, 32(3): 421–440.

Mennell, S. (1985) *All manners of food: eating and taste in England and France from the Middle Ages to the present*, New York: Blackwell.

Merton, R. (1972) "Insiders and outsiders/a chapter in the sociology of knowledge," *American Journal of Sociology*, 78(1): 9–47.

MFLW: Making Local Food Work (2009) *Simply legal: all you need to know about legal forms and organisational types for community enterprises*, Online. Available www.uk.coop/resources/documents/simply-legal (accessed September 15, 2010).

—— (2010) *Local food and climate change: the role of community food enterprises*, Online. Available www.makinglocalfoodwork.co.uk (accessed May 10, 2010).

Micheletti, M. and Stolle, D. (2008) "Fashioning social justice through political consumerism, capitalism and the internet," *Cultural Studies*, 22(5): 749–769.

Miele, M. and Murdoch, J. (2002) "The practical aesthetics of traditional cuisines: slow food in Tuscany," *Sociologia Ruralis*, 42(4): 312–328.

Miller, D. (1987) *Material culture and mass consumption*, Oxford: Blackwell.

—— (1995a) "Consumption and commodities," *Annual Review of Anthropology*, 24: 141–161.

—— (ed.) (1995b) *Acknowledging consumption*, London: Routledge.

—— (1995c) "Consumption as the vanguard of history: a polemic by way of an introduction," in D. Miller (ed.) *Acknowledging consumption: a review of new studies*, London: Routledge.

—— (1998a) "Why some things matter," in D. Miller (ed.) *Material cultures: why some things matter*, Chicago: The University of Chicago Press.

—— (1998b) *A theory of shopping*, London: Routledge.

—— (2003) "Could the internet defetishise the commodity?," *Environment and Planning D: Society and Space*, 21: 359–372.

Millward, D. J. and Garnett, T. (2009) "Food and the planet: nutritional dilemmas of greenhouse gas emission reductions through reduced intakes of meat and dairy foods," *Proceedings of the Nutrition Society*, 1–16.

Mink, G. (1995) *The wages of motherhood: inequality in the welfare state, 1917–1942*, Ithaca: Cornell University Press.

Mintz, S. (1985) *Sweetness and power: the place of sugar in modern history*, New York: Viking.

Moberg, M. (2005) "Fair trade and Eastern Caribbean banana farmers: rhetoric and reality in the anti-globalization movement," *Human Organisation*, 64(1): 4–15.

Mol, A. and Law, J. (1994) "Regions, networks and fluids: anaemia and social topology," *Social Studies of Science*, 24: 641–671.

Moore, G., Gibbon, J., and Slack, R. (2006) "The mainstreaming of fair trade: a macro-marketing perspective," *Journal of Strategic Marketing*, 14: 329–352.

Moosewood Cookbook (1977) *Moosewood cookbook: recipes from the Moosewood restaurant*, Ithaca, New York, Berkeley: Ten Speed Press.

Morgan, K. (2009) "The challenge of community food planning," paper presented at the Conference on Making Local Food Work, Bristol, September, 2009. Online. Available www.makinglocalfoodwork.co.uk/conference.cfm (accessed October 20, 2009).

Morgan, K. and Murdoch, J. (2000) "Organic vs. conventional agriculture: knowledge, power and innovation in the food chain," *Geoforum*, 31: 159–173.

Morgan, K. and Sonnino, R. (2008) *The school food revolution: public food and the challenge of sustainable development*, London: Earthscan.

Morgan, K., Marsden, T., and Murdoch, J. (2006) *Worlds of food: place, power, and provenance in the food chain*, Oxford: Oxford University Press.

Mortimer, R. and Baker, R. (2010) Fair trade gives Sainsbury's "a competitive advantage." Online. Available www.maketing week.co.uk/news/

Moseley, W. (2008) "Fair trade wine: South Africa's post-apartheid vineyards and the global economy," *Globalizations*, 5(2): 291–304.

Mulgan, G. (1989) "The power of the weak," in S. Hall and M. Jacques (eds) *New times: the changing face of politics in the 1990s*, New York: Verso.

Murdoch, J. (1997a) "Inhuman/nonhuman/human: actor-network theory and the prospects for a non-dualistic and symmetrical perspective on nature and society," *Environment and Planning D: Society and Space*, 15: 731–756.

—— (1997b) "The shifting territory of government: some insights from the rural white paper," *Area*, 29: 109–118.

Murdoch, J. and Clark, J. (1994) "Sustainable knowledge," Working Paper 9, Centre for Rural Economy, University of Newcastle-upon-Tyne.

Murdoch, J. and Miele, M. (1999) " 'Back to nature': changing 'worlds of production' in the food sector," *Sociologia Ruralis*, 39(4): 465–483.

—— (2004a) "A new aesthetic of food? Relational reflexivity in the 'alternative' food movement," in M. Harvey, A. McMeekin, and A. Warde (eds) *Qualities of food*. Manchester: University of Manchester Press.

—— (2004b) "Culinary networks and cultural connections: a conventions perspective," in A. Hughes and S. Reimer (eds) *Geographies of commodity chains*, London: Routledge.

Murdoch, J., Lowe, P., Ward, N., and Marsden, T. (2003) *The differentiated countryside*, London: Routledge.

Murdoch, J., Marsden, T., and Banks, J. (2000) "Quality, nature and embeddedness: some theoretical considerations in the context of the food sector," *Economic Geography*, 76(2): 107–125.

Murray, C. (2001) *Livelihoods research: some conceptual and methodological issues*, Background Paper 5, Chronic Poverty Research Centre, Institute of Development Policy, University of Manchester.

Mutersbaugh, T. (2002) "The number is the beast: a political economy of organic coffee certification and producer unionism," *Environment and Planning A*, 34: 1165–1184.

—— (2005a) "Fighting standards with standards: harmonization, rents and social accountability in certified agrofood networks," *Environment and Planning A*, 37: 2033–2051.

—— (2005b) "Just-in-space: certified rural products, labor of quality and regulatory spaces," *Journal of Rural Studies*, 21(4): 389–402.

Mutersbaugh, T. and Lyon, S. (2010) "Transparency and democracy in certified ethical commodity networks," *Geoforum*, 41: 27–32.

Mutersbaugh, T., Klooster, D., Renard, M.-C., and Taylor, P. (2005) "Certifying rural spaces: quality-certified products and rural governance in the global South," *Journal of Rural Studies*, 21(4): 381–388.

Nabhan, G. (2002) *Coming home to eat: the pleasures and politics of local foods*, New York: Norton.

National Agricultural Statistics Service (2002) *Agricultural statistics, 2002*, Washington, DC: United States Department of Agriculture.

Neilson, J. and Pritchard, B. (2010) "Fairness and ethicality in their place: the regional dynamics of fair trade and ethical sourcing agendas in the plantation districts of South India," *Environment and Planning A*, 42: 1833–1851.

New York Times, (1997) "The mob and the markets," Editorial, vol. 146, April 12, p. 18.

Nichols, A. and Opal, C. (2005) *Fair trade: market-driven ethical consumption*, London: Sage.

Nonaka, I. and Peltokorpi, V. (2006) "Knowledge-based view of radical innovation," in J. Hage and M. Meeus (eds) *Innovation, Science and Institutional Change*, Oxford: Oxford University Press.

Norgaard, R. (1988) "Sustainable development: a co-evolutionary view," *Futures*, 20(6): 606–620.

NOSB Hearing 2007: National Organic Standards Board Meeting (2007) Meeting transcripts: Wednesday, March 28, 2007. Online. Available www.ams.usda.gov/AMSv1.0/ams.fetchTemplateData.do?template=TemplateN&navID=NationalOrganicProgram&leftNav=NationalOrganicProgram&page=March2007Transcripts&description=NOSB%20Meeting%20transcripts:%20March%2027-29.%202007 (accessed November 19, 2008).

Nowotny, H., Scott, P., and Gibbons, M. (2001) *Rethinking science: knowledge and the public in the age of uncertainty*, Cambridge: Polity Press.

Omi, M. and Winant, H. (1996) *Racial formation in the United States: from the 1960s to the 1990s*, New York: Routledge.

Organic Trade Association (OTA) (2005a) Organic Trade Association asks Congress to take action to keep organic standards strong. Online. Available www.ota.com/news/press/181.html (accessed January 15, 2008).

—— (2005b) USDA: support organic agriculture and the organic industry through targeted programs: comments of the Organic Trade Association on "Notice of meetings and request for comments," *Federal Register*, Friday, June 17, 2005. Online. Available www.ota.com/pp/otaposition/frc/USDA12–30–05.html (accessed January 15, 2008).

OTA 2005b: Organic Trade Association (2005b) USDA: support organic agriculture and the organic industry through targeted programs: comments of the Organic Trade Association on "Notice of meetings and request for comments". *Federal Register*, Friday, 17 June, 2005. Online. Available www.ota.com/pp/otaposition/frc/USDA12-30-05.html (accessed January 15, 2008).

OTA Members/Arnold *et al.*/Center for Food Safety (2005) Open letter to the OTA and the organic community, November 18, 2005. Online. Available www.centerforfoodsafety.org/pubs/LettertoOrganicCommunityreOrganicStandards.pdf (accessed April 28, 2008).

Oudshoorn, N. and Pinch, T. (2003) *How users matter: the co-construction of users and technology*, Cambridge, MA: MIT Press.

Parrott, N., Wilson, N., and Murdoch, J. (2002) "Spatialising quality: regional protection and the alternative geography of food," *European Urban and Regional Studies*, 9(3): 241–261.

Pastor, M., Dreier, P., Grigsby, E., and Lopez-Garcia, M. (2000) *Regions that work: how cities and suburbs can grow*, Minneapolis, MN: University of Minnesota Press.

Patel, R. (2007) *Stuffed and starved: from farm to fork, the hidden battle for the world food system*, London: Portobello Books.

Paumgarten, N. (2010) "Food fighter: does Whole Foods' C.E.O. know what's best for you?," *The New Yorker*, January 4: 36–47.

People's Food Sovereignty (2009) *Declaration from Social Movements, NGOs, CSOs: Parallel Forum to the World Food Summit On Food Security*, Rome, November, 13–17, 2009. Online. Available http://peoplesforum2009.foodsovereignty.org/final_decarations (accessed December 6, 2009).

Pepper, D. (1991) *Communes and the green vision: counterculture, lifestyle and the new age*, London: Green Print.

Perez, J., Allen, P., and Brown, M. (2003) *Community Supported Agriculture on the Central Coast: The CSA Member Experience*, Research Brief Number 1, The Center for Agroecology and Sustainable Food Systems (CASFS), University of California, Santa Cruz.

Pilcher, J. (1998) *Que vivan los tamales! Food and the making of Mexican identity*, Albuquerque, NM: University of New Mexico Press.

Pinch, T. and Bijker, W. (1984) "The social construction of facts and artefacts: or how the sociology of science and the sociology of technology might benefit one another," *Social Studies of Science*, 14: 399–441.

Pinkerton, T. and Hopkins, R. (2009) *Local food: how to make it happen in your community*, Totnes, Devon: Green Books.

Piore, M. and Sabel, C. (1984) *The second industrial divide: possibilities for prosperity*, New York: Basic Books.

Platt, H. L. (2005) *Shock cities: the environmental transformation and reform of Manchester, UK and Chicago, USA*, Chicago: University of Chicago Press.

Ploeg, J. van der (2003) *The virtual farmer. Past, present and future of the Dutch peasantry*, Assen, The Netherlands: Royal Van Gorcum.

Ploeg, J. D. van der and Dijk, G. van (eds) (1995) *Beyond modernization: the impact of endogenous rural development*, Assen, The Netherlands: Van Gorcum.

Ploeg, J. D. van der and Long, A. (eds) (1994) *Born from within. Practice and perspectives of endogenous rural development*, Assen, The Netherlands: Van Gorcum.

Ploeg, J.D. van der and Renting, H. (2000) "Impact and potential: a comparative review of European development practices," *Sociologia Ruralis*, 40(4): 529–543.

Ploeg, J. D. van der, Renting, H., Brunori, G., Knickel, K., Mannion, J., Marsden, T., de Roost, K., Sevilla-Guzmam, E., and Ventura, F. (2000) "Rural development: from practices and policies towards theory," *Sociologia Ruralis*, 40(4): 391–408.

Policy Foresight Programme, (2008) *Can Britain feed itself? Should Britain feed itself?* The James Martin 21st Century School, University of Oxford, UK, October 15.

Pollan, M. (2001) "Naturally: behind the organic-industrial complex," *New York Times Magazine*, May 13.

—— (2006) *The omnivore's dilemma: a natural history of four meals*, New York: Penguin.

—— (2008) *In defense of food: an eater's manifesto*, New York: Penguin.

Polletta, F. (2002*) Freedom is an endless meeting: democracy in American social movements*, Chicago, IL: University of Chicago Press.

Popkin, B. (2009) "Reducing meat consumption has multiple benefits for the world's health," *Archives of internal medicine*, 169(6): 543–545.

Ponte, S. and Gibbon, P. (2005) "Quality standards, conventions and the governance of global value chains," *Economy and Society*, 34(1): 1–31.

Ponte, S., Richey, L., and Babb, M. (2009) "Bono's product (RED) initiative: corporate social responsibility that solves the problem of 'distant others'," *Third World Quarterly*, 30(2): 301–317.

Potter, C. (2006) "Competing narratives for the future of European agriculture: the agri-environmental consequences of neoliberalisation in the context of the Doha Round." *Geographical Journal*, 172(3): 190–196.

Potter, C. and Burney, J. (2002) "Agricultural multifunctionality in the WTO: legitimate non-trade concern or disguised protectionism?," *Journal of Rural Studies*, 18(1): 35–47.

Potter, C. and Tilzey, M. (2007) "Agricultural multifunctionality, environmental sustainability and the WTO: resistance or accommodation to the neoliberal project for agriculture?," *Geoforum*, 38: 1290–1303.

Probyn, E. (2000) *Carnal appetites: food, sex, identities*, London: Routledge.

Purvis, A. (2006) "Ethical eating/how much do you swallow?" *Observer Food Monthly*, 26 February. Online. Available www.guardian.co.uk/lifeandstyle/2006/feb/26/foodand-drink.uk.

Pykett, J. Cloke, P., Barnett, P., Clarke, N., and Malpass, A. (2010) "Learning to be global citizens: the rationalities of fair trade education," *Environment and Planning D: Society and Space*, 28: 487–508.

Quastel, N. (2008) "Ethical consumption, consumer self-governance and the later Foucault," *Dialogue*, 47: 25–52.

Rawls, J. (1971) *A theory of justice*, Boston, MA: Harvard University Press.

—— (1999) *A theory of justice. Revised edition*, Boston, MA: Harvard University Press.

Ray, C. (1998) "Culture, intellectual property and territorial rural development," *Sociologia Ruralis*, 38(1): 3–20.

—— (2000) "The EU LEADER programme: rural development laboratory," *Sociologia Ruralis*, 40(2): 163–171.

Raynolds, L. T. (2000) "Re-embedding global agriculture: the international organic and fair trade movements," *Agriculture and Human Values*, 17: 297–309.

—— (2002) "Consumer/producer links in fair trade coffee networks," *Sociologia Ruralis*, 42(4): 404–424.

—— (2004) "The globalization of organic agro-food networks," *World Development*, 32: 725–743.

—— (2009) "Mainstreaming fair trade coffee: from partnership to traceability," *World Development*, 37: 1083–1093.

Raynolds, L. and Ngcwangu, S. (2010) "Fair trade *rooibos* tea: connecting South African producers and American consumer markets," *Geoforum*, 41: 74–83.

Raynolds, L. and Wilkinson, J. (2007) "Fair trade in the agriculture and food sector: analytical dimensions," in L. Raynolds, D. Murray, and J. Wilkinson (eds) *Fair trade: the challenges of transforming globalization*, London: Routledge.

Raynolds, L., Murray, D., and Taylor, P. (2004) "Fair trade coffee: building producer capacity via global networks," *Journal of International Development*, 16: 1109–1121.

Raynolds, L., Murray, D., and Wilkinson, J. (eds) (2007) *Fair trade: the challenges of transforming globalization*, London: Routledge.

Reardon, T., Codron, J.-M., Busch, L., Bingen, J., and Harris, C. (2001) "Global change in agrifood grades and standards: agribusiness strategic responses in developing countries," *International Food and Agribusiness Management Review*, 2(3): 421–435.

Reckwitz, A. (2002) "Toward a theory of social practices: a development in culturist theorising," *European Journal of Social Theory*, 5(2): 243–263.

Reed, D. (2009) "What do corporations have to do with fair trade? Positive and normative analysis from a value chain perspective," *Journal of Business Ethics*, 86: 3–26.

Reed, M. (2001) "Fight the future! How the contemporary campaigns of the UK organic movement have arisen from their composting past," *Sociologia Ruralis*, 41(1): 130–145.

—— (2002) "Rebels from the Crown down: the organic movement's revolt against agricultural biotechnology," *Science as Culture*, 11(4): 481–504.

—— (2004) "The mobilisation of rural identities and the failure of the rural protest movement in the UK, 1996–2001," *Space and Polity*, 8(1): 25–42.

—— (2005) "Turf wars: the attempt of the organic movement to gain a veto in British agriculture," in G. Holt and M. Reed (eds) *The sociology of organic agriculture: an international perspective*, Wallingford, UK: CAB International.

—— (2008) "The rural arena: the diversity of protest in rural England," *Journal of Rural Studies*, 24(2): 209–218.

Reifsnyder, D. (2010) *Methyl bromide: remarks to the 22nd meeting of the Parties to the Montreal Protocol, 8 November 2010.* Online. Available www.state.gov/g/oes/rls/2010/150788.htm (accessed February 17, 2011).

Renard, M.-C. (1999) "The interstices of globalization: the example of fair trade coffee," *Sociologia Ruralis*, 39(4): 484–500.

—— (2003) "Fair trade: quality, market and conventions," *Journal of Rural Studies*, 19(1): 87–96.

—— (2005) "Quality certification, regulation and power in fair trade," *Journal of Rural Studies*, 21: 419–431.

Renting, H., Marsden, T., and Banks, J. (2003) "Understanding alternative food networks: exploring the role of short food supply chains in rural development," *Environment and Planning A*, 35: 393–411.

Rheinberger, H. (1997) *Toward a history of epistemic things: synthesizing proteins in the test tube*, Stanford: Stanford University Press.

Rice, A. (2009) "Agro-imperialism?," *New York Times Magazine*, November 22, 46–51.

Rice, R. (2001) "Noble goals and challenging terrain: organic and fair trade coffee movements in the global marketplace," *Journal of Agricultural and Environmental Ethics*, 14: 39–66.

Richey, L. and Ponte, S. (2008) "Better (RED) than dead: celebrities, consumption and international aid," *Third World Quarterly*, 29(4): 711–729.

Riddle, J. (2004) *Open letter to USDA: struggle over safeguarding organic standards is not over.* Online. Available www.restoreorganiclaw.org/acresusaconference.html (accessed January 15, 2008).

—— (2007) Comments at National Organic Standards Board Meeting. Public hearing, March 28, 2007.

Ritzer, G. (2000) *The McDonaldization of society*, New Century Edition, Thousand Oaks, CA: Pine Forge Press.

Rivera Escribano, M. J. (2007) "Migration to rural Navarre: questioning the experience of counter-urbanisation," *Tijdschrift voor Economische en Sociale Geografie*, 98(1): 32–41.

Robinson, P. (2009) "Responsible retailing: regulating fair and ethical trade," *Journal of International Development*, 21: 1015–1026.

Roederer-Rynning, C. (2002) "Farm conflict in France and the Europeanisation of agricultural policy." *West European Politics*, 25(3): 105–124.

Roff, R. (2007) "Shopping for change? Neoliberalizing activism and the limits to eating non-GMO," *Agriculture and Human Values*, 24: 511–522.

Rossett. P. and Altieri, M. (1997) "Agroecology versus input substitution: a fundamental contradiction of sustainable agriculture," *Society and Natural Resources*, 10(3): 283–295.

Rosset, P., Machin Sosa, B., Roque Jaime, A. M., and Rocio Lozano, D. R. (2011) "The campesino-a-campesino movement of ANAP in Cuba: social process methodology in the construction of sustainable agriculture and food sovereignty," *Journal of Peasant Studies*, 38(1), in press.

Rousseau, Jean-Jacques (1986) *The social contract*, London: Penguin.

Rudy, A. (2006) "Neoliberalism, neoconservatism, and the spaces of and for coalition," *Agriculture and Human Values*, 23(4): 4233–4425.

Rutherford, A. (2004) "A hall of mirrors: reflections on the 2003 CAP reform," *Ecos*, 25(2): 22–30.

Sage, C. (2003) "Social embeddedness and relations of regard: alternative 'good food' networks in south-west Ireland," *Journal of Rural Studies*, 18: 47–60.

Said, E. and Sjostrom, H. O. (1995) *Orientalism*, London: Penguin.

Sale, K. (1980) *Human scale*. London: Secker and Warburg.

Sandel, M. (1982) *Liberalism and the limits of justice*, New York: Cambridge University Press.

—— (1984) "The procedural republic and the unencumbered self," *Political Theory*, 12(1): 81–96.

Sanders, E. (1999) *Roots of reform: farmers, workers and the American state, 1877–1917*, Chicago: University of Chicago Press.

Sassatelli, R. (2004) "The political morality of food: discourses, contestation and alternative consumption," in M. Harvey, A. McMeekin, and A. Warde (eds) *Qualities of food*, Manchester: University of Manchester Press.

—— (2006) "Virtue, responsibility and consumer choice: framing critical consumerism," in J. Brewer and F. Trentmann (eds) *Consuming cultures, global perspectives: historical trajectories, transnational exchanges*, Oxford: Berg.

Sassatelli, R. and Davolio, F. (2008) "Politicizing food quality: how alternative is the Slow Food vision of consumption?," paper presented at the Conference on Sustainable Consumption and Alternative Agri-Food Systems, Arlon, Belgium, May, 2008. Online. Available www.suscons.ulg.ac.be/IMG/Arlon Papers/davolio Politicizing food quality how alternative is slow food.doc (accessed September 10, 2008).

—— (2010) "Consumption, pleasure and politics: Slow Food and the politico-aesthetic problematization of food," *Journal of Consumer Culture*, 10(2): 220–250.

Sassatelli, R. and Scott, A. (2001) "Novel food, new markets and trust regimes: responses to the erosion of consumers' confidence in Austria, Italy and the UK," *European Societies*, 3(2): 213–244.

Sayer, A. (2001) "For a critical cultural political economy," *Antipode*, 33(4): 687–708.

Sayre, L. (2006) "Euro-ganics." *The Natural Farmer*, Spring, 21–23. Online. Available http://www.nofa.org (accessed October 13, 2009).

Schatzki, T. (1996) *Social practices: A Wittgensteinian approach to human activity and the social*, Cambridge: Cambridge University Press.

Scherer-Haynes, I. (2007) "The impact of fair trade in the South: an example from the Indian cotton sector," in E. Zaccai (ed.) *Sustainable consumption, ecology and fair trade*, London: Routledge.

Schmelzer, M. (2010) "Marketing morals, moralizing markets: assessing the effectiveness of fair trade as a form of boycott," *Management and Organizational History*, 5(2): 221–250.

Scott, F. and Phillips, R. (2008) *Cutting our carbs: food and the environment*, London: Green Alliance.

Scott, J. C. (1976) *The moral economy of the peasant: rebellion and subsistence in Southeast Asia*, New Haven, CT: Yale University Press.

Scott, J. C. (1985) *Weapons of the weak: everyday forms of peasant resistance*, New Haven: Yale University Press.

Scott, J. W. (1988) *Gender and the politics of history*, New York; Columbia University Press.

Scrase, T. (2010) "Fair trade in cyberspace: the commodification of poverty and the marketing of handicrafts on the internet," in T. Lewis and E. Potter (eds) *Ethical consumption: a critical introduction*, London: Routledge.

Selfa, T. and Qazi, J. (2005) "Place, taste or face-to-face? Understanding producer–consumer networks in 'local' food networks in Washington State," *Agriculture and Human Values*, 22(4): 451–464.

Seyfang, G. (2005) "Shopping for sustainability: can sustainable consumption create ecological citizenship?," *Environmental Politics*, 14: 290–306.

—— (2006) "Ecological citizenship and sustainable consumption: examining local organic networks," *Journal of Rural Studies*, 22: 383–395.

Seyfang, G. and Smith, A (2006) *Community action: a neglected site of innovation for sustainable development?*, CSERGE Working Paper EDM 06–10, Centre for Social and Economic Research on the Global Environment, University of East Anglia.

Seymour, H. and Simmonds, M. "Community shares and local food," paper presented at the Conference on Making Local Food Work, Bristol, September, 2009. Online. Available www.makinglocalfoodwork.co.uk (accessed October 19, 2009).

Shah, N. (2001) *Contagious divides: epidemics and race in San Francisco's Chinatown*, Berkeley, CA: University of California Press.

Shamir, R. (2008) "The age of responsibilization: on market-embedded morality," *Economy and Society*, 37(1): 1–19.

Shaw, D., Hogg, G., Wilson, E., Shui, E., and Hassan, L. (2006) "Fashion victim: the impact of fair trade concerns on clothing choice," *Journal of Strategic Marketing*, 14(4): 427–440.

Shove, E., Watson, M., Hand, M., and Ingram, J. (2007) *The design of everyday life*, Oxford: Berg.

Shreck, A. (2002) "Just bananas? Fair trade production in the Dominican Republic," *International Journal of Sociology of Agriculture and Food*, 10: 11–21.

—— (2005) "Resistance, redistribution and power in the fair trade banana initiative," *Agriculture and Human Values*, 22: 19–29.

Siegle, L. (2004) "The food fight," *The Observer Magazine*, November 28, 22–28. Online. Available www.guardian.co.uk/magaziner/story/0,11913,1359470.00.html.

Silva Rodriguez, J. M. (2005) "In a word…," *LEADER+ Magazine*, Number 1.

Sligh, M. and Christman, C. (2003) "*Who owns organic? The global status, prospects and challenges of a changing market*," Pittsboro, NC: Rural Advancement Foundation International (RAFI)-USA. Online. Available www.rafiusa.org (accessed October 13, 2009).

Slocum, R. (2006) "Anti-racist practice and the work of community food organisations," *Antipode*, 38(2): 327–349.

—— (2007) "Whiteness, space and alternative food practice," *Geoforum*, 38(3): 520–533.

Smith, A. (2006) "Green niches in sustainable development: the case of organic food in the United Kingdom," *Environment and Planning C: Government and Society*, 24: 439–458.

—— (2008) "A response to the Adam Smith report and a new way of thinking about measuring the content of the fair trade cup," BRASS, Cardiff University. Online. Available www.brass.cf.ac.uk/uploads/TheFairCupResponsetoAdamSmithD9_1.pdf.

Smith, D. (1997) "Back to the good life: towards an enlarged conception of social justice," *Environment and Planning D: Society and Space*, 15: 19–35.

Smith, D. E. (1987) *The everyday world as problematic: a feminist sociology*, Boston: Northeastern University Press.

Smith, E. and Marsden, T. (2004) "Exploring the 'limits of growth' in UK organics: beyond the statistical image," *Journal of Rural Studies*, 20(3): 345–357.

Smith, N. (1993) "Homeless/global: scaling places," in J. Bird, B. Curtis, T. Putnam, G.

Robertson, and L. Tickner (eds), *Mapping the futures: local cultures, global change*, London: Routledge.

Smith, S. (forthcoming) "For love or money? Fair trade business models in the UK supermarket sector," *Journal of Business Ethics*.

Smith, S. and Barrientos, S. (2005) "Fair trade and ethical trade: are there moves towards convergence?," *Sustainable Development*, 13: 190–198.

Smithers, R. (2009) "Going Duchy: Waitrose and Charles in royalties deal," *Guardian*, September 13, 15.

—— (2010) "Ethical consumer spending bucks recession with 18% growth." *Guardian*, December 30.

Soil Association (2005*) Cultivating co-operatives: organisational structures for local food enterprises*, Online. Available www.uk.coop/resources/documents/cultivating-co-operatives (accessed September 17, 2010).

—— (2009a) *Organic market report 2009*, Online. Available www.soilassociation.org/Businesses/Marketinformation (accessed July 8, 2009).

—— (2009b) *Soil carbon and organic farming*. Online. Available www.soilassociation.org (accessed January 15, 2010).

—— (2010) *Organic market report 2010*. Online. Available www.soilassociation.org (accessed May 14, 2010).

Soler, L.-G. (2005) "Retailer strategies in the food marketing chain: introduction to the special issue," *Journal of Agricultural and Food Organisation*, 3(1): 1–5.

Sonnino, R. (2010) "Escaping the local trap: insights on re-localisation from school meal reform," *Journal of Environmental Policy and Planning*, 12(1): 23–40.

Sonnino, R. and Marsden, T. (2006) "Towards a new agrarian eco-economy? The evolution of alternative networks in the south-west of England," in J. Murdoch and T. Marsden (eds) *Between the local and the global: confronting complexity in the contemporary food sector*, Amsterdam: Elsevier.

Sousa, I. de and Busch, L. (1998) "Networks and agricultural development: the case of soybean production and consumption in Brazil," *Rural Sociology*, 63(3): 349–371.

Spelman, C. (2011) *Environment Secretary Caroline Spelman's speech at the Oxford Farming Conference 2011*, Online. Available www.defra.gov.uk/news/2011/01/05/Spelman-speech/ (accessed January 11, 2011).

Staeheli, L. (2008) "Citizenship and the problem of community," *Political Geography*, 27(1): 5–21.

Starr, A., Card, A., Benope, C., Auld, G., Lamm, D., Smith, K., and Wilken, K. (2003) "Sustaining local agriculture: barriers and opportunities to direct marketing between farms and restaurants in Colorado," *Agriculture and Human Values*, 20: 301–321.

Stassart, P. and Jamar, D. (2008) "Steak up to the horns!," *GeoJournal*, 73: 31–44.

Steinbrucken, T. and Jaenichen, S. (2007) "The fair trade idea: towards an economics of social labels," *Journal of Consumer Policy*, 30: 201–217.

Stern, N. (2006) *The economics of climate change*, London: HM Treasury.

Straete, E. and Marsden, T. (2006) "Exploring dimensions of qualities in food," in T. Marsden and J. Murdoch (eds) *Between the local and the global: confronting complexity in the contemporary agri-food sector*, London: Elsevier.

Stuiver, M. (2006) "Highlighting the retro side of innovation and its potential for regime change in agriculture," in T. Marsden and J. Murdoch (eds) *Between the local and the global: confronting complexity in the contemporary agri-food sector*, Oxford: Elsevier.

Subbarao, K., Kabir, Z., Martin, F., and Koike, S. (2007) "Management of soilborne diseases in strawberry using vegetable rotations," *Plant Disease*, 91: 964–972.

Sumberg, J., Okali, C., and Reece, D. (2003) "Agricultural research in the face of diversity, local knowledge and the participation imperative: theoretical considerations," *Agricultural Systems*, 76: 739–753.

Sustainable Development Commission (2008) *Green, healthy and fair: a review of the government's role in supporting sustainable supermarket food*, London: Sustainable Development Commission.

—— (2009a.) *Food security and sustainability: a perfect fit*, London: Sustainable Development Commission.

—— (2009b) *Setting the table: advice to government on priority elements of sustainable diets*, London: Sustainable Development Commission.

—— (2010) *Reducing health inequalities through sustainable development*, London: Sustainable Development Commission.

Swyngedouw, E. (1997a) "Neither global nor local: 'glocalization' and the politics of scale," in K. Cox (ed.) *Spaces of globalization*, New York: Guilford Press.

—— (1997b) "Excluding the other: the production of scale and scaled politics," in R. Lee and R. Wills (eds), *Geographies of economies*, London: Arnold.

Sylvander, B. and Kristensen, N. H. (2004) *Organic Marketing Initiatives in Europe*, School of Management and Business, University of Wales Aberystwyth.

Sylvander, B. and Schieb-Bienfait, N. (2006) "The strategic turn of organic farming in Europe: from a resource-based to an entrepreneurial approach of organic marketing initiatives," in T. Marsden and J. Murdoch (eds) *Between the local and the global: confronting complexity in the contemporary agri-food system*, Oxford: Elsevier.

Szasz, A. (2007) *Shopping our way to safety; how we changed from protecting the environment to protecting ourselves*, Minneapolis, MN: University of Minnesota.

Tallontire, A. (2000) "Partnerships in fair trade: reflections from a case study of Cafédirect," *Development in Practice*, 10(2): 166–177.

—— (2006) "The development of alternative and fair trade: moving into the mainstream," in S. Barrientos and C. Dolan (eds) *Ethical sourcing in the global food system*, London: Earthscan.

—— (2009) "Top heavy? Governance issues and policy decisions for the fair trade movement" *Journal of International Development*, 21: 1004–1014.

Tarr, J. (1996) *The search for the ultimate sink: urban pollution in historical perspective*, Akron, OH: University of Akron Press.

Taylor, P. (2005) "In the market but not of it: fair trade coffee and forest stewardship council certification as market-based social change," *World Development*, 31(1): 129–147.

Taylor, P., Murray, D., and Raynolds, L. (2005) "Keeping trade fair: governance challenges in the fair trade coffee initiative," *Sustainable Development*, 13: 199–208.

Thankappen, S. and Flynn, A. (2007) *Looking up, looking down: responsibilities for climate change in the UK food supply chains.* Working Paper Series, no. 14, The Centre for Business Relationships, Accountability, Sustainability and Society, University of Cardiff, UK.

Thatcher, J. and Sharp, L. (2008) "Measuring the local economic impact of National Health Service procurement in the UK: an evaluation of the Cornwall Food Programme and LM3," *Local Environment*, 13(3): 253–270.

The Strategy Unit (2008) *Food Matters: towards a strategy for the 21st century.* London: Cabinet Office.

Thomas, J. (2010) Sainsbury's claims to be the "world's largest fair trade retailer." Online. Available www.marketingmagazine.co.uk/news/983770/Sainsburys-claims-worlds-largest-Fairtrade-retailer/.

Thompson, E. P. (1968) *The making of the English working class*, London: Penguin Books.

Thrupp, L. (1989) "Legitimizing local knowledge: from displacement to empowerment for Third World people," *Agriculture and Human Values*, 6: 13–24.

Tovey, H. (1997) "Food, environmentalism and rural sociology: on the organic farming movement in Ireland," *Sociologia Ruralis*, 37(1): 21–37.

Tregear, A., Arfini, F., Belletti, G., and Marescotti, A. (2007) "Regional foods and rural development: the role of product qualification," *Journal of Rural Studies*, 23(1): 12–22.

Trentmann, F. (2007) "Before 'fair trade': empire, free trade and the moral economies of food in the modern world," *Environment and Planning D: Society and Space*, 25: 1079–1102.

—— (2010) "Multiple spaces of consumption/some historical perspectives," in M. Goodman, D. Goodman, and M. Redclift (eds) *Consuming space: placing consumption in perspective*, Aldershot: Ashgate.

United Nations (2009) *Report of the Special Rapporteur on the right to food, Oliver De Schutter. Addendum. Large-scale land acquisitions and leases: a set of minimum principles and measures to address the human rights challenge*, Human Rights Council, A/HRC/13/33/Add.2, December 22.

Urry, J. (2010) Presentation at the BSA Presidential Event: How to Put "Society" into Climate Change, The British Sociological Association, British Library Conference Centre, London, February 8.

USDA: United States Department of Agriculture (2009) *Facts on direct-to-consumer marketing*, Agricultural Marketing Service, Washington, DC.

Valceschini, E. "Agriculture and quality in 2015: the outlook based on four scenarios," paper presented at the Working Group on Alternative Food Networks, COST A12, Rural Innovation, 2002.

Vanclay, F. and Lawrence, G. (1994) "Farmer rationality and the adoption of environmentally sound practices: a critique of the assumptions of traditional agricultural extension," *Journal of Agricultural Education and Extension*, 1: 59–90.

Vanloqueren, G. and Baret, P. (2009) "How agricultural research systems shape a technological regime that develops genetic engineering but locks out agro-ecological innovations," *Research Policy*, 38: 9781–9983.

Varul, M. (2008) "Consuming the campesino: fair trade marketing between recognition and romantic commodification," *Cultural Studies*, 22(5): 654–679.

Vandergeest, P. and DuPuis, E. M. (1995) "Introduction," in E. M. DuPuis and P. Vandergeest (eds) *Creating the countryside: the politics of rural and environmental discourse*, Philadelphia: Temple University Press.

Von Braun, J. (2008) *Rising food prices: what should be done?*, IFPRI Policy Brief, International Food Policy Research Institute, Washington, DC.

Von Braun, J. and Meinzen-Dick, R. (2009) *"Land grabbing" by foreign investors in developing countries: Risks and opportunities*, IPFRI Policy Brief 13, April.

Vos, T. (2000) "Visions of the middle landscape: organic farming and the politics of nature," *Agriculture and Human Values*, 17: 245–256.

—— (2007) *Organic farming and the socio-ecological imaginary*, PhD Thesis, Department of Environmental Studies, University of California, Santa Cruz.

Wall, D. (1999) "Mobilising Earth First! in Britain," *Environmental Politics*, 8(1): 81–100.

Walton, A. (2010) "What is fair trade?," *Third World Quarterly*, 31(3): 431–447.

Walzer, M. (1990) "The communitarian critique of liberalism," *Political Geography*, 18(1): 6–23.

Ward, N. and Lowe, P. (2004) "Europeanising rural development? Implementing the CAP's second pillar in England," *International Planning Studies*, 9(2/3): 121–137.

—— (2007) "Blairite modernisation and countryside policy," *The Political Quarterly*, 78(3): 412–421.

Ward, N. and McNicholas, K. (1998) "Re-configuring rural development in the UK: Objective 5b and the new rural governance," *Journal of Rural Studies*, 14: 27–39.

Warde, A. (2005) "Consumption and theories of practice," *Journal of Consumer Culture*, 5(2): 131–153.

Warner, M. (2005) "A struggle over standards in a fast-growing food category," *New York Times*, November 1.

Watson, J. and Caldwell, M. (eds) (2005) *The cultural politics of food and eating: a reader*, Oxford: Blackwell.

Watson, J. L. (1997) *Golden Arches East: McDonald's in East Asia*, Stanford, CA: Stanford University Press.

Watson, M. (2006) "Towards a Polyanian perspective on fair trade: market-based relationships and the act of ethical consumption," *Global Society*, 20(4): 435–451.

—— (2007) "Trade justice and individual consumption choices: Adam Smith's spectator theory and the moral constitution of the fair trade consumer," *European Journal of International Relations*, 13(2): 263–288.

Watson, M. and Shove, E. (2006) *Materialising consumption: products, projects and dynamics of practice*. Working Paper 30, Cultures of Consumption and ESRC-AHRC Research Programme, Birkbeck College, University of London.

Watts, D., Ilbery, B., and Jones, G. (2007) "Networking practices among 'alternative' food producers in England's West Midlands region," in D. Maye, L. Holloway, and M. Kneafsey (eds) *Alternative food geographies*, Oxford: Elsevier.

Watts, D., Ilbery, B., and Maye, D. (2005) "Making reconnections in agro-food geography: alternative systems of food provision," *Progress in Human Geography*, 29(1): 22–40.

Watts, M. (1999) "Collective wish images: geographical imaginaries and the crisis of development," in J. Allen and D. Massey (eds) *Human geography today*, Cambridge: Polity Press.

Weatherall, C., Tregear A., and Allinson, J. (2003) "In search of the concerned consumer: UK public perceptions of food, farming and buying local," *Journal of Rural Studies*, 19: 233–244.

Weber, M. (1947) 'The types of legitimate domination', in T. Parsons (ed.) *The theory of social and economic organization*, New York: Simon and Schuster.

Wells, M. (1996) *Strawberry fields: politics, class and work in California agriculture*, Berkeley: University of California Press.

Whatmore, S. (2002) *Hybrid geographies*, London: Sage.

Whatmore, S. and Thorne, L. (1997) "Nourishing networks: alternative geographies of food," in D. Goodman and M. Watts (eds) *Globalising food: agrarian questions and global restructuring*, London: Routledge.

Wilkinson, J. (1997) "A new paradigm for economic analysis? Recent convergences in French social science and an exploration of the convention theory approach, with a consideration of its application to the analysis of the agro-food system," *Economy and Society*, 26(3): 305–339.

—— (2007) "Fair trade: dynamic and dilemmas of a market-oriented global social movement," *Journal of Consumer Policy*, 30: 219–239.

—— (2009) "The quality turn (around) – from niche to mainstream. The new qualification of global commodity markets – the case of soy," paper presented at the Workshop on the New Frontiers of Consumption, Warwick, Warwick University, May, 2009.

—— (2010) "Recognition and redistribution in the renegotiation of rural space: the dynamics of aesthetic and ethical critiques," in M. Goodman, D. Goodman, and M. Redclift (eds) *Consuming space: placing consumption in perspective*. Aldershot: Ashgate.

Wilson, B. (2010) "Indebted to fair trade? Coffee and crisis in Nicaragua," *Geoforum*, 41: 84–92.

Winner, L. (1980) "Do artefacts have a politics?," *Daedalus*, 109(1): 121–136.

Winter, M. (2003) "Embeddedness, the new food economy and defensive localism," *Journal of Rural Studies*, 19(1): 23–32.

—— (2006) "Rescaling rurality: multilevel governance of the agro-food sector," *Political Geography*, 25: 735–751.

Woodin, T., Crook, D., and Carpentier, V. (2010) *Community and mutual ownership: a historical review*, Institute of Education, University of London and Joseph Rowntree Foundation. Online. Available www.jrf.org.uk (accessed October 15, 2010).

Woods, M. and Goodwin, M. (2003) "Applying the rural: governance and policy in rural areas," in P. Cloke (ed.) *Country visions*. Harlow, Essex: Pearson Education.

Wright, C. (2004) "Consuming lives, consuming landscapes; interpreting advertisements for Cafédirect coffees," *Journal of International Development*, 16: 665–680.

—— (2009) "Fair trade food: connecting producers and consumers," in D. Inglis and D. Gimlin (eds) *The globalization of food*, London: Berg.

Wright, P. (2001) "Overview of anaerobic digestion systems for dairy farms," Natural Resource, Agriculture and Engineering Service (NRAES-143).

Young, I. (1990) *Justice and the politics of difference*, Princeton, NJ: Princeton University Press.

Zadek, S. and Tiffen, P. (1996) "Fair trade: business or campaign?," *Development: Journal of the Society for International Development*, 3: 48–53.

Zhang, W., McGiffen, M., Becker, J., Ohr, H., Sims, J., and Kallenbach, R. (1997) "Dose response of weeds to methyl iodide and methyl bromide," *Weed Research*, 37(3): 181–189.

Index

Page numbers in *italics* denote tables, those in **bold** denote figures.

Not all authors cited in the text are included in the index. Readers requiring a complete list of cited authors and texts should consult the reference list.